'The trouble of an index'

BYRON'S LETTERS AND JOURNALS

VOLUME 12

ANTHOLOGY AND INDEX

Juan was taught from out the best edition,
  Expurgated by learned men, who place,
Judiciously, from out the schoolboy's vision,
  The grosser parts; but, fearful to deface
Too much their modest bard by this omission,
  And pitying more his mutilated case,
They only add them all in an appendix,
Which saves, in fact, the trouble of an index.

DON JUAN, 1, 44

'The trouble of an index'

BYRON'S LETTERS AND JOURNALS

Edited by

LESLIE A. MARCHAND

VOLUME 12

*Anthology of Memorable Passages
and Index to the Eleven Volumes*

THE BELKNAP PRESS OF
HARVARD UNIVERSITY PRESS
CAMBRIDGE, MASSACHUSETTS
1982

CONTENTS

Editorial Note   vii

ANTHOLOGY OF MEMORABLE PASSAGES
IN BYRON'S LETTERS AND JOURNALS   1

INDEX TO THE ELEVEN VOLUMES   37

EDITORIAL NOTE

This volume contains a comprehensive selection of Byron's aphorisms, *bons mots*, and facetious and memorable phrases, arranged under subject headings. This is followed by a general index and subject index incorporated in a single alphabetical listing. Volume numbers are given in Arabic numerals in bold face. The volume number is not repeated for each subheading unless a different volume number has intervened; the page numbers refer to the last volume mentioned. The general index includes all proper names of persons, places, or things. Titles of books are given under the names of the authors. Subheadings are divided by semi-colons, as are also references in different volumes. The entries for recipients of letters are headed with "B's letters to" followed by volume and page numbers of all letters addressed to the recipients in the several volumes. This is followed by "biog. sketch" (when there is such) and volume and page number. Page numbers of principal biographical notes are in italics. Included in the index are the Introduction in the first volume, the text of the letters and journals, and all the notes, the biographical sketches, and the notes in "Additions and Corrections" in Volume 11. Excluded are the Editorial Note in each volume, the Chronology, the lists of letters and sources, list of forgeries, and Bibliographies. Also excluded are cross references to earlier notes unless new information is given. Subject divisions are arranged alphabetically under "Byron", under "Byron, views on", and "Byron, Works".

Anthology of Memorable Passages in
Byron's Letters and Journals

AGE

... it was one of the deadliest and heaviest feelings of my life to feel that I was no longer a boy.—From that moment I began to grow old in my own esteem—and in my esteem age is not estimable.

"Detached Thoughts", No.72 (Vol.9, p. 37)

1821. Here lies interred in the Eternity of the Past, from whence there is no Resurrection for the Days—whatever there may be for the Dust —the Thirty-Third Year of an ill-spent Life, which, after a lingering disease of many months sunk into a lethargy, and expired, January 22d, 1821, A.D. leaving a successor Inconsolable for the very loss which occasioned its Existence.

Ravenna Journal, Jan.22, 1822 (Vol.8, p.32)

[Bartolini bust] . . . it exactly resembles a superannuated Jesuit. . . . though my mind misgives me that it is hideously like. If it is—I can not be long for this world—for it overlooks seventy.

Sept.23, 1822, to Murray (Vol.9, p.213)

AMERICA

America is a Model of force and freedom & moderation—with all the coarseness and rudeness of its people.

Oct.12, 1821, to Hobhouse (Vol.8, p.240)

I would rather . . . have a nod from an American, than a snuff-box from an emperor.

June 8, 1822, to Moore (Vol.9, p.171)

ATHENS

I am living in the Capuchin Convent, Hymettus before me, the Acropolis behind, the temple of Jove to my right, the Stadium in front, the town to the left, eh, Sir, there's a situation, there's your picturesque! nothing like that, Sir, in Lunnun, no not even the Mansion House. And I feed upon Woodcocks & red Mullet every day, & I have three horses (one a present from the Pacha of the Morea) and I ride to Piraeus, & Phalerum & Munichia . . . I wish to be sure I had a few books, one's own works for instance, any damned nonsense on a long Evening.

Jan.20, 1811, to Hodgson (Vol.2, p.37)

CAVALIER SERVENTE

But I feel & feel it bitterly—that a man should not consume his life at the side and on the bosom—of a woman—and a stranger—that even the recompense and it is much—is not enough—and that this Cicisbean existence is to be condemned.—But I have neither the strength of mind to break my chain, nor the insensibility which would deaden it's weight.   *Aug.23, 1819, to Hobhouse (Vol.6, p.214)*

I am not tired of Italy—but a man must be a Cicisbeo and a singer in duets and a Connoisseur of operas—or nothing here—I have made some progress in all these accomplishments—but I can't say that I don't feel the degradation.—Better be a[n] unskilful planter—an awkward settler—better be a hunter—or anything than a flatterer of fiddlers—and a fan-carrier of a woman.—I like women—God he knows —but the more their system here developes upon me—the worse it seems—after Turkey too—here the *polygamy* is all on the female side. —I have been an intriguer, a husband, and now I am a Cavalier Servente.—by the holy!—it is a strange sensation.

Oct.3, 1819, to Hobhouse (Vol.6, p.226)

I have settled into regular Serventismo—and find it the happiest state of all—always excepting Scarmentado's.

Mar.3, 1820, to Hobhouse (Vol.7, p.51)

CHILDREN

I hear you have been increasing his Majesty's Subjects, which in these times of War & tribulation is really patriotic, notwithstanding Malthus tells us that were it not for Battle, Murder, & Sudden death, we should be overstocked, I think we have latterly had a redundance of these national benefits, & therefore I give you all credit for your matronly behaviour.   *Aug.21, 1811, to Augusta Leigh (Vol.2, p.74)*

I don't know what Scrope Davies meant by telling you I liked Children, I abominate the sight of them so much that I have always had the greatest respect for the character of *Herod*.

Aug.30, 1811, to Augusta Leigh (Vol.2, p.84)

If we meet in Octbr. we will travel in my *Vis*—& can have a cage for the children & a Cart for the Nurse.

Sept.2, 1811, to Augusta Leigh (Vol.2, p.88)

The place is very well & quiet & the children only scream in a low
voice.   *Sept.21, 1813, to Lady Melbourne (Vol.3, p.116)*

I have a particular dislike to anything of S[helley]'s being within the
same walls with Mr. Hunt's children.—They are dirtier and more
mischievous than Yahoos[;] what they can['t] destroy with their filth
they will with their fingers. . . . Poor Hunt with his six little black-
guards are coming slowly up . . . was there ever such a *kraal* out of the
Hottentot Country before?
                    Oct.4, 1822, to Mary Shelley (Vol.10, p.11)

CONSISTENCY
You accuse yourself of "apparent inconsistencies"—to me they have
not appeared—on the contrary—your consistency has been the most
formidable Apparition I have encountered.
                    Sept.7, 1814, to Annabella Milbanke (Vol.4, p.168)

COURAGE
. . . the French Courage proceeds from vanity—the German from
phlegm—the Turkish from fanaticism & opium—the Spanish from
pride—the English from coolness—the Dutch from obstinacy—the
Russian from insensibility—but the *Italian* from *anger*—so you will
see that they will spare nothing.
                    Aug.31, 1820, to Murray (Vol.7, p.169)

CUCKOLDOM
I am still remote from *marriage*, & presume whenever that takes place,
"even-handed Justice" will return me cuckoldom in abundance.
                    Nov.27, 1812, to Hobhouse (Vol.2, p.251)

DEATH
I have seen a thousand graves opened—and always perceived that
whatever was gone—the *teeth and hair* remained of those who had died
with them.——Is not this odd?—they go the very first things in youth
—& yet last the longest in the dust . . .
                    Nov.18, 1820, to Murray (Vol.7, p.228)

DON JUAN
It is called "Don Juan", and is meant to be a little quietly facetious
upon every thing.   *Sept.19, 1818, to Moore (Vol.6, p.67)*

. . . but I *protest*. If the poem has poetry—it would stand—if not—fall—the rest is "leather and prunella" . . . Dullness is the only annihilator in such cases.—As to the Cant of the day—I despise it—as I have ever done all its other finical fashions,—which become you as paint became the Antient Britons.—If you admit this prudery—you must omit half Ariosto—La Fontaine—Shakespeare—Beaumont—Fletcher—Massinger—Ford—all the Charles second writers—in short, *Something* of most who have written before Pope—and are worth reading—and much of Pope himself. . . *Jan.25, 1819, to Murray (Vol.6, p.95)*

You sha'n't make *Canticles* of my Cantos. The poem will please if it is lively—if it is stupid it will fail—but I will have none of your damned cutting & slashing. . . . So you and Mr. Foscolo &c. want me to undertake what you call a "great work" an Epic poem I suppose or some such pyramid.—I'll try no such thing—I hate tasks—and then "seven or eight years!" God send us all well this day three months—let alone years—if one's years can't be better employed than in sweating poesy—a man had better be a ditcher.—And works too!—is Childe Harold nothing? you have so many *"divine"* poems, is it nothing to have written a *Human* one? without any of your worn out machinery.
April 6, 1819, to Murray (Vol.6, p.105)

Don Juan shall be an entire horse or none. . . . I will not give way to all the Cant of Christendom.
Jan.19, 1819, to Hobhouse and Kinnaird (Vol.6, p.91)

You talk of "approximations to indelicacy"—this reminds me of George Lamb's quarrel at Cambridge with Scrope Davies—"Sir—said George—he *hinted at my illegitimacy*," "Yes," said Scrope—"I called him a damned adulterous bastard"—the approximation and the hint are not unlike. *May 21, 1819, to Murray (Vol.6, p.138)*

. . . you are too earnest and eager about a work never intended to be serious;—do you suppose that I could have any intention but to giggle and make giggle?—a playful satire with as little poetry as could be helped—was what I meant. . . *Aug.12, 1819, to Murray (Vol.6, p.208)*

As to "Don Juan"—confess—confess—you dog—and be candid—that it is the sublime of *that there* sort of writing—it may be bawdy—but is it not good English?—it may be profligate—but is it not *life*, is it not *the thing*?—Could any man have written it—who has not lived in the world?—and tooled in a post-chaise? in a hackney coach? in a

Gondola? Against a wall? in a court carriage? in a vis a vis?—on a table?—and under it?   *Oct.26, [1819], to Kinnaird (Vol.6, p.232)*

There has been an eleventh commandment to the women not to read it—and what is still more extraordinary they seem not to have broken it.——But that can be of little import to them poor things—for the reading or non-reading a book—will never keep down a single petticoat. . . .   *Oct.29, 1819, to Hoppner (Vol.6, p.237)*

The truth is that *it is too true*—and the women hate every thing which strips off the tinsel of *Sentiment*—& they are right—or it would rob them of their weapons.   *Oct.12, 1820, to Murray (Vol.7, p.202)*

The 5th. is so far from being the last of D. J. that is is hardly the beginning.—I meant to take him the tour of Europe—with a proper mixture of siege—battle—and adventure—and to make him finish as *Anacharsis Cloots*—in the French revolution.—To how many cantos this may extend—I know not—nor whether (even if I live) I shall complete it—but this was my notion.—I meant to have him made a Cavalier Servente in Italy and a cause for divorce in England—and a Sentimental "Werther-faced man" in Germany—so as to show the different ridicules of the society in each of those countries——and to have displayed him gradually gaté and blasé as he grew older—as is natural.—But I had not quite fixed whether to make him end in Hell— or in an unhappy marriage,—not knowing which would be the severest. —The Spanish tradition says Hell—but it is probably only an Allegory of the other state.   *Feb.16, 1821, to Murray (Vol.8, p.78)*

D[on] Juan will be known by and bye for what it is intended a *satire* on *abuses* of the present *states* of Society—and not an eulogy of vice;—it may be now and then voluptuous—I can't help that—Ariosto is worse —Smollett (see Lord Strutwell in vol 2d. of R[oderick] R[andom]) ten times worse—and Fielding no better.——No Girl will ever be seduced by reading D[on] J[uan]—no—no—she will go to Little's poems—& Rousseau's romans—for that—or even to the immaculate De Stael—— they will encourage her—and not the Don—who laughs at that—and —and—most other things.   *Dec.25, 1822, to Murray (Vol.10, p.68)*

DRINKING
Like other parties of the kind, it was first silent, then talky, then argumentative, then disputatious, then unintelligible, then altogethery,

then inarticulate, and then drunk. When we had reached the last step of this glorious ladder, it was difficult to get down again without stumbling;—and, to crown all, Kinnaird and I had to conduct Sheridan down a d——d corkscrew staircase, which had certainly been constructed before the discovery of fermented liquors, and to which no legs, however crooked, could possibly accomodate themselves. . . . Both he and Colman were, as usual, very good; but I carried away much wine, and the wine had previously carried away my memory; so that all was hiccup and happiness for the last hour or so, and I am not impregnated with any of the conversation.

Oct.31, 1815, to Moore (Vol. 4, pp.326–327)

ENNUI

J[ohn] Claridge is here, improved in person a good deal, & amiable, but not amusing, now here is a good man, a handsome man, an honourable man, a most inoffensive man, a well informed man, and a *dull* man, & this last damned epithet undoes all the rest; there is S[crope] B[erdmore] D[avies] with perhaps not better intellects, & certes not half his sterling qualities, is the life & soul of me, & every body else; but my old friend with the soul of honour & the zeal of friendship & a vast variety of insipid virtues, can't keep me or himself awake.

Sept.20, 1811, to Hobhouse (Vol.2, pp.102–103)

I shall not entertain you with a long list of *attributes* [of Lady Oxford], but merely state that I have not been guilty of once *yawning* in the eternity of two months under the same roof—a phenomenon in my history. . . .   *Dec.31, 1812, to Lady Melbourne (Vol.2, p.265)*

FREEDOM

There is no freedom in Europe—that's certain—it is besides a worn out portion of the globe.

Oct.3, 1819, to Hobhouse (Vol.6, pp.226–227)

FRIENDSHIP

I have always laid it down as a maxim—and found it justified by experience—that a man and a woman—make far better friendships than can exist between two of the same sex—but *then* with the condition— that they never have made—or are to make love to each other.— Lovers may [be]—and indeed generally are—enemies—but they never can be friends—because there must always be a spice of jealousy—and a something of Self in all their speculations.—Indeed I rather look

upon Love altogether as a sort of hostile transaction—very necessary to make—or to break—matches and keep the world a-going—but by no means a sinecure to the parties concerned.

Dec.1, 1822, to Lady Hardy (Vol.10, p.50)

GAMBLING

I have a notion that Gamblers are as happy as most people—being always *excited*;—women—wine—fame—the table—even Ambition—*sate* now & then—but every turn of the card—& cast of the dice—keeps the Gambler alive—besides one can Game ten times longer than one can do any thing else.

"Detached Thoughts", No.33 (Vol.9, p.23)

GREEKS

The supplies of the Committee are some useful—and all excellent in their kind—but occasionally hardly *practical* enough—in the present state of Greece—for instance the Mathematical instruments are thrown away—none of the Greeks know a problem from a poker—we must conquer first—and plan afterwards. The use of the trumpets too may be doubted—unless Constantinople were Jericho.

Dec.26, 1823, to Bowring (Vol.11, p.83)

The opposition say they want to cajole me—and the party in power say the others want to seduce me. . . . It is not of their ill-usage (which I should know how to repel or at least endure perhaps) but of *their good* treatment that I am apprehensive—for it is difficult not to allow our private impressions to predominate—and if these Gentlemen *have* any undue interest and discover my weak side—viz—a propensity to be governed—and were to set a pretty woman or a clever woman about me—with a turn for political or any other sort of intrigue—why—they would make a fool of me—no very difficult matter probably even without such an intervention.——But if I can keep passion—at least that passion—out of the question—(which may be the more easy as I left my heart in Italy) they will not weather me with quite so much facility.

Oct.25, 1823, to Barry (Vol.11, pp.54–55)

As I did not come there to join a faction but a nation—and to deal with honest men and not with speculators or peculators—(charges bandied about daily by the Greeks of each other) it will require much circumspection to avoid the character of a partizan. . . . Whoever goes into Greece at present should do it as Mrs. Fry went into Newgate—not

in the expectation of meeting with any especial indication of existing probity—but in the hope that time and better treatment will reclaim the present burglarious and larcenous tendencies which have followed this General Gaol delivery.

Journal in Cephalonia, Sept.28, 1823 (Vol.11, p.32)

HOMOSEXUALS

[Veli Pasha] He said he wished all the old men . . . to go to his father, but the young ones to come to him, to use his own expression "vecchio con vecchio, Giovane con Giovane". . . . All this is very well, but he has an awkward manner of throwing his arm round one's waist, and squeezing one's hand in *public*, which is a high compliment, but very much embarrasses *"ingenuous youth"*. . . . He asked if I did not think it very proper that as *young* men (he has a beard down to his middle) we should live together, with a variety of other sayings, which made Stranè stare and puzzled me in my replies.

Aug.16, 1810, to Hobhouse (Vol.2, p.10)

At Vostitza I found my dearly-beloved Eustathius—ready to follow me not only to England, but to Terra Incognita. . . . The next morning I found the dear soul upon horseback clothed very sprucely in Greek Garments, with those ambrosial curls hanging down his amiable back, and to my utter astonishment and the great abomination of Fletcher, a *parasol* in his hand to save his complexion from the heat.

July 29, 1810, to Hobhouse (Vol.2, p.6)

But my friend as you may easily imagine is Nicolo, who by the bye, is my Italian master, and we are already very philosophical.—I am his "Padrone" and his "amico" and the Lord knows what besides, it is about two hours since that after informing me he is most desirous to follow *him* (that is me) over the world, he concluded by telling me it was proper for us not only to live but "morire insieme".

Aug.23, 1810, to Hobhouse (Vol.2, p.12)

ILLNESS

Here be also two physicians, one of whom trusts to his Genius (never having studied) the other to a campaign of eighteen months against the sick of Otranto, which he made in his youth with great effect.— When I was seized with my disorder, I protested against both these assassins, but what can a helpless, feverish, toasted and watered poor wretch do? in spite of my teeth & tongue, the English Consul, my

Tartar, Albanians, Dragoman forced a physician upon me, and in three days vomited and glystered me to the last gasp.—In this state I made my epitaph, take it,

> Youth, Nature, and relenting Jove
> To keep my *lamp in* strongly strove,
> But Romanelli was so stout
> He beat all three—and *blew* it *out*.—

But Nature and Jove being piqued at my doubts, did in fact at last beat Romanelli, and here I am well but weakly, at your service.

Oct.3, 1810, to Hodgson (Vol.2, pp.18–19)

I am in bad health & worse spirits, being afflicted in body with what Hostess Quickly in Henry 5th. calls a villainous *"Quotidian Tertian."* It killed Falstaff & may me. I had it first in the Morea last year, and it returned in Quarantine [at Malta] in this infernal oven, and the fit comes on every other day, reducing me first to the chattering penance of Harry Gill, and then mounting me up to a Vesuvian pitch of fever, lastly quitting me with sweats that render it necessary for me to have a man and horse all night to change my linen.

May 15, 1811, to Hobhouse (Vol.2, p.44)

ITALIANS
As a very pretty woman said to me a few nights ago, with the tears in her eyes, as she sat at the harpsichord, "Alas! the Italians must now return to making operas." I fear *that* and macaroni are their forte...
[On the failure of the Carbonari uprising]

April 28, 1821, to Moore (Vol.8, p.105)

LANGUAGES
By way of divertisement, I am studying daily, at an Armenian monastery, the Armenian language. I found that my mind wanted something craggy to break upon; and this—as the most difficult thing I could discover here for an amusement—I have chosen to torture me into attention.

Dec.5, 1816, to Moore (Vol.5, p. 130)

... I fell in love ... I shall think that—and the Armenian Alphabet—will last the winter—the lady has luckily for me been less obdurate than the language—or between the two I should have lost my remains of sanity.

Dec.4, 1816, to Murray (Vol.5, p. 138)

LIFE AND CHARACTER
... I am so convinced of the advantages of looking at mankind instead

of reading about them, and of the bitter effects of staying at home with all the narrow prejudices of an Islander, that I think there should be a law amongst us to set our young men abroad for a term among the few allies our wars have left us.

Jan.14, 1811, to Mrs. Byron (Vol.2, p. 34)

... anything that confirms or extends one's observations on life & character delights me even when I don't know people. ...

Oct.1, 1813, to Lady Melbourne (Vol.3, p. 129)

All are inclined to believe what they covet, from a lottery-ticket up to a passport to Paradise,—in which, from description, I see nothing very tempting.

Journal, Nov.27, 1813 (Vol. 3, p.225)

When one subtracts from life infancy (which is vegetation),—sleep, eating, and swilling—buttoning and unbuttoning—how much remains of downright existence? The summer of a dormouse.

Journal, Dec.7, 1813 (Vol.3, p.235)

... but what is Hope? nothing but the paint on the face of Existence; the least touch of truth rubs it off, and then we see what a hollow-cheeked harlot we have got hold of.

Oct.28, 1815, to Moore (Vol.4, p.323)

... whenever I meet with any-thing agreeable in this world it surprizes me so much—and pleases me so much (when my passions are not interested in one way or the other) that I go on wondering for a week to come. *June 6, 1819, to Hoppner (Vol.6, p.147)*

The lapse of ages *changes* all things—time—language—the earth—the bounds of the sea—the stars of the sky, and every thing "about, around, and underneath" man, *except man himself*, who has always been, and always will be, an unlucky rascal. The infinite variety of lives conduct but to death, and the infinity of wishes lead but to disappointment. All the discoveries which have yet been made have multiplied little but existence. *Jan.9, 1821, Journal (Vol.8, pp.19–20)*

What a strange thing is the propagation of life!—A bubble of Seed which may be spilt in a whore's lap—or in the Orgasm of a voluptuous dream—might (for aught we know) have formed a Caesar or a Buona-

parte—there is nothing remarkable recorded of their Sires—that I know of—   *"Detached Thoughts"*, *No.102* (*Vol.9, p.47*)

LITERATI
[No affectations in Scott, Gifford, and Moore] . . . as for the rest whom I have known—there was always more or less of the author about them—the pen peeping from behind the ear—& the thumbs a little inky or so.   *Mar.25, 1817, to Murray* (*Vol.5, p.192*)

In general I do not draw well with Literary men—not that I dislike them but—I never know what to say to them after I have praised their last publication.   *"Detached Thoughts"*, *No.53* (*Vol.9, p.30*)

LITERATURE
But I hate things *all fiction* . . . there should always be some foundation of fact for the most airy fabric—and pure invention is but the talent of a liar.   *April 2, 1817, to Murray* (*Vol.5, p.203*)

If I live ten years longer, you will see, however, that it is not over with me—I don't mean in literature, for that is nothing; and it may seem odd enough to say, I do not think it my vocation.
                    Feb.28, 1817, to Moore (*Vol.5, p.177*)

LONDON
And so—you want to come to London—it is a damned place—to be sure—but the only one in the world—(at least in the English world) for fun—though I have seen parts of the Globe that I like better—still upon the whole it is the completest either to help one in feeling oneself alive—or forgetting that one is so.
                    Mar.1, 1816, to James Hogg (*Vol.5, p.38*)

LOVE
. . . to give you some idea of my late life, I have this moment received a prescription from Pearson, not for any *complaint* but from *debility*, and literally *too much Love.*—You know my devotion to woman, but indeed Southwell was much mistaken in conceiving my adorations were paid to any Shrine there, no, my Paphian Goddesses are elsewhere, and I have sacrificed at their altar rather too liberally.—In fact, my blue eyed Caroline, who is only sixteen, has been lately so *charming*, that though we are both in perfect health, we are at present commanded to *repose*, being nearly worn out. *Feb.26, 1808, to Becher* (*Vol.1, p.157*)

Bland (the *Revd*) has been challenging an officer of Dragoons, about a *whore*, & my assistance being required, I interfered in time to prevent him from losing his *life* or his *Living*.—The man is mad, Sir, mad, frightful as a Mandrake, & lean as a rutting Stag, & all about a bitch not worth a Bank token.—She is a common Strumpet as his Antagonist assured me, and he means to marry her, Hodgson meant to marry her, the officer meant to marry her, her first Seducer (seventeen years ago) meant to marry her, and all this is owing to the *Comet*!

Nov.16, 1811, to Hobhouse (Vol.2, pp.129–130)

It is true from early habit, one must make love mechanically as one swims, I was once very fond of both, but now as I never swim unless I tumble into the water, I don't make love till almost obliged. . . .

Sept.10, 1812, to Lady Melbourne (Vol.2, p.193)

I . . . determined—not to *pursue*, for pursuit it was not—but to *sit* still, and in a week after I was convinced—not that [Caroline] loved me—for I do not believe in the existence of what is called Love—but that any other man in my situation would have believed that he *was* loved.

Sept.13, 1812, to Lady Melbourne (Vol.2, p.194)

As to *Love*, that is done in a week (provided the Lady has a reasonable share) besides marriage goes on better with esteem & confidence than romance, & she is quite pretty enough to be loved by her husband, without being so glaringly beautiful as to attract too many rivals.

Sept.18, 1812, to Lady Melbourne (Vol.2, p.199)

I cannot exist without some object of Love.

Nov.9, 1812, to Lady Melbourne (Vol.2, p.243)

. . . but hatred is a much more delightful passion—& never cloys—it will make us all happy for the rest of our lives.

April 19, 1813, to Lady Melbourne (Vol.3, p.41)

[Lady Charlotte Harley, Lady Oxford's daughter] . . . whom I should love forever if she could always be only eleven years old—& whom I shall probably marry when she is old enough & bad enough to be made into a modern wife. *April 5, 1813, to Lady Melbourne (Vol.3, p.36)*

. . . one generally *ends & begins* with Platonism—& as my proselyte is only twenty—there is time enough to materialize—I hope neverthe-less this spiritual system won't last long—and at any rate must make

the experiment.—I remember my last case was the reverse—as Major O'Flaherty recommends "we fought first and explained afterwards."
Oct.8, 1813, to Lady Melbourne (Vol.3, p.135)

This business is growing serious—& I think *Platonism* in some peril.
Oct.8, 1813, to Lady Melbourne (Vol.3, p.136)

We have progressively improved into a less spiritual species of tenderness—but the seal is not yet fixed though the wax is preparing for the impression.   *Oct.14, 1813, to Lady Melbourne (Vol.3, p.145)*

I do detest everything which is not perfectly mutual.
Oct.21, 1813, to Lady Melbourne (Vol.3, p.151)

. . . if people will stop at the first tense of the verb "aimer" they must not be surprised if one finishes the conjugation with somebody else.
Jan.13, 1814, to Lady Melbourne (Vol.4, p.28)

. . . the fact is that my wife if she had common sense would have more power over me—than any other whatsoever—for my heart always alights upon the nearest *perch*. . . .
April 30, 1814, to Lady Melbourne (Vol.4, p.111)

[To a Swiss girl] Excepting your compliments (which are only excusable because you don't know me) you write like a clever woman for which reason I hope you *look* as *un*like one as possible—I never knew but one of your country—Me. de Stael—and she is frightful as a precipice. . . . . If you will become acquainted with me—I will promise not to make love to you unless you like it. . . .
June 8, 1814, to Henrietta D'Ussières (Vol.4, p.122)

[Francis Hodgson] . . . an excellent-hearted fellow, as well as one of the cleverest; a little, perhaps, too much japanned by preferment in the church and the tuition of youth, as well as inoculated with the disease of domestic felicity, besides being over-run with fine feelings about women and *constancy* (that small change of Love, which people exact so rigidly, receive in such counterfeit coin, and repay in baser metal).
Nov.17, 1816, to Moore (Vol.5, p.131)

. . . my Goddess is only the wife of a "Merchant of Venice"—but she is pretty as an Antelope,—is but two & twenty years old—has the large black Oriental eyes—with the Italian countenance—and dark

glossy hair of the curl & colour of Lady Jersey's—then she has the voice of a lute—and the song of a Seraph (though not quite so sacred) besides a long postscript of graces—virtues and accomplishments—enough to furnish out a new Chapter for Solomon's song.—But her great merit is finding out mine—there is nothing so amiable as discernment.   *Nov.25, 1816, to Murray (Vol.5, pp.133–134)*

I meant to have given up gallivanting altogether—on leaving your country—where I had been totally sickened of that & every thing else but I know not how it is—my health growing better—& my spirits not worse—the "besoin d'aimer" came back upon my heart again—after all there is nothing like it. *Nov.27, 1816, to Kinnaird (Vol.5, p.135)*

. . . I have fallen in love with a very pretty Venetian of two and twenty with great black eyes—she is married—and so am I—which is very much to the purpose—we have found & sworn an eternal attachment—which has already lasted a lunar month—& I am more in love than ever—& so is the lady—at least she says so—& seems so,—she does not plague me (which is a wonder—) and I verily believe we are one of the happiest—unlawful couples on this side of the Alps.
                         Dec.18, 1816, to Augusta Leigh (Vol.5, p.141)

[Claire Clairmont] You know—& I believe saw once that odd-headed girl—who introduced herself to me shortly before I left England—but you do not know—that I found her with Shelley and her sister at Geneva—I never loved nor pretended to love her—but a man is a man —& if a girl of eighteen comes prancing to you at all hours—there is but one way—the suite of all this is that she was with *child*—& returned to England to assist in peopling that desolate island . . . This comes of "putting it about" (as Jackson calls it) & be damned to it—and thus people come into the world. *Jan.20, 1817, to Kinnaird (Vol.5, p.162)*

I have fallen in love within the last month with a Romagnuola Countess from Ravenna—the Spouse of a year of Count Guiccioli—who is sixty the Girl twenty—he has eighty thousand ducats of rent—and has had two wives before—but he is Sixty—he is the first of Ravenna Nobles but he is sixty—She is fair as Sunrise—and warm as Noon—we had but ten days—to manage all our little matters in beginning middle and end, & we managed them;—and I have done my duty—with the proper consummation.
                         April 24, 1819, to Kinnaird (Vol.6, p.114)

Farewell, my dearest *Evil*—farewell, my torment—farewell, my *all* (but *not all mine!*) I kiss you more often than I have ever kissed you—and this (if Memory does not deceive me) should be a fine number, counting from the beginning.

Aug.7, 1819, to Countess Guiccioli (Vol.6, p.203)

I am all for morality now—and shall confine myself henceforward to the strictest adultery—which you will please to recollect is all that that virtuous wife of mine has left me.

Oct.29, 1819, to Hoppner (Vol.6, p.238)

. . . my attachment has neither the blindness of the beginning—nor the microscopic accuracy of the close of such liaisons. . . .

Jan.10, 1820, to Hoppner (Vol.7, p.24)

I verily believe that nor you, nor any man of poetical temperament, can avoid a strong passion of some kind. It is the poetry of life. What should I have known or written, had I been a quiet, mercantile politician or a lord in waiting? A man must travel, and turmoil, or there is no existence. Besides, I only meant to be a Cavalier Servente, and had no idea it would turn out a romance, in the Anglo fashion.

Aug.31, 1820, to Moore (Vol.7, p.170)

It is awful work, this love, and prevents all a man's projects of good or glory. I wanted to go to Greece lately (as every thing seems up here) with her brother, who is a fine, brave fellow (I have seen him put to the proof), and wild about liberty. But the tears of a woman [Countess Teresa Guiccioli] who has left her husband for a man, and the weakness of one's own heart, are paramount to these projects, and I can hardly indulge them.   *Sept.19, 1821, to Moore (Vol.8, p.214)*

I can say that without being so *furiously* in love as at first—I am more attached to her [Countess Guiccioli]—than I thought it possible to be to any woman after three years.

Oct.5, 1821, to Augusta Leigh (Vol.8, p.234)

MARRIAGE
[Newstead Abbey] . . . the premises are so delightfully extensive, that two people might live together without ever seeing hearing or meeting,—but I can't feel the comfort of this till I marry.—In short it would be the most amiable matrimonial mansion, & *that* is another great in-

ducement to my plan,—my wife & I shall be so happy,—one in each
Wing.   *Aug.30[31?], 1811, to Augusta Leigh (Vol.2, p.86)*

Besides I do not know a single gentlewoman who would venture upon
me, but that seems the only rational outlet from this adventure [his
love affair with Lady Caroline Lamb].——I admired your niece, but
she is engaged to Eden——Besides she deserves a better heart than
mine. What shall I do—shall I *advertise*?
           [Sept.30 ?], 1812, to Lady Melbourne (Vol.2, p.222)

. . . as Moore says "a pretty wife is something for the fastidious vanity
of a roué to *retire* upon."
           Jan.16, 1814, to Lady Melbourne (Vol.4, p.34)

I have great hopes that we shall love each other all our lives as much
as if we had never married at all.
           Dec.5, 1814, to Annabella Milbanke (Vol.4, p.239)

MATHEMATICS
I thank you again for your efforts with my Princess of Parallelograms
[Annabella Milbanke], who has puzzled you more than the Hypothen-
use; . . . her proceedings are quite rectangular, or rather we are two
parallel lines prolonged to infinity side by side but never to meet.
           Oct.18, 1812, to Lady Melbourne (Vol.2, p.231)

I agree with you quite upon Mathematics too—and must be content to
admire them at an incomprehensible distance—always adding them to
the catalogue of my regrets—I know that two and two make four—&
should be glad to prove it too if I could—though I must say if by any
sort of process I could convert 2 & 2 into *five* it would give me much
greater pleasure.—The only part I remember which gave me much
delight were those theorems (is that the word?) in which after ringing
the changes upon—A–B & C–D &c. I at last came to "which is
absurd—which is impossible" and at this point I have always arrived
& I fear always shall through life . . .
           No.10, 1813, to Annabella Milbanke (Vol.3, p.159)

MEMORY
It is singular how soon we lose the impression of what ceases to be
constantly before us.—A year impairs, a lustre obliterates.—There is
little distinct left without an *effort* of memory,—*then* indeed the lights

are rekindled for a moment—but who can be sure that the Imagination is not the torch-bearer?   *"Detached Thoughts"*, *No.51* (*Vol.9, p.29*)

MISCELLANY

As for expectations, don't talk to me of "expects" . . . the Baronet is eternal—the Viscount immortal—and my Lady (*senior*) without end.— They grow more healthy every day and I verily believe Sir R[alph] Ly. M[ilbanke] and Lord W[entworth] are at this moment cutting a fresh set of teeth and unless they go off by the usual fever attendant on such children as don't use the "American soothing syrup" that they will live to have them all drawn again.

Jan.26, 1815, to Hobhouse (*Vol.4, p. 260*)

. . . if I could but manage to arrange my pecuniary concerns in England —so as to pay my debts—& leave me what would be here a very fair income—(though nothing remarkable at home) you might consider me as posthumous—for I would never willingly dwell in the "tight little island".   *Nov.27, 1816, to Kinnaird* (*Vol.5, p.136*)

Lord G[uilford] died of an inflamation of the bowels: so they took them out, and sent them (on account of their discrepancies), separately from the carcass, to England. Conceive a man going one way, and his intestines another, and his immortal soul a third!—was there ever such a distribution? One certainly has a soul; but how it came to allow itself to be enclosed in a body is more than I can imagine. I only know if once mine gets out, I'll have a bit of a tussle before I let it get in again to that of any other.   *April 11, 1817, to Moore* (*Vol.5, p.210*)

An old Woman at Rome reading Boccaccio exclaimed "I wish to God that this was saying one's prayers."

July 30, 1819, to Hobhouse (*Vol. 6, p.190*)

The Cardinal [at Ravenna] is at his wit's end—it is true—that he had not far to go.   *July 22, 1820, to Murray* (*Vol. 7, p.137*)

Your letter of excuses has arrived.—I receive the letter but do not admit the excuses except in courtesy—as when a man treads on your toes and begs your pardon—the pardon is granted—but the joint aches —especially if there is a corn upon it.

Feb.2, 1821, to Murray (*Vol.8, p.73*)

As to Lady Noel—what you say of her declining health—would be very well to any one else—but the way to be immortal (I mean *not* to die at all) is to have me for your heir.—I recommend you to put me in your will—& you will see that (as long as *I* live at least) you will never even catch cold.   *Mar.23, 1821, to Kinnaird (Vol.8, p.96)*

MONEY
Whatever Brain-money—you get on my account from Murray—pray remit to me—I will never consent to pay away what I *earn*—that is *mine*—& what I get by my brains—I will spend on my b——ks— as long as I have a tester or a testicle remaining.
                    Jan.19, 1819, to Kinnaird (Vol.6, p.92)

I have imbibed such a love for money that I keep some Sequins in a drawer to count, & cry over them once a week. . . .
                    Jan.27, 1819, to Kinnaird (Vol.6, p.98)

If you say that I must sign the bonds—I suppose that I must—but it is very iniquitous to make me pay my debts—you have no idea of the pain it gives one.   *Oct.26, 1819, to Kinnaird (Vol.6, p.232)*

I believe M[urray] to be a good man with a personal regard for me.— But a bargain is in its very essence a *hostile* transaction. . . . do not all men try to abate the price of all they buy?—I contend that a bargain even between brethren—is a declaration of war.—
                    July 14, 1821, to Kinnaird (Vol.8, p.153)

I will trust no man's honour in affairs of barter.—I will tell you why.— A state of bargain is Hobbes's "state of nature—a state of war."—It is so with all men.—If I come to a friend—and say "friend, lend me five hundred pounds!" he either does it or says he can't or won't.— But if I come to Ditto—and say "Ditto,—I have an excellent house— or horse—or carriage—or M.S.S. or books—or pictures—&c. &c. &c. &c. &c. honestly worth a thousand pounds, you shall have them for five hundred["]———what does Ditto say?—Why he looks at them —he *hums*—he *ha's*—he *humbugs*—if he can—because *it is* a bargain— this is the blood and bone of mankind—and the same man who would lend another a thousand pounds without interest—would not buy a horse of him for half it's value if he could help it.—It is so—there's no denying it—& therefore I will have as much as I can—& you will give

as little.—And there's an end.—All men are intrinsical rascals,—and I am only sorry that not being a dog I can't bite them.—

Oct.20, 1821, to Murray (Vol.8, pp.244–245)

As my notions upon the score of monies coincide with yours and all men's who have lived to see that every guinea is a philosopher's stone —or at least his *touch*-stone—you will doubt me the less when I pronounce my firm belief that Cash is Virtue.

Feb.23, 1822, to Kinnaird (Vol.9, p.113)

I always looked to about thirty as the barrier of any real or fierce delight in the passions—and determined to work them out in the younger ore and better veins of the Mine—and I flatter myself (perhaps) that I have pretty well done so—and now the dross is coming— and I loves lucre. . . . *Jan.18, 1823, to Kinnaird (Vol.10, p.87)*

OPINIONS

Opinions are made to be changed—or how is truth to be got at? we don't arrive at it by standing on one leg? or on the first day of our setting out—but though we may jostle one another on the way that is no reason why we should strike or trample—*elbowing's* enough.—I am all for moderation which profession of faith I beg leave to conclude by wishing Mr. Southey damned—not as a poet—but as a politician.

May 9, 1817, to Murray (Vol.5, p.221)

PAINTING

. . . as for Rubens . . . he seems to me (who by the way know nothing of the matter) the most glaring—flaring—staring—harlotry imposter that ever passed a trick upon the senses of mankind—it is not nature— it is not art—with the exception of some linen (which hangs over the cross in one of his pictures) which to do it justice looked like a very handsome table cloth—I never saw such an assemblage of florid nightmares as his canvas contains—his portraits seem clothed in pulpit cushions. *May 1, 1816, to Hobhouse (Vol.5, p.73)*

You must recollect however—that I know nothing of painting—& that I detest it—unless it reminds me of something I have seen or think it possible to see—for which [reason] I spit upon & abhor all the saints & subjects of one half the impostures I see in the churches & palaces. . . . Depend upon it of all the arts it is the most artificial & unnatural—& that by which the nonsense of mankind is the most imposed upon.

April 14, 1817, to Murray (Vol.5, p.213)

19

PEOPLE

COGNI, MARGARITA

... with great black eyes and fine [figure]—fit to breed gladiators from.   *Mar.11, 1818, to Murray* (*Vol.6, p.23*)

In the autumn one day going to the Lido with my Gondoliers—we were overtaken by a heavy Squall and the Gondola put in peril—hats blown away—boat filling—oar lost—tumbling sea—thunder—rain in torrents—night coming—& wind increasing.—On our return—after a tight struggle: I found her on the steps of the Mocenigo palace on the Grand Canal—with her great black eyes flashing through her tears and the long dark hair which was streaming drenched with rain over her brows & breast;—she was perfectly exposed to the storm—and the wind blowing her hair & dress about her tall thin figure—and the lightning flashing round her—with the waves rolling at her feet— made her look like Medea alighted from her chariot. . . . Her joy at seeing me again—was moderately mixed with ferocity—and gave me the idea of a tigress over her recovered Cubs.

Aug.1, 1819, to Murray (*Vol.6, p.196*)

LAMB, LADY CAROLINE

Then your heart—my poor Caro, what a little volcano! that pours *lava* through your veins, & yet I cannot wish it a bit colder . . . I have always thought you the cleverest most agreeable, absurd, amiable, perplexing, dangerous fascinating little being that lives now or ought to have lived 2000 years ago.

[April, 1812?], to Lady Caroline Lamb (*Vol.2, pp.170–171*)

[*Glenarvon*] It seems to me that, if the authoress had written the *truth* and nothing but the truth—the whole truth,—the romance would not only have been more *romantic*, but more entertaining. As for the like- ness, the picture can't be good—I did not sit long enough.

Dec.5, 1816, to Moore (*Vol.5, p.131*)

LEIGH, HON. AUGUSTA

I have received all your letters—I believe—which are full of woes—as usual—megrims & mysteries—but my sympathies remain in suspense —for—for the life of me I can't make out whether your disorder is a broken heart or the ear-ache. . . .

June 3, 1817, to Hon. Augusta Leigh (*Vol.5, p.231*)

To Lady Melbourne I write with most pleasure—and her answers, so sensible, so *tactique*—I never met with half her talent. If she had been a few years younger, what a fool she would have made of me, had she thought it worth her while,—and I should have lost a valuable and most agreeable *friend*.   *Journal, Nov.24, 1813 (Vol.3, p.219)*

MILBANKE, ANNABELLA

I have no desire to be better acquainted with Miss Milbank[e], she is too good for a fallen spirit to know or wish to know, & I should like her more if she were less perfect.

May 1, 1812, to Lady Caroline Lamb (Vol.2, p.176)

As to Annabella she requires time & all the cardinal virtues, & in the interim I am a little verging towards one who demands neither, & saves me besides the trouble of marrying by being married already.

Sept.25, 1812, to Lady Melbourne (Vol.2, p.208)

I congratulate A[nnabella] & myself on our mutual escape.—That would have been but a *cold collation*, & I prefer hot suppers.

Nov.14, 1812, to Lady Melbourne (Vol.2, p.246)

. . . here is the strictest of St. Ursula's what do you call 'ems [St. Ursula and her 11,000 virgins]—a wit—a moralist—& religionist— enters into a clandestine correspondence with a personage generally presumed a great Roué—& drags her aged parents into this secret treaty . . . but this comes of *infallibility*.

Sept.28, 1813, to Lady Melbourne (Vol.3, pp.124–125)

I am not now in love with her—but I can't at all foresee that I should not be so if it came "a warm June" (as Falstaff observes) and seriously —I do admire her as a very superior woman a little encumbered with Virtue. . . .   *April 29, 1814, to Lady Melbourne (Vol.4, p.109)*

WEBSTER, JAMES WEDDERBURN

His wife is very pretty, & I am much mistaken if five years from hence she don't give him reason to think so.—Knowing the man, one is apt to fancy these things, but I really thought, she treated him even already with a due portion of conjugal contempt, but I dare say this was only the megrim of a Misogynist.——At present he is the happiest of men, & has asked me to go with them to a tragedy to see his *wife cry*.

Nov.3, 1811, to Hobhouse (Vol.2, p.126)

POETS

BURNS

What an antithetical mind!—tenderness, roughness—delicacy, coarseness—sentiment, sensuality—soaring and grovelling, dirt and deity—all mixed up in that one compound of inspired clay! It is strange; a true voluptuary will never abandon his mind to the grossness of reality. It is by exalting the earthly, the material, the *physique* of our pleasures, by veiling these ideas, by forgetting them altogether, or, at least, never naming them hardly to one's self, that we alone can prevent them from disgusting.   *Journal, Dec.13, 1813 (Vol.3, p.239)*

COLERIDGE

"Christabel"—I won't have you sneer at Christabel—it is a fine wild poem.   *Sept.30, 1816, to Murray (Vol.5, p.108)*

HUNT, LEIGH

He is a good man, with some poetical elements in his chaos; but spoilt by the Christ-Church Hospital and a Sunday newspaper,—to say nothing of the Surry Jail, which conceited him into a martyr. But he is a good man. When I saw "Rimini" in MSS., I told him that I deemed it good poetry at bottom, disfigured only by a strange style. His answer was, that his style was a system, or *upon system*, or some such cant; and, when a man talks of system, his case is hopeless.

June 1, 1818, to Moore (Vol.6, p.46)

. . . I cannot describe to you the despairing sensation of trying to do something for a man who seems incapable or unwilling to do any thing further for himself,—at least, to the purpose. It is like pulling a man out of a river who directly throws himself in again.

April 2, 1823, to Murray (Vol.10, p.138)

KEATS

Johnny Keats's *p–ss a bed* poetry. . . .

Oct.12, 1820, to Murray (Vol.7, p.200)

The Edinburgh praises Jack Keats or Ketch or whatever his names are;—why his is the *Onanism* of Poetry. . . .

Nov.4, 1820, to Murray (Vol.7, p.217)

. . . such writing is a sort of mental masturbation—he is always f—g-g—g his *Imagination*.—I don't mean that he is *indecent* but vici-

He is certainly a prepossessing person to look on, and a man of talent and all that, and—*there* is his eulogy.

Sept.27, 1813, to Moore (Vol.3, p.122)

His appearance is *Epic*; and he is the only existing entire man of letters. All the others have some pursuits annexed to their authorship. His manners are mild, but not those of a man of the world, and his talents of the first order. His prose is perfect. Of his poetry there are various opinions: there is, perhaps, too much of it for the present generation; posterity will probably select. He has *passages* equal to any thing. At present, he has a *party*, but no *public*—except for his prose writings. The life of Nelson is beautiful. *Journal, Nov.22, 1813, (Vol.3, p.214)*

With regard to Southey please to recollect that in his preface to his "Vision"—he actually called upon the legislature to fall upon Moore[,] me—& others—now such a cowardly cry deserves a dressing.—He is also the vainest & most intolerant of men—and a rogue besides.

Nov.16, 1821, to Kinnaird (Vol.9, p.62)

WORDSWORTH

... his performances since "Lyrical Ballads"—are miserably inadequate to the ability which lurks within him—there is undoubtedly much natural talent spilt over "the Excursion" but it is rain upon rocks where it stands & stagnates—or rain upon sands where it falls without fertilizing—who can understand him?—let those who do make him intelligible.   *Oct.30, 1815, to Leigh Hunt (Vol.4, p.324)*

POETRY

I by no means rank poetry high in the scale of intelligence——this may look like Affectation—but it is my real opinion—it is the lava of the imagination whose eruption prevents an earth-quake....

Nov.29, 1813, to Annabella Milbanke (Vol.3, p.179)

I am glad you like it [third canto of *Childe Harold*]; it is a fine indistinct piece of poetical desolation, and my favourite. I was half mad during the time of its composition, between metaphysics, mountains, lakes, love unextinguishable, thoughts unutterable, and the nightmare of my own delinquencies. I should, many a good day, have blown my brains out, but for the recollection that it would have given pleasure to my mother-in-law; and, even *then,* if I could have been certain to haunt her. ...   *Jan.28, 1817, to Moore (Vol.5, p.165)*

I can never get people to understand that poetry is the expression of *excited passion*, and that there is no such thing as a life of passion any more than a continuous earthquake, or an eternal fever. Besides, who would ever *shave* themselves in such a state?

July 5, 1821, to Moore (Vol.8, p.146)

POLITICS

... my parliamentary schemes are not much to my taste—I spoke twice last Session—& was told it was well enough—but I hate the thing altogether—& have no intention to "strut another hour" on that stage.   *Mar.26, 1813, to Augusta Leigh (Vol.3, p.32)*

I have declined presenting the Debtor's Petition, being sick of parliamentary mummeries.   *Journal, Nov.14, 1813 (Vol.3, p.206)*

But Men never advance beyond a certain point;—and here we are, retrograding to the dull, stupid old system,—balance of Europe— poising straws upon kings' noses instead of wringing them off! Give me a republic, or a despotism of one, rather than the mixed government of one, two, three. A Republic!—look in the history of the Earth. . . . To be the first man—not the Dictator—not the Sylla, but the Washington or the Aristides—the leader in talent and truth—is next to the Divinity!   *Journal, Nov.23, 1813 (Vol.3, p.218)*

... I have simplified my politics into an utter detestation of all existing governments; and, as it is the shortest and most agreeable and summary feeling imaginable, the first moment of an universal republic would convert me into an advocate for single and uncontradicted despotism. The fact is, riches are power, and poverty is slavery all over the earth, and one sort of establishment is no better, nor worse, for a *people* than another.   *Journal, Jan.16, 1814 (Vol.3, p.242)*

... we have had lately such stupid mists—fogs—rains—and perpetual density—that one would think Castlereagh had the foreign affairs of the kindgom of Heaven also—upon his hands.

July 29, 1816, to Rogers (Vol.5, p.86)

Weather cold—carriage open, and inhabitants somewhat savage— rather treacherous and highly inflamed by politics. Fine fellows, though,—good materials for a nation. Out of chaos God made a world, and out of high passions comes a people.

Ravenna Journal, Jan.5, 1821 (Vol.8, p.13)

The king-times are fast finishing. There will be blood shed like water, and tears like mist; but the peoples will conquer in the end. I shall not live to see it, but I foresee it.

Ravenna Journal, Jan.13, 1821 (Vol.8, p.26)

It is no great matter, supposing that Italy could be liberated, who or what is sacrificed. It is a grand object—the very *poetry* of politics. Only think—a free Italy!!!

Ravenna Journal, Feb.18, 1821 (Vol.8, p.47)

There is, in fact, no law or government at all [in Italy]; and it is wonderful how well things go on without them.

Jan.2, 1821, to Moore (Vol.8, p.55)

God will not be always a Tory. . . .

Feb.2, 1821, to Murray (Vol.8, p.74)

. . . after all it is better playing at Nations than gaming at Almacks or Newmarket or in piecing or dinnering. . . .

Dec.23, 1823, to Kinnaird (Vol.11, p.80)

RELIGION
As to miracles, I agree with Hume that it is more probable men should *lie* or be *deceived*, than that things out of the course of nature should so happen.   *Sept.13, 1811, to Hodgson (Vol.2, p.97)*

And our carcases, which are to rise again, are they worth raising? I hope, if mine is, that I shall have a better *pair of legs* than I have moved on these two-and-twenty years, or I shall be sadly behind in the squeeze into Paradise.   *Sept.13, 1811, to Hodgson (Vol.2, p.98)*

. . . there is something Pagan in me that I cannot shake off. In short, I deny nothing, but doubt everything.

Dec.4, 1811, to Hodgson (Vol.2, p.136)

I am no Bigot to Infidelity—& did not expect that because I doubted the immortality of Man—I should be charged with denying ye existence of a God.—It was the comparative insignificance of ourselves & *our world* when placed in competition with the mighty whole of which it is an atom that first led me to imagine that our pretensions to eternity might be overrated.

June 18, 1813, to William Gifford (Vol.3, p.64)

My restlessness tells me I have something within that "passeth show". It is for Him, who made it, to prolong that spark of celestial fire which illumines, yet burns, this frail tenement; but I see no such horror in a "dreamless sleep", and I have no conception of any existence which duration would not render tiresome.

Journal, Nov.27, 1813 (Vol.3, p.225)

Is there any thing beyond?—*who* knows? *He* that can't tell. Who tells that there *is*? He who don't know. And when shall he know? perhaps, when he don't expect it, and, generally when he don't wish it. In this last respect, however, all are not alike; it depends a good deal upon education,—something upon nerves and habits—but most upon digestion.

Journal, Feb.18, 1814 (Vol.3, p.244)

. . . if ever I feel what is called devout—it is when I have met with some good of which I did not conceive myself deserving—and then I am apt to thank anything but mankind . . . why I came here—I know not—where I shall go it is useless to enquire—in the midst of myriads of the living & the dead worlds—stars—systems—infinity—why should I be anxious about an atom?

Mar.3, 1814, to Annabella Milbanke (Vol.4, p.78)

I remember a methodist preacher who on perceiving a profane grin on the faces of part of his congregation—exclaimed "no *hopes* for *them* as *laughs*" . . .

Dec.19, 1816, to Augusta Leigh (Vol.5, p.144)

. . . when I turn thirty—I will turn devout—I feel a great vocation that way in Catholic Churches—& when I hear the Organ.

April 9, 1817, to Murray (Vol.5, p.208)

. . . I do not know what to believe—which is the devil—to have no religion at all—all sense & senses are against it—but all belief & much evidence is for it—it is walking in the dark over a rabbit warren—or a garden with steel traps and spring guns.—for my part I have such a detestation of *some* of the articles of faith—that I would not subscribe to them—if I were as sure as St. Peter *after* the Cock crew.

April 14, 1817, to Hobhouse (Vol.5, p.216)

Some of the epitaphs at Ferrara pleased me more than the more splendid monuments of Bologna—for instance

"Martini Luigi
Implora pace."
"Lucrezia Picini
Implora eterna quiete."

Can any thing be more full of pathos! those few words say all that can be said or sought—the dead had had enough of life—all they wanted was rest—and this they *"implore"*. there is all the helplessness—and humble hope and deathlike prayer that can arise from the Grave— *"implore pace"*. I hope, whoever may survive me and shall see me put in the foreigners' burying-Ground at the Lido—within the fortress by the Adriatic—will see those two words and no more put over me. I trust they won't think of "pickling and bringing me home to Clod or Blunderbuss Hall". I am sure my Bones would not rest in an English grave—or my Clay mix with the earth of that Country.

June 7, 1819, to Murray (*Vol.6, p.149*)

It has been said that the immortality of the soul is a "grand peut-être"—but still it is a *grand* one. Everybody clings to it—the stupidest, and dullest, and wickedest of human bipeds is still persuaded that he is immortal.   *Ravenna Journal, Jan.25, 1821* (*Vol.8, p.35*)

. . . the Padre Pasquale Aucher . . . assured me "that the terrestrial Paradise had been certainly in *Armenia*"—I went seeking it—God knows where—did I find it?—Umph!—Now & then—for a minute or two.   *"Detached Thoughts", No.55* (*Vol.9, p.31*)

A *material* resurrection seems strange and even absurd except for purposes of punishment—and all punishment which is to *revenge* rather than *correct*—must be *morally* wrong—and *when* the *World is at an end*— what moral or warning purpose *can* eternal tortures answer?

"Detached Thoughts", No.96 (*Vol.9, p.45*)

I cannot help thinking that the *menace* of Hell makes as many devils as the severe penal codes of inhuman humanity make villains. Man is born passionate of body—but with an innate though secret tendency to the love of Good in his Main-spring of Mind.—— But God help us all!— It is at present a sad jar of atoms.

"Detached Thoughts", No.96 (*Vol.9, p.46*)

I am always most religious upon a sunshiny day. . . .

"Detached Thoughts", No.99 (*Vol.9, p.46*)

. . . I am really a great admirer of tangible religion; and am breeding one of my daughters a Catholic, that she may have her hands full. It is by far the most elegant worship, hardly excepting the Greek mythology. What with incense, pictures, statues, altars, shrines, relics, and the real presence, confession, absolution,—there is something to grasp at. Besides, it leaves no possibility of doubt; for those who swallow their Deity, really and truly, in transubstantiation, can hardly find any thing else otherwise than easy of digestion.

Mar.8, 1822, to Moore (Vol.9, p.123)

REVIEWS

Reviews & Magazines—are at the best but ephemeral & superficial reading—*who thinks* of the *grand article* of *last year*—in any *given review?* in the next place—if they regard *myself*—they tend to increase *Egotism*, if favourable—I do not deny that the praise *elates*—and if unfavourable that the abuse *irritates*—the latter may conduct me to inflict a species of Satire—which would neither do good to you nor to your friends. . . . The same applies to opinions *good—bad* or *indifferent* of persons in conversation or correspondence; these do not *interrupt* but they *soil* the *current* of my *Mind.* . . . You will say—"to what tends all this?—" I will answer *that*——to keep my mind *free and* unbiased—by all paltry and personal irritabilities of praise or censure;— to let my Genius take it's natural direction,—while my feelings are like the dead—who know nothing and feel nothing of all or aught that is said or done in their regard. . . . all reading either praise or censure of myself has done me harm.—When I was in Switzerland and Greece I was out of the way of hearing either—& *how I wrote there!*

Sept.24, 1821, to Murray (Vol.8, pp.220–221)

SELF-ANALYSIS

. . . we are all selfish & I no more trust myself than others with a good motive. . . .   *Sept.28, 1813, to Lady Melbourne (Vol.3, p.124)*

I hate sentiment—& in consequence my epistolary levity—makes you believe me as hollow & heartless as my letters are light—Indeed it is not so.   *[Oct.25, 1813?] to Lady Melbourne (Vol.3, p.155)*

It is odd I never set myself seriously to wishing without attaining it— and repenting.   *Journal, Nov.14, 1813 (Vol.3, p.205)*

. . . I will *not* be the slave of *any* appetite.

Journal, Nov.17, 1813 (Vol.3, p.212)

I only go out to get me a fresh appetite for being alone.
Journal, Dec.12, 1813 (Vol.3, p.238)

My great comfort is, that the temporary celebrity I have wrung from the world has been in the very teeth of all opinions and prejudices. I have flattered no ruling powers; I have never concealed a single thought that tempted me. *April 9, 1814, to Moore (Vol.4, pp.92–93)*

. . . it is her fault if she don't govern me properly—for never was anybody more easily managed.
Oct.7, 1814, to Lady Melbourne (Vol.4, p.199)

. . . I am about to be married—and am of course in all the misery of a man in pursuit of happiness.
Oct.15, 1814, to Leigh Hunt (Vol.4, p.209)

. . . it is odd but agitation or contest of any kind gives a rebound to my spirits and sets me up for a time. . . .
Mar.8, 1816, to Moore (Vol.5, p.45)

. . . I was not, and, indeed, am not even *now*, the misanthropical and gloomy gentleman he takes me for, but a facetious companion, well to do with those with whom I am intimate, and as loquacious and laughing as if I were a much cleverer fellow.
Mar.10, 1817, to Moore (Vol.5, p.186)

[Carnival adventures] I will work the mine of my youth to the last vein of the ore, and then—good night. I have lived, and am content.
Feb.2, 1818, to Moore (Vol.6, pp.10–11)

My time has been passed viciously and agreeably—at thirty-one so few years months days hours or minutes remain that *"Carpe diem"* is not enough—I have been obliged to crop even the seconds—for who can trust to *tomorrow? tomorrow* quotha? *to-hour—to-minute*—I can *not* repent me (I try very often) so much of any thing I have done—as of any thing I have left undone—alas! I have been but idle—and have the prospect of early decay—without having seized every available instant of our pleasurable year. *Aug.20, 1819, to Hobhouse (Vol.6, p.211)*

I am afraid that this sounds flippant, but I don't mean it to be so; only my turn of mind is so given to taking things in the absurd point of view, that it breaks out in spite of me every now and then.
Mar.8, 1822, to Moore (Vol.9, p.123)

SENSATION
The great object of life is Sensation—to feel that we exist—even though in pain—it is this "craving void" which drives us to Gaming—to Battle—to Travel—to intemperate but keenly felt pursuits of every description whose principal attraction is the agitation inseparable from their accomplishment.

Sept.6, 1813, to Annabella Milbanke (Vol.3, p.109)

And yet a little *tumult*, now and then, is an agreeable quickener of sensation; such as a revolution, a battle, or an *aventure* of any lively description.   *Journal, Nov.22, 1813 (Vol.3, p.213)*

SERVANTS
Besides the perpetual lamentations after beef & beer, the stupid bigoted contempt for every thing foreign, and insurmountable incapacity of acquiring even a few words of any language, rendered him [Fletcher] like all other English servants, an incumbrance.

Jan.14, 1811, to Mrs. Byron (Vol.2, p.34)

SEVILLE
Seville is a fine town, and the Sierra Morena, part of which we crossed a very sufficient mountain,—but damn description, it is always disgusting.   *Aug.6, 1809, to Hodgson (Vol.1, p.216)*

SOCIETY
The truth is, my dear Moore, you live near the *stove* of society, where you are unavoidably influenced by its heat and its vapours. I did so once—and too much—and enough to give a colour to my whole future existence. As my success in society was *not* inconsiderable, I am surely not a prejudiced judge upon the subject unless in its favour; but I think it, as now constituted, *fatal* to all original undertakings of every kind. I never courted it *then*, when I was young and in high blood, and one of its "curled darlings"; and do you think I would do so *now*, when I am living in a clearer atmosphere?

Mar.4, 1822, to Moore (Vol.9, p.119)

SPONTANEITY
. . . I can't *furbish*—I am like the tyger (in poesy) if I miss my first Spring—I go growling back to my jungle.

Nov.18, 1820, to Murray (Vol.7, p.229)

... it will be difficult for me not to make sport for the Philistines by pulling down a house or two—since when I take pen in hand—I *must* say what comes uppermost—or fling it away. "Lara" . . . I wrote while undressing after coming home from balls and masquerades in the year of revelry *1814*.   *June 6, 1822, to Murray (Vol.9, p.168)*

STIMULANTS
How do you manage? I think you told me, at Venice, that your spirits did not keep up without a little claret. I *can* drink, and bear a good deal of wine (as you may recollect in England); but it don't exhilarate —it makes me savage and suspicious, and even quarrelsome. Laudanum has a similar effect; but I can take much of *it* without any effect at all. The thing that gives me the highest spirits (it seems absurd. but true) is a dose of *salts*—I mean in the afternoon, after their effect. But one can't take *them* like champagne.
Oct.6, 1821, to Moore (Vol.8, p.236)

THEATRE
I am acquainted with no *im*material sensuality so delightful as good acting. . . .   *[May 8?, 1814], to Moore (Vol.4, p.115)*

. . . I could not resist the *first* night of any thing. . . .
April 23, 1815, to Moore (Vol.4, p.290)

TRAVEL
I remember my friend Hobhouse used to say in Turkey that I had no notion of comfort because I could sleep where none but a *brute* could— & certainly where *brutes did* for often have the *Cows* turned out of their apartment *butted* at the door all night extremely discomposed with the unaccountable ejectment.—Thus we lived—one day in the palace of the Pacha & the next perhaps in the most miserable hut of the Mountains—I confess I preferred the former but never quarrelled with the latter. . . .   *Aug.23, 1813, to Lady Melbourne (Vol.3, p.97)*

Now my friend Hobhouse—when we were wayfaring men used to complain grievously of hard beds and sharp insects—while I slept like a top—and to awaken me with his swearing at them—he used to damn his dinners daily both quality & cookery and quantity—& reproach me for a sort of "brutal" indifference as he called it to these particulars . . . *he* knows that I was always *out* of bed before him—though it is true

that my ablutions detained me longer in dressing—than his noble contempt for that "oriental scrupulosity" permitted.

Nov.9, 1820, to Murray (Vol.7, pp.223–224)

VENICE

[Venice] has always been (next to the East) the greenest island of my imagination. *Nov.17, 1816, to Moore (Vol.5, p.129)*

Venice pleases me as much as I expected—and I expected much—it is one of those places which I know before I see them—and has always haunted me the most—after the East——I like the gloomy gaiety of their gondolas—and the silence of their canals . . .

Nov.25, 1816, to Murray (Vol.5, p.132)

VICE AND VIRTUE

I should wish to gaze away another [year] at least in these evergreen climates, but I fear Business, Law business, the worst of employments, will recall me. . . . If so, you shall have due notice, I hope you will find me an altered personage, I do not mean in body, but in manner, for I begin to find out that nothing but virtue will do in this damned world.

May 5, 1810, to Hodgson (Vol.1, p.241)

Every day confirms my opinion on the superiority of a vicious life—and if Virtue is not it's own reward I don't know any other stipend annexed to it. *Dec.18, 1813, to Henry Drury (Vol.3, p.202)*

I am as comfortless as a pilgrim with peas in his shoes—and as cold as Charity—Chastity or any other Virtue.

Nov.16, 1814, to Annabella Milbanke (Vol.4, p.232)

The general race of women appear to be handsome—but in Italy as on almost all the Continent—the highest orders are by no means a well looking generation . . . Some are exceptions but most of them as ugly as Virtue herself. *Nov.25, 1816, to Murray (Vol.5, p.134)*

In England the only homage which they pay to Virtue—is hypocrisy.

May 11, 1821, to Hoppner (Vol.8, p.113)

WOMEN

I only wish she [an Italian women] did not swallow so much supper, chicken wings—sweetbreads,—custards—peaches & *Port* wine—a

woman should never be seen eating or drinking, unless it be *lobster sallad* & *Champagne*, the only true feminine & becoming viands.

Sept.25, 1812, to Lady Melbourne (Vol.2, p.208)

There is something to me very softening in the presence of a woman,— some strange influence, even if one is not in love with them,—which I cannot at all account for, having no very high opinion of the sex. But yet,—I always feel in better humour with myself and every thing else, if there is a woman within ken. *Journal, Feb.27, 1814 (Vol.3, p.246)*

... the women [in Venice] *kiss* better than those of any other nation— which is notorious—and is attributed to the worship of images and the early habit of osculation induced thereby.

Mar.25, 1817, to Murray (Vol.5, p.193)

I should like to know *who* has been carried off—except poor dear *me*— I have been more ravished myself than anybody since the Trojan war. . . . *Oct.29, 1819, to Hoppner (Vol.6, p.237)*

Your Blackwood accuses me of treating women harshly—it may be so —but I have been their martyr.—My whole life has been sacrificed *to* them & *by* them. *Dec.10, 1819, to Murray (Vol.6, p.257)*

WRITING
I have but with some difficulty *not* added any more to this snake of a poem [*The Giaour*]—which has been lengthening its rattles every month. . . . *Aug.26, 1813, to Murray (Vol.3, p.100)*

All convulsions end with me in rhyme; and, to solace my midnights, I have scribbled another Turkish story. . . .

Nov.30, 1813, to Moore (Vol.3, p.184)

... I do think . . . the mighty stir made about scribbling and scribes, by themselves and others—a sign of effeminacy, degeneracy, and weakness. Who would write, who had any thing better to do?

Journal, Nov.24, 1813 (Vol.3, p.220)

To withdraw *myself* from *myself* (oh that cursed selfishness!) has ever been my sole, my entire, my sincere motive in scribbling at all . . . . If I valued fame, I should flatter received opinions, which have gathered strength by time, and will yet wear longer than any living works to

the contrary. But for the soul of me, I cannot and will not give the lie to my own thoughts and doubts, come what may.

Journal, Nov.27, 1813 (Vol.3, p.225)

I can forgive whatever can be said of or against me—but not what they make me say or sing for myself—it is enough to answer for what I have written—but it were too much for Job himself to bear what one has not—I suspect that when the Arab Patriarch wished that "his Enemy had written a book" he did not anticipate his own name on the title page.

July 22, 1816, to Murray (Vol.5, pp.84–85)

... but poetry is—I fear—incurable—God help me—if I proceed in this scribbling—I shall have frittered away my mind before I am thirty,—but it is at times a real relief to me.

Oct.5, 1816, to Murray (Vol.5, p.112)

I feel exactly as you do about our "art", but it comes over me in a kind of rage every now and then, like * * * *, and then, if I don't write to empty my mind, I go mad. As to that regular, uninterrupted love of writing, which you describe in your friend, I do not understand it. I feel it as a torture, which I must get rid of, but never as a pleasure. On the contrary, I think composition a great pain.

Jan.2, 1821, to Moore (Vol.8, p.55)

I sent two more Poeshies to A[lbemarle] Street—"Cain", a tragedy in three acts—[and] "a Vision of Judgment" by way of reversing Rogue Southey's—in my finest ferocious Caravaggio style. . . .

Oct.12, 1821, to Hobhouse (Vol.8, p.240)

Index to the Eleven Volumes

Abel, **9**, 53, 54
Abdiel, **3**, 225
Abercromby, Miss, **3**, 222, 223
Aberdeen, **3**, 222; **5**, 26n; **7**, 204; **9**, 87; B.'s account in journal, **1**, 25; B. at school, **8**, 99n, 107–8, 238
Aberdeen, George Hamilton Gordon, 4th Earl of, **1**, *254 and n*; **2**, *156n*, 190; **3**, 91 and n; **8**, 73; proposes B. for Athenian Society, **2**, 156 and n; attacked in *Childe Harold*, **2**, 156–7
Aberdeenshire, **1**, 275; **2**, 174n
Abortions, **7**, 138
Abraham, **3**, 164; **5**, 116
Abydos, B.'s swimming feat, **1**, 237 and n, 240, 242, 243, 246, 247–8, 250, 253, 255; **2**, 18, 30, 34, 53, 59; **11**, 157
Acarnania, **1**, 233, 237, 249; **11**, 23, 30, 31, 32, 41, 45, 73, 80
Accademia delle Belli Arte, Venice, **11**, 228
Acerbi, Giuseppe, **5**, 124 and n
Achaean League, **11**, 70n
Achelous, **1**, 237; **11**, 34
Acheron, **2**, 58
Achilles, **1**, 238, 250; **5**, 238n; **8**, 115
Acklom, Esther, **4**, 91 and n
Acropolis, **1**, 3; **2**, 11n, 37, 234n; **3**, 248
Actium, **1**, 237
Actium, Battle of, **1**, 225, 229
Acts of the Apostles, **5**, 205; **11**, 228
Adair, James MacKittrick, *An Essay on Diet and Regimen*, **2**, 191 and n, 197
Adair, Robert, **1**, 236n
Adair, Sir Robert, B.'s letter to, **1**, 256; mentioned, **1**, 236 and n; **2**, 3, 8, 9, 23n, 132, 261 and n; **4**, 262 and n; **11**, 158; Ambassador at the Porte, **1**, *236 and n*, 239, 242 and n, 243, 254, 256 **and n**
Adam and Eve, **3**, 164; **9**, 46, 53
Adam Bey, **2**, 21, 125
Adam, General Sir Frederick, **11**, 23
Adam, William, **4**, 253 and n; **6**, 86
Addington, Henry, **3**, 237n
Addison, Joseph, **2**, 210 and n; **4**, 19; **8**, 110 and n, 120–1; marriage to Countess of Warwick, **7**, 117 and n; attacked by Pope, **8**, 85n; 'little Senate at Buttons', 148 and n; *Cato*, **2**, 179; **5**, 276 and n; *Drummer*, **9**, 196 and n; *Spectator*, **8**, 239 and n

Adolfo (German Philhellene), **10**, 180
Adonis, **6**, 206n
Adriatic, **4**, 93; **5**, 249, 251; **6**, 10, 16, 17, 21, 44, 65, 149, 181, 188, 237; **7**, 63; **8**, 194, 239
Adventurer, The, **4**, 11
Ægean, **2**, 181
Ægina **11, 41**
Ægina, Gulf of, **2**, 27
Ægina marbles, **2**, 29n, 30n
Aeneas, **8**, 115
Aeolian lyre, **11**, 234
Aeschylus, **3**, 221; Promethean theme in B.'s poetry, **5**, 297; Prometheus compared to Manfred, **5**, 268; B. compared to, **9**, 11; *Prometheus*, **8**, 67; **9**, 43, 53; *Seven before Thebes*, **5**, 268
Aesietes, **1**, 250
Aeson, **11**, 156
Aetna, **5**, 210
Aetolia, **1**, 233, 237; **5**, 205; **11**, 32, 45
Africa, **1**, 221, 230, 237; **2**, 4 and n; **3**, 236; **8**, 14n; **9**, 41
Agag, **11**, 197
Agamemnon, **9**, 29; **11**, 85n
Agar, Mr., *see* Ellis, George Agar
Agar, Mr., engraver, **4**, 144n
Agen, Bishop of, **3**, 251n
Agincourt, **10**, 137
Agis IV, King of Sparta, **7**, 132 and n
Aglietti, Carlotta, **6**, 190 and n
Aglietti, Dr. Francesco, **5**, 197; **6**, 77; **7**, 48, 153; **10**, 76 and n; collection of MS letters, **6**, 30 and n, 60, 64; recommended by B., 64, 167, 175; attends Teresa Guiccioli, 176, 239, 241; and Allegra, 245
Aigion, *see* Vostitza
Ailesbury, Lady, **4**, 112n
Airlie, Mabel, Countess of, *In Whig Society*, **3**, 72n
Ajax, **1**, 238; **3**, 107
Ak-Deniz, **3**, 213 and n; **11**, 224
Alacrity, gun-brig, **11**, 100n, 101n, 102
Alamanni, Luigi, **8**, 124
Alban mount, **5**, 221, 227, 233
Albania, **2**, 10, 21 and n, 53, 58, 102n, 113, 125, 134, 262, 263; **3**, 111; **4**, 299; **5**, 205; **7**, 179; **8**, 219; B. visited Ali Pasha, **1**, 3, 226 and n, 254; B. travelling in, 233, 235, 237, 242, 254, 255; B.'s letters from, 234, 235, 249; **2**, 75; saw more of than any other

Albania—*continued*
Englishman, **1**, 237 and n, 248; Lord Aberdeen's explorations, 254n

Albanians, **2**, 13, 21; **11**, 34, 157; description of, **1**, 227, 228 and n, 229; soldier attended B., 228 and n; B.'s servants, **2**, 7, 9, 10 and n, 19, 27, 31, 34, 123; **11**, 157

Albanian dress, **1**, 231 and n; given to Mercer Elphinstone, **4**, 112–13; Phillips portrait, 112n, 113, 250

Albano, **5**, 221

Albany, N.Y., **3**, 229

Albany House, **3**, 255n; **4**, 124n, 147, 175, 232, 264, 281; B. took bachelor quarters in, **4**, 87 and n, 91 and n

Albaro, **10**, 77; **11**, 76

Albemarle Street, **1**, 124; **2**, 53, 55, 57, 125n, 286; **3**, 6, 11, 13; **4**, 87n, 142; **6**, 166, 235n, 240; **7**, 190, 218; **8**, 162, 193n, 239, 240; **9**, 61, 73, 83, 122, 209; **10**, 42, 116; **11**, 24; Murray moving to, **2**, 235 and n

Albemarle, William Charles, 4th Earl of, **3**, 116n; **11**, 224

Albergo Imperiale, **7**, 13n, 25

Alberoni, Cardinal, **6**, 181; **8**, 36 and n, 39; **11**, 231

Alberoni, Giulio, **3**, 213 and n

Alborghetti, Count Giuseppe, B.'s letters to, **6**, 171, 177; **7**, 237, 243; **8**, 124, 140, 142, 180; biog. sketch, **6**, 275; mentioned, 262 and n; **7**, 35, 51, 125n, 134; **8**, 13, 21, 48–9; **9**, 181 and n; a trimmer, **8**, 18 and n; and Gigante, 124 and n; and Tita's arrest, 140 and n, 142 and n

Albrizzi, Count Giuseppe, **5**, 293

Albrizzi, Count Giuseppino, B.'s letters to, **6**, 57, 74, 90; **8**, 51, 52; mentioned **6**, 57n, 90n; **8**, 52n, 125 and n

Albrizzi, Countess Isabella Teotochi, biog. sketch, **5**, 293; mentioned, 182, 183, 193, 275–6, 277; **6**, 8, 18, 19, 38n, 42, 75 and n, 90n, 93, 96, 184, 238; **8**, 125; **9**, 31; **10**, 130; **11**, 197; bust of Canova, **5**, 132n, 133, 148; friendship with B., 142, 146, 148, 151; called De Staël of Venice 148, 293; asked for B.'s works, 163; illustrator of Canova, 207; her *conversazioni*, 293; **6**, 19, 20, 90n; character study of B., 58; B. met Teresa at her house, 107, 117, 277; *Ritratti*, **5**, 277n, 293

Alcibiades, **1**, 238; **5**, 186; **9**, 48

Aldea Gallega, **1**, 219

Alder, William, **10**, 119n, 129 and n

Aleppo, **10**, 57

Alesia, **9**, 48

Alexander, Czar, **4**, 132n

Alexander the Great, **2**, 190; **3**, 145; **5**, 237, 238n; **6**, 91; **8**, 27, 238; **11**, 74

Alexander, Dr. James, B.'s letters to, **10**, 106(2), 147, 186, 196, 202; mentioned, 106, 128; **11**, 82; medical supplies for Greeks, **10**, 186–7, 188, 195, 196–7, 202; recommended Dr. Bruno, 194n, 206; consulted by B. on wart, 147, 148

Alexander VI, Pope, **5**, 114, 123

Alexandria, **6**, 244n

Alexandrine, **5**, 262

Alfieri, Count Vittorio, **3**, 133, 245; **5**, 216, 218, 293, 295; **6**, 145, 181, 276; **7**, 150, 182; **8**, 57, 93, 152, 164, 218; incest theme, **3**, 196 and n, 199; and Comtesse d'Albany, **8**, 14 and n; B. likened to, **9**, 11; *Filippo*, **8**, 12 and n, 15n, 210; *Mirra*, **6**, 206 and n, 217; **8**, 210

Alfred Club, *see under* Byron, Clubs

Algarotti, Francesco, **6**, *30 and n*, 60; **7**, 184; *Opere*, **6**, 30n

Algeciras, **1**, 221

Algiers, **2**, 36; **5**, 107n, 125

Ali Pasha, B.'s letter to, **4**, 299; mentioned, **1**, 225, *226n*, 231 and n, 237; **2**, 21 and n, 22n, 83, 102 and n, 262n; **3**, 110–11, 111–12; **4**, 299; **6**, 4n; **10**, 180n; **11**, 158; receives B., **1**, 227–8, 234; knew B. to be of noble birth, 227, 238, 249, 254; and young Bossari, **2**, 11; marries Giaffer Pasha's daughter, 114; letter to B., 113, 124 and n, 263

Alkmaar, **2**, 112

Allan, Mr., **6**, 223

Allegra, *see* Byron, Allegra

Allen, John, **3**, *239 and n*

Allingham, John Till, *The Weathercock*, **1**, 101n; **9**, 37

Allsop, Mr., B.'s letter to, **11**, 189

Almack's, **1**, 17; **3**, 70, 272; **7**, 169n, **11**, 80

Alma Mater, **1**, 108, 111, 163, 193, 197; **10**, 63; **11**, 176

Alpine Journal, **1**, 20; **5**, 96–105, 188, 268; **8**, 176

Alpine journey, **1**, 20

Alphonso III, **4**, 251n

Alps, **5**, 75, 80, 90, 92, 99, 100, 114, 123, 154, 170, 188, 227; **6**, 9, 126, 174, 216; **7**, 17, 76; **8**, 176, 225; **10**, 162; **11**, 163, 167

Altamont, Peter Howe Browne, Lord, *see* Sligo, Marquis of

Althorp, John Charles Spencer, Viscount (later 3rd Earl Spencer), marriage, **4**, *91 and n*; sublets apartment to B., **3**, 255 and n; **4**, 91n

Alvanley, Lord **9**, 22 and n, 83 and n; **10**, 141; **11**, 58
Alvisi, **6**, 92
Amadis de Gaule, **5**, 262n
Amalekites, **5**, 232
Ambracian Gulf, **1**, 233
Ambrose, **1**, 171
Ambrosian Library, **5**, 114, 116, 123
Amcotts-Ingilby, Sir John, **2**, 131n
America, *see also* Byron, views on; **1**, 209n; **2**, 28n, 219; **3**, 218, 236, 249n; **4**, 93, 198n, 251; **6**, 131, 209; **7**, 44; **8**, 36; **9**, 41, 49, 179, 192; **10**, 157, 170, 204n, 208; B.'s popularity in, **9**, 52, 162 and n, 163; **10**, 36, 131, 153; "a model of force and freedom", **1**, 16; **8**, 240; B.'s desire to go to, **10**, 86, 118; B. thought of purchasing land in, **11**, 49
Americans, **4**, 184; **9**, 161 and n, 164, 208; **10**, 131, 202; **11**, 229; B. liked their praise, **3**, 236; **9**, 17, 20–21, 162 and n, 164; 'a nod from an American', 171
American Negro, **11**, 31 and n
American squadron, **9**, 161 and n, 162, 164, 171, 179
American War, **2**, 215n; **4**, 243; **8**, 40n; **9**, 25n; **10**, 196n
Americani, **8**, 39, 43, 48, 197
Amicable Society, **7**, 231
Amphion, **8**, 114
Amphissa, **11**, 134n
Amsterdam, **2**, 112n; **3**, 180n
Anabaptists, **2**, 112n
Anacharsis, **2**, 32n
Anacreon, **1**, 115, 118; **2**, 97, 123 and n, 284–5, **3**, 49
Anak, **2**, 95; **3**, 210 and n
Anarghiro, Signor, **11**, 52n, 68, 134n
Anatoliko, **11**, 34, 79n, 80, 90, 106 and n, 150n
Ancona, **8**, 33, 34; **10**, 151, 162, 169, 180; **11**, 20, 30, 78
Anderson Galleries, **1**, 163n
Andes, **6**, 212
Andrews, Miles Peter, *Better Late than Never*, quoted, **1**, 122 and n
Angelo, Henry, B.'s letter to, **1**, 92; fencing master, *92 and n*, 162n; **6**, 218 and n; **7**, 118; **9**, 12
Angelina, **6**, 108 and n, 133–4
Angostura, **9**, 173 and n
Anguish, Catherine, **1**, 45n; **6**, 62n
Aniello, Tommaso (Massaniello), **8**, 36 and n
Ann (storeship), **11**, 31n, 105n, 111n, 217
Anne, Queen, **5**, 218, 265
Annesley, Lady Catherine (sister of Lady Webster), **3**, 127 and n, 141, 142,

208, 237 and n; **4**, 31–2; last Lord Bury, **3**, 116, 133; B. alleged pretendant to her hand, **3**, 151, 153
Annesley, Lady Frances Caroline (later Lady Webster), **2**, 126 and n, 287
Annesley Hall, **1**, 43n, 173n
Annesley, Lady Juliana (sister of Lady Webster), **3**, 208, 223, 241; **4**, 36
Annual Register, The, **2**, 215n; **3**, 102n
Anstey, Christopher, *New Bath Guide*, **6**, 91, 94, 234, 253; **7**, 101; **10**, 98 and n
Anti-Byron, **4**, 81 and n, 82
Anti-Corn Law League, **10**, 230
Anti-Jacobin Review, The, **1**, 144 and n, 147; **2**, 197 and n; **3**, 66n, 144, 208n, 216n; **4**, 95 and n, 96, 287n, **5**, 59n, 260; **8**, 11n; **11**, 226
Antilochus, **1**, 236, 237, 238
Antinous, **5**, 218
Antioch, **9**, 150
Anton, Miss, **1**, 195n
Antonines, **8**, 107
Antonio, servant, **6**, 175
Antonio, Carlo, **5**, 293
Antony, Mark, **3**, 207; defeat at Actium, **1**, 229
Antwerp (Anvers), **3**, 180n; **5**, 72, 73, 74, 75, 76, 217
Apennines, **5**, 211, 217, 234; **9**, 50, 53, 55, 66
Aphrodite, **1**, 237n
Apocalypse, **5**, 101
Apollo, **6**, 145n; **8**, 132, 189; **9**, 41
Apollo Belvedere, **3**, 75n; **5**, 227
'Apollo and Hyacinth', **1**, 207n
Apollonius of Tyana, *Life*, **8**, 127 and n, 238 and n
Apreece, Jane (née Kerr), **11**, 180 and n
Aquinas, Thomas, **11**, 159
Arabia, **11**, 107
Arabian Nights, **3**, 164; **4**, 62 and n
Arachova, **6**, 173 and n
Arbuthnot, Dr. John, **2**, 114
Arcadia, **2**, 16n; **5**, 99
Archimedes, **11**, 108
Archipelago, **2**, 41, 126; **11**, 72, 80
Arethusa, Fountain of, **11**, 30
Aretino, Pietro, **9**, 11
Arezzo, **7**, 47
Argentiere, Aiguille de, **5**, 96
Argonauts, **1**, 245 and n; **8**, 100n; **11**, 156n
Argos, **2**, 9, 11, 13, 16, 137; **10**, 180, 181; seat of legislative body, **11**, 72n
Argostoli, **11**, 15n, 16n, 18, 20n, 29, 31, 46n, 23, 58, 66, 86n, 87n, 89n, 91, 96 and n, 99; Chalandritsanos family, 213
Argyle Institution, **2**, 168 and n, 169; **3**, 170; **9**, 22

Argyrocastro, **5**, 76
Ariadne, **6**, 21
Arianism, **3**, 63 and n; **9**, 86
Aricia, **5**, 221
Arimaspians, **8**, 208 and n; **10**, 116 and n
Ariosto, Ludovico, **1**, 13, 94; **2**, 63; **3**, 221; **6**, 147; **8**, 53, 210; **10**, 68, 132; **5**, 217, 266; Titian's portrait of, 213; bust of, **6**, 8 and n, 14; freedom in writing, 77, 91, 95, 234; *Orlando Furioso*, **6**, 145; **7**, 124n
Aris, Governor, of Coldbath Fields prison, **5**, 233 and n
Aristides, **1**, 20; **3**, 218; **10**, 59
Aristippus, **1**, 148
Aristophanes, **8**, 132
Aristotle, **8**, 115, 141, 223; Tyrnhill's (Tyrwhitt's) ed., **5**, 36; on melancholy of geniuses, **9**, 47
Armenia, **5**, 156; Earthly Paradise in, **1**, 22; **5**, 157; **9**, 31
Armenian and English Grammar, **5**, 142 and n, 146, 152, 156, 157 and n, 179, 193, 235; **6**, 9n; **9**, 31; **10**, 112
Armenian language, **5**, 130–31, 137, 140–41, 142, 146, 152, 160, 162, 179, 274; **7**, 60; **8**, 237; **11**, 164; B.'s study of, **1**, 22; B.'s translations from, **5**, 201, 238; **6**, 29, 38
Armenian monastery, **5**, 130–31, 137, 140
Armenians, **2**, 35; **5**, 157n; **6**, 29
Armida, **2**, 108, 238 and n, 250, 261, 286; **10**, 131
Armstrong and Crooke, B.'s letter to, **5**, 51; sale of B.'s books, 42n, 51
Armstrong, Col., **9**, 18
Armstrong, F. C., B.'s letter to, **9**, 116
Arnauts (Arnaouts), **2**, 113, 118, 123, 132; **5**, 92
Arnaut Beligrade, **2**, 114
Arnaut garments, **4**, 112–13
Arno, **4**, 93, **8**, 39, 246; **9**, 61, 66, 74, 105, 185
Arnold, Samuel James, **5**, *107 and n*; *The Prior Claim*, 107n
Arqua, **5**, 217, 264; **6**, 17
Arrian, **8**, 58
Arta, **10**, 179n, 180; **11**, 23n, 143
Artemesia, **5**, 125
Artificers, going home, **11**, 118, 119n, 124; returned home, 125, 127, 133, 142
Artillery Brigade, **11**, 152; paid by B., 142, 145
Asham, [J.?], B.'s letter to, **3**, 198
Asham, T., **3**, 198 and n
Ashbourne, **4**, 270
Ashburton, John Dunning, 1st Baron, **9**, 47n

Ashe, Thomas, B.'s letters to, **3**, 197; **4**, 15; *Memoirs and Confessions, The Spirit of 'The Book'*, **3**, *197n*; B. lends him money, **4**, 15
Asia, **1**, 216; **2**, 9, 92; **3**, 179, 236; **6**, 64n; **8**, 80; **9**, 17; **11**, 58; B. intends to enter, **1**, 178, 230, 232; B. will not proceed further into, 250; B. has been in, **2**, 4
Asia Minor, **1**, 237, 251, 254n, 255; **2**, 17; **3**, 207; **5**, 99; **8**, 219
Asiatics, **3**, 218; **11**, 35
Asmodius, **2**, 251; **3**, 16
Aspasia, **2**, 283; **7**, 143
Assisi, **7**, 229
Assyrians, **8**, 26, 126
Astakos (Dragomestri), **11**, 88 and n
Astley, Philip, **6**, 27n; **8**, 224n; **9**, 36
Aston Hall, **2**, 287; **3**, 120, 123, 125, 130, 131, 132, 138, 139, 152, 154, 155, 193; **4**, 22, 36, 40, 67, 125; Webster's residence, **3**, 81n, 114n; where B.'s father adulterated, 81n, 122; B. at, 115–16, 132–6, 139–45, 148, 193
Athanasius, Creed of, **4**, 109, 172
Atheism, **3**, 251; **4**, 50, 51; **8**, 96; **9**, 97 and n; Matthews an atheist, **2**, 76
Athenaeus, **4**, 104 and n, 106
Athenian Society, **1**, 254n; **2**, 156 and n
Athens, **2**, 10, 14, 46, 57, 60, 190, 198, 262; **3**, 27, 57n, 155n, 199n, 230, 248; **4**, 161, 215, 299n; **5**, 42n, 219; **6**, 66; **7**, 60n, 179; **8**, 59, 237; **9**, 237; **10**, 57, 180; **11**, 134n, 138n, 146n, 157; B. describes life in, **1**, 3; B. headed for, 225, 233, 246; B. to study modern Greek in, 230, 232; Greek girls in, 240; B. ten weeks at, 234, 235, 237, 239, 255; compared to Troad, 236; B. wrote from, 249; B. has seen, 251; B. returned to from Constantinople, **2**, 3, 8; B. met Sligo in, 5, 8; B. returning to from Morea, 7, 8, 16; B. at, 11–14, 23–44, 50; B. met Lady Hester Stanhope, 21; governor of, 27; B.'s headquarters in, 17, 18; English in, 23, 31, 33n, 42, 43; females in, 31; Hobhouse knows, 33; Bruce in, 49 and n; robbery of ruins, 66n; B.'s poems written at, 78; notes to *Childe Harold* written in, 102, 115–17; British Embassy at, **3**, 68n; relief of, 1827, **11**, 39n; Trelawny with Odysseus in, **9**, 237; **11**, 23n, 137n; Stanhope left for, 138, 218
Atherton, John, Bishop of Waterford, **2**, 132 and n
Athlone, Earl of, **6**, 252 and n
Atkinson, Joseph, friend of Moore, **4**, 253 and n

Atlantic Ocean, **1**, 239; **4**, 152; **9**, 174
Attica, **1**, 237, 238, 239; **2**, 13, 31, 34
Atticus, Titus Pomponius, **6**, 89
Aubonne, **5**, 104
Aucher, Padre Pasquale, **1**, 22; **9**, 31;
  10, 112, 128; B.'s Armenian tutor, **5**,
  137, 142 and n, 152, 157n; helps B.
  translate two Epistles, 201 and n,
  238; Armenian-English Grammar,
  146, 152, 156–7, 157n, 179, 235; **6**,
  9 and n
Aufrere, A., **9**, 156n
Augustine, coachman, **6**, 150, 162, 163
Augustus, Emperor, **1**, 25, 229; **4**, 54;
  6, 9; **8**, 47, 106–7
Aurelius, Marcus Aurelius Antoninus,
  9, 45
Austerlitz, **9**, 48
Australia, **4**, 187n; **8**, 215n
Austria, Emperor of, **4**, 298n; **8**, 12n;
  11, 223
Austrian monarchy, **11**, 139 and n
Austrians, **5**, 117n, 121, 122, 126, 132,
  146, 235, 295; **6**, 108, 240; **7**, 178,
  190, 210, 211, 212, 213, 236; **8**, 20,
  36, 105n, 108n, 121, 122n, 154, 155;
  10, 179, 180, 181, 189 and n; B.'s
  hatred for, **7**, 77, 82, 85, 152n, 179
  and n, 183, 206, 237, 238–9; **8**, 26,
  44, 79, 84, 96, 125; (Germans), 33,
  43, 84, 106, 126, 130, 134
Austrian journal, **9**, 175–6
Aveiron, **5**, 94, 206
Aventicum, **5**, 78; **11**, 227
Avranches, **8**, 20n
Ay, Lady (Aylesford?), **3**, 86 and n

Babylon, **2**, 211; **5**, 252; **7**, 125, 258
Bacchus, **6**, 12
Bacon, Francis, Baron Verulam, on ass-
  assination, **7**, 184, 249; B. alleges
  inaccuracies, **8**, 14, 18, 162 and n, 192,
  194; 'Of Revenge', **11**, 233
Baden, **5**, 77
Bagdad, **3**, 27
Bagnacavallo, Convent School of San
  Giovanni Battista, **8**, 91 and n, 97,
  226, **9**, 146, 148
Bailen, battle of, **8**, 126n
Baillie, Joanna, **3**, 109, 180 and n; **4**, 86,
  236 and n, 290; **5**, 203; **8**, 207, 219;
  De Montfort (*Plays of the Passions*),
  4, 336–7, 337n; **8**, 208 and n, 210
Baillie, 'Long', **2**, 28 and n, 33, 84,
  114,129; **5**, 144 and n, 183 and n, 198;
  7, 225, 233; **9**, 19; **11**, 163 and n, 165
  and n
Baillie, Dr. Matthew, examines B.'s
  club foot, **1**, 41n; consulted by Lady
  B., **5**, 33 and n
Bainbridge, Mr., **5**, 30 and n

Bairaktar, Pasha of Rouschouk, **3**, 58n
Bajazet, Ottoman ruler, **9**, 155 and n
Bakewell, **5**, 131n; **7**, 253
Balaam, **5**, 159
Balani, accident victim, **8**, 165
Balatreri, Signor, **9**, 126, 211
Balcarres, James Lindsay, 5th Earl of,
  4, 103n
Baldwin, Mr., libels Lady Frances
  Webster, **5**, 28 and n; **10**, 48n
Baldwin, W. J., B.'s letter to, **3**, 164;
  King's Bench prisoner, his petition, **3**,
  164 and n, 165 and n, 193n, 206n,
  228–9, 233
Baldwin, Craddock & Joy, publishers,
  5, 205n; **11**, 228
Balfour, Mr., **8**, 88
Ball, Admiral Sir Alexander, **1**, *230 and
  n*, 239n; death, **2**, 8 and n
Balliol College, Oxford, **5**, 136n
Baltimore, **4**, 198n
Baltimore, Francis Calvert, 7th Lord,
  1, 145 and n
Bambas (Vambas), Neophytos, **11**, 126
  and n, 132
Banbury, **6**, 243n
Bancroft, George, visits B. at Villa
  Dupuy, **9**, 164 and n, 165
Bandello, Matteo, Italian novels, **3**, 251
  and n, 252; **5**, 132 and n
Banff, **3**, 222
[Banier?], Mr., **11**, 100
Banker (creditor), **10**, 96
Bankes, George, quotes *English Bards*,
  8, 79 and n
Bankes, William John, B.'s letters to, **1**,
  110, 112, 198; **2**, 172, 173 (2), 214,
  261; **6**, 243; **7**, 39, 45; **8**, 228; mentioned, **2**, 87, 162, 214–15, 261, 262;
  3, 15 and n; **4**, 66; **6**, 12, 200, 243n;
  8, 228; B. fears his criticism, **1**, *110*,
  111; invites B. to 'one of my places',
  2, 84; **11**, 160 and n; rejected by
  Miss Milbanke, **3**, 103; in quarantine in Trieste, **6**, 240, 245; to return
  to England, 243; return from the
  East, **7** 27 and n: left for Florence,
  28; B.'s praise of, 39n, 150, 168, 195,
  225; invited to Ravenna, 39 and n; at
  Venice and Ravenna with B., 51; at
  Cambridge with Matthews, 230–31
Barbarossa, Horuc, **3**, 213 and n
Barbary, **1**, 221
Barbauld & Co., **1**, 225, 234
Barber, John Vincent, **2**, 113n
Barberini, Princess, **6**, 149
Barbieri, Giovanni Francesco (il Guer-
  cino), **5**, 116 and n
Barcelona, **8**, 77, 84
Barclays Bank, **11**, 155
Bardi, print seller, **9**, 214

Barff, Samuel, B.'s letters to, **11**, 99, 100, 110, 115 (2), 118, 119 (2), 128, 130, 137, 138, 139, 141, 150, 152 (2); biog. sketch, 154; B.'s banker at Zante, 16n, 63, 65 and n, 75, 89n, 93, 94, 107, 109, 135, 137; offered B. his country house, 131; and Greek loan, 146n; partner of Hancock, 16n, 65 and n, 89, 214

Baring Brothers, **11**, 147 and n

Barnard, Lady Anne, authoress of *Auld Robin Gray*, **4**, 103n

Barnard, Mother, **1**, 68 and n

Barras, Paul-Jean, vicomte de, **3**, 210 and n

Barrett, **9**, 194

Barrow [Anna Maria], B.'s letter to, **3**, 5; mentioned, 5n

Barrow, Sir John, **3**, 5n; **5**, 169; **8**, 151 and n, 155, 163

Barry, Charles F., B.'s letters to, **10**, 159, 161, 185, 187, 194, 195, 201; **11**, 16, 43, 52, 75, 81, 153; biog. sketch, **10**, 228; mentioned, 183, 199, 200, 205, 206, 210; **11**, 152; B. opened mind to, **1**, 17; finds vessel for B., **10**, 151, 159 and n, 185, 228; recommends advocate, 161; credits for B.'s Greek venture, 177, 186, 188, 228; sale of B.'s snuff boxes, 81, 185 and n, 194–5; B.'s banker friend and confidant, 228; and B.'s possessions in Genoa, **11**, 55, 76, 153

Barthelemi, **2**, 12

Bartley, George, actor, B.'s letter to, **4**, 293; mentioned, 293 and n; Falstaff, 313n

Bartley, Mrs. (née Smith), **4**, 290 and n, 293n, 314

Bartolini, Lorenzo, B.'s letter to, **9**, 57; busts of B. and Teresa, 57–8n, 121–2, 121n, 136 and n, 157, 216–17; **10**, 18; B.'s bust resembles Jesuit, **9**, 213, 214, 215; engraving by Morghen, 214

Barton, Bernard, B.'s letters to, **2**, 178; **4**, 97; mentioned, **2**, 178n; **4**, 97 and n; **5**, 89–90; *Metrical Effusions*, **2**, 178n

Basinghall St., **3**, 29

Basle, **5**, 78, 86

Bassae, **2**, 30n

Bassano, **6**, 96; **8**, 81

Batavia, **9**, 30

Bath, **2**, 144; **8**, 217; **9**, 207; order of the, **3**, 249n

Bathurst, Allan, Lord, **11**, 220

Bathurst, Capt. Walter, B.'s letter to, **1**, 244; mentioned, 242n, *244n*; **7**, 99; **8**, 80, 83, 121

Batt's Hotel, **2**, 251; **3**, 14

Battailin, Count, **10**, 103

Battersby, madman, **9**, 28

Battuzzi, **9**, 135

Baudry, publisher, **10**, 204n

Bavaria, **3**, 158; **10**, 180, 181

Baxter, coachmaker, **2**, 68; **4**, 333 and n; **5**, 72 and n, 73, 278; **10**, 27, 74, 91, 110 and n, 111, 113, 118, 153, 159

Bayard, le Chevalier, **2**, 246 and n

Bayes, **7**, 181

Bayle, Pierre, **8**, 237; **9**, 76; *Dictionnaire Historique*, 102 and n, 106; **8**, 238 and n

Baylen, battle of, **1** 221n

Bayman, footman to B., **5**, 75

Baynes, Mr., **11**, 115

Bayonne, **4**, 102 and n

Beattie, James, **6**, 85; *The Minstrel*, **7**, 42

Beauclerk, Topham, **6**, 166; **7**, 16n; **9**, 89n

Beaumarchais, Pierre Augustin, **2**, 142 and n

Beaumont, F. and Fletcher, J., **6**, 95; *Philaster* (prologue), **2**, 210 and n; **5**, 173 and n

Beaumont, Sir George and Lady, **3**, 214 and n

Beauvais, Bishop of, **9**, 26

Beccaria, Cesare Bonesana, Marchese di, **5**, 117 and n; *Dei Delitti e delle Pene*, 117n

Becher, Anne, **1**, 125 and n, 126

Becher, Rev. John Thomas, B.'s letters to, **1**, 157, 162, 170; mentioned, 7, 97n, 123 and n, 125n, *126 and n*; **2**, 72; objects to 'To Mary', **1**, 97n, 123n; asked to read proof, 137, 138; his interest in B.'s poems, 158

Becher, Richard Turner, **1**, 125n

Becher, Sherard, **1**, 94 and n, 104 and n, 126–7, 136 and n

Beckford, William, **11**, 230; and Lord Courtney, **1**, 210 and n; B.'s interest in his tales, **6**, 17 and n; *Vathek*, **2**, 107; **3**, 164; **6**, 17n, 18; **11**, 76 and n

Bective, Lord, **1**, 151 and n, 152 and n

Bedford, Duke of, **3**, 70

Bedlam, **7**, 159

Beefsteak Club, **3**, 79n

Bees, on *Bolivar*, **10**, 36, 37, 39–40, 43–44, 45, 75

Behman (Boehme) Jacob, **2**, 82 and n; **4**, 324; **6**, 47

Belcher, Tom, **7**, 233 and n; bout with Dan Dogherty, **1**, 162 and n

Belem Castle, **1**, 215n

Belfast, **7**, 74

Belgrade, **1**, 250

Belham Scholarship, **1**, 184n

Bell, Henry Nugent, *Huntingdon Peerage*, **7**, 196 and n

Bell, John, solicitor, **9**, 209, 212, 213; **10**, 47; **11**, 233; B. sought his counsel on Hanson's account, **7**, 198

Bellamy, pastry cook, **7**, 205; **9**, 14 and n

Bellamy, Mr., **10**, 65, 74

Bellamy, Mrs., **10**, 16–17

Bellasyse, Mr., **4**, 198

Bellingham, John, **2**, 177 and n

Belmont, Hertfordshire, **1**, 277

Beloe, Rev. William, ed. *The British Critic*, **6**, 11n; *The Sexagenarian*, 11 and n, 12 and n

Belzoni, Giovanni Battista, *Narrative of the operations . . . in Egypt and Nubia*, **8**, 79 and n

Bembo, Cardinal, letters from Lucretia Borgia, **5**, 114, 116 and n, 123

Benacus (Lago di Garda), **5**, 123 and n

Bendall, Newstead tenant, **4**, 293 and n

Bender, W., *The Armenian* (trans.), **5**, 203n

Benedetto Theatre, **5**, 143 and n, 182

Benedictines, **6**, 8n

Benini (later Ovioli), Rosa, dialogue with B. on the Pope, **9**, 51

Bennet, C. E., **2**, 14n; **9**, 39n

Bennet Street, **3**, 41, 61, 115, 117, 148

Bent, Jeffrey Hart, **2**, 45 and n; **11**, 220

Bentham, Jeremy, **3**, 225n

Bentham, Sir Samuel, **3**, 225 and n

Benthamites, **11**, 217

Bentinck, Lord Frederick, **5**, 95 and n

Bentinck, Lord William Cavendish, **3**, 86n; **5**, 171 and n; **7**, 184 and n

Benzoni, Countess Marina Querini, B.'s letter to, **8**, 137; biog. sketch, **6**, 276; mentioned, 32, 38n, 92, 96, 177 and n, 179, 184, 191; **7**, 226; **8**, 130 and n, 135, 180 and n, 241; **10**, 130; her *conversazioni*, **6**, 37, 107, 108, 114, 140, 276; a Venetian Lady Melbourne, 40, 97; B. met Teresa at her house, 107, 108, 111n, 114; and the Fornarina, 195

Benzoni, Count V., **8**, 135

Berat, **2**, 21, 114

Berdmore, Samuel, **11**, 155

Berdmore, Scrope, **11**, 155

Berdmore, Thomas, **11**, 155

Berdmore, William, **11**, 155

Beresina, **6**, 51n, 60

Berg Collection, N.Y. Public Library, **1**, 109n, 152n

Bergami, Bartolommeo, alleged lover of Queen Caroline, **7**, 122, 153, 213, 214 and n; **8**, 100 and n, 147n

Bergamo, **8**, 53n

Berge (telescopes), **10**, 82

Berger, B.'s Swiss guide, **5**, 60 and n, 71, 97, 144

Berkeley, Col., seducer, **8**, 140 and n

Berkeley, Sir George, **10**, 30n, 130n

Berkeley, Lord, of Stratton, **10**, 30n

Berkeley Square, **3**, 248; **4**, 19

Berlin, **5**, 14n, 216n; **8**, 164

Bermuda, **3**, 45; **4**, 243 and n; **6**, 67n, 205 and n; **8**, 251; **9**, 69

Bernadotte, Count, **3**, 107 and n, 172, 211

Bern, **5**, 86, 100, 103; **6**, 238

Bernese Alps, **5**, 93, 94, 104, 108, 109, 205; **8**, 11, 113

Berni, Francesco, **6**, 77; adaptation of Boiardo's *Orlando Innamorata*, 24 and n

Bernini, Giovanni Lorenzo, **6**, 149 and n

Berri, Duc de, assassination, **7**, 50 and n

Berry, the Misses, **3**, 97n, 214 and n, 228, 231, 244; **4**, 65, 105, 112n

Berry, Mary, **2**, 174 and n; *Journal and Correspondence*, 170n, 174n; **3**, 44 and n

Bertrand, Gen. Henri Gratien, **4**, 126 and n

Berwick, Rev. Edward, **8**, 127n

Berwick-upon-Tweed, **2**, 65n

Bess, maid at Newstead, **2**, 155

Bessborough, Frederick Ponsonby, 3rd Earl of, **1**, 125n; **2**, 217, 244, 283

Bessborough, Lady (née Lady Henrietta Frances Spencer), m. of Caroline Lamb, **2**, 174n, 184 and n, 283; **3**, 10, 42n, 69, 129, 171; **4**, 87, 132; **5**, 204; **7**, 169; **8**, 155; her daughter's affair with B., **2**, 184, 186, 187 and n, 193, 194, 195, 196, 200, 202, 203, 217, 222, 239, 243, 244, 245, 247, 248, 249, 250, 252, 254, 256, 258, 259; nicknamed by B. "Lady Blarney", 185 and n, 235, 240, 246; **3**, 23, 27, 37, 40, 90, 126, 170; **4**, 136, 158, 258; on B.'s deficiency in Romance, **3**, 16; B.'s antipathy to, 23, 27, 31, 40–41, 53

Bettesworth, Capt. George Edmund Byron, **1**, *135 and n*; **11**, 158n, death, off Bergen, **1**, 209n

Bethlehem Hospital (Bedlam), **2**, 207 and n; **5**, 179n, 208, 238n

Betty, William Henry West ('Young Roscius'), **1**, *67 and n*; B. on, **2**, 192, 193, 213, 214 and n

Bey of Corinth, **4**, 46n

Beyle, Henri, B.'s letter to, **10**, 189; Hobhouse on, 189n; *Histoire de la Peinture*, 189; *Rome, Naples, and Florence in 1817*, 189 and n; **11**, 76 and n

Bianchetti, **9**, 66

Bianchi, Marechal, **6**, 40

Bianchini, the, danseuse, **6**, 165, 176 and n, 190

43

Bianchoni (Bianchini), Francesco, **6**, 8 and n, 14
Bible, **8**, 238; **9**, 198
Bible Society, **11**, 132 and n
Bibulus, **6**, 209 and n
Bickerstaffe, Isaac, *Love in a Village*, **1**, 240; **2**, 48; **5**, 182 and n; **11**, 220, 221
Bickersteth, Henry, **6**, 187 and n
Bindlose (née Delawarr), Cecilie, **1**, 55n
Bindlose, Sir Francis, **1**, 55n
Bingen, **5**, 76
Biographica Britannica. **4**, 92
Biographica Dramatica, **7**, 61n
Birch, Alderman, **2**, 250 and n
Birch, J., B.'s letter to, **1**, 174; mentioned, 101 and n, 102, 120, 174 and n, 205n; **2**, 190 and n
Birch of Stockport, **6**, 211
Birmingham, **3**, 127
Birmingham University, **7**, 252n
Biron, Marshal, **10**, 208
Biron, Princess, Duchess of Hohen, **4**, 128 and n
Biscay, Bay of, **4**, 151, 152, 263
Bishop's Castle, **2**, 282; **5**, 168n; **6**, 200n, 210, 212; **7**, 75, 95
Black, John, **8**, 165n
Black John, lugger, **2**, 30, 36
Black Prince, **5**, 142n
Black Sea, **1**, 245 and n, 250; **2**, 84; **3**, 180n; **11**, 157
Blackburne, **1**, 160
Blacket, Joseph, **1**, 194n; **2**, 53 and n, 76, 80, 82, 132, 175; **3**, 89n, 110 and n
Blackett, artisan, **11**, 94 and n, 96, 97, 115 and n
Blackmore, Sir Richard, **8**, 23
Blackwell, **9**, 35
Blackwood's Edinburgh Magazine, **3**, 217n; **5**, 249 and n, 268n, 269n; **6**, 3n, 126, 212n, 257 and n; **7**, 49, 195; **8**, 88, 99n, 144, 156, 164 and n; **10**, 206; Murray's partnership in, **6**, 3n; reviews *Don Juan*, 257n; **7**, 60n; **9**, 190; B.'s reply to, **7**, 59, 114n, 201 and n, 205, 212; **8**, 197 and n; **9**, 58 and n, 190 and n; **10**, 64–5; on B. and Moore, **7**, 245n; and B.'s geese, **9**, 83 and n; review of Moore's *Irish Melodies*, 117 and n; Wilson's savage reviews, **10**, 81n
Blackwood, William, **3**, 238 and n
Blair, Hugh, sermons, **5**, 97
Blake, barber, **3**, *3 and n*; **5**, 135 and n, 190; **6**, 222 and n; **7**, 227, 228
Blake, Mr. **2**, 153
Bland, Rev. Robert, **2**, 20 and n, 55, 127, 142, 149, 156; **3**, *130 and n*, 235; **11**, 179; English chaplain in Holland, **2**, 109 and n, *112 and n*; translation

of *Charlemagne*, 136 and n, 137, 141 and n, 146; prevented from duelling by B., 129–30, 132, 148; **9**, 26; *Collections from the Greek Anthology*, **1**, 241, 246 and n; **2**, 112n; **3**, 7 and n; *Four Slaves of Cythera*, **2**, 112n
Bland, Thomas Davison, Lady Byron's trustee, **7**, 40 and n; **10**, 95, **11**, 135, 227, 235; and an Irish loan, **8**, 61–2, 72, 76, 87, 135, 210
Blaquiere, Edward, B.'s letters to, **10**, 139; **11**, 15; mentioned, **10**, 126, 142, 143, 144, 147, 149, 150, 152–3, 170, 171, 173, 176, 177, 184, 186, 187, 203, 214; **11**, 29 and n; one of the founders of London Greek Committee, **10**, 139n, 229; called on B. in Genoa, *139 and n*; at Rome, 151, 153; on way to Greece, 169; at Corfu, 179; **11**, 16 and n, 29 and n; at Zante, **10**, 195, 196, 199, 200; urged B. to go to Greece, 199; urged loan to Greek government, 210, 211; on way home, **11**, 20, 22, 29; returned to England, 41; his report to Committee, 55; invited Mavrocordatos to England, 104 and n; Parry thinks him a humbug, 108
Blessington, Earl of, B.'s letters to, **10**, 138, 139, 141, 146, 148 (2), 156, 157, 167, 171, 183, 192; biog. sketch, 229; mentioned, **7**, 106, 116, 136, 210, 240, 248; **8**, 61–2, 65, 69; **10**, 141 and n,145, 174; owner of Ormond Quays, **7**, 70 and n; arrival in Genoa, **10**, 135n, 136, 229; death of his son, 141 and n; bought B.'s schooner, 182n, 194, 214 and n; marriage, 229; delay in paying for *Bolivar*, **11**, 81; and purchase of *Bolivar*, 153
Blessington, Marguerite, Countess of, B.'s letters to, **10**, 163 (2), 166, 192; biog. sketch, 228–9; mentioned, **1**, 1; **2**, 283, 286; **7**, 138n, 161n, 165n; **9**, 100n; **10**, 138, 140, 142, 145, 148, 157, 163, 167–8, 174, 183; arrival in Genoa, 135 and n, 136, 229; described by B., 137, 197; defended B., 163; her verses, 168; Lawrence's portrait of, 174–5, 229; Teresa jealous of her, 175, 177; sold Arabian horse to B., 183 and n; parting gift from B., 192 and n; B. not in love with, 197; bored with husband and D'Orsay, 197; her past history, 229; *Journal of the Conversations of Lord Byron*, **3**, 128n, 273; **10**, 135n, 229; leaving Genoa, 183
'Blessington Circus', **10**, 228
Blidworth Land purchase, **4**, 163

Blinkensop, unidentified, **3**, 73
Blomfield, Edward Valentine, reviews *Géographie de Strabon*, **2**, 102 n
Bloomsbury, Maryland, **6**, 123n
Bloomsbury Square, **3**, 248; **4**, 237; **9**, 205
Blücher, Gerhard von, Marshal, **3**, 246; **4**, 37 and n, 128, 302; **5**, 76, 98 and n; B. on, **9**, 49
Bluebeard, **2**, 212n
Blümel, Dr., of Breslau, **1**, 71n
Boa Constrictor, **5**, 159, 172, 243; **6**, 59; **11**, 163 and n, 165
Board of Longitude, **6**, 29 and n
Boatswain, B.'s dog, **2**, 26n, 72, 94; **4**, 256 and n; **7**, 225; B.'s Newfoundland dog, **1**, 120 and n, 123 and n, 127, 132; death and tomb inscription, 176 and n, 178 and n, 202n
Boccaccio, Giovanni, **6**, 188n; Boccaccian tales, **2**, 45, 127; **3**, 251n; scene of Boccaccio's tale, **6**, 166, 168, 181; **7**, 252; old woman reading, **6**, 190; *Decameron*, **5**, 251; **8**, 48 and n
Bodleian Library, **5**, 88n
Boeotia, **1**, 238
Boffini, Signor, **6**, 74
Bohemia, **2**, 199
Boiardo, Matteo Maria, **6**, 77; *Orlando Innamorato*, 24n
Boileau, Nicolas, **3**, 213n
Boisragon, Dr. Henry Charles, **2**, 222
Boissy, Count de, **6**, 278
Bokara, **2**, 91
Bolgheri, **9**, 102 and n
Bolingbroke, Henry St. John, 1st Viscount, **9**, 116
Bolívar, The, (Schooner), **9**, 87, 113, 116, 137 and n, 149, 178, 181, 184 and n, 186 and n, 192 and n, 197 and n, 203 and n; **10**, 11–12, 12n, 25 and n, 36–7, 43–4, 45, 60; laid up at the arsenal, **10**, 40, 43, 60, 102, 182n; B.'s intention to take to Greece, 134, 182 and n; hoisting a 'pendant', [pennant] 165–6; sale to Lord Blessington, 182n, 194, 200, 214 and n; **11**, 55, 153; at Lerici, 196
Bolívar, Simon, **6**, 225; **9**, 173
Bolívar (city), **6**, 240
Bologna, **5**, 211, 216, 231, 234, 295; **6**, 39, 128, 141, 142, 144, 145, 146, 147, 149, 151, 154, 156, 157, 162, 163, 198 and n, 240, 260; **7**, 14, 25, 27, 40, 100, 104, 109, 163 and n, 228; **8**, 12, 14, 43, 131, 159, 161, 168, 169–70, 175, 245, 246, 247; **9**, 12, 30n, 49, 50, 53, 54, 56, 66, 167n; **10**, 130; **11**, 163; B. to meet Guicciolis in, **6**, 200 and n, 201, 202, 203, 204, 206; B. out of sorts at, 214,

215, 216–17, 224, 225; B. in, 146–50, 206–24, 259–60; picture galleries, **7**, 45; Carbonari failed to strike, 172, 177; Allegra to be brought to, **11**, 192 and n
Bologna cemetery, **6**, 148–9, 217
Bologna Telegraph, **7**, 49
Bolognese, **8**, 34
Bolton, Samuel, B.'s letters to, **2**, 71, 73 (2); **11**, 177; mentioned, **2**, 68; and B.'s will, 71–3
Bombard, taken by Turks, **11**, 86n, 87 and n, 88, 89, 102; released by Turks, 90, 91 and n
Bombay, **3**, 104n
Bonaldo, **7**, 203
Bond St., **3**, 216n; **10**, 53
Bonivard, François, **5**, 87
Bonn, **5**, 76, 78
Bonneval, C. A. Comte, **3**, 213 and n
Bonstetten, Charles Victor de, **5**, 86 and n, 87, 205, 207n
Booth, G., **8**, 129n
Bordeaux, **5**, 81
Boreham Wood, Herts, **4**, 213n
Borgia, Caesar, **5**, 114
Borgia, Lucretia, Duchess of Ferrara, letters to Cardinal Bembo, **5**, 114–15, 116, 118 and n, 123
Boringdon, Lord, B.'s debt to, **3**, 29 and n, 30
Borromean Islands, **5**, 114, 115, 117, 125
Borromeo, Carlo, **5**, 125 and n
Borst, William A. *Lord Byron's First Pilgrimage*, **2**, 27n
Bosnia, **2**, 113
Bosnians, **2**, 123
Bosphorus, **1**, 245 and n, 250; **3**, 180, 184, 212; **8**, 194, 239
Bossari, **2**, 11
Bossi, Giuseppe, *Life of Leonardo*, **8**, 13 and n
Bossons Glacier, **5**, 102
Boston, **8**, 146; **10**, 131n
Boswell, James, **1**, 163n; **2**, 132n; **8**, 110; **9**, 86; journals compared with B.'s, **1**, 1; *Life of Johnson*, **3**, 67n; **4**, 74n, 278n, 290n, 315n; **6**, 166n, 208 and n; **7**, 16n, 191 and n, 205, 229 and n; **8**, 12; **9**, 89 and n, 99n
Boswell, James the younger, **3**, 80n
Bosworth Field, **1**, 136
Botany Bay, **5**, 15n; **8**, 215n
Botherby, W., 'Song of Triumph,' **7**, 73
Botsaris, Constantine ('Kosta'), **11**, 41
Botsaris, Marco, **11**, 41; killed in battle, 23 and n, 40, 54; his last letter 26, 32
Botsaris, Noti (Noto), **11**, 143

Boulogne, **11**, 53 and n
Bounty, The, **10**, 89n
Bourbons, **1**, 16; **3**, 257; **4**, 94, 101, 157 and n, 179, 317; **5**, 76; **7**, 207; **11**, 53n
Boussa, **6**, 244n
Bow Church, **8**, 101
Bow Street, **2**, 204n
Bowdlerizing, **1**, 4, 24, 26
Bowen, possible identity, **2**, 133 and n
Bowers, 'Bodsy', **8**, 107–8
Bowman, Newstead tenant, **1**, 251 and n, 252; **2**, 52; **4**, 41 and n
Bowood Park, **2**, 223; **5**, 200n; **6**, 24n
Bowles, William Lisle, **1**, 188n; **2**, 66n, **4**, 286; **5**, 111n, 240–1; **8**, 132, 145, 201, 207, 213, 236; B.'s letter on Pope, **3**, 145n, 171n; **7**, 61n; **9**, 58, 68, 84, 93, 98; **10**, 134; and the woods of Madeira, **7**, 220; B. on his attack on Pope, 229, 245; *Quarterly* on, 253; B.'s 1st and 2nd letters to Murray on Bowles, *see under* Byron, Works; dispute with Campbell over Pope, **8**, 43, 50, 76n, 110; and Moore, 109 and n, 110, 134 and n, 146; his civil reply to B., 111 and n, 116, 136, 141, 145; **9**, 67; anecdote of his youth, **8**, 111–12; attack on Gilchrist, 111n, 199n, 200; and Hobhouse, 126 and n, 130, 134, 143, 239; *Invariable Principles of Poetry*, **7**, 217 and n; *The Missionary of the Andes*, **5**, 187 and n, 193, 199; **8**, 111 and n; *Spirit of Discovery*, **5**, 241n; 'Strictures on the Life and Writings of Pope', **8**, 53n, 76n; 'Two Letters to the Right Honourable Lord Byron', 126n
Bowring, John, B.'s letters to, **10**, 168, 179, 212, 213; **11**, 64, 72, 73, 76, 82, 101, 129, 139, 145; biog. sketch, **10**, 229–30; mentioned, **11**, 27, 74, 80, 119, 131, 144, 151, 153, 218; and London Greek committee, **1**, 17; **10**, 168 and n, 179 and n, 184, 211, 229, 230; **11**, 50, 53 and n; prospect of a Greek loan, 41; arrested by French at Calais, 53n; *Specimens of the Russian Poets*, 85 and n, 147 and n
Boyce, Francis (Frank), **1**, 79 and n, 98–99, 100; deportation, 79n, 100n, 107, 116
Boyce, Susan, actress, **6**, 97 and n; B.'s affair with, **8**, 185 and n
Boyd, Hugh S., *Writings of St. Chrysostom*, **4**, 252 and n
Boyd, Henry, **7**, 58
Boyne (ship), **3**, 76, 84 and n, 88, 106
Bozzi, Count, **7**, 65–6
Bracchi, Cardinal, **5**, 219, 224
Bracciaferro, Count of Ravenna, **3**, 253

Braccio di Montone, **3**, 253
Bradford, Lord, **9**, 131
Bradshaw, Hon. Augustus Cavendish, **4**, 296 and n, 297
Braemar, **9**, 87
Braganza, **4**, 161
Braham, John, 'Entusymusy', **3**, 209 and n; **4**, 263 and n, 274; **5**, 218; **8**, 114; **10**, 84; **11**, 20, 108
Braithwait, Richard, **3**, 95n
Bramber, **6**, 96n
Bran (?B.'s dog), **1**, 123 and n, 127, 132
Branksome Castle, **1**, 227
Brazil, **5**, 163, 183, 272; **6**, 172n; **11**, 163, 164
Brême, Luigi (Ludovico), the Abbate, **5**, 124 and n, 181; **6**, 63; **8**, 172–3; defence of Italian writers, **6**, 51, 53, 56, 90n, 91, 93; illness, 96
Brême, Marchese di, **5**, 121, 124n
Brenta (river), **5**, 234, 237, 238, 242; **6**, 17, 147, 192; **9**, 18; B.'s palace on **11**, 166, 198
Brera Gallery, Milan, **5**, 116
Brescia, **5**, 151
Breslaw's Last Legacy, **2**, 97 and n.
Brest, **2**, 58
Briareus, **4**, 46, **9**, 30 and n
Brick, Windsor, **1**, 62 and n
Bridgeman, **1**, 139
Bridge of Sighs, **5**, 244
Bridge Street, **8**, 181; **9**, 200; **10**, 67 and n, 68, 98
Bridges, Thomas, *Homer Travestie*, **8**, 22 and n
Brientz, **5**, 102, 103, 205
Brighthelmstone, **5**, 74; **7**, 99; **9**, 39
Brighton, **1**, 167 and n, 168, 170, 180; **2**, 62, 162n; **3**, 94, 235; **4**, 212, 256n, 257; **7**, 222, 224; **9**, 35, 82, 88; B. at, **11**, 176
Bristol, **2**, 166; **7**, 63n
Bristol, 4th Earl of, **3**, 174n; **5**, 270n
Britain, **4**, 12
British Constitution, **7**, 244
British Critic, The, **2**, 174 and n; **3**, 209 and n; **4**, 205n, **6**, 11n
British Institution, **3**, 46n
British Library, **11**, 223
British Museum, **10**, 142n
British Press, **2**, 166
British Review, The, **2**, 175, 181 and n; **3**, 141 and n; **6**, 213n; **9**, 58 and n
Brock, **3**, 212
Brocket Hall, **2**, 260; **3**, 93, 123, 154; **4**, 199; Lady Caroline Lamb at, **11**, 182
Brockman, W., **1**, 71 and n, 75
Broglie, Albertine, Duchesse de (née de Staël), **5**, 86 and n, 88n, 111; **6**, 127 and n; **8**, 167 and n, 172; **9**, 47

Brompton, **1**, 167n, 170; **2**, 155; **5**, 97; B.'s lodgings in, **11**, 161

Brønsted, Peter Oluf, **2**, 27n, **37** *and n*, 43

Brook, Master, **2**, 141; **11**, 179

Brook Street, **8**, 25

Brooke, Fulke Greville, 1st Baron, **3**, 62 and n; MS poem, **2**, 249

Brookman, **7**, 229

Brooks's Club, **3**, 249; **5**, 188, 194; **11**, 158

Brothers, Richard, **2**, 97 and n; **5**, 267 and n

Brothers, Messrs., **2**, 52 and n

Brougham, Henry (later Baron Brougham and Vaux), B.'s letter to, **7**, 95; mentioned, **1**, 193 and n; **7**, 180; **8**, 100; **9**, 14; reviews *Hours of Idleness* (in *Edinburgh Review*), **1**, 157 and n, 177n, 255n; **3**, 203n; **6**, 86n; **11**, 188n; obtains Hunt's acquittal, **3**, *203n*; loses his seat, 249 and n; B.'s hatred of, **5**, 184n, 223, 225; B.'s 'character' of, **6**, 85, 86–7; B. intends to challenge, 188–9, 242 and n, 246; **7**, 95–6, 96n, 153–4, 178, 188–9; **10**, 89n, 126; **11**, 168n; defender of Queen Caroline, **7**, 153 and n, 178; B. calls him blackguard, 181; stanzas on in *Don Juan*, 188 and n

Broughton, **5**, 97

Broughton, Baron (John Cam Hobhouse), *Recollections of a Long Life*, **2**, 258n; **5**, 62n; **7**, 231n; **8**, 121n

Brown, Rawdon, **5**, 147n

Brown, Thomas, *see* Moore, Thomas

Brown, Tom, *Works*, **5**, 179n

Brown, Col., and Queen Caroline, **8**, 65 and n

Brown and Henshaw, **4**, 301 and n

Brownbill, blacksmith, **11**, 106, 126, 133

Browne, Mr., **5**, 90

Browne, Dominick, **1**, 139n, 158 and n

Browne, Isaac Hawkins, **2**, 221 and n, 228

Browne, James Hamilton, **11**, 72, 93; arrived in Cephalonia, 52 and n; trip to Ithaca, 18 and n; in the Morea, 23 and n, 26, 33, 38, 57; returned to Cephalonia and England, 23 and n; treated well by Greek Government, 52 and n; to negotiate B.'s bills, 61, 62; offers services to Greek committee, 66

Browne, William George, **6**, 244 and n

Bruce, Michael, **2**, 21n, 49 and n; **4**, 215 and n; **6**, 200–1

Bruen, George H., B.'s letters to, **9**, 162, 174; Portrait of B., 162 and n, 164 and n; offers passage to America, 179

Bruges, **1**, 184n; **5**, 71, 72; **7**, 50, 63, 100

Brummell, George Bryan, 'Beau', **4**, 117n; **7**, 50 and n; **10**, 141; in France, **9**, 21–2; 'Dandy', 22n

Bruno, Dr. Francesco, **11**, 79, 82, 86n, 89n, 92, 133; B.'s personal physician, **10**, 194n; on the *Hercules*, 210n; trip to Ithaca, **11**, 18n; and Gamba's order for red cloth, 96 and n; and B.'s last illness, 217

Brunswick, **8**, 251

Brunswick family, **4**, 154n

Brussels, **3**, 232n; **5**, 80n; B. at, 72–6 **11**, 190n; after Waterloo, 28n

Brutus, **3**, 207, 218, 228, 243; **8**, 107

Bryant, Jacob, *Dissertation concerning the War of Troy*, **8**, 22 and n

Bryce, Rev. Dr., Letter to, **9**, 83

Brydges, Sir Samuel Egerton, *Letters on ... Lord Byron*, **3**, *217n*; *The Ruminator*, 217 and n

Buc (Buck), Sir George, *History of ... Richard the 3rd*, **5**, 111 and n; **6**, 140 and n

Bucke, Charles, *Philosophy of Nature*, **3**, 41 and n

Buckingham, George Nugent-Temple Grenville, 1st Marquis of, **3**, 232 and n

Buckingham, Duke of, **2**, 15n; **3** 116

Buckingham, George Villiers, 2nd Duke of, **11**, 220; *The Rehearsal*, **8**, 120 and n

Buffini, **7**, 25, 28

Buffon, George Louis, Comte de, **3**, 234; **8**, 222

Bugden, **3**, 117

'Bull and Mouth', **5**, 262

Bülow, General, **3**, 180n

Buonaparte, Louis, *Documents Historiques*, **8**, 44 and n

Buonaparte, Lucien, **2**, *28 and n*; *Charlemagne*, 136n, 137, 141n, 197n; **3**, 97, 101n, translations, 78 and n, 97n, 150 and n

Buonaparte, Napoleon, **2**, 52; **3**, 78, 86, 95, 107, 125, 157–8, 218, 242, 243–4, 246, 249n, 256; **4**, 53, 60, 63, 125n, 282, 330n; **5**, 14 and n, 34n, 73, 74, 157, 169n, 205, 213, 277n; **6**, 51, 60, 100n, 209, 279; **7**, 50, 137, 152n, 154; **8**, 107, 182; **9**, 21, 22, 29, 47, 74, 77, 155, 171n; **11**, 22, 49, 74, 223; his last twelvemonth, **1**, 20; threatened invasion, 77n; the chin of, 118; Austrians beating, 206; incensed with Mrs. Smith, 224; gave snuffbox to Ali Pasha, 228; imprisoned Cazenoves, **2**, 41n; **4**, 305n; 'direful foe', **2**, 197 and n; dark and diabolical,

Buonaparte, Napoleon—*continued*
203; B. will back him against the
field, 261; Mamaluke Guard, **3**, 28;
B.'s bust of him, 210; portrait print,
248 and n; abdication, 256; **4**, 90 and
n, 91, 93, 98n, 101, 284–5, 284n;
B.'s Ode to, **3**, 257; **4**, 94 and n, 98
and n, 99, 102 and n; and de Staël, **3**,
273; his fall prophesied, **4**, 19; his
spirit seems broken, 27; Moscow
retreat, 39; seems to be reviving, 46;
report he has lost his senses, 126;
escape from Elba, 283 and n, 284 and
n, 285, 287n; nicknamed 'Jack', 306
and n; triumphal arch, **5**, 114, 117;
before Marengo, 125; B. accused of
being his panegyrist, 198, 201, 204;
on St. Helena, 215 and n; snuff box
with his portrait, **6**, 221 and n, 223;
10, 185 and n; **11**, 81; death, **8**, 166
and n, 225n; B. compared to **9**, 11;
as general, 26, 48; transported to St.
Helena, 116n; memoirs of, **10**, 82 and
n, 108; cameo of, 192 and n; campaign in Italy, **11**, 34 and n; sent copy
of Hobhouse's book, 228–9
Burckhardt, John Lewis, **6**, 244 and n
Burdett, Sir Francis, **1**, 16, *186 and n*,
209n; **2**, 22, 167, 174 and n, 286; **3**,
18 and n; **4**, 122 and n; **5**, 172 and n,
182, 233; **6**, 63, 107, 109, 232; **7**, 44,
45, 49, 62, 63, 70n, 86; in Parliament
for Westminster, **1**, 186n; **6**, 59 and
n; genteel reformer, **1**, 186n; **7**, 44;
8, 240; as B.'s arbiter, **6**, 79; **9**, 73,
105 and n, 106–16, *passim*, 124, 137,
138, 144–5, 151, 152–3, 176, 194,
212; **10**, 58, 73, 75; B.'s admiration
for, **6**, 166, 233; duel with Paull, **8**,
144n; and Canning, 144 and n, 145,
149; as orator, **9**, 14; marriage to
Sophia Coutts, **1**, 186
Burdett (née Coutts), Lady Sophia, **9**,
138n
Burgage Manor, Mrs. Byron rented
house, **1**, 44 and n, 93n, 277
Burges, Sir James Bland, B.'s letters to,
4, 288, 327, 328 (2); **5**, 26; mentioned, 26 and n; **7**, 178; **8**, 61;
Wentworth's executor, **4**, 288, 309
and n, 327–9; literary ambitions, 328
and n; **9**, 35 and n
Burges, Lady (nee Hon. Elizabeth
Noel), **4**, 288n
Burgundians, **5**, 78; **8**, 20n; **11**, 227
Burke, Edmund, **3**, 80n, 225; **4**, 105n,
326 and n; **6**, 48, 89; **7**, 63n; B.
compared to, **2**, 167; as orator, **9**, 13,
14
Burke's Peerage, **1**, 50n
Burlington House, **4**, 135n; **10**, 141

Burnet, Bishop, *History of My Own
Times*, **5**, 67n
Burney, Fanny (Mme D'Arblay)
Cecelia, **2**, 143; **5**, 98; *The Wanderer,
or Female Difficulties*, **2**, 143n, 146,
147; **3**, 204n; **4**, 86 and n, 87, 146
and n
Burns, Robert, **3**, 114; **6**, 85; **8**, 93; **9**,
11; his unpublished letters, **1**, 19;
3, 202 and n, 239; B. on his character,
207, 239; 'Tam O'Shanter', **4**, 56 and
n; and whisky, 85
Burrows, **1**, 139
Burton, Sir Richard, *Arabian Nights*, **4**,
62n
Burton, Robert, *Anatomy of Melancholy*,
3, 243 and n; **8**, 238 and n
[Burwash?], Sussex, **10**, 97
Bury, Augustus Frederick, Viscount,
11, 224
Bury, Lord, **11**, 224
Bury, Viscount, s. of 4th Lord Albe-
marle, **3**, 116 and n, 133
Bury (Berry), Navy Surgeon, **7**, 193
Bury Street, **5**, 188
Busby, Dr. Thomas, **2**, 227; **3**, 210 and
n, 211; **4**, 81 and n, 82 and n, 93; his
rejected address, **2**, 228n, 235, 250
and n
Bushe, Charles Kendal, **11**, 225
Bute, Lord, **2**, 180n
Butler, Mr. C., **9**, 136, 137
Butler, Charles, *Historical Memoirs
respecting the … Catholics*, **8**, 144
and n
Butler, Lady Eleanor, **1**, *125 and n*
Butler, Dr. George, **1**, *53n*; **2**, 155;
succeeds Drury, **1**, *64 and n*; lampooned by B. as Pomposus, 64n, 111
and n, 133n, 145n, 146, 153, 155;
speechday, 69; B. reconciled to, 145n,
153–4, 154–5 and n; recommends
Friese, 206 and n, 208; presented B.
a gold pen, 216, 239
Butler, Joseph, *Analogy of Religion*, **4**,
60
Butler, Samuel, **6**, 85; *Hudibras*, **2**, 126;
3, 52 and n; **4**, 28 and n; **7**, 234 and n;
8, 53; **9**, 25 and n
Butler, Dr. Samuel, B.'s letter to, **3**,
150; and Lucien Buonaparte, 130 and
n; translates *Charlemagne*, **2**, 136n,
141n, 197n; **3**, 97n, 130n, 150 and n
Button's Coffee House, **8**, 148n
Büyükdere, village, **3**, 180 and n
Byrne, Oscar, ballet-master, **4**, 330 and
n; **9**, 36
Byron, Allegra, **5**, 264n, 295; **7**, 186,
209; **9**, 120; birth, **5**, 228n, 294, 296;
the Shelleys and, 296, 297–8; her
name, **6**, 7; B.'s plans for, 7; d. of B

and Claire Clairmont, 10, 171, 175 and n, 204; to be sent to B., 14, 17, 20, 25, 37; in Venice, 39 and n, 41, 42, 212, 228, 230; resembles Lady Byron, 62; appearance, 67, 150, 223, 238; with her mother at Este, 69; miniature, 74; to be brought to Bologna, 198, 218; **11**, 192; to have a governess, **6**, 212–13; in Bologna, 223, 226; B. to take her to South America, 226, 228, 235, 236, 242; to accompany B. to England, 242, 245; illness, 242, 245, 247, 249, 253, 255, 259; **7**, 147, 148, 149, 151, 162, 167, 176; **11**, 195; health and character, **7**, 15, 17, 66, 78, 80, 119, 227; Hoppners gave toys to, 25; riding with Teresa, 35, 36, 66; spoilt, 80, 166; her up-bringing, 80, 251; to country house, 152, 157–8; Claire's letters to B. about, 174; B.'s concern for her morals, 174; **8**, 140; and Elise, **7**, 191n; education, **8**, 29, 76, 87, 98, 112; B's concern for, 33; at Bagna-cavallo, 91 and n, 97 and n, 98, 103, 112–13, 130, 138, 139; B. wants potrait by Holmes, 95; to become a Catholic, 98; **9**, 119, 123; future plans for, **8**, 125, 171; B.'s legacy, 125; **10**, 162; and Shelley, **8**, 171; letter to B., 226 and n; death, **9**, 146 and n, 147, 148 and n, 151, 170, 193n; **10**, 55, 162; body shipped to England, **9**, 163 and n; burial in Harrow church, 146–7, 163–4, 166; **10**, 54–5; funeral of, 64; no memorial in-scription, **9**, 164n; **10**, 65; **11**, 224

Byron, Anne Isabella, Lady (Noel) (née Anne Isabella [Annabella] Milbanke, q.v.) B.'s letters to, **4**, 287, 309; **5**, 15, 21, 22, 24, 26, 30, 33, 38, 40, 41, 46, 51, 54, 56 (2), 61, 62, 66, 120, 180; **6**, 80, 180, 260; **7**, 40, 68 (2), 210, 248, 256; **8**, 61, 89, 209; **9**, 64 and n, 65; mentioned, **4**, 253, 307n; **5**, 23, 39, 122, 162; **6**, 65, 79, 80, 84, 235; **8**, 75, 91, 95, 132, 139, 234–5; **9**, 35n, 194; **10**, 30, 162, 176, 178; **11**, 120; copied B.'s poems, **4**, 249 and n, 277; **5**, 13 and n; marriage arrangements, **4**, 249–51; honeymoon, 249–51, 252, 254, 262; 'Treaclemoon', 263; her title older than B.'s, 254; has her own way, 258; heir to Lord Wentworth, 264–5, 285, 288; saved B. from suffocating, 267–8; marriage settle-ment, 270, 272, 273, 298n, 300n, 326, 327–8, 329; **8**, 72n; a woman of learning, **4**, 271; to remain at Seaham, 276; Prince de Ligne's

autograph, 283 and n; pregnancy, 285, 289, 291, 294, 297, 303, 310, 317n, 318, 323, 327, 328; receipt of Stothard's drawings, 292 and n; not a 'fine lady', 294–5; not a scribbler, 310; has a copy of *English Bards*, 318, 321; gives birth to daughter, 338; to go to Kirkby with Ada, **5**, 15 and n, 20; B. says she is truth itself, 20 and n; proposes separation, 21, 23, 29 and n; praised by B., 20–1, 21–2, 23, 44, 55; B. pleads with her to return, 22, 23–4, 24–5, 26–7, 33, 38–9, 40–1; legal affairs, 46–50; deed of separation, 65 and n, 69 and n, 91–2, 242, 255–6; urged to be kind to Augusta, 66; **7**, 41, 212, 256–7; B. on her illness, **5**, 87–8, 89, 91, 109; on a reconciliation, 87–8, 120–1, 175, 180; kind to Augusta, 91; 10, 14; opens B.'s letter trunks, **5**, 93; B.'s afterthoughts, 94, 104–5, 119, 120, 188, 228; B.'s fear she would take Ada to Continent, 109–10, 118, 121, 128–9, 144–5, 150–1, 153–4, 160, 189, 223, 224–5, 242; 'moral Clytemnestra', 144, 186, 191, 198; **6**, 150; **7**, 51; **10**, 142; **11**, 197; 'She's a fool', **5**, 175; B.'s worst enemy, 190; her 'magnanimity', 232; **7**, 208; **8**, 60; B. on her silence, **5**, 255–6; 'mathematical Medea', **6**, 17, 23, 133; **8**, 74, 86, 240; **11**, 197; Allegra resembles, **6**, 62; a cold blooded animal, 70; Romilly her adviser, 78n, 80, 90; efforts at reconciliation by Hanson and Webster, 78n, 227–8; as Donna Inez in *Don Juan*, 95n, 257n; **7**, 208, 239 and n; correspond-ence with B., **6**, 126–7; 'fiend', 129, 131; B.'s settlement invested, 136, 247, 252; refuses character for Fletcher's wife, 171; B.'s wish for a divorce, 171; separation discussed in Germany, 223; her jointure, 247–8; offered view of B.'s Memoirs, 257; **7**, 16–17, 68 and n, 102; B. on their financial affairs, 14, 15, 40, 41, 44, 68, 71, 210–11, 213–14, 221, 240, 252; B. would not attend coronation with, 41, 42, 50; an equinoctial line between her and B., 42; declines to read Memoirs, 68n; B. sends word he wishes to remarry, 91n; Brougham her adviser, 95–6; the 'White Devil', 123 and n, 124; reaction to 'Fare Thee Well', 199 and n; called 'Mathematician', 199, 214, 220, 221; date of leaving B., 207; old starch obstinacy, 208; and Augusta's family, **8**, 62; B. regrets their meeting, 62,

Byron, Anne, Isabella—*continued*
63, 69; B.'s letters and verses, 176–7,
221, 227, 228 and n; B.'s novel on
separation, 196n; and Augusta, 217;
Teresa champions her, 234–5; verses
on by German Baroness, **9**, 24; on
B.'s melancholy, 38; an only child,
52, 77; B. on their separation, 65–6;
B. insures her life, 105, 106, 107–8,
112, 113, 114, 115, 124, 127, 141, 151,
158, 166, 188, 206, 211, 214; **10**, 20,
26, 35, 38, 43, 49, 60, 61, 67, 74,
143, 196; B. did not marry her for
money, **9**, 108–9; her dowry, 108–9,
141, 187, 195; division of Noel
property, 108–9, 111–13, 198; **10**,
115, 149, 150; **11**, 42; B.'s feelings
about, **9**, 120; ill health, 138, 141,
145, 166; **10**, 163; and church living
at Kirkby, 14–15, 54, 203 and n,
204; in Harrow Church, 54–5, 64;
on Cunningham, 65; B.'s income only
during her life, 85; Augusta passed
B.'s letters to, 111n; B. wants her
miniature, 163; letters to B. returned,
163; B.'s unsent letter to, 167 and n;
offered view of B.'s letter, **11**, 45;
employs physician for Ada, 46; B.
leaves direction of Ada to her, 47; B.
wanted to send Hatagée to, 111n,
120; report on Ada's health, 120;
Satire on in *Don Juan*, 171 and n;
'mathematical Blue Devil', 197;
marriage settlement trustees, 227;
jeu d'esprit on, 227
Byron, Hon. Augusta, (later Hon. Mrs.
George Leigh), see also Leigh, Hon.
Augusta; B.'s letters to, **1**, 44, 45, 46,
48, 52, 53, 55, 57, 58, 60, 62, 65, 66,
68, 69, 72, 73, 75, 79, 85, 86, 87;
biog. sketch, 273; conflicting relations
with B., 19, 66, 274; marriage, 44
and n; various 'homes', 46n, 60n, 65
and n, 76n; unhappiness in love, 52
and n, 69; income, 52n; at Castle
Howard, 57 and n, 75n; attachment
to her cousin George, 60n; half-
brothers and half-sisters, 60n; bore-
dom with Garter Installation, 67 and
n; letter from Mrs. Byron, 68; misses
Harrow speech-day, 69 and n; asked
by B. to guarantee a loan, 86–7, 87n,
90n; B.'s attack on Carlisle, 255–6
Byron, (Augusta) Ada (later Lady
Lovelace), d. of B. and Annabella, **2**,
284; **4**, 338; **5**, 27, 30, 39, 45, 69, 70,
71, 72, 74, 90, 118, 175; **6**, 62, 150,
171, 228; **7**, 123, 208; **8**, 140; **9**,
120; **10**, 55; birth, **5**, 14 and n, 37;
B. sends presents for her, 93, 95,
114, 120; B. objects to her going

abroad, 144–5, 153–4, 160; with
Lady Noel, 36; to be left with her
mother, 109, 110, 154; source of her
name, 127; **7**, 196; B.'s stanzas to, **5**,
139, 159–60; birthday, 139, 141, 153,
154–5; **6**, 90; **7**, 207; **9**, 65; **10**, 52;
B.'s paternal rights, **5**, 180, 189, 190,
223–4; made a chancery ward, 198,
224; little legitimate, **6**, 10; her
portrait, 182, 223, 249, 260; **7**, 41,
60, 168, 207, 211; **9**, 77; **10**, 31; **11**,
47, 76; to learn Italian, **6**, 182; **7**, 251;
8, 210; B.'s fear for guardianship,
256; **7**, 196 and n; **9**, 54; resembles
her mother, **7**, 165, 168, 207, 211;
B. leaves education to Lady Byron,
251; **10**, 163; B.'s exchange of hair
with, **8**, 209–10; **9**, 57, 64–5, 83; an
only child, 52, 77; **10**, 31; her
character, **9**, 77; provisional heir, 105,
141; B.'s portrait not to be shown to
her, 127 and n, 164; prejudiced
against her father, 127–8; B. wants
Mrs. Clermont kept away from her,
128, 145; illness, **11**, 33, 44, 120;
disposition, 47; B. wanted to send
Hatagée to, 111n, 120, 126, 127; B.'s
love for, 169, 197
Byron, Bernard, **5**, 89
Byron, Catherine Gordon (B.'s
mother), B.'s letters to, **1**, 39, 41,
43 (2), 49, 88, 171, 172, 195, 203,
206, 218, 223, 226, 234, 235, 236,
242, 243, 249; **2**, 3, 8, 17, 34, 39, 40,
51, 61; biog. sketch, **1**, 273–4; mentioned, 41, 225; **5**, 26n; **7**, 198, 204
and n; **9**, 52, 77; at Newstead, **1**, 39–
41; dislikes her son's companions,
43–4; at Burgage Manor, Southwell,
44–201, 44n, 46n, 48, 53, 65–6, 93n,
102n, 277; gives party at Southwell,
48; her character described by B.,
53–4, 55–6, 57, 72–3, 74, 75–6; relations with B., 53, 54, 55–6, 81, 82;
misrepresents her age, 55; in love
–with Lord Grey, 55; B. to avoid her
if possible, 56; her temper and disposition, 56–58; appetite for scandal,
57, 59; disapproved Augusta's marriage, 59, 61; threatened to write
Drury, 62 and n; conduct described to
Augusta, 68; disapproves of Lord
Carlisle, 67, 76 and n; does not like
Augusta, 68, 76; and B.'s relationship with Augusta, 68–9, 72; and
B.'s holidays, 70, 73–4; Civil List
pension, 74n, 76n, 80, 89 and n; and
B. at Cambridge, 79–80, 83, 84;
threatened visit to B. at Cambridge,
83; her indulgence and harshness, 85;
quarrel with B., 93 and n, 94–95;

followed B. to London, 96–7; ignorant of Rochdale value, 99; borrowed £60 from B., 116; borrowed money for B., 120–21, 149 and n, 196 and n; and B.'s allowance, 128; review sent to, 144; to be warned of hostile review, 157; likens B. to Rousseau, 171 and n; **9**, 11; at Newstead while B. is abroad, **1**, 175, 203–57; **2**, 3–67; B. avoids her society, **1**, 179; recommends B. marry for money, 181n; in B.'s will' 202n; B.'s long letter to about Ali, 226–31; B. asks Hanson to supply her, 243; failure to receive B.'s letters, 249; at Newstead, 4, 9, 35, 51–2, 62; on the value of B.'s property, **2**, 46; attacked by Hewson Clarke, 65 and n, 67; death, 65n, 67–9, 74, 77, 120n; on Col. Leigh, 85n; her ancestry, 68 and n; her Scotch property, 72 and n, 133 and n, 153, 156; on Mary Duff, **3**, 222–23, 258; Gight estate, **8**, 73; and B.'s father, **10**, 208

Byron, Charlotte Augusta, marriage to Christopher Parker, **4**, 184n

Byron crest, **7**, 95

Byron, Eliza, **3**, 161 and n, 205, 206, 208, 209

Byron, Frances (later Mrs. Charles Leigh), **1**, 44n

Byron, Col. Geoffrey, heir apparent, Byron Pedigree, **4**, 303 and n

Byron, the Hon. George, **1**, 121n

Byron, the Hon. Mrs. George, **1**, 120, 121n, 149 and n, 172 and n, 196n; **4**, 259; **5**, 189 and n, 222

Byron, George Anson, (f. of 7th Baron), **1**, 274; **2**, 82n

Byron, George Anson (later 7th Baron), B.'s letter to, **1**, 41; mentioned, *41 and n*; **4**, 143, 147 and n; **5**, 67, 181, 244; B.'s heir, **1**, 41 and n, 165 and n, 166; **2**, 71, 81–2; **3**, 227 and n, 229, 236; **4**, 236 and n; B.'s loan to, 213–14, 303n; marriage to Elizabeth Pole, **5**, *39 and n*, 222; his conduct in separation, **7**, 208; **11**, 169 and n

Byron, George Gordon (Noel), 6th Baron

Age
feels 60 instead of 29, **5**, 120; on 33rd birthday, **8**, 31–2, 43, 67; Bartolini bust makes him look seventy, **9**, 213

Ambitions
'the way to *riches* to *Greatness*', **1**, 49; oratory, 48, 63 and n, 67n; **9**, 16, 37, 42–3; 'politics and decorum', **1**, 241; no ambition, **3**, 217; **5**,

135; **6**, 214; not in literature, **5**, 177

Amours
at Southwell, **1**, 103ff, 131; in London, 7, 157 and n, 158–9, 161, 167 and n, 170n; in Athens, 240; **2**, 13, 14, 23, 46; Newstead maids, 105–6; Lucy, **1**, 187, *189 and n*, 191, 232n; **2**, 105 and n, 106, 131; Susan Vaughan, 131 and n, 151 and n, 155 and n, 157 and n, 158, 159 and n, 160 and n, 162, 163; Angelina (Venice), **6**, 108 and n, 133–4; *see also* Byron, dissipations

Ancestry
The Gordons, **2**, 68; **7**, 204, 212; the Byrons, **4**, 219–20

Animals
at Zoo, **3**, 206–7; **4**, 278n; **5**, 214; eagles on Parnassus, **3**, 253; **9**, 41; shot eaglet, 253; *see also* Byron, Menagerie

Annuity
B. wants to buy, **10**, 86, 133

Appearance
hair, **1**, 119; **5**, 120, 127; **6**, 174, 259; **7**, 227, 228; **8**, 233; **9**, 57; weight (*see* Dieting); height, **3**, 251; described by Newton Hanson, **6**, 78n; alteration at Venice, 173–4; Bartolini bust, **9**, 213, 214, 215, 216–17; thinner at Genoa, **10**, 82, 111, 112, 137; small ears, white hands, **1**, 227, 238, 249

Arms (Heraldic)
described, **1**, 50 and n; **9**, 87; crest on carriage, **7**, 95; addition of Noel arms, **9**, 107, 115

Bible
B.'s knowledge of, **8**, 238

Books
to go to Murray's, **3**, 56, 60, 61; preparation to sell, **5**, 36 and n, 37, 42, 51, 52–3, 57–8; **11**, 184–5 and n; Evans sale, **5**, 57–8, 62; purchased from Murray, 57; **8**, 232, 239; Hanson left B.'s books in England, **6**, 77, 82; sent by Murray, **6**, 83–4; **8**, 135, 144; B. specifies books wanted and unwanted, 219–21

Boxing
'Gentleman' Jackson, **1**, *162n*; interest in prize fights, 182 and n; to prevent obesity, **2**, 70, 84, 94; sparring with Jackson, **3**, 251, 253, 255, 257; **4**, 91, 106, 114, 117, 129

Boys, B.'s attachment to
in Greece, **1**, 207 and n, 221–2 232n; **2**, 6–7, 10, 11, 12–14 and n' 23, 29 and n, 124; Delawarr, **1**, *53'*

Byron George Gordon—*continued*
55; Edleston, 88n, 110n, 117n,
118n, 122 and n, 123, 124–5, 129n;
Edleston accused of indecency,
257n; Edleston (the Cornelian), **2**,
110 and n, 119–20; as 'Thyrza',
139–40; death of, 114, 116 and n,
117 and n, 119–20; memories of at
Cambridge, 117, 141 and n, 163;
B.'s note to in cypher, **11**, 173 and
n; Rushton, **1**, 187 and n; connection with prostitutes, 203–4 and
n; to Gibraltar with B., **1**, 206 and n,
222; in B.'s will, **2**, 71, 232, and
Susan Vaughan, 157, 158; Hyacinth,
1, 207 and n; **2**, 124 and n; Ali's
grandson, **1**, 231, 249–50, 254;
Nicolo Giraud, **2**, 10 and n, 12–13,
14, 16, 21, 29; in B.'s will, 71;
Claridge, 102–3, 113n, 115, 126
and n; De Bathe, 126 and n;
Harness, 136, 137, 140, 141, 145,
148–50, 155; Lukas, **11**, 213–14
Cambridge degree
struggle to obtain it, **1**, 161 and n,
164, 193, 197 and n; **2**, 96, 142;
11, 176–7
Cavalier Servente
to the Countess Guiccioli, **1**, 8;
reluctance to take the role, **5**, 145;
6, 108; chafing under it, 214, 226;
learning to perform the part, 262;
7, 28; 'the happiest state of all',
51; 'Cavalier Schiavo', 195
Character potrayal
1, 9–11
Charities and gifts
Hodgson, **1**, 196n, 198, 276; **2**, 27n;
3, 130n, 187 and n, 210n, 228 and
n; **8**, 156; Coleridge, **5**, 16n, 17;
9, 206–7, 208; Lady Falkland, **1**,
195n; Godwin, **5**, 16 and n, 17;
10, 18; Hunt, **10**, 13, 60, 66, 105,
138; Maturin, **4**, 337; **5**, 16n;
Harriette Wilson, **7**, 64–5, 100;
Irish woman in Paris, 104 and n;
Madame de Yosy, **10**, 22–3, 64;
gifts to poor men and women, **8**,
35, 96; Greek refugees, **11**, 19 and
n, 23, 32, 57, 77
Clubs
Alfred, **2**, 125 and n, 128, 131,
140n, 141, 145 and n, 148; **9**, 22,
23; **11**, 179; proposed for Athenian,
2, 156 and n; Cocoa Tree, **3**, 255;
4, 86 and n; **9**, 23; **11**, 156, 162;
Cambridge Whig Club, **1**, 125n,
139 and n, 158 and n, 159–60; **6**,
166; **7**, 230–1; **9**, 23; Hampden,
23; Owls, 23; Pugilists, 23;
Ratchets (Brighton), 23; Union,

23; Watiers, **4**, 117 and n; **9**, 22; **10**,
41, 141
Composition
can't revise, **1**, 13; **7**, 82, 86, 229;
8, 65; **9**, 54; wrote better in 1811,
7, 179; Drury Lane Address, **11**,
181; comedy, **3**, 205, 209; tale in
prose, 205, 209, 217; threw poem
into fire, 210, 235; 'a devil of a
mannerist', **5**, 185; 'I can write
cheerfully', **6**, 25.
Copyrights
6, 252; **8**, 231, 232; and Galignani,
72, 74; **9**, 84; **10**, 134, 204
Conversation
1, 1
Cosmopolitanism, **1**, 248; **2**, 34–5; a
citizen of the world, 40–1; **6**, 259;
9, 78
Cricketer
Harrow-Eton match, **1**, 70–1; **7**, 229
Dandyism
a tinge of it, **9**, 22
Debts
of his minority, **1**, 121, 163, 198; at
Harrow, 68 and n, 88; at Cambridge
88–9 and n, 116, 149; creditors
pressing, 256–7n; **2**, 3, 57, 62, 66,
99, 153 and n, 162; borrowed from
mother, **1**, 196n; daily increasing,
202; Brothers, upholsterer, 256n;
memoir on debts and annuities, **2**,
154–5; duns, **1**, 192, 201; **11**, 185;
userers, **1**, 86–7 and n, 88–9 and n,
90 and n, 93 and n, 182 and n,
204–5 and n, 257n; **2**, 60, 62, 122–3,
139, 146 and n, 147, 152, 154–5,
156, 231, 255; **3**, 29–30; **10**, 16–17,
146–7; total in 1809–10, £10,000,
1, 163, 257n; to Davies, **2**, 28 and
n, 45 and n, 123 and n, 162, 238
and n, 241, 248; **3**, 255; **11**, 157 and
n, 160–1, 162 and n; debts reduced,
4, 190, 200, 266; not less than
£30,000 in 1815, 259; creditors
closing in, 317n, 333 and n; to break
up household because of, **5**, 15n, 20;
tenth excution, 42, summarized for
Kinnaird, 247; **6**, 222 and n; summarized for Hanson, **5**, 278; **6**, 222
and n; to be paid from surplus of
Newstead sale, 6, 42–3, 79; his
creditors, **10**, 26–7, 110 and n,
113–14, 127; B. to liquidate, 42,
43, 47, 71, 74, 87, 91, 110–11, 113,
118; usurers must wait, 65–6, 74
Depression of spirits, *see* Byron,
Melancholy
Dieting
lost 18 pounds, **1**, 113–14; continued loss of weight with violent

exercise, 115, 117, 119, 121–2, 122–3, 133, 144–5; tea and biscuits, 3, 212, 226; tea and soda water, 235; wishes he could leave off eating, 237; biscuits and soda water, 257; vegetable diet, 2, 131; 11, 180; fasting and purgatives, 8, 165

Dissipation
in London, 1, 103, 113, 124, 126, 157, 158, 159, 160–1, 163, 164–5; in Greece, 2, 6–7, 23 and n, 27, 29, 46; in Venice, 5, 259; 6, 14, 19, 40, 62, 66, 92, 133; period of ended, 10, 87, 128

Dogs
B. a 'friend of the dog', 4, 255n; offer of bulldogs from Murray, 7, 41, 48; Boatswain, 1, 120 and n, 132; 2, 72, 94; 4, 256 and n; Boatswain's death, 1, 176 and n; his vault at Newstead, 178; 7, 225; Dutch mastiff, 2, 94; Fanny, 1, 126 and n; greyhound, 180; 2, 59; Lyon, 10, 164 and n, 210n; 11, 86n; Moretto, 6, 235; 10, 210n; Mutz, 5, 103, 127, 144, 217; 6, 108, 235; Nettle (poodle), 3, 118 and n, 122, 126, 127; Savage, 1, 120, 123n; Smut, 132; B. wants a terrier and a Newfoundland, 6, 138, 140

drinking
wine, 1, 114; 2, 70, 95; intoxicated, 1, 158; at Cambridge, 78, 80, 124, 135; 4, 234, 235; Turkish wine bad, 1, 242; Davies drunk, 2, 117; left off wine, 131, 133; at Newstead, 155; 'nipperkin of Grog', 3, 15; eating and drinking when wretched, 91; to drink more than is prudent, 92; drinking with Davies, 114, 255; 11, 166; emptied skull cup, 3, 145; detests drinking in general, 146; three bottles of claret, 213; drank more than I like, 221; drinking with Sheridan, 249, 272; 4, 326–7; all night at the Cocoa Tree, 91–2; tumbler of brandy, 124n; two bottles of claret, 144; with Moore, 240; a holiday drinker, 243; Kinnaird's brandy, 264; 6, 34, 37; will get drunk, 4, 298; drunk at party, 326–7; at Kinnaird's party, 334; spirits of wine, 8, 13, 51; wanted to get drunk with Scott, 13; effect on B., 16, 27, 236; soda water, 42; Imola wine, 50, 51; drunk with Hobhouse and Davies, 9, 39; temperate in general, 125; not temperate as formerly, 11, 113; abstinence, 126

Duels

mediator or second, 2, 129–30, 132, 148; 3, 85–6 and n, 93–4, 95; 9, 25–6; intended challenge to Brougham, 5, 184n; 6, 189 and n; 7, 95–6, 96n, 153 and n, 154, 178, 188–9; 8, 92, 100; 10, 89 and n; 11, 167–8 and n; Capt. Cary apologized, 1, 224 and n, 239, 240, 11, 158; challenge to Hewson Clarke, 167 and n; 2, 68; with Croker considered, 4, 73; threatened with young Grattan, 2, 256n; threatened with Col. Greville, 168 and n, 169; with Leacroft avoided, 1, 104 and n, 105–6; near duel with Moore, 2, 118n, 118–19, 120–1, 123 and n, 152 and n; 3, 94–5; contemplated with Schlegel, 8, 172–3; challenge to Southey, 7, 96n; 9, 95n, 100, 102 and n, 109–10, 160 and n; 10, 89 and n; challenge to Twiddie, 1, 150; possible duel with Webster, 3, 143, 144, 146, 174, 209; 4, 16n; Caroline Lamb's relatives, 24

Engagement
B.'s letters before and after, 1, 5; tentative proposal accepted, 4, 174–8, 180, 188; marriage settlement, 180, 186; announcement made, 185, 186; contradicted, 192–3, 196–7; first visit to Seaham, 228–31; go on extremely well, 229–30; doubts about marriage, 231

Eyesight
B.'s remarkable distance vision, 9, 12

Fencing
lessons with Angelo, 1, 92 and n, 162n; fencing daily, 4, 100, 106, 129

Gambling
gave up, 1, 158, 160, 165; loved rattle of dice, 9, 23; at Brighthelmstone, 39

Health
'too much love', 1, 157, 158, 160; seasick, 216; fever at Patras, 2, 14–16, 18–19, 27, 42, 44; 4, 26–7; gonorrhea, 2, 48, 54, 56; 6, 14, 19, 25; 11, 159; catarrh and piles, 2, 42; 'well but weakly', 11, 179; 2, 141; tertian fever, 44, 53, 54, 56; 6, 239, 240, 242, 243, 244, 253, 259; 7, 17, 48, 136, 139; hemorrhoids, 2, 54, 56, 58; exercise and abstinence, 94; kidney stone, 161, 162, 163, 167–8, 221; 3, 34; digestion spoiled by feasting, 230, 233; in robust health, 60, 246; 4, 65, 162; 5, 222, 227, 231; liver trouble, 33, 36; ill from excesses of

Byron, George Gordon—*continued*
Carnival, 176, 178, 179; fever, 185, 186, 187, 189, 190, 191–2, 194, 197, 200, 206, 207–8; **11**, 163, 165; fits of giddiness, **5**, 119, 124, 127; abstemiousness, **7**, 83; swelled face, **8**, 115; **10**, 106, 112, 126, 127, 128, 135, 137; scarlet fever, **9**, 87; ill at Lerici, **10**, 11, 12–13, 14, 19, 28, 56, 62; not well since summer, 56, 62, 112, 117, 137; skin eruptions, 57, 62–3; warts on face, 147, 148, 149; chilblains, 82, 100; suffers from excessive dining, 157; headaches in youth, **11**, 44; convulsive attack, 113, 117, 118, 122, 123, 125
Homosexual tendencies
Lord Grey's advances, **1**, 45n, 46, 54, 55, 168 and n; veiled references, 206–7 and n, 208; **2**, 23; *see also* Byron, Boys, B.'s attachment to
Honeymoon
at Halnaby, **4**, 249, 252; the treaclemoon is over, 262, 263
Humanitarianism
Nottingham weavers, **1**, 16; **2**, 165; auto-da-fé, **9**, 78–9 and n, 81; civilize their mode of treating prisoners, **10**, 152; **11**, 98, 118; Turkish prisoners returned, 98, 118
Humour
muted or casual, **1**, 6; absurd point of view, 7; **9**, 123
Journals
general nature, **1**, 18–23, 25–6; '. . . reasons in favour of a change', **2**, 47–8; carried by Mawman, **8**, 196, 198, 217; 1813–14, **3**, 204–8; given to Moore, **4**, 126 and n; **6**, 235 and n; **8**, 11, 176; Alpine journal, **1**, 20; **5**, 96–105, 108, 109, 114, 188, 268; **8**, 11 and n, 176, 217; 'My Dictionary', 105–8; Ravenna diary, **1**, 20, 25; **4**, 25n, 117n; **8**, 11–51, 105, 141, 176, 217; 'Detached Thoughts', **1**, 21, 156n, 165n, 171n, 184; **2**, 125n, 128n, 215n, 287; **3**, 48n, 128n, 273; **4**, 117n, 330n; **8**, 105n, 146n, 245 and n; **9**, 11–52, 80n, 83n, 118n, 168 and n; carried to England by Clare, 168 and n, 172, 188 and n; journal in Cephalonia, **11**, 29–35, 90n; final entry, 1824, 113–14
Lameness
treated by Lavender, **1**, 39n; brace by Sheldrake, 41 and n, 43; and Hanson, 275; 'bodily inferiority',

2, 47; a better pair of legs, 98; mentioned, 108; the devil boiteux, **4**, 50, 51 and n; **10**, 136
Languages
B.'s wish to study, **3**, 217; **9**, 31; Albanian, **2**, 81, 84, 102, 104, 113 and n, 135, 155 and n; **9**, 31; Arabic, 31; Armenian, **5**, 130–1, 137, 138, 140–1, 142, 146, 152, 160, 162, 193; **9**, 31; **11**, 164; B.'s translations **5**, 201 and n, 238; **8**, 237; English, B. continues to write in, 210; '*our* barbarous language', **10**, 156; writes to Teresa in, 212; **11**, 137; 'the language of birds', 137; French, **4**, 132; **6**, 17, 18; **9**, 31; B.'s knowledge of, **2**, 105; **3**, 184; **8**, 91; **10**, 207; German, **7**, 113; **8**, 25–6; Greek (modern), **1**, 230, 232, 238, 241; **2**, 30, 34, 134, 135; **9**, 31; **11**, 157, 158; B. studying with a master, **2**, 32 and n, 37; Italian, 29, 32, 34, 37, 47, 59, 208, 217; **3**, 240; **4**, 132; **5**, 125, 133, 138, 140–1; **6**, 17–18, 32–3, 42, 105, 215; **9**, 31; **10**, 18, 168, 170; B.'s knowledge of, **6**, 111n; **8**, 35, 91, 210, 228; taught by Nicolo, **2**, 12–13, 16, 29; B. spoke Venetian, **9**, 19; B. writes Italian to English and Greeks, **11**, 137; Latin, 30, 32, 37; Lingua Franca, **2**, 37; Portuguese, **4**, 37 and n; Romaic (*see also* Greek, modern), **1**, 238; **2**, 32 and n, 34, 37, 59, 104, 134, 135; **4**, 32, 97 and n, 268; **10**, 168, 201; Spanish, **9**, 31; Turkish, **1**, 238; **2**, 37; **9**, 31
Lawsuits
threatens chancery suit over Ada, **5**, 189–90; Merryweather, **6**, 213 and n, 233–4; **7**, 79, 103, 106 and n; **11**, 194–5 and n; Dupuy, **10**, 152 and n, 160, 161; **11**, 140 and n; *see also* Rochdale, lawsuit, in general index
Loans to friends
to Hobhouse, **3**, 212; to Bland, 130 and n; to Webster, 138–9, 144 and n, 152, 172 and n, 212; **4**, 83–4; **5**, 68 and n; **7**, 71; **9**, 73; **10**, 48–9, 60–1
Letters
not cautious, **1**, 1; **10**, 83; letters less gloomy than poems, **1**, 1; characteristics, 1–8, 11–12, 17–18; editions, 24–5; forgeries, 26; his chief correspondents, **8**, 226–8
Marriage
described, **4**, 249, 252; marriage forfeit, 222–3, 256–7, 260;

Midianite marriage, **5**, 232; anniversary, 153, 154–5; **7**, 16; **8**, 86; wishes to marry again, **6**, 171; B.'s wish to marry Teresa, **7**, 91 and n, 109 and n; verses on, **8**, 86, 87; not for money, **9**, 108–9; 'funeral' with Miss M., **11**, 167; *see also* Byron, views on, marriage

Melancholy
confessed in journals, **1**, 21–2; **8**, 11, 15–16, 37, 42; **9**, 38, 47; early 'bad spirits', **1**, 63; bad news from England, 256–7 and n; at Malta, **2**, 47; confessed to Teresa, **7**, 185, 186–7, 189; increasing depression of spirits, **8**, 216–17, 230, 236, 241; **9**, 64; confession to Davies, **11**, 165

Memoirs
first mention, **6**, 59 and n; begun, 61; continued, 62 and n, 63–4; **7**, 207, 219, 244; given to Moore, **1**, 25–6; **6**, 59 and n, 232, 235 and n, 257; **7**, 169; not confessions, **6**, 236, 261; contents, 63–4, 235 and n, 236, 261; **8**, 54, 91, 164 and n, 226; sold to Murray by Moore, **6**, 235n, **7**, 244n; **8**, 103, 176 and n, 177, 182, 188, 225, 227 and n, 228–9; **9**, 68–9, 70, 84–5, 85n, 182; **10**, 22, 33; hermetically sealed, 146; Ms. burned, **1**, 276; **2**, 285; **6**, 235n; **7**, 244n; offer to let Lady Byron read, **6**, 257, 261; **7**, 16–17, 68 and n; copy to be made, 125, 207 and n; additions to, **8**, 105, 134, 196n; shown to Lady Holland, 164 and n; possible editor, 216; omitted consequential parts of his life, **9**, 38; Moore to edit, 57; Hobhouse objects to sale, 68–9, 70, 88 and n; not to be published in B.'s lifetime, 172, 191; B. never read over, 57.

Menagerie
bear at Cambridge, **1**, 135 and n, 136, 167n; the bear is dead, **2**, 64; land tortoises, 48, 59, 94, 106; hedgehog, 106; at Venice, **6**, 108, at Ravenna, 171; **7**, 105, 209, 227; **8**, 13, 15, 46, 139, 222

Military plans
11, 35, 102; B. to lead the Suliotes, 107; Commander-in-Chief, Western Greece, 115

Money
B.'s love of, **1**, 12; **6**, 91, 92, 96, 98, 101, 232; **7**, 115, 170 and n; **8**, 153, 244; **9**, 62, 108, 114 and n, 207; **10**, 87, 128; **9**, collects gold coins, 63; cash is virtue, 113

Motto
Crede Byron, **8**, 160

Music
B.'s liking for, **8**, 15, 20, 21, 24, 27, 28, 30, 36, 43

Mustache
twirl mustachios, **1**, 240; B. to grow one again, **3**, 28

Napoleonic carriage,
ordered from Baxter, **5**, 72 and n; lost its splendour, **6**, 176; imperial carriage, **9**, 202; Barry to keep it for B., **11**, 76, 153

Nostalgia
for the East, **1**, 3; **2**, 95, 141, 190; **3**, 28, 30, 34–5, 40, 43, 63, 90, 217; **11**, 159, 179; for London, **1**, 3, 21; **8**, 43; **9**, 168, 170, 171

Pistol shooting, **3**, 82; sent pistol to Ali Pasha, **4**, 299; in the Pineta, **7**, 140, 141, 167, 207; **8**, 27, 28, 30, 31, 32, 35

Plagiary
B. charged with, **8**, 186

Poems
see under Byron, Works

Politics
to strut no more on that stage, **1**, 16; **3**, 32; **4**, 63n; B. attends debates, **1**, 67 and n; debtors' petition, **3**, 164 and n, 165 and n, 193n, 206n, 228–9, 233; never consistent in anything but, 204; sick of parliamentary mummeries, **1**, 16; **3**, 206; parliamentary speeches, **1**, 16; **2**, 165–6; **3**, 55 and n, 193, 206; **7**, 205 and n; **9**, 16; Lady Oxford urged B. to engage in, **3**, 229; B. a Jacobin, **4**, 102; dullness of House of Lords, **5**, 19 and n; ambition to have a fling, **9**, 119; could not help Hobhouse in election, **11**, 168–9; *see also* Byron, views on, politics

Portraits
Newstead miniature seized by Caroline, **3**, 3, 8, 10, 12, 14, 15, 17, 25, 26, 31, 36 and n; three miniatures, 60; to Lady Frances, 224 and n; miniature sent from Venice, **6**, 74; not to be shown to Ada, **9**, 127 and n, 145 and n, 164; Count D'Orsay, **10**, 167 and n; **11**, 235; Friedel, 128n; Harlow, **6**, 192n, 259 and n; Holmes, **3**, 170, 224n; **5**, 190 and n, 212, 242; **6**, 26; **10**, 175, and n, 176; Phillips, **3**, 68 and n, 70 and n. 113, 167 and n, 198, 248; **4**, 250; **5**, 106; owned by Chandos Leigh, **4**, 43n; nose turned up, 79; Phillips, in Albanian dress, **1**, 231n; **4**, 112n, 113, 250; engraving by Agar, 144n, 145 and n,

Byron, George Gordon—*continued*
146, 248, 287 and n; given to Murray, **5**, 28 and n, 106; two portraits, **11**, 187; Prepiani, **5**, 191 and n, 212, 242; Sanders, **1**, 197n, 206n, 243, 251; **2**, 4, 18, 224 and n, 234; **3**, 10, 33 and n, 41; West, **9**, 162 and n, 164 and n, 171; **10**, 18 and n, 198; Westall, **3**, 33, 41, 198; **11**, 187; *see also* Bartolini and Thorwaldsen in general index
Prose story, **8**, 196n
Punctuation
  3, 100, 166; **4**, 24, 94, 96, 132
Religion
  see Byron, views on, religion
Residences
  Athens
    Macri house, **1**, 240 and n; Capuchin convent (monastery), **2**, 11–14, 37
  Bologna
    with the Guicciolis, **6**, 206–223
  Cambridge
    Trinity College, **1**, 78–85, 92–3, 121–6, 133–4, 135–42, 167, 169
  Cheltenham
    High Street, **2**, 189–235
  Constantinople
    Pera, **1**, 241–57
  Dulwich
    Dr. Glennie's school, **1**, 40–1
  Geneva
    Villa Diodati, **5**, 79–113
  Genoa (Albaro)
    Casa Saluzzo, **10**, 11–212
  Halnaby, Yorkshire
    honeymoon, **4**, 249–57
  Harrow
    Henry Drury's pupil, **1**, 41–3, 49; Mr. Evan's house, 42 and n, 52–60; last term, 68–70
  Janina
    [Argyri house], **1**, 226
  Leghorn (Montenero)
    Villa Dupuy, **9**, 161–178
  Lisbon
    [Barnewell's hotel], **1**, 214–16
  London
    Albany, **3**, 255 and n, 255–8; **4**, 87 and n, 91, 124n, 147, 175, 87–246; Batt's Hotel, **1**, 201–3; **2**, 251, 252–5; **3**, 14; Bennet St., St. James's, **3**, 41, 61, 115, 117, 148, 20–33, 43–115, 119–31, 150–255; Dorant's Hotel, **1**, 134–5, 142–66. Gordon's Hotel, 126–33; 16 Piccadilly (Mrs. Massingberd's), 85–91, 92–9; 13 Piccadilly Terrace, **4**, 278–9, 283n, 285, 317n, 283–338; **5**, 13–69;

Reddish's Hotel, St. James's, **1**, 169, 189–95; **2**, 49, 57, 59–67; 8 St. James's St., **1**, 195–98, 203–5; **2**, 120–51, 153–89; **5**, 188
  Malta
    Strada di Torni, **1**, 223–5
  Metaxata, Cephalonia, **11**, 20 and n, 86
  Mira, La
    Villa Foscarini, **5**, 237–66; **6**, 224–38
  Missolonghi
    last residence, **11**, 90–154
  Newstead Abbey
    in 1798, **1**, 39; after Lord Grey, 170–89, 199–201; after his mother's death, **2**, 68–116, 151–3; **4**, 35–47, 161–78
  Nottingham
    with Parkyns family, **1**, 39–40
  Pisa
    Casa Lanfranchi, **9**, 61, 66, 74 and n, 75, 49–160, 179–219
  Ravenna
    Albergo Imperiale, **6**, 150–206; 260–2; **7**, 13n, 25, 13–34; Guiccioli Palace, 13n, 33n, 34–258; **8**, 11–251
  Rome
    66 Piazza di Spagna, **5**, 219–27, 225n
  Seaham, Durham
    before marriage, **4**, 228–31; after marriage, 248–9, 258–81
  Smyrna
    with Werry, **1**, 234–6
  Southwell
    Burgage Manor, **1**, 44 and n, 45–8, 50–1, 63–8, 70–8, 100–21
  Venice
    Segati house, Frezzeria, **5**, 129–216, 229–37, 264–79; **6**, 3–45; Palazzo Mocenigo, **6**, 25n, 39n, 40, 43, 65, 45–143, 224–59
Reviews
  send no periodical works, **8**, 219–21; won't read, **9**, 55; of early poems, **1**, 130–1, 147, 159 and n, 162–3, 167n; **8**, 102, 103, 173; **11**, 174 (*see also* Byron, Works); reviews by B., **2**, 156 and n, 164, 167 and n; **3**, 7 and n; **9**, 42; offered to review Moore in *Quarterly*, **3**, 50–1 and n
Riding
  on first pilgrimage, **1**, 216, 217, 219, 226; **2**, 3, 5, 6; Veli Pasha gave B. a horse, 9, 11, 37; daily ride to Piraeus, 13, 37; in Rome **5**, 219, 221, 223, 227; on Lido, Venice, **6**, 7, 10, 17, 20, 43–4, 65,

237; at La Mira, **5**, 238, 248, 251; **6**, 192, 194; **11** 167; in Ravenna, the Pineta, **6**, 162, 163, 181, 186, 219; **7**, 57, 101, 112, 128, 130, 197, 209; **8**, 13, 14, 28, 29, 30, 31, 32, 35, 43, 44, 45, 48, 49, 50, 115, 236; in Pisa, **9**, 128, 218; at Genoa, **10**, 82, 148; at Metaxata, **11**, 31, 45, 52; at Missolonghi, 116, 132

Self-analysis
easily managed, **1**, 5; **2**, 194, 199, 240; **3**, 241; **4**, 199, 218, 219, 258; cynical, **2**, 86; not 'melancholic', 87; gloomy, 110; growing nervous, 111, 117; a facetious personage, **3**, 109, 159; 'restless doctrines', 119; must have object of attachment, **2**, 243; **3**, 142, 178; flattery pleasing, 227, 235–6; self-contradictions, 233; ennuyé, **2**, 112; **3**, 236; merry and conceited, 131; temper, 258; not popular, **4**, 21; shyness, 22, 127, 182, 187, 234, 236; made a devil by a bad passion, 34; repugnance to making new acquaintances, 71; has a heart, 77; quite irresolute, 109; his indifference, 121; melancholy, **9**, 38; early passions, 40; can't keep resentment, **10**, 18

Separation
mentioned, **1**, 276; **9**, 128n; Mme. de Staël's attempt at reconciliation, **3**, 273; **5**, 87–8; proposed by Sir Ralph Milbanke, 20–1; B.'s first letter to Annabella on, 21–2; appeals to Lady B. to return, 22, 24–5, 26–7, 33, 38–9, 40–1; battle of lawyers, 26 and n, 46; Murray's concern, 29 and n; Lord Holland as mediator, 30 and n, 31; Hunt's sympathy, 32–3; rumours circulated, 32, 35; Moore's inquiry, 35 and n; B. asks for interview, 38–9, 44; revokes agreement, 39–40; agreed in principle, 48; has not spoken ill of Lady B., 53 and n, 54–5, 56, 57; deed signed, 65 and n, 69 and n; has broken his heart, 91; irrevocable after first year, 223; consequence to B., 228; B.'s statement on, 255–6; desolation brought him, **6**, 69; Brougham's remarks on, **7**, 95–6; Webster's attempt at reconciliation, 111; stories told in Rome, 197 and n; B.'s epigram on, 219; B.'s novel on, **8**, 196n; for a year considered reunion possible, **9**, 65

Servants
fourteen servants in Venice, **6**, 65; Albanian soldiers, **11**, 157; Augustine, coachman, **6**, 150, 162,

163; **7**, 66; Boyce, Francis, **1**, 79 and n, 98–9, 100 and n, 107, 116; Charles, 98–9; Falcieri, Giovanni Battista (Tita), *see under* Falcieri in general index; Gaetano, **11**, 81; Fletcher, William, *see under* Fletcher in general index; Friese, **1**, 206 and n, 208; George, dragoman, 235n; in Greece, 228, 238; **2**, 9, 13 and n, 19, 27, 29, 32 and n, 34, 48; James, **1**, 65 and n; Lewis, Benjamin, **11**, 31; Lionardo, courier, **6**, 166 and n; Luigi, **7**, 128, 139–40, 149, 197; **8**, 12; Marietta, housemaid, dismissed, **6**, 20; Murray, Joe, *see under* Murray, Joseph (Joe) in general index; Papi, Vincenzo, **7**, 78, 79, 125, 135; sent home from Greece, **11**, 81; Masi assailant, 194 and n; Saraci, Spiro, **2**, 48 and n, 51, 59, 94, 153n, 157 and n, 167 and n; Stevens, **6**, 20; Tahiri, Dervise, **2**, 13, 19, 27. 29, 34, 262; Tita, *see under* Falcieri; Valeriano, **7**, 128, 129, 130; Viscillie, **2**, 10 and n, 13, 19, 27, 29, 34, 262; Zambelli, Lega, *see under* Zambelli, in general index; Zantachi, Andreas, **1**, 235n; **2**, 10 and n, 13 and n, 16, 29, 32 and n; Zograffo, Demetrius, 48 and n, 51, 59, 94, 102, 103, 113 and n, 118, 124, 129, 130, 150, 153n, 155, 162, 167 and n, 262 and n; **9**, 23

Signature
in Greek, **2**, 23 and n; Greek monogram, 152 and n; as Noel Byron or N. B., **9**, 106 and n, 107, 115, 171 and n

Skepticism
apology for, **2**, 76, his skeptical creed, 88–9; doubt everything, 136; Sir W. Drummond, 140; and Dr. Kennedy, **11**, 215; *see also* Byron, views on, religion,

Swimming
in the Thames, **1**, 132, 247 and n; Tagus, 215 and n; **8**, 81; Hellespont, **1**, 215n, 237, 240, 242, 243, 247–8, 250, 253, 255; **2**, 34, 53, 59, 200; **11**, 157; swims like a duck, **4**, 122; Turner's comment on, **8**, 80–3; with Nicolo at Piraeus, **2**, 14; contest with Mengaldo, **6**, 51, 52, 54–5, 60, 191; **8**, 81–2; B. an expert, **6**, 126; raises B.'s spirits, **8**, 16; at Viareggio, **9**, 194, 197 and n, 201–2; **10**, 56, 62, 82, 112, 137

Teeth
5, 80; **6**, 17, 223 and n; **7**, 113, 150, 227, 228; grinds them in sleep, **3**,

Byron, George Gordon—*continued*
245; 'loosish', **5**, 120; has not lost
any, **10**, 111
Theatre
saw young Roscius, **1**, 67 and n,
2, 192, 193; Southwell theatricals,
1, 101 and n; **9**, 37; theatricals at
Newstead, **1**, 170; **11**, 175 and n;
saw Robert Coates at Haymarket, **2**,
143 and n, 149; saw Kemble and
Siddons, 147 and n; Kemble in *Coriolanus*, 149; first night with Lewis,
3, 4–5; *Antony and Cleopatra* with
Lewis, 207; Kean in *Richard III*, 244;
4, 110, 111; to Drury Lane with
Henry Fox, **3**, 224 and n, 226;
Sheridan's *Trip to Scarborough*, 249
and n; to *Othello* with Moore, **4**,
115 and n; to Covent Garden with
Moore, 114, 115; *The Child of
Nature*, 118 and n; saw Kean's
Macbeth, 235, 242; urged Coleridge
to write a tragedy, 286; saw Mrs.
Wilmot's tragedy damned, 290 and
n; B. as actor, **9**, 37; private box
with Davies, **11**, 161; Goldoni
comedies in Venice, 189 and n;
theatre with Lewis, 183; Alfieri's
Mirra in Bologna, **6**, 206 and n;
Drury Lane Address (*see under*
Drury Lane Theatre in general
index); on Drury Lane Committee,
4, 285n, 296 and n, 301n, 302,
309n, 311–12, 319, 322–3, 334,
336; **9**, 35–6; La Scala, Milan, **5**,
119, 121, 125; at Ravenna, **6**, 152;
7, 25; *see also under* Drury Lane
Theatre, Fenice Theatre, San Benedetto Theatre in general index
Tobacco
smoking, **1**, 240, 241; chewing, **2**,
94, 141 and n, 143; **11**, 179; cigars,
3, 235, 243
Travel
first voyage to the East, **1**, 214–57;
travel plans, 131–2, 135, 151, 172
and n, 173, 175, 176; **2**, 163; **3**,
19, 22, 23–4, 25, 27, 29, 30–1, 33,
34, 35, 38, 39, 42, 56, 59, 75, 76, 82,
83, 84, 88, 92, 93, 95, 106, 205;
5, 15n, 20, 24, 53; to go to
Holland, **3**, 176 and n, 180, 184,
187, 212–13, 218, 223, 234, 235;
4, 54; not going to Paris, 96; to go
abroad with W. Clark, **3**, 63 and n,
74, 84 and n, 115 and n, 176 and n,
180, 181, 199n; **4**, 99–100 and n,
223n; B. an uncomplaining traveller, **3**, 97; **7**, 221–2, 223–4; six
years a Gypsy-ing, 86; Albania, **1**,
225–33; Alpine journey, **5**, 94–105,

106, 109; Athens, **1**, 234; **2**, 3,
11–14, 23–44; Bologna, **5**, 216–17;
6, 146–50; **9**, 53; Brussels, **5**, 72–6;
Cephalonia, **11**, 15–86; Cape
Colonna, **2**, 30–1, 36; Constantinople, **1**, 241–57; **2**, 3, 8, 18, 34, 37;
Corinth, 6; Ephesus, **1**, 235;
Ferrara, **5**, 217; **6**, 145–9; Florence,
5, 216–17; **9**, 50; Gibraltar, **1**,
218–22; Ithaca, **11**, 18, 19, 30–1;
Malta, **1**, 223–5; **2**, 44–8; Milan,
5, 113–22, 206; Morea, **2**, 3–11,
23–4, 34; Missolonghi, **1**, 233; **11**,
90–154; Patras, **1**, 233; **2**, 5–9, 21–
3, 23–4; Portugal, **1**, 214–16, 218;
plans to go to Rome, **5**, 187, 197,
206, 208, 210, 211, 212, 214–15,
216; Rome, 219–27; Smyrna, **1**,
234–5; Spain, 218–21; Switzerland,
5, 79–113; firman for Syria and
Egypt, **2**, 38–9, 40, 41; Tripolitza,
9–10; Troy, **1**, 236, 238; **2**, 3, 34
Tutors
at Harrow, Henry Drury, **1**, 41–2
and n; Evans, 42n; at Cambridge,
Rev. Thomas Jones, 79 and n, 80,
100 and n, 108–9
Wills
of 1809, **1**, 178n; alterations, 191;
codicil for Davies, 213–14, **11**,
156 and n; of 1811, **1**, 178n, 222;
2, 71–3 and n; of 1813, **3**, 126 and
n; last will, 1815, **4**, 298n, 303;
codicil for Allegra, **8**, 125; **10**,
162; proposed new will, **9**, 193
and n
Women
had more than 200 in Venice, **6**,
66; list of in Venice, 92; has
given up concubinage, 83; *see also*
Byron, views on women,
Byron views on
Age, **9**, 37
America and Americans, 'a model
of force and freedom', **1**, 16, **8**, 240;
B. liked their praise, **3**, 236; **9**,
17, 20–1, 52, 162 and n, 163, 164;
10, 131; Anglo-Americans a little
too coarse, **6**, 225; Mr. Coolidge,
8, 146; **9**, 20–1; 'a nod from an
American', 171
Anonymity, **8**, 223, 232, 233; **9**, 54,
99, 104
Assassination, **6**, 188–9; **7**, 184, 249
Bargaining, **1**, 12; **8**, 143, 144, 153,
244; **9**, 62
Burial, his, **6**, 147, 149; **10**, 157
Cambridge, **1**, 79, 80–1, 89, 122,
124, 135–6, 147
Cant, **7**, 181; **8**, 146, 237; **9**, 196;
11, 147, 171; 'the million's cant-

ing', **1**, 13; **6**, 192; B. an enemy of cant, **1**, 17; 'all the cant of Christendom', **6**, 91; 'the Cant of the day', **6**, 95; **8**, 21; 'will never flatter *Cant*', **6**, 104; 'Cant is so much stronger . . .', 232; 'pretty Cant', 234; 'Cant is up', 256; and hypocrisy in England, **7**, 121

Character, **1**, 9–11; **3**, 129; **6**, 134

Children, **1**, 6, 10; respect for character of Herod, **2**, 84; should be provided with gag, 85; a cage for the children, 88; Leigh Hunt's 'little Yahoos', 282; **10**, 11; only scream in a low voice, **1**, 6; **3**, 116; B.'s dislike of, 15, 93; little squallers, **4**, 137–8, 140

Christianity, **2**, 89, 97–8; **3**, 73, 120; **7**, 245; **8**, 35, 98; **9**, 46, 119n; 123; **10**, 52, 137–8; **11**, 46, 56, 87n, 215

Criticism, **4**, 68–9

Cruelty, **8**, 26

Death and dying, **2**, 68–71, 77, 102; **4**, 26–7; death of Edleston, **2**, 110, and n, 114, 116 and n, 117 and n, 119, 121 and n, 124, 141, and n, 163–4 and n

Democracy, **8**, 107

Description, **1**, 2–3, 216

Drama, **8**, 56–7, 78, 203, 210, 223; **9**, 84; **10**, 116

Duelling, **6**, 188–9; **7**, 184

Elgin Marbles, **2**, 65–6 and n, 156; 157, 172n

English climate, **2**, 88

English high life, **10**, 116, 139–40

Executions, **5**, 229–30

Fame, **3**, 225; **5**, 201; **6**, 98, 148; **9**, 24; **11**, 188

Field sports, **1**, 47, 48, 51, 60, 181; given up sporting, **3**, 253; **4**, 166; not amused by hunting, 176

Fortune (Goddess), **5**, 164–5; **9**, 41

Friendship, **3**, 67; **10**, 34; friendship of men and women, 50

Gambling, **1**, 198; **4**, 117; **9**, 23; not one of his amusements, **4**, 176

Greeks (modern), **1**, 23, 225, 238; **2**, 115, 125; **11**, 17, 29n, 32–3, 40, 56, 58, 77

Irish, the, **3**, 128

Literati, **1**, 14; **3**, 251–2; **5**, 192, 193; **9**, 30

Literature, 'hate things all fiction', **1**, 13; **5**, 203; 'not my vocation', 177

Love, **1**, 8–9, 52, 53; one must make love from habit, **2**, 193: does not believe in, 194; 'cannot exist

without some object of love', **1**, 5; **2**, 243; 'any woman can *make* a man in *love* with her', 209; danger and difficulty make more piquant, **3**, 142; advice to love-sick friend, 250; 'never could love but that which *loves*', **4**, 229; 'after all there is nothing like it', **5**, 135; suffers so much in loving, **6**, 160; 'a sort of hostile transaction', **10**, 50; dread of new love, 197; could not fall in love with an English woman again, 197

Low life, **3**, 47, 107, 173, 216–17, 221

Marriage (*see also* Byron, marriage), 'that worst of evils', **1**, 180, 254; thinks of marrying for money, **2**, 62, 75, 84, 85, 86, 88, 109, 115; on Webster's marriage, 87, 126 and n, 131; **3**, 116–17, 123–4, 129, 135, 137, 142, 143, 149, 171, 172; must marry, **2**, 127; better with esteem than romance, 199; advantage of affair with married woman, 208, 217; nothing but marriage can save B., 218, 222; expects cuckoldom in, 251; cannot fortune-hunt, **3**, 32; bad enough to be a modern wife, 36; conceived delight of in country, 100–1; no one improved by matrimony, 206; no good comes from a young wife, 210; ideal confessed to Annabella, 178; a wife would be his salvation, 241; queer ceremony, 248; wishes he was married, **4**, 29; moderate expectations, 30, 34; means to marry, 92, 93; foxes who have cut off their tails, 151–2; so much ceremony should not be made of it, 185, 196, 204, 213; one ought to marry upon lease, 263; advised Hobhouse not to marry, 283n; 'funeral', **5**, 204; the way to hate each other, **8**, 234; thought of marrying again, **9**, 138, 141

Mathematics, **1**, 108, 148; facetious remarks to Annabella, **3**, 159, 160

Memory, **9**, 29–30

Miracles, **2**, 97; **3**, 120

Mistresses, **3**, 240; a mistress can never be a friend, 219

Money, *see* Byron, money

Napoleon, **3**, 256–7; *see also* Buonaparte, Napoleon, in general index

Newspapers in Greece, **11**, 132 and n, 138–9

Orators and oratory, **1**, 170n; **3**, 219; **9**, 13–14

Byron's views on—*continued*
Orientalizing, **3**, 101, 104
Painting, **1**, 94n; Titian, **5**, 213; Giorgione, 213, Rubens, 73, 74, 213; Murillo, 213; Van Dyke, 74; Velasquez, 213; most artificial and unnatural, 73, 74–5, 116–17, 213
Physicians, **2**, 18–19; **6**, 239–40
Platonism, **3**, 135; **4**, 22
Poets and poetry, **1**, 12–13; **7**, 182; poetic philosophy in letters, **1**, 12–13; Miss Milbanke's poetry, **2**, 175–6; advice to Bernard Barton, 179; 'the lava of the imagination', **3**, 179; on Moore's songs and poems, 193–5, 215; on Southey, 214 (*see also* Southey in general index); on Sotheby, 214; **9**, 29 (*see also* Sotheby in general index); one should not be a rhymer, **3**, 217, 220; Gradus ad Parnassum, 219–20; no great esteem for poets, 221; **4**, 183; dislikes talking about his rhymes, **3**, 231; no poetical envy, 233; on verse forms, **4**, 13; **11**, 183; likes rhyme no better than a grocer likes figs, **4**, 109; Milton, 84; Shakespeare, 50, 84–5, 301; Wordsworth, 84–5, 167, 317 and n, 324–6; can't rhyme on a subject on which his heart is set, 226; would not take money for poems, **5**, 13n; could write only from experience, 14; the East source of his poetical feelings, 45; **8**, 221; *Christabel*, **5**, 108; poesy 'the dream of my sleeping passions', 157; does not consider literature his vocation, 177; a devil of a mannerist, 185; too much of the author about them, 192; all upon a wrong system, 265–6; Crabbe and Rogers, **6**, 10; on Pope, 31; sweating poesy, 105; 'no poetry is generally good', **7**, 83–4; What is poetry?, **8**, 37; poetry next best to action, 104–5; on Bowles and Campbell, 110; expression of excited passion, 146; his not a high age of English poetry, **9**, 35; 'who was ever altered by a poem?' 53; poetry is a distinct faculty, 64; Coleridge's lecture, **11**, 179; Gally Knight, 188, (*see also* general index)
Politics, maiden speech, **1**, 16; **2**, 148n, 150 and n, 155, 158n, 160–1 and n, 165 and n, 166 and n, 167 and n, 281; B.'s Whiggish views,

1, 16; humanitarian views, 16–17; House of Lords, **5**, 19; French Revolution, 16; **7**, 80–1; **8**, 240; 'the very poetry of politics', **1**, 17; **8**, 47; detestation of existing governments, **1**, 20; **3**, 242; independent views, **1**, 186–7; for Catholics, **2**, 162; does not wholly agree with Lady Oxford, 263; more radical than Lord Holland, 281; Madame de Staël's, **3**, 66; peoples' indifference to government, 117; Baldwin's petition, 164–5 and n; parliamentary ambitions, 217; to be a leader, 218; a republic, 218, 242, 243, 244; **8**, 240; restoration of Bourbons, **3**, 257; **4**, 100 and n; *see also* Byron, politics
Popularity, **9**, 92–3, 94; **10**, 36, 109
Prince Regent, **2**, 180 and n, 182 and n, 183 and n, 250 and n; **4**, 37 and n, 42 and n, 80 and n, 120 and n; **6**, 209; **7**, 214n
Public opinion, **9**, 94, 125, 152, 161, 173; B. thought it against him, **10**, 47
Publication, not to print physically impossible, **3**, 206, 225
Radicals and radicalism, **1**, 16; **6**, 187 and n; **7**, 44, 48, 63, 80–1, 95, 99, 252; **8**, 240 and n; **9**, 50
Reform and reformers, **6**, 165–6, 187 and n; **7**, 44–5, 49–50, 59 and n, 62–3, 80–1, 99
Religion, **1**, 14–16, 22; **2**, 99, 104, 107; **9**, 45–7; B.'s scepticism, **1**, 14–15; Catholicism, *see under* Catholicism and Catholics in general index; immortality, **1**, 14–16, 22; **2**, 88–9, 98; **9**, 45–6; will turn devout at thirty, **1**, 15; **5**, 208; B. gives views to tutor, **1**, 108; to Long, 114; to Dallas, 148; his unorthodox views, **2**, 88–9, 97–8; in *Childe Harold*, 91; will turn Mussulman, 94; dislike of Calvinism, **3**, 119; opinions undecided, 119–20; **4**, 177; confessed to Miss Milbanke, 60, 101, 109; never can derive comfort from, 78; not an atheist, 81, 82; report he is turning Methodist, 87; **10**, 128; to be treated with respect, 101; does not know what to believe, **5**, 216; shocked by Shelley's rage against, 297; accused of irreligion, **7**, 49; letter to Shepherd, **9**, 76–7; not such as in *Cain*, 118; no enemy to, 119; admirer of tangible religion, 123

Revolutions, **7**, 14–15, 237; **8**, 240
'Scorching and drenching', **6**, 207
Scotland, **1**, 75; **9**, 87
Sculpture, **8**, 53; on his own bust, **9**, 21
Sentiment, **3**, 155, 239
Servants, English servants bad travellers, **1**, 235; an incumbrance, **2**, 34; seldom think, **4**, 123
Siesta, **10**, 140
Slavery, **9**, 41
Society, not a social animal, **2**, 79, 108, 111; *ennuyer*, 112; parties, 169–70, 173–4; high life in England, **10**, 139–40, 156
Solitude, **1**, 181; **2**, 77; **3**, 237, 238, 243, 246, 257; **4**, 211
Sonnets, **3**, 240
Stage, the, **5**, 196
Suicide, **4**, 26
Teeth and hair, **7**, 227, 228
Tragedy, **8**, 115
Travel books, **7**, 200; **8**, 219, 220
War, **1**, 117–18
Whisky, **4**, 85
Women, **1**, 4–5, 6, 7–9; eating habits, 7; **2**, 208, 219; pursued by women, **1**, 8; **6**, 237, 257; in the East, **2**, 79, 95; **8**, 15; hate women, **2**, 127; 'scribbling woman', 132; 'damned, deceitful —delightful woman', 160 and n; through with, 163; any woman can make a man in love with her, 209; something of the woman about Annabella, 229; be only a friend to, 236 and n; easily deceived by them, **3**, 98; literary women or 'Blues', 221, 228; hates an esprit in petticoats, 241; superior woman, **4**, 109; would have preferred Medea, **6**, 69; **11**, 196–7; B.'s good opinion of after thirty, **8**, 75–6; exalt sentiment of the passions, 148
Writing, resolves to write no more, **4**, 13, 35, 37, 44–5, 58, 92, 94, 102; will not accept money for himself for poems, 14–15, 35, 63; can't do anything he is asked to do, 107; motives for writing, **3**, 225; **6**, 61; 'a great pain', **8**, 55; writing is nothing but a knack, 133; **11**, 34
Byron (works)
Address to Neapolitan insurgents, **7**, 187–8, 188n
Address Spoken at the Opening of Drury Lane Theatre, **2**, 204–14 *passim*, 219–27 *passim*
Age of Bronze, The, **10**, 83, 90, 111,

121, 127, 128, 133, 159, 166n, motto for, 81 and n; additional lines, 94 and n; to be published alone, 110, 114, 115, 118; printer's blunders, 117; published by John Hunt, 150n, 151, 155, 182; 2000 copies sold, 154, 158, 161
American edition, **9**, 163, 164
'As the liberty lads', **5**, 149
'Away, Away, ye notes of woe', **2**, 139–40 and n; **11**, 178
'The Barmaid' (unpublished) **2**, 91n
Beppo, **1**, 94n; **2**, 128n; **5**, 125n, 213n, 237n; **6**, 4n, 39, 59, 67, 76; **8**, 114, 200, 239; **9**, 11; and Frere's 'Whistlecraft', **3**, 80n, 216n; **5**, 59n, 267 and n, 269; 'bustling Botherby' (Sotheby), **4**, 118n, 311n; publication, **6**, 3n; sent to Murray, 3n, 7–8; politics and ferocity, 9; misprints, 7–8, 15, 16, 19; insertions and alterations, 21–2, 24, 26; conditions of publication, 34–5; copyright to cancel Murray's bills, **9**, 84, 93; MS. given to Ada, 127n
Blues, The, **8**, 172 and n; **10**, 108, 122 and n, 151; Lydia White satirized, **3**, 214n; not meant for publication, **8**, 216
'Bosworth Field' (unpublished), **1**, 131 and n, 132, 136
'Braziers, The, it seems', **8**, 58, 68
Bride of Abydos, The, **1**, 226n; **4**, 63, 71n; **5**, 29, 188n, 239; **8**, 191; composition, **3**, 156 and n, 157, 160, 161, 168, 194, 202, 208; sent to Gifford, 161–2, 163; publication questions, 162, 163, 166, 168, 181n, 189, 230; dedication, 163 and n, 169; alterations and corrections, 163–4, 165, 172–3, 183, 188, 190–1, 192, 201; payment for,166–7, 167n, 176–7, 187–8, 212; copies given, 170, 175 and n, 176, 184, 187, 197, 200, 228; printing, 170, 173, 175, 177, 181n, 182n; Selim-Zuleika relationship, 175n, 196n, 199, 205, 230; title, 205 and n, 206, 232–3; B. advised not to publish, 206; tribute to de Staël, 226–7, 235; 1000 guineas offered for *Bride* and *Giaour*, **4**, 63, 71n, 71–2, 107; written in four days, 77; reviewed in the *Anti-Jacobin*, 95 and n, 96, in *Edinburgh Review*, 87 and n, 92 and n, 142n, in *Quarterly Review*, 90 and n, in *Scottish Review*, 107 and n
'Bright be the place of thy soul', **5**, 255 and n

Byron's works—*continued*

'British Bards', **1**, 136n, 141 and n, 276

Cain, **7**, 244n, **8**, 210, 240, 248, 250; **9**, 59, 81, 118, 154; Murray alarmed at, **1**, 11; **9**, 56, 60; religious problems in, **1**, 14; dedicated to Scott, **4**, 358; **8**, 198 and n, 205; **9**, 54 and n, 86 and n; lines for, **8**, 38; sent to Murray, 205–6, 208, 223, 224, 225, 230, 233, 240; additions, 206; theme, 215–16; 'the politics of Paradise', 216; character of Lucifer, **9**, 53; character of Cain, 53–4; Eve's curse, 54; orthodox, 56; B. insists it is pious, 60; praised by Gifford, Moore, Matthews, 60, 61, 64, 67; publication by Murray, 62, 88, 89; Hobhouse on, 67, 70, 101 and n, 124; Murray's offer for, 71; Murray to be prosecuted for, 88, 89, 103 and n; outcry of parsons, 95 and n, 100 and n, 110; attacked by Oxoniensis, 100n, 103n, 142 and n; Lucifer and Satan, 103; Moore's protest, 111n; pirated, 115–16, 152; Shelley's supposed influence on, 119n; war of church and state against, 122, 123; attacks on, 141; defended by Harroviensis, 142 and n, 145 and n, 146, 151 and n, 152, 156, 167; reviewed by *Edinburgh*, 159 and n; German translation, 165n; B. willing to omit passage, **10**, 12; *Quarterly* review of, 18, 68n; theological problems in, **11**, 215

'Charity Ball, The', **8**, 228n

Childe Harold (Cantos I and II), **1**, 101n, 215n, 274; **2**, 32n, 111, 113, 135n, 176, 210, 212, 281; **3**, 34 and n, 44, 60n, 100, 168, 237, 238; **4**, 16, 35, 36, 37n, 43n, 49, 52, 64, 89, 94, 165, 253, 308n, 314n; **5**, 29, 186, 192; **8**, 162; **9**, 16, 40; tortured spirit, **1**, 1; B.'s Childe Harold moods, 3; B. made famous by, 8; **3**, 271; praised by Jeffrey, **1**, 11; **11**, 188n; B. lionized after publication, **1**, 19; note on Lisbon, 215n; ridicules Sir John Carr, 217n; Cintra, 218n; 'Florence', 224n; on Zitza, 226n; Basili, 228n; Mount Tomerit, 237n; tribute to Matthews, 277; on Fauvel, **2**, 11n; notes, 59, 100, 102 and n, 103, 104 and n, 115 and n, 130, 146, 151, 172n, 178; submitted to Miller, 63 and n; Elgin, 65–6, 156, 172n; title page, 75–6, 83; to be shown

to Gifford, 78, 80 and n, 91–2, 98–9, 101, 109, 130; commemorative stanzas, 81, 84; reviews of: *Anti-Jacobin Review*, and *Quarterly Review*, 197 and n; *British Critic*, 174n; *British Review*, 181 and n; *The Satirist*, 225 and n, 228–9; Spenser's measure, 210; parodied in 'Cui Bono', 221n; **3**, 7 and n, 11 and n; later editions, **2**, 224, 234, 235, 258; on literature of modern Greeks, 91; defended by B. against Dallas, 92; changes in proof, 96 and n; 103 and n, 104, 105, 106, 109, 115–17; Edleston, 116n, 121 and n; Wingfield, 81, 118n; **3**, 106n; identification of Harold, **2**, 122 and n; nears publication, 130, 151; Dodona, 134n; Earl of Aberdeen, 156 and n; publication (Cantos I and II), 167 and n, 168, 283, 284, 285; Caroline Lamb read early copy, 169n; reviewed in *Edinburgh Review*, 174n; **3**, 224n; Scott's praise of, **2**, 182n; preface to 2nd ed., 246n; 'To Ianthe', 258n; **3**, 33n, 201n; race horse named for **2**, 260n; B. will not continue, **3**, 8; 7th ed., 33n, 201 and n; **4**, 16n, 45, 46, 47; always will be unconcluded, **3**, 182; reviewed in *Quarterly Review*, 208n; B. identified with, **4**, 13–14; out of print, 30; facsimile of Greek letter, 46 and n; copyright given to Dallas, 71 and n; B. believed most original, 107; Mildmay compared himself to, 242; Hodgson's critique, **8**, 112 and n, 114; alleged plagiarism in, 164 and n; B. said to resemble, **9**, 11; lines to Parnassus, 41; German translation, 164; refused by half the trade, **10**, 62, 67, 70

(Canto III), **5**, 144, 153, 196, 262n; **8**, 185; Waterloo, **11**, 190 and n; 'piece of poetical desolation', **1**, 6; **5**, 165; tribute to Frederick Howard, **4**, 302n; **1**, 61n; portrait of Rousseau, 171n; 3rd canto reviewed by Scott, **4**, 358; finished, **5**, 80, 82, 83, 87; MS. sent by Shelley, 90, 115; payment for, 105–7, 266; delights Gifford, 105 and n; fair copy of MS carried by Davies, 108, 110, 115; stanzas to his daughter, 113, 139, 159; published by Murray, 153; to be published without omissions, 154, 159–60; first draft sent by St. Aubyn, 155; B. thought his best, 159, 165; omissions on Gifford's advice, 169 and n; reviewed by Jeffrey in *Edinburgh*, 170

and n, 183 and n, 185, 198; reviewed by Scott in *Quarterly*, 178 and n, 183 and n, 184, 185, 198; B. accused of praising Buonaparte in, 201–2, 204; corrections, 220, 264; **11**, 190; Shelley's influence on, **5**, 297; General Marceau, **10**, 165 and n; B.'s fair copy of MS., **11**, 155

(Canto IV), **5**, 157, 174n, 196, 267, 269, 279; **6**, 32, 36–7, 45–6, 105; **7**, 201n, 202; **9**, 72; composed a La Mira, **5**, 237n, 249, 251; 'I stood in Venice . . .', 244; finished, 253–4, 261; notes by Hobhouse, **1**, 276; **5**, 255, 263, 265, 269 and n, 272; **6**, 7, 8 and n, 14 and n, 20, 51 and n; B. on merits of, **5**, 264–5; MS. sent by Hobhouse, 266; **6**, 3 and n; dedicated to Hobhouse, 16n, 59 and n, 75n; reference to Candia, 23 and n; Leoni's translation, 42 and n; **7**, 97 and n; **9**, 157n; **11**, 194 and n; B.'s anxiety about success, **6**, 53; corrections and alterations, 70–1, 75 and n; reviewed by *Edinburgh*, **9**, 11; reviewed by Scott in *Quarterly*, 85 and n, 86; 'Apostrophe to Ocean', **10**, 93n; B. has no intention to continue, 108, 126, 127; possible 5th and 6th cantos, 69

'Childish Recollections', **1**, 53n, 64n, 65n, 101n, 111 and n, 133n, 147n; **8**, 23 and n; omission from *Poems Original and Translated*, **1**, 142 and n, 143 and n, 145n, 154–5; suggested alterations, 143, 152; 'lordly preface', 157n, 159n

'Consolatory Address to Sarah Countess of Jersey', **4**, 149 and n, printed in the *Champion*, 120 and n, 152 and n, 154

'The Cornelian', **1**, 110 and n, 118 and n, 123n

Corsair, The, **2**, 228n, 234n, 285; **3**, 242n, 243, 255; **4**, 35, 36, 37 and n, 49, 54, 56, 107, 126n, 165, 253; **5**, 29, 85n, 110n, 153 and n, 154, 265; **7**, 214n; **10**, 90; identified with B. **3**, 250; mottoes from Dante, **4**, 11 and n; **6**, 170n; dedication to Moore, **4**, 12–14, 16, 17, 18 and n, 19, 20, 32 and n; **9**, 190 and n; B. gives Dallas copyright, **4**, 14n, 71n; heroine's name, 17 and n; additions and corrections, 22, 24, 33, 48; included 'Weeping' poem, 42 and n, 49, 50, 52; first day's sale, 44n; **10**, 161; new ed., **4**, 45, 46, 65, 96 and n, 167; written in 10 days, 77;

notes for, 95, 167, 250–1; reviewed in *Anti-Jacobin*, 95 and n, 96, in *Edinburgh Review*, 87 and n, 92 and n, 142n, 147; in *The Quarterly*, 145n; similarity to *Ivan*, 314, 315–16; sale of, **6**, 237; Medora's song, **9**, 24; personified by Trelawny, 236

Curse of Minerva, The, **2**, 131, 136, 228 and n, 234; **3**, 132 and n; **4**, 26; events of its publication, **5**, 42 and n

'Dear Doctor—I have read your play', **5**, 258–61

'Death of Calmar and Orla, The', **1**, 130n

Deformed Transformed, The, **10**, 182 and n; copied by Mary Shelley, 33n; published by Hunt, 90 and n

Devil's Drive, The, **3**, 240

Don Juan (general), **1**, 162n, 226n; **2**, 13n, 128n, 141n; **3**, 122n, 123n, 207n; **6**, 88, 212; **7**, 201n, 207; **8**, 14, 65, 92, 101; **9**, 59, 60, 87n, 104, 200; and B.'s letters, **1**, 3; deflated sentiment, 6; shocking to Romantics and Victorians, 7; Murray's timidity in publishing, 11

(Cantos 1 and 2), B.'s friends against publication, **1**, 12; **6**, 97 and n, 99, 101; **11**, 171 and n, 172; B. defends, **1**, 13; **11**, 147 and n; no 'cutting and slashing', **1**, 13; **6**, 91, 105; 'a little quietly facetious', **1**, 13, **6**, 67; a human poem, **1**, 13; **6**, 105; 'giggle and make giggle', **1**, 13; **6**, 208; a '*satire* on *abuses*', **1**, 13; **10**, 68; 'sha'n't make Canticles of my Cantos', **1**, 13; **6**, 105; 'it is *too true*', **1**, 13; **7**, 202; 'will never flatter the million's canting', **1**, 13; **6**, 192; ridicules *British Review*, **2**, 181n; St. Francis, **4**, 28 and n; Mirabeau, 74 and n, 256n; Motto, 320n; **6**, 139; modelled on 'Whistlecraft', **5**, 59n; begun at Villa Foscarini, 237n; the Shelleys and, 296, 297; plans for, **6**, 105, 207–8; **8**, 78, 231; payment for, **6**, 137–8, 139, 143, 145, 221; **8**, 76, 77–8, 185, 187n, 191; **9**, 71, 72; to remain anonymous, **6**, 214, 215, 216, 236n; disparaged by Mr. Saunders, **7**, 39n; Canto I, parody of Ten Commandments, 196 and n; B. promises not to continue, **8**, 145 and n, 147–8, 198, 235; alleged plagiarism in, 186 and n; misprints and errors, 192–3, 194, 196, 197, 209, 244, 248; unacknowledged by Murray, **9**, 54, 55, 71, 82, 84, 104;

Byron's works—*continued*
   general approval, 55; might visit
   Rome, 66; lines on Castlereagh,
   124–5n; **11**, 171 and n; *Edinburgh*
   called it pernicious, **9**, 159n;
   German admirers, 165; Teresa's
   embargo, 182, 188n; permission to
   continue, 182, 187–8, 188n, 198;
   B.'s offer to alter or omit, **10**, 20;
   inspired love letter from Pimlico,
   29; misprints, 41; Kinnaird to
   arrange publication, 47, 62, 66, 70,
   72–3, 74, 80, 96, 108, 110, 115,
   145, 154; plans for publication, 51,
   52–3, 58, 61, 67, 76; criticized in
   Quarterly, 68; passages deleted by
   B., 69; Murray declined publishing,
   70; payment for, 78; revision, 87;
   B. wants to try copyright, 98;
   appropriate time for publication,
   92, 115; satire on affectations, 116;
   must be published, 126, 127, 132;
   valuable as B.'s last work, 134, 151,
   153; popular in Paris, 134, 145,
   146; B. to continue as long as he can
   write, 135; a poetical *Tristram
   Shandy*, 150; B. will write 100
   cantos, 150; B. will not mollify
   bigotry, 160; and piracy 159; cheap
   edition to prevent piracy, 181–2;
   begun, **6**, 59 and 'n; 1st canto
   finished, 67 and n, 68, 71; dedicated
   to Southey, 68, 76, 91 and n; free
   and bitter, 76–7; additions, 85, 98–
   9; 2nd Canto, 91, 94, 96, 104, 105,
   107, 109. 114, 131, 139; B.'s
   defense against charges of indecency, 91, 94, 95, 125, 207–8,
   234; omissions, 91, 94, 132; copyright, 91, 166, 252, 256; fifty copies
   to be printed, 94; varied decisions
   on publication, 95, 100, 101, 132;
   satire on Lady Byron, 95n, 257n;
   11, 171 and n; 2nd canto finished,
   96; omissions, 104, 123, 127; **11**,
   171 and n; B.'s instructions, **6**, 105,
   109, 114, 122, 123, 125, 131, 132,
   148; will make 50 cantos, 105;
   reference to Lord Kinnaird, 165n;
   publication, 200 and n, 205, 236
   and n; reviewed by *British Review*,
   213 and n, 214; B. praises its
   poetry, 232; admired by Hoppner,
   234; not well received, 234, 237;
   Paris edition, 238; alterations,
   238–9, does well financially, 252–3,
   253n; reviewed by *Blackwood's*,
   257 and n; **7**, 60n, 106; **9**, 190 and
   n; Canto 1, suppressed stanzas, **7**,
   188 and n, 189; French translation,
   197 and n, 201, 202, 207; **8**, 147,

148, 235; Teresa's opinion of, **7**,
   202; Lady Byron as Donna Inez,
   239 and n; B. thought his best, **8**,
   65; success on publication, 193 and
   n, 209, 233; not as indecent as
   Pope, 200; less coarse than Johnson,
   11, 171–2; pirated editions, **8**, 223;
   'dry-bob', **11**, 171 and n; ship-
   wreck, 171; affected by reception of
   Cantos 1 and 2; **6**, 234, 235;
   piracies and forgeries, 236 and n,
   237
   (Cantos 3, 4 and 5), **6**, 237; 3rd
   canto completed, 253, 256; dull, **8**,
   65; debt to Tully's *Tripoli*, 186 and
   n; Wellington, 225 and n; Fricker
   sisters, **9**, 207 and n; (Cantos 3
   and 4), **4**, 74 and n, 256n; **7**, 34–5,
   42, 47. 49, 51, 57, 59, 63, 64, 75,
   85, 111, 150, 182, 238; 4th Canto,
   9, 153 and n; (Cantos 3 and 4),
   'Arcades Ambo', **7**, 81 and n; B.
   can't furbish, 82, 86, 229; B. on, 82,
   83–4, 85–6, 162; Murray need not
   publish, 82, 96, 114, 115; half good,
   83–4; to be anonymous, 121, 250n;
   Westall's drawings, 165 and n 168;
   stanzas on Brougham 188 and n;
   protest against Bryant, **8**, 22n;
   (Canto 5), **7**, 239–40, 245, 250 and
   n, 255, 256, 257; Mary Montagu,
   5, 275n; Semiramis stanza suppressed, **7**, 258 and n; additional
   stanzas, **8**, 50 and n, 76, 87 and n,
   162n; sent to Kinnaird, 56, 60, 73,
   91; on Bacon's inaccuracies, 58 and
   n, 162 and n, 192, 194; Murray
   offers 1000 gns per canto, 76; not
   the last, 78; stanzas to be omitted,
   147 and n, 148 and n, 192; (Cantos
   3, 4, 5) their success, 109, 211;
   careless printing, 192, 193, 248,
   251; B.'s pride in, 192, 198, 209;
   Mawman's copy, 196 and n
   (Cantos 6–11), Dudu in Harem
   (Canto 6), **2**, 13n; Canto 6 proofs,
   10, 94; stanzas to Wellington
   (Canto 9), **8**, 225n; **9**, 182–3, 183n,
   11, 197; new cantos, **9**, 199, 204–6,
   208, 211, 214; **10**, 12, 23 and n,
   26, 27; St. Ursula, (Canto 10), **3**,
   124 and n; 'Gentleman' Jackson,
   1, 162n; (Cantos 10 and 11), **10**,
   18, 19, 26, 35, 42; (Canto 11), **8**,
   163n
   (Cantos 12–17), 12th Canto
   completed, **10**, 51, 52, 59, 60, 66,
   80, 86, 87, 162; English ennui, 139
   and n; English high society, 146
   and n; Canto 13 completed, 104,
   109, 117, 121, 127; friends and

lovers (Canto 14), 50 and n; (Canto 14), 119, 121, 127, 135; (Canto 15), 127, 132, 135, 144, 159; (Canto 16), 151, 159, 200, 201, 206, 212; 17th Canto not finished, 206, 212; publication by John Hunt, **9**, 188 and n; 234; **11**, 24, 75; more cantos written, **9**, 187–8, 191, 195–6, 198, 209, 211, 218; consigned to J. Hunt, **10**, 23n; Hunt possible publisher, 66, 133, 162; proofs corrected, 96, 99, 104, 166, 177, 181, 187; 11 new cantos to be published, 149, 150; to be corrected through press by John Hunt, 158; Hunt to publish for 15 per cent, 182 and n, 201; Hunt's injunction against pirates, **11**, 24, 49; last cantos published by Hunt, 75, 110n; Turkish girl rescued by Juan, 111 and n; not continued in Greece, 125; carried to England by Lauderdale, 170; Cantos 1 and 2, B.'s defense of, 171–2; cosmological problems in, 215

'Dream, The', **5**, 160, 178n

'Elegy on the recovery of Lady [Noel]', **8**, 126, 128

'Elegiac Stanzas on the death of Sir Peter Parker', **1**, 39n; **4**, 198n, 201–2

Endorsement to the Deed of Separation, **7**, 219

English Bards and Scotch Reviewers, **1**, 136n, 141 and n, 192 and n, 274; **2**, 43, 45n, 75, 281, 285; **3**, 60n, 61, 101, 107n; **4**, 62, 63, 95n, 107, 165, 318 and n; **5**, 91, 269–70; **7**, 60n, 217 and n, 229; **8**, 79 and n, 102; attack on Jeffrey, **1**, 11; **9**, 86 and n; **11**, 188n; 2nd edition, **1**, 136n, 167n, 251, 252–3 and n; on Pye, 188n; Brougham, 194n; Hobhouse on Bowles's Pope, 188 and n; **8**, 126 and n; on Gell, **1**, 238n; **3**, 234n; **4**, 97n; on Wright, **1**, 248n; on Lord Aberdeen 254n; Carlisle, 255n; B. will give satisfaction to critics, **2**, 26, 28, 29; later editions, 44, 53, 57, 127, 131; Hewson Clarke, 65n; Bloomfield, 76n; Kirke White, 76n; **4**, 332 and n; on Lord Carlisle, **2**, 85, 88; **3**, 255 and n; **4**, 61 and n, 134n; makes Augusta angry, **2**, 88; attack on Moore, 118n; **9**, 190 and n; Sotheby, **2**, 128n; praises Campbell and Rogers, 128n, 286; Lord Holland and *Edinburgh* reviewers, 168n; offended Col. Greville, 168n; attack on Scott, 182 and n; **4**, 358; **9**, 86 and n; *Edinburgh*

reviewers, **3**, 60n; American ed. 204 and n; suppression of, 208; **4**, 59, 320, 332; **9**, 98–9; in an Albany (US) reading-room, **3**, 229–30, 236; on Gifford, 271; ridicules Fitzgerald, **4**, 19 and n; **6**, 47n, 209 and n; Irish piracy, **4**, 98, 220–1; ridicules Coleridge, 285n, 286 and n; B. regrets its publication, 286, 318; sent to Hunt, 318 and n, 320 and n, 332; reviewed by *Poetical Register*, 205n; ridicules Pye, **5**, 107n; Della Cruscan poets, 233n; ridicules Bowles, 241 and n; models for, **7**, 175n; B. threatens a new satire, **8**, 206–7, 221, 224, 236–7; admired by Sheridan, **9**, 16; pirated in Ireland, 99; refused by half the trade, **10**, 62, 67, 70; 3rd edition, **11**, 158

Epistle to Augusta, **5**, 90–1, 91n, 106, 110

Epistle to Corinthians, (translation), **11**, 164

'Epistle to Dr. Polidori from Mr. Murray', **4**, 91n

Epitaphs for Castlereagh and Pitt, **7**, 17 and n

'Fare thee well', **5**, 51 and n, 52, 58n, 61; effect on Teresa, **7**, 199 and n

'The Farewell, to a Lady', **11**, 175–6 and n

'Farewell to Malta', **2**, 126 and n

'Farewell to the Muse', **1**, 118n

'For Orford and for Waldegrave', **8**, 187, 191

Francesca of Rimini, **7**, 58, 59, 64, 73, 75, 83, 106; **8**, 37; **9**, 118, 125, 155, 178

French edition, **9**, 79n

French translation, **10**, 95, 204, 207n

Fugitive Pieces, **1**, 96 and n, 97n, 100n, 112n, 117n; 'To Mary', 97n, 103n, 123n; **6**, 143n; 'To a Beautiful Quaker', **1**, 100n; poems addressed to 'Caroline', 103n, 116; suppressed by B., 103n, 123n; 'The Cornelian', **2**, 119n

Giaour, The, **3**, 37, 48, 126n, 131 and n, 168, 169, 194, 228 and n, 236, 237; **4**, 165, 215; **5**, 29, 186, 192, 239; **8**, 191; **9**, 80; first draft, **3**, 28 and n; private circulation, 33n, 34, 40, 57 and n, 88; publication and dedication, 44 and n, 59, 63, 69, revisions and additions, 51 and n, 54 and n, 57n; 59, 87n, 88 and n, 105, 111, 124, 125, 131, 132, 141, 157 and n, 177, 218; **11**, 184 and n; written in fragments, **3**, 62 and n, 105; later editions, 65 and n, 66n,

Byron's Works—*continued*
100 and n, 163, 166, 175, 208; 'this
snake of a poem', 100; **11**, 183n;
and Sligo's letter, **3**, 102 and n,
105, 155n, 156, 200, 230; **11**, 186
and n; payment for, **3**, 167 and n,
176, 187–8, 212; reviewed by *British
Review*, 141 and n, *Christian
Observer*, 189n, *Edinburgh Review*,
94 and n, 236, *The Monthly Review*,
57 and n; *The Satirist*, 69 and n,
84 and n, 197 and n; B. identified
with hero, **4**, 13, 208; B. offered
1000 gns. for *Bride* and, 63, 71n,
71–2, 107; similar to Knight's tale,
80; reviewed in *Quarterly*, 90 and
n, 107
'Granta: A Medley', **1**, 111 and n
Heaven and Earth, **3**, 102n; **9**, 82, 84
and n, 91, 92, 93, 94, 118, 121 and
n, 122; **10**, 13, 23, 24, 134; religious
problems in, **1**, 14; **11**, 215;
published in *The Liberal*, **9**, 58n;
10, 39n, 66; suggested publication,
9, 58–9 and n, 81, 125, 142, 146,
151, 155, 159, 166; on the Deluge,
59, 81, 100, 118; to be sent to
Moore in Paris, 93, 94; 'pious
enough', 136, B. willing to omit
passages, **10**, 12, 18; publication,
18n; offered to J. Hunt, 27;
Kinniard in raptures over, 109,
134, 136; *Edinburgh* review of, 166
Hebrew Melodies, **2**, 282; **3**, 209n;
4, 250, 260, 268, 274, 277 and n,
293; **10**, 134; music by Nathan, **4**,
187n, 220; praised by Jeffrey, 330
and n; 'In the Valley of Waters',
249 and n; offered to *Poetical
Register*, **5**, 43 and n
'He has twelve thousand pounds a
year', **6**, 27–8, 27n
'Here's a happy new Year', **7**, 16
Hints from Horace, **2**, 42 and n, 43,
53–4, 58, 59, 75, 103, 127, 131; **3**,
3n; **5**, 144n; **7**, 60 and n, 114, 178,
179, 183, 192, 222, 224, 238, 251;
8, 21, 33 and n, 56, 65, 79, 92,
211; **9**, 118; **10**, 25, 39; addressed
to Hobhouse, **2**, 45–6, 49; 'Ad
Pisones', 49; with Cawthorn, 59,
74, 80, 81, 83n, 87, 90, 104, 109,
111; Townsend, 82n; ridicules
Southey, 101n; Methodism, 112
and n; *Edinburgh Annual Register*,
112 and n; proofs, 112; **8**, 60 and n,
61 and n, 69, 77; delayed publication, 59 and n, 88n; Latin version,
79, 88; MS. variants, 88 and n;
omissions, 178; note on Stickles, **11**,
160n

'His father's Sense . . .', **11**, 191 and n
Hours of Idleness, **1**, 75n, 110n, 112n,
125n, 126n, 127n, 129n, 190 and n;
2, 174n; **6**, 86n; **11**, 173n, 174n;
laudatory reception, **1**, 130–1, 136,
139; variation in private and public
editions, 134; abused, 136 and n;
alterations and new title to 2nd
edition, 137 and n, 138–9, 140,
141, 162 and n; reviewed by: *The
Anti-Jacobin*, 144 and n, 147, *The
Critical Review*, 147 and n; *The
Eclectic Review*, 147 and n, 167n;
Monthly Literary Recreations, 130
and n, 147; *The Monthly Mirror*,
150n, 167n, 190n, *The Monthly
Review*, 141 and n; caustic critique
in *Edinburgh Review*, 157 and n,
158n, 159, 162–3, 167n, 177n, 239
and n, 255n; **3**, 203n, 213; published
by Ridge, **4**, 46n, 47; reviewed by
Poetical Register, 205n
'How goes the arbitration', **9**, 138
'Huzza! Hodgson, we are going', **1**,
211–13
'The Incantation', **5**, 170 and n
'Inscription on the Monument of
Newfoundland Dog', **4**, 33n
The Irish Avatar, **8**, 213 and n, 214;
9, 71, 80; alterations, **8**, 214–15,
219; sent to Moore, 225, 236 and
n; to Murray, 238, 240, 245
The Island, **10**, 117–18, 121, 133,
134, 135, 145, 150, 153, 154, 158,
159, 166, 182, 206; B.'s intentions
in, 89n, 90; payment for, **11**, 75
'I speak not, I trace not, I breath not
thy name', **4**, 114 and n
'I wander near the fount of waters'
(translation), **4**, 97 and n, 268 and
n
'I would I were a careless child', **1**,
155 and n
Journals, *see under* Byron, Journals
'Juvenilia' (*Poems on Various
Occasions*), **1**, 103 and n, 110
'Lachin y Gair', **1**, 75n
Lament of Tasso, **5**, 217–18, 219,
220, 225–7, 229, 232, 239–40, 246,
254, 255, 256, 263, 266; **6**, 42n,
158–9; Italian translation, **9**, 157n;
inspired by visit to Ferrara, **11**,
190 and n
Lara, **4**, 129, 140–1, 156, 165, 173,
253; **5**, 29; **8**, 73 and n, 115 and n;
9, 11, 168, 170; **10**, 117; published
with *Jacqueline*, **2**, 287; **4**, 126 and
n, 132 and n, 133n, 138 and n, 140,
147, 148, 150, 152; **11**, 196 and n;
misprints, **4**, 132; name only is
Spanish, 143–4; reviewed in

Quarterly, 145 and n; to be separated from *Jacqueline*, 157; earns B. £700, 171; admired by Hunt, 295
'Letter to the Editor of *My Grandmother's Review*', **6**, 214n, 215, 216, 224 and n; **9**, 58 and n
Letter to John Murray (on Bowles and Pope), *see also* under Bowles, W. L., B.'s first letter to Murray, **8**, 44, 50, 53 and n, 76 and n, 77, 79, 95, 100n, 101, 102 and n, 109 and n, 113, 114, 122, 134, 191, 212, 239; additions, 85 and n, 90, 92, 94; B.'s second letter to Murray, 54n, 99 and n, 111 and n, 166 and n, 172; dispute over Pope, **9**, 58, 84, 93, 98
'Lines to a Lady Weeping', **4**, 37 and n, 46 and n, 49, 50, 51, 80, 82; **5**, 276n; **7**, 214n; distorted in *Moniteur*, **3**, 254n; called 'impudent doggerel' by *Courier*, **4**, 42 and n, 63, 70, 134n; causes an uproar, 41, 51, 54n; defended in the *Morning Chronicle*, 52 and n
'Lines Written in an Album, at Malta', **1**, 224n
'Love's Last Adieu', **1**, 139
'Magdalen' (privately printed), **4**, 105n
'Maid of Athens', **1**, 240n
'To Genevra' (sonnets), **3**, 240 and n
Manfred, **5**, 173–4, 177–8, 179, 203, 204, 209, 225, 251; **6**, 14; **7**, 182; **8**, 157, 206; **9**, 96, 165; **10**, 134; safety valve for feelings, **1**, 1; religious problems in, 14; Alpine inspiration, 20; **5**, 99n, 188, 194–5, 268 and n; payment for, 183 and n, 192–3, 239, 246, 254, 263, 266; B. speaks slightingly of, 194–5 196, 259; B. rewrites Act III, 211 and n, 212, 214, 219, 220, 229, 238; supposed origin, 249 and n; reviewed by *Blackwood's*, 249 and n, 268, 269n, 270; copies arrive, 256–7; last line omitted, 257 and n; not taken from Faust, 268, 270; Italian version, **6**, 15 and n; reviewed by Goethe, **7**, 106 and n, 113, 220 and n; German translation, 201, 203, 206; germs in Alpine journal, **8**, 176; metaphysical style, 36, 205, 208, 215, 224; two acts sent to Murray, 11, 164 and n; Davies got MS. from Murray, 105; 3rd act not finished, 190; must astonish Moore, 197
Marino Faliero, **4**, 161n; **5**, 174n, 203, 293; **6**, 207n; **7**, 57n, 74, 98, 117, 121, 122, 127, 146, 150, 158, 178–9,

191, 251; **8**, 21, 44 and n, 53, 103, 149, 157, 211, 223; **9**, 59, 82; compares Venice to Sodom, **7**, 25 and n; title page motto, 123n; task of copying, 130, 131, 136, 137; historical sources, 131 and n, 132, 141–2, 238 and n; preface, 162, 182; additions and alterations, 164–5, 168, 169–70, 203–4; end note attack, 173 and n, 175, 183 and n; Gifford praised its diction, 175, 194, 205; **8**, 114; Teresa's interruptions, **7**, 182, 195; not for stage, 182; unpopular politics, 184, 190; defended by B., 194–5; burial of the Doges, 201; dedicated to Goethe, 206 and n; B. objects to stage preśentation, **8**, 22–3, 59–69 *passim*, 73, 90, 112, 136, 181, 210; praise of Albrizzi in note, 52 and n; notes to, 52, 102, 124 and n, 130 and n, 141 and n, 149, 225, 244; dramatic principles in, 56–7, 78; Drury Lane performance, 66n, 116–19, 122–4, 127–8, 132, 133, 208; publication, 66n, 69 and n, 132; Murray's offer, 73, 76, 122; alterations and additions, 73–4, 76–7, 94; copyright fee, 96n; Cogni frontispiece, 136; success, 136, 137, 144; sale of, 158; appendix, 161 and n, 162; dedicated to Kinnaird, 195 and n, 196, 198 and n; **9**, 55 and n; note on woman writer revoked, 67, 182; not plagiarized from Procter's *Mirandola*, 83; attacked by *Edinburgh*, 158
Mazeppa, **5**, 296; **6**, 59n, 71, 76, 88, 92, 100, 101, 109, 123, 126n, 127, 132, 142, 187; **7**, 44, 58; B. opposes separate publication, **6**, 95–6; carried to England by Lauderdale, **11**, 170 and n
Memoirs, see under Byron, *Memoirs*
Miscellanies (projected), **9**, 58, 71
'Mr. Hoby the Bootmaker', **7**, 159, 171
'Mrs. Wilmot sate scribbling a play', **6**, 28–9
'Monody on the Death of the Right Hon. R. B. Sheridan', **5**, 82n, 83–4, 106, 107, 110, 111–12, 136n, 255
Morgante Maggiore, trans. of Pulci, **4**, 12n; **7**, 35 and n, 39, 42, 45, 46, 47, 49, 51, 54, 57, 58, 59, 61, 64, 73, 75, 83, 97, 106, 115, 117, 150, 162; **8**, 76, 88, 92, 114, 118n, 206, 211; **9**, 92, 93, 94, 101, 118, 125, 136, 146, 155, 182; **10**, 24, 118; B.'s pride in, **7**, 182; **8**, 65; published in *The Liberal*, **10**, 24–5,

Byron's Works—*continued*
39, 66, 81, 83, 110, 115, 118, 120, 121, 122n, 182; to be published with original, 25

'My boat is on the shore', **5**, 250, **8**, 85

'My Boy Hobbie O', **7**, 59 and n, 62, 99, 102, 104, 224; ridicules Hobhouse, **9**, 88 and n, 101n

'My dear Mr. Murray', **6**, 3–6

'My Grandmother's Review', **2**, 181n

'Napoleon's Farewell', published (anon) in *Examiner*, **4**, 307 and n

'No more shall Mr. Murray', **7**, 62

'Nose and chin, would shame a knocker', **7**, 181 and n

'Ode from the French', **5**, 33–4, 34n; **7**, 84 and n

Ode on Venice, **5**, 296; **6**, 58, 76, 101, 123, 126n, 127, 132, 142, 187, 234; **7**, 44; B.'s instructions, **6**, 95 and n; carried to England by Lauderdale, **11**, 170 and n

Ode to Napoleon Buonaparte, **3**, 257; **4**, 94 and n, 98 and n, 99, 100n, 102 and n, 126 and n, 284; **10**, 134; Murray asks for more stanzas, **4**, 104 and n, 107; decried by 'J.R.', 298 and n; reviewed in the *Morning Chronicle*, 102 and n; new stanzas, **11**, 187 and n

'An Ode to the Framers of the Frame Bill', **2**, 166 and n

Oeuvres Complète (Paris edition), **8**, 114 and n

'Of Turdsworth the great Meta-quizzical poet', **8**, 66, 68

'Oh! talk not to me of a name great in story', **9**, 51–2, 80 and n

'Oh you, who in all names can tickle the town', **3**, 49–50

'On the Bust of Helen by Canova', **5**, 132 and n, 133

'On a Change of Masters at a Great Public School', **1**, 64n

'On Leaving Newstead Abbey', **1**, 96n, 147n

'On this day I complete my thirty-sixth year', **11**, 214

'Parenthetical Address, by Dr. Plagiary', **2**, 228 and n

Parisina, **4**, 331n; **5**, 219; **6**, 59, 182; **8**, 73; incest theme, **5**, 13n; copied by Lady Byron, 13 and n; published with *Siege of Corinth*, 13n, 22n, 28 and n; payment for, 13n, 16 and n, 17–18; lines similar to *Marmion*, 22 and n; setting of at Ferrara, 217, 255

Poems on his Domestic Circumstances, **2**, 126 and n

Poems on Various Occasions, **1**, 96n, 102n, 103n, 109n, 111n, 112n

Poems Original and Translated, **1**, 117n, 142n; **4**, 274n; **11**, 174 and n; second edition of *Hours of Idleness*, **1**, 137n, 162 and n; omission of the preface, 137n; dedication, 155 and n; alterations in, 138, 139, 140

Poetical Works, Paris ed., **3**, 38n

The Prisoner of Chillon, **5**, 83, 87, 89n, 153, 160; inspiration, 80n; MS. sent to England by Shelley, 90; published by Murray, 144; Gifford's suggested omission, 169 and n; laudatory review in *Edinburgh*, 170n; praised in *Quarterly*, 178n; and Mr. De Luc, 209; Italian piracy, 222; Sotheby's criticism, **6**, 18, 33, 35

Prophecy of Dante, **6**, 235, 239; **7**, 44, 57 and n, 59, 64, 73, 75, 83, 96, 115, 158, 162, 172, 182, 205, 238, 251; **8**, 65, 69 and n, 73, 130, 132; **9**, 58, 118, 125, 155, 178; published with *Marino Faliero*, **7**, 57 and n, 115 and n; B.'s 'best thing', 59; American edition, **10**, 93 and n

Prose story contained in paper books, **8**, 196 and n

'Question and Answer' (on Sam Rogers), **2**, 287; **9**, 213 and n

'Remember him . . .', **4**, 36

'Romaic love-song' (translation), **4**, 33n

Sardanapalus, **8**, 26, 143, 144, 187n; **9**, 60, 71; composition, **8**, 27, 28, 31, 36–7, 45, 119 and n, 125, 126–7; sent to Murray, 128, 129, 130, 131, 134–44 *passim*, 147, 149; historical source, 128–9n; proofs, 151, 153, 155–6; alterations, 152; Gifford's opinion, 156, 158; publication, 157, 198; dedication, 198 and n; approved by Moore, 250; dedication to Goethe omitted, **9**, 91, 93, 163, 167, 182; **10**, 64; reviewed by *Edinburgh*, **9**, 159n; reviewed in *Quarterly*, **10**, 68n

'Saucy Tom' and 'Billy Bowles', **8**, 85, 110

'She Walks in Beauty like the Night', **3**, 140n; inspiration, **4**, 97n, 124n, 290n; **5**, 47n

The Siege of Corinth, **5**, 158, 219; **8**, 73; resemblance to *Christabel*, **4**, 321 and n, 322; publication, 331 and n; proposed opening lines, 337 and n; published with *Parisina*, **5**, 13n, 22n, 28n, 32 and n; payment for, 13n, 16, 17–18, 22n; metrical form, 29; *Christabel* praised in note, 150n, 153

'A Sketch' ('Born in the garret'), **5**, 58 and n, 60 and n
Skull cup lines, **4**, 47, 52 and n
'Some Observations upon an Article in Blackwood's Magazine', **7**, 60n, 64, 73, 83, 94, 96–7, 102, 106, 195, 201; contents, 114n; not to be published, 116, 121; posth. publication, **9**, 190n
Sonnet: 'To be the father of the fatherless', **6**, 209
'Sons of the Greeks, arise!', **2**, 135n
'So we'll go no more a-roving', **5**, 176
'The Spell is broke, the charm is flown', **1**, 224n
'Stanzas Addressed to the Earl of [Clare]: **1**, 140 and n
'Stanzas Composed During a Thunderstorm', **1**, 224n
'Stanzas to Augusta', **5**, 68n, 89 and n, 106, 111; **7**, 224 and n; Augusta objects to their publication, **5**, 91n, 110
'Stanzas to Jessy', **1**, 129n
'Stanzas to the Po', **7**, 97, 111, 115, 150, 191; **8**, 211; **9**, 118, 125, 155, 167, 178, 182
'Stanzas Written in Passing the Ambracian Gulph', **1**, 224n
'Strahan—Tonson—Lintot of the times', **6**, 29
'Sympathetic Address to a Young Lady', **2**, 183n; **3**, 242 and n
'There's not a joy the world can give', **4**, 277 and n, 330n; **5**, 45
'Thou art not false', **3**, 186–7; **4**, 16 and n
'Thoughts Suggested by a College Examination', **1**, 111 and n, 118n, 139
'Through life's road, so dim and dirty', **8**, 32, 67
'To a Beautiful Quaker', **1**, 100n
'To E——', **1**, 117n
'To Edward Noel Long', **1**, 116 and n, 119n; **8**, 23n
'To Genevra' (sonnets), **4**, 17n
'To George, Earl Delawarr', **1**, 53n
'To Harriet', **1**, 127n
'To Ianthe', **2**, 258n
'To a Lady on Being Asked my Reason for Quitting England in the Spring', **1**, 173n, 179
'To a Lady Who Presented the Author with a Lock of Hair', **1**, 94n
'To Florence', **1**, 224n
'To Marion', **1**, 127n
'To Mary', **1**, 97n, 103n, 123n
'To Mrs. M.C.' **11**, 175–6 and n
'To My Son', **1**, 189n
'To Penelope', **7**, 219

'To Thyrza', **4**, 308 and n
'Tu mi chamas' (translation), **4**, 37 and n
Two Foscari, The, **8**, 181, 250; **9**, 60, 71; composition, **8**, 143 and n, 144, 147, 150; sent to Murray, 151–2, 153, 155, 157, 158, 162; publication, 157, 198 and n; proofs, 178, 208; payment offered, 187 and n; dedication, 197, 198 and n, 205; dramatic aim, 218; offered Scott the dedication, **9**, 54, 86; attack on Southey, 86, 95 and n, 104; reviewed by *Edinburgh*, 159 and n; reviewed in *Quarterly*, **10**, 68n
'Upon this day I married', **8**, 86
'A Very Mournful Ballad on the Siege and Conquest of Alhama (trns. from the Spanish), **5**, 174 and n, 196; **6**, 71 and n
Vision of Judgment, The, **2**, 282; **9**, 91, 93, 151, 155; *lèse-majesté* of, **1**, 13; lines on Pye, **1**, 188n; theme, **8**, 229–30; with pseudonym 'Quevedo', 229 and n; **9**, 61, 64, 71, 72, 125; sent to Murray, **8**, 232, 233, 235, 236, 238, 245, 247, 248; 'ferocious Caravaggio style', 240; B. seeks a publisher, **9**, 61, 62, 84, 88, 92, 100, 115, 136, 142, 168; Kinnaird delighted with, 92; to be sent to Moore in Paris, 94; ridicules Southey, 95n; publication plans, 100, 125, 146, 159; appalled the Row, 118; given to John Hunt, 179, 181–2; published in *The Liberal*, 183, 234; **10**, 13n, 47n, 66; Murray delivered without preface, 16, 17, 18, 21, 22, 24, 25, 26, 27, 158; corrections, 25; Hunt prosecuted for publishing, **8**, 181n; **10**, 39n, 47 and n, 57, 66, 67n, 68, 72, 98 and n; B.'s opinion of, 59
Waltz, **2**, 228 and n, 229, 234; **3**, 41 and n, 94n
'Well! Thou Art Happy!', **1**, 173n
Werner, **8**, 224 and n, 237; **9**, 81, 90; **10**, 23, 24, 27, 28, 42, 53, 95, 158; composition, **9**, 88, 89, 90, 91; publication matters, 92; MS sent to Moore in Paris, 93, 94, 100, 115, 116 and n, 118; MS returned to Murray, 117n, 120, 121, 125, 136; to be published by Murray, 142, 146, 151, 155, 159; dedication to Goethe, 163, 167, 179; **10**, 60, 63–4 and n; misprints, **9**, 166 and n; **10**, 41; B. urges publication, 12, 13, 17; publication, 18 and n; offered to J. Hunt, 27; published by Murray, 39 and n, 40; liked by

Byron's Works—*continued*
Augusta, *55*; Kinnaird said 6000 copies sold, 60, 70 and n, 71 and n, 110, 134, 154–5, 159; **11**, 24 and n; payment for, **10**, 61, 74, 78, 99, 153, 159, 200; **11**, 42, 50, 74
'What are you doing now?', **5**, 148–9
'When I Roved a Young Highlander', **1**, 117n
'When a man hath no freedom', **7**, 219
'When ——[Thurlow] this damn'd nonsense sent', **3**, 55
'When we two parted', **5**, 28n; **10**, 198
'When youthful Keppel's name was lost', **10**, 88 and n
'Who killed John Keats?', **8**, 163
'Windsor Poetics', **3**, 38 and n, **4**, 80
'You ask for a "Volume of Nonsense"', **7**, 183
Byron, Major George Gordon (De Gibler), forger, **1**, 26; **9**, 100n
Byron, Rev. Henry, **3**, 161n, 205 and n, 208, 209
Byron, Hon. Isabella, **1**, 76n
Byron, Sir John, first owner of Newstead, **7**, 204n
Byron, 'Little' Sir John, **7**, 204n
Byron, Sir John, 1st Baron Byron of Rochdale, **1**, 55n; **5**, 19n
Byron, Admiral, poet's grandfather, **1**, 53n, 121n; **4**, 184n; marriage to Sophia Trevanion, **1**, 135n, 195n; **5**, 117n; and Patagonian giants, **6**, 212 and n
Byron, Capt. John, f. of B. and Augusta, **1**, 44n, 45n, 60n, 274; **3**, 122; **6**, 62n; B. defends his character, **10**, 207–8, 207n
Byron, Julia, **1**, 165 and n; **2**, 82 and n; **3**, 45 and n
Byron, Juliana Elizabeth, **10**, 208n, 209
Byron, Richard, 2nd Lord, **1**, 55n, 82n
Byron, Richard (brother of B.'s grandfather), **1**, 191 and n; **3**, 161n, 205n
Byron, Sophia Maria, **1**, 53 and n; **5**, 141, 175; **8**, 235
Byron, Sophia Trevanion, **1**, 53 and n; *see also* Trevanion, Sophia
Byron, William, 3rd Baron, **10**, 209n
Byron, William, 4th Baron, **10**, 30n, 130n
Byron, William, 5th Baron, **1**, 45n, 183, 203 and n; **3**, 161n, 258; **4**, 189n; **7**, 146n; sold Rochdale leasehold, **1**, 76n; B. on his character, **10**, 130, 208–9
Byron Room (at John Murray's), **3**, 68n, 167n

Bysshe, Edward, *The Art of English Poetry*, **5**, 29 and n
Byzantium, **1**, 215

Cade, Jack **7**, 63, 81 and n
Cadel and Davies, publishers, **2**, 164, 196n
Cadiz, **1**, 2, 216, 217, 220–1, 225, 239; **2**, 5n, 37, 53; **3**, 92
Caesar, Julius, **1**, 97; **2**, 14 and n; **3**, 194n; **4**, 13; **7**, 62n; **8**, 47, 107; **9**, 47, 48, 77, 89 and n
Cagliari, **1**, 221, 224; **2**, 28, 31, 42; **3**, 29, 174; **5**, 81
Caher, Richard Butler, Baron (of Ireland), **4**, 114n
Caher, Lady (née Emily St. John Jeffries), **4**, 114 and n
Cain, **3**, 164; **9**, 53
Cairo, **2**, 38
Calabria, **2**, 155n; earthquake, **9**, 30
Calais, **6**, 9, 241, 242, 246, 251, 252, 253; **7**, 50; **8**, 99; **11**, 53n, 195
Calcutta, **1**, 172; **10**, 68n
Calderon de la Barca, Pedro, **9**, 93
Caldwell, Mr., **2**, 117
Caligari, **6**, 92
Caligula, **8**, 107, 119n
Callaghan, L., Irish Committee, **9**, 183
Callao, **8**, 126n
Callcott, Augustus, painter, **6**, 172n
Callcott (née Dundas), Mrs. María, *Little Arthur's History of England*, **6**, 172n
Calvinism, **2**, 174n; **3**, 64, 119; **7**, 101; **8**, 117
Calvinists, **11**, 56
Cam (river), **8**, 24
Cambon, Signor, **5**, 143
Cambridge, (University), **2**, 5n, 46, 47, 50, 55, 66n, 69, 76 and n, 83, 102n, 112, 133, 134, 136 and n, 142, 148, 163, 168, 177, 282, 287; **3**, 59, 63n, 83, 115, 181, 197, 199n, 271; **4**, 90, 135, 156–7, 216, 220, 223, 233n, 234 and n, 308n; **5**, 156; **6**, 138, 218n, 243; **7**, 230, 232, 234; **8**, 23, 24, 250n; **9**, 25, 37, 82; **10**, 61; **11**, 164, 228, 179; developed B.'s skepticism, **1**, 14; Hanson recommended to B., 63; B. entered name, 69, 71, 72; B.'s life at, 78ff.; B.'s expenditures at, 78–80, 81–4, 88–9 and n; B.'s debts at, 80, 88–9 and n, 116, 149; college bills paid by B., 88; Edleston at, 88n, 122, 123, 124–5, 232n; **11**, 173n, 213; B.'s views of, **1**, 89, 147; Angelo in, 92; B. wretched at going to, 108 and n; **7**, 230; B. and Long at, **1**, 110n; B. can't return, 113; B. to quit, 116; Petty lost seat, 118n; B.

to settle affairs at, 121; B. at 121–6, 133–4, 135–42, 167, 169n; **11**, 179; B. to return, **1**, 124; B. sends Fletcher for plate, 162, 163; B.'s bear, 167n; Arabic Professor, 172 and n; Harness at, 197; Hobhouse, B.'s friend at, 275; B.'s letters from, to E. Pigot, 277; Matthews at, 277 (second printing); **11**, 159; B. invited to by Davies, **2**, 77, 80, 85, 86, 88, 89, 98, 105, 107, 108, 110, 114, 115; **11**, 160; B.'s M. A. degree, **1**, 95–6; **11**, 176–7; B.'s sad remembrance of Edleston at, **2**, 114, 124, 141 and n, 163; **8**, 24 and n; B. visited, **2**, 116–20, 124; Person at, 124n; E. N. Long at, **1**, 73 and n; 95 and n, 110n; **8**, 23–4; B. weaned from, **11**, 177

Cambridge Chronicle, The, **5**, 137 and n

Cambridge, Duke of, **6**, 18n

Cambridge Whig Club, **1**, 125n, 139 and n, 158 and n, 159–60; **6**, 166; **7**, 230–1; **9**, 23

Cameron, Miss, **1**, 167 and n, 170 and n; **2**, 8 and n

Cameron, Kenneth Neill, ed., *Shelley and His Circle*, **5**, 51n

Cameronians, **11**, 46

Campbell, Mr. of Glensaddle, **10**, 101

Campbell, Augustus, **1**, 121 and n

Campbell, Thomas, **2**, 127, 128 and n; **3**, 217; **4**, 86, 87, 115; **5**, 242, 260, 265; **6**, 47; **8**, 21, 61, 110, 207, 211, 219; to read *Childe Harold* MS, **2**, 130; attacked by Coleridge, 140, 141, 142, 147; **11**, 179; at Sydenham, **2**, 147 and n, 149; B. evaluates, **3**, 220, 232; jealous of B.'s fame, 233; and Merivale's review of Grimm, 247 and n; controversy with Bowles over Pope, **8**, 76n, 85, 134; *Gertrude of Wyoming*, **8**, 22 and n; 'Lines on Leaving a Scene in Bavaria', **4**, 164 and n; *Pleasures of Hope*, **2**, 147; **3**, 107 and n; **9**, 17 and n; *Specimens of the British Poets*, **7**, 101 and n, 102; **8**, 20 and n, 22, 211

Campus Martius, **5**, 227

Canada, **5**, 182; **7**, 44

Canarioti [?], Pano, **11**, 183

Candia, (Crete), **6**, 23 and n; **11**, 94

Candidus, B.'s pseudonym, **11**, 182 and n

Cannae, **9**, 48

Cannes, **10**, 108

Canning, George, **1**, 214n, *242n*; **2**, 23n; **3**, 80; **4**, 287n; **5**, 59n, 260n; **6**, 5, 11n, 86, 208; **7**, 222, 223; **9**, 14, 101; **10**, 83; *Anti-Jacobin*, **3**, 66n, 216n; and *The Bride of Abydos*, 162n, 170, 173 and n, 175; and Hobhouse,

8, 120 and n, 121, 123, 149; **10**, 176; duel with Castlereagh, **8**, 143, 144; quarrel with Burdett, 144n, 145; Hobhouse's Philippic on, **9**, 138; B.'s praise of, **10**, 166 and n; *The Rovers*, **8**, 11n

Canning, Stratford (later Viscount Stratford de Redcliffe), B.'s letters to, **2**, 23, 40; mentioned, **1**, 242n; **2**, 23n, 40, 261 and n, 262n; suitor of Annabella, **3**, 160n; *Bonaparte*, **4**, 106 and n, 117 and n, 164

Cannstatt, **2**, 37n

Canterbury, **5**, 71; **8**, 227

Canterbury, Archbishop of, *see* Manners-Sutton, Charles

Canova, Antonio, **5**, 132n, 148, 207, 216, 218, 235, 293; **6**, 190, 191; **8** 79; **9**, 26; B. subscribed to proposed memorial, **10**, 21, 76

Canton, **6**, 64n

Cape Colonna, **1**, 238; **2**, 30, 36

Cape Matapan, **2**, 112

Cape St. Angelo, **2**, 112

Cape St. Vincent, **1**, 220n; **2**, 50

Capo d'Istria, **7**, 132

Capra, Countess, **7**, 143

Caprea, **3**, 234, 256; **8**, 37

Capuchin Convent (monastery), Athens, **1**, 3; **2**, 11n; **4**, 161; B.'s life in, **2**, 12–13, 16, 37, 50

Capudan, Pasha, **1**, 242 and n, 243, 254

Capulets, **5**, 123, 126

Carapanos, Constantin, and Dodona, **2**, 134n

Caravaggio, Michelangelo Amerighi, **8**, 240

Carbonari, the, **7**, 155n, 162 and n, 249, 255, 272, 273; **8**, 17, 32, 43, 45, 47, 48, 49, 109n, 116n, 126, 130 and n, 156, 158, 166n; **9**, 23; **10**, 177; B.'s connections with, **1**, 17, 20; **6**, 229, 276; deposited arms with B., **1**, 21; time for uprising set, **7**, 162 and n, 167, 169; passwords, **8**, 40; B. as chief, 197–8

Carey, Henry ('Sig. Carini'), *see Wantley, The Dragon of*

Cargill, **5**, 13n

Carhais, Cornwall, **1**, 195n, 196; **5**, 117n

Carhampton, 2nd Earl of, **3**, 97n; **7**, 165n

Carlisle, Henry Howard, 4th Earl of, marriage to Isabella Byron, **1**, 76n

Carlisle, Frederick Howard, 5th Earl of, **1**, 46n; **2**, 85 and n; **3**, 214; **4**, 53, 127n; **6**, 134n; **11**, 225; B.'s guardian, **1**, 52, 56, 57, 61, 63, 66, 67, 155 and n, 275; B. did not dislike, 56, 57, 58; B. considers him a friend, 59; allowed B. to choose university, 63;

Carlisle, Frederick Howard—*continued*
Augusta at town house, 65 and n; at
Knights of Garter installation, 67 and
n; relation to B., *76n*; receipt of
Hours of Idleness, 133; B. dedicates
poems to, 137 and n, 155 and n; B.'s
presentation in the Lords, 186n, 196
and n, 251, 255n; in *English Bards*,
190, 193, 194 and n, 196 and n, 255n;
and Augusta, 273; marriage, **3**,
236n, 254n; Augusta urged B. to
make up with, 255 and n; B. refuses
reconciliation, **4**, 61, 64–5, 73, 128
and n, 191 and n; Poems, **5**, 36
Carlile, Richard, **6**, 240n; trial and
imprisonment, *240 and n*, 256; *The
Republican*, 240n
Carlotta, **6**, 92
Carlton House, **2**, 144n; **3**, 240; **6**, 123;
9, 96
Carlsruhe, **5**, 76–7, 78, 81
Carlyle, Thomas, **3**, 16n; *Frederick the
Great*, **9**, 121n
Carmarthen, Francis Godolphin,
Marquis of (later 5th Duke of Leeds),
1, 46n, 60n, 273; marriage to
Catherine Anguish, 45n, Kiveton
home, 60n; friendship with Augusta,
60n; children by Lady Carmarthen,
60n
Carmarthen, Marchioness of, **1**, 60n;
3, 81n, 122, 140; **8**, 34n; **10**, 207n,
208
Carnarvon, Earl of, **7**, 114n
Carnival, in Venice, **5**, 133, 143, 145–6,
148, 149, 151, 155, 160, 163, 165,
168, 171, 174, 175, 176, 178, 181,
197; **6**, 8, 9, 10–11, 14, 17, 19, 95, 99,
100; **11**, 163
Carnival, Ravenna, **7**, 18, 27, 35; **8**,
45, 55
Carnivals, **7**, 43
Caro, Annibale, trns. *Œneid*, **8**, 25 and n
Caroline (early love of B.), **1**, 7, 157
'Caroline' unidentified, **1**, 103–4 and n,
117n
Caroline, Princess of Wales, B.'s letter
to, **3**, 18; mentioned, **2**, 263 and n,
265, 286; **3**, 44n; **4**, 103, 104, 112n,
158; **5**, 155, 241n; **11**, 222; asks B.'s
advice, **3**, 18 and n; and B.'s relations
with Annabella, 19 and n; alleged
adultery, 25 and n, 197n; and 'The
Corsair', 255
Caroline, Queen, **1**, 255n; **6**, 69; **7**,
172, 191, 213, 238, 245, 252; **10**, 56;
becomes thin and gracious, **3**, 127;
death, **6**, 90; **8**, 187 and n, 189, 192,
213n, 225n; trial, **7**, 120n, 130 and
n, 149, 153 and n, 158, 159, 176,
177, 224, 227, 253; **10**, 116; Teresa

on her guilt, **7**, 122; arrival in
England, 122; acquitted of adultery
130n, 214, 237 and n, 243–4 and n;
8, 58 and n, 147n; incident at Lady's
Oxford's, **7**, 139; scandalizes England,
141, 208; B. furnished evidence for,
153, 180, 190, 204–5, 222; defended
by Brougham, 153 and n, 178, 208;
B.'s feeling for, 153, 191, 208, 218,
220, 237, 253; B.'s verses on, 159,
171; **8**, 58 and n, 66, 68; B. reported
in England on her business, **7**, 173,
177; Italian interest in trial, 180;
publication of evidence, 207; Moore's
epigram on, 218, second reading of
the bill, 238, 255, 256, 257; thanks-
giving at St. Paul's, 243 and n;
B.'s Stanza on in *Don Juan*, 258; **8**,
148 and n, 194; Italian witnesses,
65 and n; Brandenburgh House, 68
and n; and Bergami, 100n; her
funeral, **10**, 114n; B.'s jests on, **11**, 197
Carpenter, J. and T. **1**, 132 and n
Carpentiere (Carpenter), **2**, 154
Carr, Sir John, *The Stranger in France,
A Tour of Holland, Descriptive Travels
in the Southern and Eastern Parts of
Spain*, **1**, *217 and n*, 221
Carranza, Jerónimo, swordsman, **9**,
101 and n
Carrascosa, **8**, 122 and n
Carrington, Robert Smith, 1st Baron,
3, 116n
Carridi (Carrithi), banker, **11**, 16, 17,
56
Cartagena, **8**, 126n
Carthage, **7**, 50, 62n
Cartwright, Major John, his petition
supported by B., **3**, 55 and n, 193,
229; **6**, 165n; **7**, 205n; challenge to
Hobhouse, **6**, 165 and n, 168, 187,
211–12, 220; Radical, **8**, 240 and n
Cary, Capt., B.'s letter to, **1**, 224;
challenged by B., 224–5, 239 and n,
240
Cary, Rev. H. F., translator of Dante,
7, 58
Casa Magni, **9**, 147n, 178n
Cassius, **3**, 218; **8**, 107
Castaños, General Francisco Janier de,
Duke of Baylen, **1**, *221 and n*
Castellan, A. L. *Moeurs, usages costumes
des Othomans*, **3**, 102 and n, 104
Castelli, advocate, **6**, 213, 234, 254–5;
7, 25, 28, 65, 79, 103
Castellini, Artemesia, **10**, 56n
Casti, Giambattista, 'Animali Parlanti',
5, 80, 262n; **6**, 24n; *Novelle Amorose*,
5, 80 and n
Castiglione, Marchesa, **5**, 147 and n
Castle Eden, **4**, 26n, 232

Castle Howard, **1**, 57, 60, 75n; **4**, 127n

Castlecomer, Lord, **7**, 100; **11**, 232

Castlereagh, Robert Stewart, Viscount, 2nd Marquess of Londonderry, **1**, 186n; **4**, 298 and n, 300, 302, 323; **5**, 86, 214; **6**, 86, 89, 143; **7**, 25, 97–8; **8**, 225; **9**, *124–5n*; **11**, 64n; stanzas on in *Don Juan*, **6**, 91, 94, 105; **11**, 171 and n; B.'s opinion of, **6**, 104, 229; epigrams, **10**, 173 and n; epitaph by B., **7**, 17 and n; **9**, 209–10; duel with Canning, **8**, 143, 144; his death, **9**, 197 and n; **11**, 198

Castor, **3**, 221

Castri, (Delphi), **3**, 253; **9**, 41

Catalani, Mme Angelica, **1**, 159 and n, 195 and n; **5**, 160, 163, 168, 182–3

Cataline, **2**, 261; **4**, 161; conspiracy of, **8**, 14

Cateaton Street, **7**, 50

Catesby, **4**, 41

Catherine II, **4**, 290

Catholic churches, **5**, 208

Catholic Claims, **1**, 67n, 148; **3**, 22n

Catholic countries, **9**, 147

Catholic emancipation, **3**, 232n; **4**, 244n; **8**, 229

Catholic question, **1**, 67 and n; **2**, 160; **7**, 205n; **9**, 28

Catholic riots, **7**, 45n

Catholicism, **6**, 44; **7**, 35, 299; 'the best religion', **1**, 14; **8**, 98; B. facetious about, **1**, 15; a fascinating religion, **3**, 119; Allegra to be raised as a Catholic, **5**, 228, 260; **8**, 98; **9**, 119; Claire Clairmont, **5**, 294; 'most elegant worship', **9**, 123

Catholics, **2**, 12, 108, 155, 162; **5**, 200, 210, 216n; **6**, 172; **8**, 144 and n

Cato, **7**, 62n

Cato Uticensis, **8**, 85 and n

Cato street conspiracy, **7**, 62 and n

Catullus, **3**, 50 and n; **5**, 36; 'Sirmio', 123 and n

Cavalier Servente (Cicisbeo), **6**, 18, 108, 214, 226, 262; **8**, 78; described, **5**, 145, 156, 189; Italian spelling of, **6**, 32–3; B. learning to become one, **7**, 28, 195

Cavalier Serventi, **1**, 8, 9

Cavalier Serventismo, **7**, 42, 43–4, 51, 138

Cavalli, Marchese Antonio, **6**, 262 and n; **8**, 159 and n, 170, 235

Cavalli, Marchesa Clelia, **7**, 13, 18, 53; **8**, 50

Cavalli, Marchese Giovanni Battista, **7**, 18, 78; **8**, 33, 159, 170, 235

Cavendish Square, **2**, 245, 248, 260

Cawdor, John, 1st Lord, marriage, **1**, 52n

Cawthorn, James, B.'s letters to, **1**, 252; **2**, 44, 57, 73, 81, 83, 87, 90; **4**, 220; mentioned, **2**, 101, 104, 106, 114, 126, 133; **3**, 197, 202n, 203 and n; **4**, 74, 165; **5**, 91, 108–9, 139, 270; **8**, 79; publisher of *English Bards*, **1**, 248, 252–3, 253n, 274; **2**, 44, 53, 57–8, 131; *Hints from Horace*, 58, 59, 74, 80, 81, 83 and n, 90, 104, 107, 109, 111; Hobhouse's *Journey*, 61 and n, 113, 124, 128, 132, 151, 155; Hobhouse's 'Weeks at Bath', 65 and n

Caylus, Comte de, **6**, 205 and n

Cazenove, James, B.'s letter to, **4**, 305; mentioned, **2**, 41 and n

Cazenove brothers, **4**, 305n, 305–6

Cazotte, Jacques, *Le Diable Amoureux*, **3**, 101 and n

Cecil, duellist, **7**, 178 and n

Centlivre, Mrs. Susanna, **2**, 244n; *A Bold Stroke for a Wife*, **6**, 148n; **7**, 61n; **11**, 32 and n; *The Busy Body*, 61n; **8**, 57 and n; *The Wonder*, **7**, 61n; **8**, 57n

Cephalonia, **11**, 15n, 18, 19n, 21, 26 and n, 32, 43n, 45, 53, 61, 63n, 64n, 72n, 76, 89, 92, 96, 101, 109, 125, 126n, 132n, 214, 216; journal in, **1**, 22–3, 25–6; **11**, 29–35, 113; B. in, 15–86; Napier Governor of, 20n, 45; earthquake, 43 and n, 46, 51, 52; Chalandritsanos family, 213

Cerberus, **8**, 230

Ceriga, (island), **2**, 112

Certosa Cemetery, Ferrara, **1**, 15–16; **6**, 147, 149; **9**, 66

Cervantes Saavedra, Miguel de, **3**, 220–1; *Don Quixote*, **2**, 194; **10**, 116 and n

Cesena, **8**, 45

Cesto, **5**, 113, 116, 117

Ceylon, **2**, 89n

Chalandritsanos family, **11**, 19 and n, 23, 32; B.'s aid to, 63–4

Chalandritsanos, Lukas, biog. sketch, **11**, 213; mentioned, 86n, 87; B.'s page, 19n; sent to Missolonghi, 88, 90, 92 and n; ill, 106; his death, 214

Chaldaic, **2**, 151

Chalmers, Alexander, ed. of the 'Tatler', **4**, 11

Chalmers, George, *Life of Mary Queen of Scots*, **6**, 4 and n

Chalmers, Dr. Thomas, **5**, 277

Chamouni, **5**, 86, 89, 93, 94, 97, 102, 106, 108, 188, 206; **9**, 97n

Champs Elysees, **8**, 56

Champion, The, **4**, 115 and n, 120n, 152 and n, 154

Chancery Lane, **4**, 141; **6**, 32, 77, 78n, 82; **9**, 32, 205; **10**, 154; **11**, 185

Chantrey, Sir Francis, **5**, 260n, 269

Chaonia, **1**, 237

Chardin, Jean, *Voyage en Perse*, **3**, 252 and n

Charing Cross, **2**, 217

Charlemagne, **5**, 127, 221; **7**, 45, 196

Charl emont, Francis William Caulfield, 2nd Earl of, **3**, 171n, 214n

Charle mont, Lady (née Bermingham), **3**, *171 and n*, 214 and n, 228; **8**, 54 and n

Charles, servant, **1**, 98

Charles I, **1**, 55 and n; **3**, 37, 38 and n; **4**, 80n, 278n; **5**, 19, 97

Charles II, **5**, 19n, 218; **6**, 95; **8**, 122 and n; **10**, 156 and n

Charles V, **3**, 256

Charleville, Lady, B.'s letter to, **4**, 107; mentioned, 105 and n, 107

Charlotte, Pri ncess, **3**, 242, 254n; **4**, 60, 144n; death. **5**, 276 and n; **6**, 90

Charlotte Augusta , Princess, **1**, 63 and n; **2**, 183n, 263

Charlotte, Queen, **5**, 209n; **9**, 190n; **10** 208

Charon, **9**, 34

Charterh ouse, **11**, 155

Charybd is, **11**, 172

Chateau briand, François René, Vicomte de, **5**, 34 and n

Chatham, **1**, 115 and n, 151; **9**, 35

Chatham, William Pitt, 1st Earl of, **6**, 30; **9**, 14, 155

Chatsworth, **4**, 263 and n, 267, 269n

Chatterton, Thomas, **2**, 82; **4**, 332; **6**, 85; **9**, 11

Chaucer, Geoffrey, **6**, 91, 94; **8**, 101; Wife of Bath, **9**, 62

Chauncey, Capt. Isaac, **9**, 164, 179

Chaworth, Elizabeth, **10**, 209n

Chaworth, Mary (*see also* Chaworth-Musters, Mary), **3**, 99n, 178 and n; B. in love with, **1**, 43n, 173 and n, 174; B.'s po ems to, 116–17 and n, 173n, 179; **11**, 1 75–6 and n; B.'s attachment, **4**, 20, 27, 55–6; **9**, 24; **10**, 209 and n; and B. in a boat, **9**, 34

Chaworth, John Viscount, **10**, 209n

Chaworth, William, duel with 5th Lord Byron, **10**, 208 and n, 209

Chaworth-Musters, John, **1**, 183 and n, 189

Chaworth-Musters, Mary (*see also* Chaworth, Mary), **1**, 116–17 and n, 183n; **2**, 248; visited by B. and Hobhouse, **1**, 173–4; **11**, 176n; her letters to B., **4**, 17, 19, 29; separated from her husband, 19–20, 21, 56; wants to see B., 19–20, 21,

23, 28, 56; B. feels only friendship for, 21, 23, 28, 29, 35; to go to London, 39; B. did not see her, 48; B. would like to see her, 125; in London, 143; her illness, 224, 226–7; mad in town, 228; B.'s letters to offered to Murray, **8**, 227

Cheapside, **5**, 143, 151, 158

Chelsea, **8**, 207n

Cheltenham, **2**, 189n, 192, 201, 206, 222, 235, 236, 241, 245, 246, 247, 248, 250, 251, 252; **3**, 12, 13, 42, 47; **5**, 79n; **9**, 35

Chénier, Marie André, **9**, 11

Cheops, **6**, 99

Cheronea, **5**, 76

Cheshire, **4**, 45, 47

Chester (city), **2**, 67 and n, 93

Chester, 'Cheeks', **9**, 44–5; **10**, 125

Chesterfield, Philip Stanhope, 2nd Earl of, **3**, 146 and n, 148 and n

Chesterfield, Philip Dormer Stanhope, 4th Earl of, **4**, 226 and n; **10**, 171 and n; **11**, 226

Chiarenza, **11**, 30

Chichester, **4**, 316

Chiesa Nuova, **5**, 227

Chile, **3**, 249n; **6**, 172n

Chillingworth, William, **9**, 76 and n

Chillon, Chateau de, **5**, 82, 97, 98, 209

Chimborazo, **3**, 233

China, **6**, 60; **8**, 107; **9**, 30; **10**, 230

Chios, **11**, 59n

Choiseul-Gouffier, Count, *Voyage Pittoresque de la Grêce*, **2**, 11n

Chrisso (Chrysso), Bishop of, **2**, 59, 60; **3**, 61n, 253

Christ, **2**, 26, 89, 98, 112; **6**, 256

Christ's College, Cambridge, **1**, 154n

Christ Church, Oxford, **1**, 108n

Christianity, **2**, 89, 97–8; **3**, 73, 120; **7**, 245; **8**, 35, 98; **9**, 46, 119n, 123; **10**, 52; **11**, 87n; and Kennedy, 46, 214

Christians, **2**, 40, 98, 114; **7**, 113

Christian Observer, The, **3**, 189 and n, 190 and n

Christie, J. H., duellist, **8**, 99n

Christ's Hospital, School, **1**, 10; **2**, 281; **6**, 46

Churchill, Charles, **2**, 206, 207 and n; **9**, 11; and 'Hell-Fire Club', **1**, 161n

Church, Edward, B.'s letter to, **10**, 202; mentioned, 202 and n, 203

Church of England, **1**, 274

Cibber, Colley, **8**, 112; improvements to Shakespeare, **4**, 77n, 85; *Richard III*, **3**, 184 and n; *The Careless Husband*, **11**, 222

Cibber, Theophilus, *Lives of the Poets*, **2**, 197n

Cicero, **3**, 207; **6**, 89; **7**, 81n, 174; **9,**

17; *De Oratore*, **2**, 138n; *Tusculanae Disputationes*, **9**, 117 and n; **11**, 233

Cicognara, Count Leopoldo, B.'s letter to, **10**, 21; mentioned, 76 and n

Cicognara, Mme., **7**, 25

Cincinnatus, Lucius, **5**, 168

Cintra (Sintra), **1**, 215, 218 and n, 226; **2**, 106, 187; **5**, 76

Cirencester, **2**, 223

City Road, **2**, 265n

Clairmont, Claire, B.'s letters to, **5**, 59 (2); biog. sketch, 293–4; mentioned, **9**, 205 and n; B. never pretended to love her, **1**, 9; **5**, 162; besieges B., **5**, 59 and n, 293, 296; B.'s affair with in Geneva, 92; **6**, 76, 82, 126; with child by B., **5**, 141–2, 143, 162, 228n, 295; bears B.'s daughter, 228 and n; Allegra with at Este, 264n; **6**, 69; later years, **5**, 294; and the Shelleys, 295, 296, 297, 298; her daughter Allegra sent to B., **6**, 39n; and Southey's 'League of Incest', 76, 82, 126; and guardianship of Allegra, **7**, 80, 174–5; **8**, 113; her insolent letters to B., **7**, 162, 174; alleged child by Shelley, 191 and n; **8**, 97 and n; letter to B., 97n

Clara, maid, **7**, 147

Clare, John Fitzgibbon, 2nd Earl of, B.'s letters to, **1**, 101, 106, 129, 133; **3**, 5; **8**, 228; **9**, 167; **11**, 148; mentioned, **2**, 149, 230 and n, 235, 259; **3**, 5; **6**, 86; **9**, 67; **10**, 30, 57; **11**, 66, 148n; met B. on road to Pisa, **1**, 22; **9**, 49, 53, 56, 118, 167n; favourite of B. at Harrow; **1**, *101 and n*, 129; **9**, 44, 49–50; as Lycus, **1**, 101n, 109n; B.'s apologies to, 133–4; stanzas to, 140 and n; bequeathed library to, 202n; At Rome, **9**, 67, 117–18; visit with B. at Montenero, 167 and n, 170, 175, 201; carried 'Detached Thoughts' to England, 168, 172, 188; on B. and Tuscan government, 175; B.'s friendship for, **10**, 34

Clare, Lady, **2**, 235

Clarence, Duke of, **3**, 249n; **6**, 18n

Clarens, **5**, 81, 82, 95, 96, 97, 98, 108, 113, 205, 220, 264

Claridge, J. F., **1**, 176n

Claridge, George, **1**, 176n

Claridge, John Thomas, **1**, *176 and n*, 239; **2**, 101 and n, 102–3, 108, 113n, 115, 126 and n, 127

Clark, J. W., *Cambridge, Brief Historical and Descriptive Notes*, **1**, 79n

Clark, Dr. William, B.'s letters to, **3**, 74, 83, 84, 176, 180; **4**, 99; mentioned, **3**, 147, 197; **4**, 233n; plans to go abroad with B., **3**, *63 and n*, 74, 84, 115 and n, 176 and n, 180, 181, 199n; **4**, 99–100 and n, 233n; B. voted for at Cambridge, 235 and n

Clarke, physician, **3**, 147

Clarke, Edward Daniel, B.'s letters to, **2**, 156, 169, 171; 178, 180; **3**, 62, 199 **4**, 338; **11**, 180; mentioned, **2**, 103, 117 and n, 124, 157; **3**, 63n, 84, 197, 199 and n; **4**, 146, 234 and n, 338; **6**, 56; **8**, 93; **11**, 164; and *Childe Harold*, **2**, 169 and n, 171 and n; B. quotes his letter, 172 and n, 178; *Travels* (6 vols.), 61 and n, *66 and n*, 117n, 125, 180 and n, 181 and n

Clarke, Mrs. Edward Daniel, **2**, 178; **3**, 200

Clarke, Hewson, B's letter to, **1**, 167; abuses *Hours of Idleness* in *The Satirist*, 136 and n, 167n; challenged by B., *167 and n*; personal attack on B. in *The Scourge*, **2**, 65 and n, 67 and n, 68

Clarke, James Stanier, *Naufragia*, **3**, 62 and n

Clarke, Mr. and Mrs., **9**, 34

Clarke, Mrs. (m. of Mary Chaworth), **2**, 248

Clarke, Mary Ann, mistress of Duke of York, **1**, 197n; **2**, 194 and n, 255n

Clarke, Samuel, **3**, *63 and n*; **9**, 76 and n

Clarke, T. [J?], B.'s letters to, **3**, 76; **11**, 185

Clarke Library, U. of Cal., **3**, 72n

Claudianus, Claudius, **5**, 123, 265; **6**, 95

Claughton, Thomas, B.'s letters to, **4**, 165, 282; mentioned, **2**, 231, 233–4; **4**, 24, 29, 30, 31, 86n, 89, 147, 211, 238, 239, 254, 255, 258; **6**, 102; **7**, 116, 235, 239, 240; **9**, 56, 73, 82, 201, 217, 218; **10**, 46, 48, 86; purchase of Newstead, **2**, 28n, 188n, 189, 190 and n, 238 and n, 241, 248, 255; **3**, 6, 22, 24, 28 and n, 29, 32, 33, 38, 39, 56, 76–7, 138; **11**, 157n, 185; inclined to settle, **4**, 25, 38; coming to Newstead, 40–1; not real purchaser of Newstead, 43 and n; at Newstead, 45, 47, 121; failure to make payments, 96n, 106, 124; part of downpayment, 116n, his procrastination, 125, 140, 141–2; unable to complete purchase, 139, 281, 282, 283; to forfeit £25,000, 143, 150, 152, 155, 156, 168, 190, 216, 218, 258, 260, 299n; his possession of Newstead, 148, 165–6, 281; tries to complete purchase, 156, 160, 163, 170, 273, 282; renews offers, 179, 186, 188–9, 240–1, 243, 245, 253,

Claughton, Thomas—*continued*
264, 265, 270, 271, 272; contradiction of B.'s engagement, 195, 198, 200, 204; dawdles over Newstead, 238; makes reduced offer, 240–1; about to complete, 270, 277; one time bidder for Newstead, 5, 89, 151, 161, 261; debt to B., 245 and n, 278; in debt over Newstead, 8, 62, 63, 101, 208; his bills discounted, 11, 162; defaulted on Newstead purchase, 189n

Clayton, 9, 44

Clemilda, 7, 38

Cleopatra, 3, 207 and n

Clerkenwell, 8, 207n

Clermont, Mary Anne, maid to Lady Noel, 5, *31 and n*, 36, 56, 208, 224, 231, 232; B.'s satire on, 58n, 60; accused by B., 62–4; not to come near Ada, 9, 128 and n, 145

Cleveland, John, 4, 93

Clifford, Capt. R. N., B.'s letter to, 11, 27

Cline, C. L., 9, 100n; *Byron, Shelley and their Pisan Circle*, 128n, 133n, 150n, 161n

Clitumnus, 5, 233

Clodius, Publius, 7, 81 and n

Clogher, Bishop of, 8, 228

Clonmell, Lady, 2, 183

Clootz, Jean Baptiste, (Anacharsis), 2, 32n; 8, 78 and n

Close, 2, 45

Club foot, 1, 41 and n, 43

Clubs (*see also under* Byron, Clubs), Pugilistic Club, 1, 162n; Brookes's (Brooks's) Club, 256

Clutterbuck, Wortley, B.'s pseudonym, 9, 58 and n

Clytemnestra, 5, 144, 186, 191, 198; 6, 131; 11, 197

Coates, Robert, 2, 143 and n, 144, 149

Cobbett, William, 3, 169, 185, 210; 7, 17, 50, 63 and n, 80, 81

Coblenz, 5, 76, 77, 160; 10, 165n

Cobourne (Cockburn), Mrs., 1, 116 and n

Cocker, Edward, 5, 266; 10, 61 and n, 62

Cockerell, Charles Robert, 2, 24n, 29n, 30 and n, 37 and n, 46, 48, 60

Cochrane, Thomas, Lord (later 10th Earl of Dundonald), 3, *249 and n*; and *Esmeralda*, 8, 126 and n

Cocoa Tree Club, *see under* Byron, Clubs

Cogni, Margarita, 1, 3; 6, 23, 68 and n, 69, 92, 237; described by B., 68–9, 69–70, 192, 193; a 'gentle tigress', 1, 8; 6, 195, 196; B. tells

her story, 192–8, 205; stories about her and B., 237, 238; her picture as frontispiece, 192 and n; 7, 59; 8, 136

Cohen, Francis, *see* Palgrave, Sir Francis

Coimbra, 2, 69n, 70, 84; 3, 34n

Coke, Rev. Richard, 2, 95n; 3, 7 and n

Coke, Thomas William (later Earl of Leicester), 10, 88 and n

Colborne, Ridley, 9, 207 and n; (Cobourne), 10, 95; 11, 235

Colburn, Henry, publisher, 5, 137; 6, 126; *Biographical Dictionary*, 7, 79 and n

Coldbath Fields Prison, 2, 281; 5, 233 and n

Coldham, Mr., 2, 165

Coleridge, E. H., 1, 136n; ed., *The Works of Lord Byron . . . Poetry*, 39n, 129n, 157n, 228n; 3, 38n; 5, 174n, 213n; 7, 188n, 206n

Coleridge, John Taylor, 6, 83n

Coleridge, Samuel Taylor, B.'s letters to, 4, 285, 318, 321; 11, 188; mentioned, 3, 220; 4, 72, 85; 5, 30, 274; 6, 83; 7, 84; 8, 207; secretary to Sir Alexander Ball, 1, 230n; lectures on Shakespeare, 2, 138 and n, 140 and n, 141, 142, 147 and n, 149; projected tragedy, 4, 322 and n; B. urged Moore to review C., 324; financial aid from B., 5, 16n, 17; 9, 206–7, 208; B.'s comments on, 5, 267 and n; B. asked for tragedy for Drury Lane, 9, 35; marriage to Miss Fricker, 207 and n; B. to attend his lecture, 11, 179; *Biographia Literaria*, 5, 267 and n; *Christabel* 'a fine wild poem', 1, 14; B.'s admiration for *Christabel*, 4, 285n, 318–19, 318n, 321 and n 331 and n; 5, 15 and n, 108, 187, 193, 208; cut up by *Edinburgh*, 150, 153; praised by B., 150 and n, 177, 199; 8, 31 and n, 66 and n, 250 and n; with Southey 'The Devil's Thoughts' 3, 240n; *Kubla Khan*, 4, 285n, reviewed by *Edinburgh*, 5, 170n; *Lay Sermons, A Statesmen's Manual*, 170 and n, 252 and n; 'Love', 4, 319; *Remorse*, 286 and n, 313n; *Rime of the Ancient Mariner*, 285n, 319; 9, 24 and n; 'To a Young Ass', 4, 285n, 286 and n

Coligny, 5, 94 and n

Coliseum, 5, 227

Collège de France, 7, 104n

Collet of Staines, 2, 95

Collina, 8, 98

Collini, Lorenzo, lawyer, and Masi Affray, 9, 142 and n, 143, 144, 147, 149, 157, 159, 169, 180; said to be 'profligate', 175

Collins, William, **3**, 179; **4**, 12–13, 332; **6**, 85; **8**, 21

Colman, George, the Elder, **2**, 210 and n; **4**, 326 and n; (with Garrick), *The Clandestine Marriage*, **3**, 216n; **5**, 273–4 and n; **9**, 44 and n; *John Bull*, 69 and n

Colman, George, the younger, **1**, 22; **2**, 178; **4**, 11, 315, 326, 330; **8**, 164; **9**, 14, 16n; drinking with Sheridan and B., 48; *Bluebeard, or Female Curiosity*, **2**, 20n; **11**, 151 and n; *Broad Grins*, **8**, 146 and n, 164; *The Heir-at-Law*, **4**, 280 and n; *John Bull*, **7**, 105 and n; **8**, 233 and n; *Love Laughs at Locksmiths*, **5**, 233–4, 234n; **8**, 246 and n; *The Review, or Wags of Windsor*, **2**, 138 and n; **4**, 258 and n; **7**, 84 and n; **8**, 34 and n

Cologne, **3**, 124n; **5**, 76–7; **10**, 156n

Cologny, **7**, 113

Colombani, **7**, 146

Colonel ——, B.'s letter to, **6**, 74

Comacchio, **8**, 44

Commandant, shot at B.'s door, **7**, 245–6, 247, 248–9, 250–1; **8**, 12, 56, 85, 125

Commons, House of, **1**, 66n; **3**, 22 and n, 226n, 249n; **4**, 298n; **6**, 86, 88n, 96n, 106–7; **7**, 16n, 17, 50, 70n, 73, 205; **8**, 79 and n, 214; **9**, 13 and n; **11**, 49n

Complete Peerage, The, **2**, 185n

Concanen, Matthew, *La Pie Voleuse*, **4**, 315 and n, 316

Confucius, **1**, 148; **2**, 26

Congreve, William, **2**, 206; **3**, 249; **6**, 253; **7**, 61; **8**, 57 and n

Congreve Rockets, **11**, 39, 40 **4**, 285n, 318–19, 318n, 321 and n,

Constant, Benjamin, **8**, 54; *Adolphe*, **5**, 86 and n, 87; **7**, 161 and n, 163 and n; **10**, 167 and n

Constantine, **5**, 221

Constantinople, **1**, 223, 224, 225, 227n, 233, 234, 239; **2**, 3 and n, 8, 11, 12n, 17, 18, 19, 23n, 24n, 33n, 34, 35, 37, 38, 39, 40, 42, 43, 50, 53, 92, 198, 261n; **3**, 27, 58n, 180 and n; **4**, 215, 262n; **5**, 144, 210, 219, 227; **7**, 234; **8**, 80n, 215n; **11**, 17, 157, 213; not Jericho, **1**, 17; **11**, 83; letters of credit at, **1**, 202, 207, 245, 247; B. on way to, 206, 210, 214, 216, 236, 240; B. at, 241–56; descriptions of, 250; Lady Hester Stanhope going to, **2**, 21; Rome beats it, **5**, 221, 276n; plague, **9**, 30; Mavrocordatos educated at, **11**, 215; Millingen in, 216

Constitution (American frigate), **9**, 161 and n, 162n, 165

Constitutional Association, **8**, 181 and n, **10**, 47n, 67 and n, 80n, 98 and n

Contarini, Mme, **6**, 194, 205

Conversazioni, **5**, 142, 146, 193, 238, 293; **6**, 17, 19, 37, 96, 107, 108, 114, 117, 146, 177; **7**, 43, 51, 65, 73, 78; **10**, 56, 130

Conyers, Amelia D'Arcy, Baroness, **9**, 52, 77; m. of Augusta, **1**, 60n, 273; elopement with Capt. Byron, 45n; children by Duke of Leeds, 60n

Cooke, George Frederick (actor), **4**, 67; **5**, 124; **9**, 31; *Memoirs*, **3**, 95 and n, 229–30, 230n, 245

Coolidge, Mr., of Boston, **8**, 146; **9**, 20

Cooper, Major, **9**, 39

Copenhagen, **8**, 23

Coppet, **3**, 273; **5**, 85, 86, 87, 92, 107, 109, 110, 111, 114, 124, 131, 205, 207, 260; **6**, 127; **8**, 164

Coray, M. translator of Strabo, **2**, 102n

Corbet, Mr., B.'s letter to, **3**, 24; mentioned, 17 and n, 24 and n

Cordova, Admiral, **1**, 220 and n

Cordova, Signorita, **1**, 220–1

[Core?], Waddy, **1**, 139

Corfe Castle, **8**, 79n; **11**, 160

Corfu, **1**, 229; **2**, 5n; **3**, 199n; **4**, 172; **5**, 148, 166, 199n, 293; **6**, 92; **8**, 34; **10**, 143, 151, 169, 171, 184; **11**, 15, 20n, 25, 30, 56, 58, 64, 95, 138n; Lord Aberdeen's explorations, **1**, 254n; Blaquiere at, **11**, 15, 16.

Corgialegno, Geronimo, B.'s letter to, **11**, 63; mentioned, 16 and n, 17, 19, 52, 56; asked exorbitant exchange, 52–3, 58, 75–6; his scheming, 69; B.'s banker in Cephalonia, 32, 88, 93, 94, 107, 109

Corinth, **2**, 27; **3**, 256; **4**, 321; **10**, 180; **11**, 127n, 157; Sligo travels with B. to, **2**, 5–6, 7, 8; taken by Greeks, **11**, 65, 66, 72, 80

Corinth, Bey of, **2**, 24, 40 and n

Corinth, Gulf of, **1**, 226n; **2**, 18; **11**, 91n, 104n, 148

Corinth, Isthmus of, **5**, 208

Cork, **2**, 81

Cork and Orrery, Countess (née Hon. Mary Monckton), w. of 7th Earl, **4**, 278 and n

Cork Chronicle, **2**, 65

Corneille, Pierre, *Polyeucte*, **8**, 94 and n

'Cornelian' (Edleston), **1**, 110 and n; **2**, 119–20

Cornhill, **2**, 250n

Cornwall, **5**, 117n; **8**, 104; **9**, 28

Cornwall, Barry, *see* Procter, Bryan Waller

Corpus Christi College, Oxford, **1**, 214n; **2**, 181n

Corresponding Society, **5**, 15n

Corri, Domenico, **4**, 187n

Corsica, **5**, 14; **9**, 173; **11**, 29

Corsini, Port, **7**, 171

Cortesi, **7**, 131

Cortez, Hernando, **6**, 216n

Corunna, battle of, **11**, 25 and n

Costa, Professor Paolo, **8**, 160 and n, 170; **11**, 21, 56, 79, 137

Coul Pasha, **2**, 114, 125

Coulmann, J. J., B.'s letters to, **10**, 207 (2); mentioned, 207n

Courier, The, B.'s letters to, **4**, 41; **9**, 95; mentioned, **2**, 144n, 192; **3**, 90n, 254; **4**, 45, 52n, 57, 65, 134 and n; **5**, 184, 276; **6**, 119n; **7**, 76, 214n; **8**, 67; **9**, 50, 95n; **11**, 162; B.'s answer to, **4**, 41–3; attacks B.'s lines on Prince Regent, 50, 51, 53, 63, 70, 96

Court of Chancery, **1**, 78n, 82n, 202n; **5**, 138n

Courtenay, John, **9**, 12–13, 12n

Courtney, Lord, **1**, 210 and n; **2**, 124 and n

Coutts (née Mellon) Harriet, widow of Thomas, **9**, 138 and n

Coutts (later Burdett), Sophia, d. of Thomas, **9**, 138n; mentioned, **1**, 186n

Coutts, Thomas, **1**, 186n; **9**, 138n

Covent Garden, **2**, 210; **3**, 107n; **5**, 15

Covent Garden Theatre, **1**, 19, 67n, 159n, 165; **2**, 192, 207, 212n, 221; **3**, 79n, 95n, 131, 171, 215, 223, 240, 249n; **4**, 114, 115, 118; **5**, 72n, 182n, 198, 238n; **6**, 18 and n; **8**, 60n; **9**, 83n; riots at, **4**, 297 and n, 337

Coventry, **1**, 209n

Cowell, John, B.'s letters to, **2**, 162, 164; **4**, 222; mentioned, **1**, *182 and n*, **2**, 162 and n, 164n; **4**, 139 and n, 222 and n

Cowley, Abraham, **6**, 85; *Epitaphium vivi Auctoris*, **8**, 50 and n

Cowper, Lady (née Emily Mary Lamb), **2**, 215n, 232 and n, 237, 261, 264; **3**, 22, 50, 97, 154n, 236; **4**, 132, 133–4, 185, 188, 189, 196, 205, 267; **10**, 140n; nicknamed Countess of Panshanger, **3**, 92 and n; possessor of B.'s letters to Lady Melbourne, **8**, 226

Cowper, Peter, 5th Earl of, **2**, 215n, 232n, 237, 260–1; **4**, 132, 133, 205 and n, 206, 218, 250 and n, 251; **10**, 140 and n

Cowper, William, **3**, 179; **4**, 332; **5**, 37; **6**, 85; **8**, 93; 'Friendship' quoted, **1**, 110 and n; 'The Garden', **7**, 246 and n; *John Gilpin*, 16 and n; *Retirement*, 101 and n; translation from Homer, **6**, 47n; 'To Mary', **11**, 234

Coxe, William, *Kings of Spain* ... **4**, 161 and n

Crabbe, George, **1**, 190; mentioned, **5**, 260, 265, 266; **6**, 10, 47, 95, 206; **7**, 201n; **8**, 132, 219, 238; **10**, 59; 'Parish Register', 63 and n; *Resentment*, **3**, 141 and n

Crabtree, **9**, 188; **10**, 60, 75 and n, 78, 98–9, 126, 135, 136, 155; **11**, 25, 116

Cranidi, Greek Government at, **11**, 143

Cranstoun, Lord, **4**, 271

Crawford, Dr., James, **9**, 129, 132, 154; **11**, 195n

Crayon, Geoffrey, *see* Irving, Washington, **7**, 200 and n

Cretans, **11**, 33

Crewe, Frances Anne, Lady, **4**, 105 and n

Cribb, Thomas, pugilist, **3**, 216 and n, 221

Crimea, **11**, 71

Critical Review, The, **1**, 136 and n, 147 and n; **2**, 135; **11**, 174

Croker, John Wilson, B.'s letters to, **3**, 76, 84; mentioned, 5n, 76; **4**, 32, 72–3; **5**, 220, 260; **6**, 11 and n, 24, 208; **7**, 223; and B.'s passage abroad, **3**, 84 and n; reviews Hobhouse in the *Quarterly*, **5**, 169 and n; and B. in *Morning Chronicle*, 184 and n; review of Keats's *Endymion*, **8**, 163n; reviewer of Webster, **11**, 163 and n

Croly, Rev. George, **7**, 201 and n, 225; *The Modern Orlando, 201n*; 'Paris in 1815', **5**, 262 and n; **7**, 201n

Cropley, Bill, fights Dutch Sam, **1**, 162 and n

Crosby, Ben, B.'s letters to, **1**, 129 (2), 140; **11**, 173; mentioned, **1**, 126 and n, 129n; **11**, 174n; *Hours of Idleness*, **1**, 130n, 130–1, 132, 138

Crousaz, Jean Pierre de, *Examen de l'Essai de Monsieur Pope sur l'homme* **9**, 146 and n

Cruger, Henry, **4**, 326n

Crusades, **3**, 254

Cumberland, **2**, 80, 111

Cumberland, Richard, **2**, 82 and n; *Wheel of Fortune*, **1**, 101 and n; **7**, 211 and n; **9**, 37

Cumberland, William Augustus, Duke of, **2**, 263 and n; **11**, 222

Cunegonde, **3**, 111

Cunningham, John William, **11**, 190; reviews *The Giaour*, **3**, 190 and n; vicar of Harrow, denies Allegra an inscription, **9**, 164n; *De Rancy*, **10**, 65

Cunningham, Peter ed. Horace Walpole's Letters, **11**, 232

Curioni, Alberico, **8**, 77 and n; recommended to Murray and others, 77, 83, 86, 101, 113–14, 129 and n
Curll, Edmund, **5**, 143; **10**, 28
Curll and Osborne, **11**, 24 and n
Curran, John Philpot, **3**, *128 and n*, 130–1; **6**, 86, 237–8, 243; **8**, 230 and n, 246; **9**, 20; on the Prince's corpulence, **3**, 128; in 'Detached Thoughts', **8**, 245; mimic, **9**, 26–7
Curtis, Lewis Perry, ed., *Letters of Laurence Sterne*, **9**, 49n
Curzon, B.'s Harrow classmate, **9**, 42
Curzon, N., **9**, 105, 112
Cuvier, Léopold Chrétien, **9**, 53 and n; 'Essay on the Theory of the Earth', **8**, 216 and n
Custom House, **4**, 60, 63 and n
Cyanean Rocks, **1**, 245, 246; **2**, 59
Cyclades, **2**, 31
Cyprus, **3**, 31; **7**, 40
Cyprus, Queen of, **5**, 213
Czar of Russia, **8**, 12n; **11**, 147
Czartoryski, Prince Adam Jerzy, **4**, *132 and n*

D., Mr., possible identity, **3**, 198 and n
D., Mrs., **2**, 45
da Bezzi, Eleanora, **6**, 92
Dacre, Lord, **9**, 138 and n, 145 and n, 151, 152–3
d'Albany, Comtesse, **8**, *14 and n*
Dalbiac, Col., **4**, 317 and n, 327, 337
Dallas (later Byron), Henrietta Charlotte, **1**, 274; **2**, 82n
Dallas, R., **9**, 11
Dallas, Robert Charles, B.'s letters to, **1**, 146, 147, 189 (2), 191, 192, 193 (3), 194 (2), 195, 201, 247; **2**, 52, 70, 75, 79, 81, 90. 91, 96, 99 ,100 (2), 102, 103, 104, 106, 109, 110, 115, 116 (2), 118, 120, 121, 135, 146, 151, 169; **3**, 202; **4**, 11, 63, 64; **8**, 228; biog. sketch, **1**, 274–5; mentioned, **2**, 29, 44, 53n, 58, 84, 114, 148, 175n, 285; **3**, 89, 201, 205, 206; **4**, 18, 33, 38, 89, 296; **9**, 11; and *Hours of Idleness*, **1**, 146 and n; and *English Bards*, 189–90, 190n, 192, 248; his farce, **2**, 20 and n, 132; in B.'s will, 72 and n; *Childe Harold*, 63n, 75, 78, 83, 91, 92, 98, 100, 101, 104, 124; recommended to Southwell, 110–11; 'a *damned* nincom', **3**, 15; arrival of his nephew, 229; and Murray, **4**, 14 and n, 15, 45; B. gave copyrights to, 14n, 45, 63–4, 64n, 71n, 72; **5**, 17; public acknowledgment of B.'s gifts, **4**, 64n, 69–70, 71n, 75; corrects B.'s punctuation, 132;

first to mention Miss Milbanke to B., 235 and n; accuses B., **7**, 47–8; knowledge of B.'s family, **11**, 187; *Aubrey*, **1**, 146 and n; *Correspondence of Lord Byron with a Friend*, 190n; **3**, 202n, 203n; *Miscellaneous Works and Novels*, **4**, 64 and n; *Percival*, **1**, 146 and n, 147 and n; *Recollections of the Life of Lord Byron . . .*, **11**, 185n
Dallas, Mrs. Robert Charles, and her son's poems, **4**, 159 and n, 160
Dallaway, James, *Letters . . . of Lady Mary Wortley Montagu*, **5**, 276 and n
Dalmatia, **5**, 48, 92, 108
Dalmatian coast, **8**, 54n
Dalrymple, Mr., **4**, 257
Dalrymple, Sir Hew, Convention of Cintra, **1**, 218 and n
Dalrymple, Capt. John Henry William, **2**, 108 and n
D'Alton, John, *Dermid*, **4**, 298 and n
Dalton, Edward T., **3**, 79 and n
Dalyell, Sir J. G., *Shipwrecks and Disasters at Sea*, B.'s debt to, **8**, 186 and n
Damascus, **2**, 39
Damer, Anne (née Ailesbury), **4**, *112 and n*, 229
da Mosta, Elena, **6**, 14, 19, 92
Dance, George, **3**, 198n
Dandies, **1**, 21; **3**, 244; **9**, 22, 29; **10**, 141
Dandy Ball, **3**, 80
Danes (in Greece), **2**, 35, 37
d'Angoulême Duc de, **10**, 140n
Daniel, William Barker, *Rural Sports*, **1**, 142 and n
Danish Consul, **5**, 163, 183, 272
Dante, **3**, 133, 221; **6**, 122, 154, 181, 188, 189, 200, 235; **7**, 45; **8**, 39–40, 48, 93, 130; **9**, 178; **11**, 232; mottoes for *The Corsair*, **4**, 11 and n; his tomb, **7**, 39, 252; Taaffe's translation and Commentary, **9**, 63–4, 90, 122, 123, 126; *Commedia*, **6**, 188n; *Francesca of Rimini*, B.'s translation, **7**, 58 and n, 59, 64, 73, 83, 106; *Inferno*, **1**, 94; **3**, 36, 70; **6**, 129; **7**, 68 and n, 73, 170 and n, 209 and n, **11**, 232; *Purgatorio*, **11**, 232
Danube, **2**, 9, 16, 21; **6**, 51
Da Ponte, L., *La Profezia di Dante*, **10**, 93 and n
D'Arblay, Mme, *see* Burney, Fanny
Darby and Joan, **11**, 179
Dardanelles, **1**, 237, 240, 242, 243, 247–8; **8**, 82
Darien, **2**, 7
Darnely, Henry Stewart, Lord, **4**, 91
Darnley, John Bligh, 4th Earl of, **10**, 140 and n

Daru, Pierre Antoine, Count, **7**, 132; *History of Venice*, **8**, 124 and n, 151

Darwin, Charles Robert, *Origin of Species*, **2**, 7n, 132n

Darwin, Erasmus, *The Botanic Garden*, **2**, 7n

Darwin, Dr. Francis, **2**, 7 and n

Dashwood, Sir Francis, **1**, *161 and n*; **9**, 186n

Datchet, **1**, 247

Davenport, Richard A., B.'s letter to, **5**, 43; mentioned, , 43 and n; *A Dictionary of Biography*, 43n

Davey, creditor, **6**, 222

David, (King), **3**, 164, 168; **4**, 220

Davies, Edward, on *Church Union*, (*British Critic*), **2**, 174 and n

Davies, Goose, **7**, 100

Davies, Richard, **11**, 155

Davies, Scrope Berdmore, B.'s letters to, **1**, 184; **2**, 68; **4**, 86; **11**, 156, 157, 159, 160, 161 (2), 162 (2), 163, 164, 166, 168 (2), 170; biog. sketch, 155; mentioned, **1**, 187; **2**, 20, 26, 64, 76, 84, 114, 127, 141, 143, 169; **4**, 243, 256n, 257, 272; **5**, 49, 56, 64n, 71, 72, 74, 77, 78, 79, 80, 182, 194, 195, 196–7, 236, 257, 274; **6**, 14, 19, 20, 21, 33, 34, 60, 88, 89, 94, 132, 201; **7**, 221, 224, 233; **10**, 56; told Augusta B. liked children, **1**, 6; **2**, 84; anecdotes of in 'Detached Thoughts', **1**, 21; **9**, 19, 21–2, 25, 38–9; new Cocoa Tree Club, **1**, 150 and n, 246 and n; to accompany B. to Harrow, 152; 'a very profane scoffer', 161; 'Bilious Birdmore', 161; his drinking, 165 and n; **2**, 60, 117, 118; **3**, 114, 213; **5**, 77; **6**, 25, 39; **9**, 38–9; and money-lenders, **1**, 166 and n; **11**, with B., 156n; at Brighton, **1**, 167n; not at Newstead, 179; aids B. financially, 184n; **11**, 156 and n; genealogy, **1**, 187; 'the immortal Davies', 199; 'pledged for £6000', 213 and n; B.'s debt to, **2**, 28 and n, 45 and n, 123 and n, 162, 238 and n, 241, 248; **3**, 255 and n; **5**, 247; **11**, 157 and n; to marry an heiress, **2**, 29, 32; on Matthew's death, 69, 83; in B.'s will, 71, 72–3; at Newstead, 77, 83; invited B. to Cambridge, 77, 85, 89, 95; **11**, 160; his conversation, **2**, 93; in Cambridge, 117, 118, 148; character, 102–3; at Newmarket, 124; his facetiousness, 112; B.'s second, 123, 129; quarrel with Lord Foley, **3**, 85–6, 86n, 93, 95; B.'s debt finally paid, **4**, 86 and n, 259; **11**, 157n, 162 and n; his finances, **5**, 80, 215; carried gifts to England for

B., 89, 91, 93, 94, 95, 114, 115, 118, 127; and MS of *Childe Harold*, 108, 110, 113, 115, 137; his bons mots, 159; pronunciation of name, 168 and n; B. wishes he would marry, 168 and n; wanted to see a boa constrictor, 159, 172; **11**, 163 and n, 165; wanted copy of B.'s verse on Croker, **5**, 184; possible visit to Italy, 209, 222; **11**, 166; B.'s miniature by Holmes done for him, **6**, 26; 'everybody's Huncamunca', 32; his gambling, 37, 74; **7**, 50 and n, 253; **9**, 38–9; **11**, 156 and n; his God, **6**, 77; against publication of *Don Juan*, 97 and n; **11**, 171 and n, 172; never writes to B., **6**, 109; quarrel with George Lamb, 138; ill and out of spirits, 187; B.'s debt to his landlord, 233; B. wants him for second, 242, 245; **11**, 167–8 and n; B.'s regard for, **7**, 50; **11**, 169; unknown whereabouts, **7**, 63, 86, 253; and Matthews, 233; his wit, **9**, 19, 21–2, 25; B. postponed seeing him, **11**, 161; stood by B. during separation, 169; interesting and invalid, 179

Davila, *Enrico Caterino, Istoria delle Guerra Civile di Francia*, **4**, 161 and n

Davison, Maria Rebecca, **5**, 82 and n

Davison, Thomas, Murray's printer, **3**, 132n; **5**, 42n; printer's errors, **3**, 157 and n; **11**, 190 and n; printer to the 'Board of Longitude', **6**, 29n; and to Murray, 200n; suspected spy of Murray, **9**, 199 and n, 200; **10**, 96, 98, 104, 108

Davison, Mr. (Davidson) (*see also* Bland, Thomas Davison), **4**, 337; **5**, 38 and n; and Lady Noel's estate, **9**, 176, 177, 193–4, 195, 209, 211–12, 213

Davy, Sir Humphry, **3**, 44n, 48; **4**, 122; **7**, 122; **9**, 16, 34; in Ravenna, **7**, 78, 95, 105; and Teresa's foolish request, 98; marriage to Jane Apreece, **11**, 180 and n

Davy, Sir Humphry and Lady, **8**, 29

Davy, Lady, (Jane Apreece, née Kerr), B.'s letters to, **3**, 44, 48; mentioned, **7**, 122; as hostess, **3**, *44 and n*; and Maria Edgeworth, 48 and n; **7**, 217

[Davy?] John, **10**, 97

Dawe, George, **3**, 198n

Dawes, **2**, 10

Dawkins, Edward, British chargé d'affaires, B.'s letters to, **9**, 129, 130, 132, 135, 139, 142, 144, 147, 148 (2), 149, 150, 157, 168, 174, 178, 179, 180, 184 (2), 185; **10**, 103; and Masi affray, **6**, 142 and n; **9**, 129–50

passim, 154, 158, 168–9, 179–80; and party against B. in Pisa, 150 and n

Dawson, Capron and Rowley [Barley?], attorneys, **7**, 71; **9**, 73

Day, The, **3**, 21 and n; **2**, 166; Editor of, B.'s letter to, **3**, 21

Day and Martin, **8**, 150

Dean's Court, Wimborne, **2**, 108 and n

Dearden, James, **2**, 201, 231 and n; **11**, 25; Rochdale coal mines, **4**, 189 and n; and Rochdale, **9**, 127, 128; and Rochdale accommodation, **10**, *35 and n*, 49, 59, 61, 73, 74, 75–6, 77, 84, 86, 88, 89, 91, 99, 108, 109, 110, 111, 113, 114, 118, 121, 124, 126 127, 135, 143, 145, 150, 155; purchased Rochdale, **11**, 47 and n, 48, 51, 57

De Bathe, Sir James Wynne, Bt., B.'s letter to, **1**, 151; mentioned, 109 and n; **2**, 126 and n; **7**, 99

Defoe, Daniel, *Robinson Crusoe*, **3**, 62 and n

De Gramont, *see* Gramont

D'Egville (Harvey), James, **1**, *159 and n*, 180; **2**, 8; *Don Quichotte*, **1**, 195n

Deighton, Mr., B.'s letter to, **2**, 127

Deists, **1**, 115

Dejean, Jacques, **6**, 74 and n

De la Croix, Petite, *Contes Persans* **5**, 192n

Delaney, Mrs., **3**, 4n

Delaval, Sir F. B., **8**, 42

Delawarr, Thomas, 3rd Earl, **1**, 55n

Delawarr, George John, 5th Earl, **2**, 149; **3**, 106; at Harrow, **1**, *53 and n*, 55, 109–10; character and appearance, 53, 54; at Windsor Castle, 63 and n; misunderstanding with B., 106, 134, 143n; represented as 'Euryalus', 143 and n

Delawarr, Lady, **1**, 53

Della Cruscan poets, **2**, 53n; **5**, 233 and n; **6**, 63

Delladecima, Count, Demetrius, **11**, 89 and n, 95, 97, 109, 133; advisor to B., 54 and n; recommended Mavrocordatos, 216

Della Scala family, tombs, **5**, 126 and n

Dellvalley, money-lender, **2**, 154

Delphi, (Castri), **1**, 237, 238, 251; **2**, 59; **6**, 173n; **9**, 41

De Luc, John Andre, **5**, 209 and n

Delvin, Lord, **9**, 39

Delvinachi, **2**, 125; **5**, 76

Demetrius Poliorcetes, **2**, 113 and n

Demper, Madame, **6**, 177

Democracy, **8**, 107

Democritus, **3**, 103

Demosthenes, **3**, 220; **4**, 231; **9**, 14

Demosthenes' 'Lantern', **2**, 12 and n

Denen, Mr., agent to Duchess of Devonshire, **5**, 23, 70, 271 and n

Denina, Carlo Giovanni Maria, **4**, 162 and n

Denman, Thomas, **10**, 72; defends Queen Caroline, **7**, 252 and n

Denmark, **6**, 180

Dennis, John, **4**, 314, 315; **5**, 28; *Appius and Virginia*, **4**, 280 and n

Denon, Dominique Vivant, Baron de, **5**, *277 and n*

Dent, John ('Dog Dent'), **5**, 260 and n

Dent D'Argent, **5**, 101

Dent Jamant, **5**, 98, 205, 268

De Pauw, **2**, 106

De Quincey, Thomas, *Autobiographical Sketches*, **3**, 102n

Derbyshire, **3**, 73n, 81n; **4**, 253n, 263, 270; **5**, 131, 200n, 201, 211n; **9**, 34

Dermody, Thomas, **2**, 175 and n

Dersofi, Nancy, **6**, 221n, 247n, 251n, 255n, 259n; **7**, 11n, 47n, 97n, 156n, 157n, 172n, 243n; **8**, 138n

DeRuyter, *see* Ruyter

Descartes, René, **9**, 113

Deshayes, André, dancer and ballet master, **1**, 195n

De Silver & Co., Philadelphia, **5**, 42n

'Detached Thoughts', (*see under* Byron, journals)

Deutsche Gazette, **7**, 106

Devis, Arthur W., **3**, 198n

Devon, **4**, 222n, 226

Devonshire, Elizabeth, 2nd Duchess of, (née Elizabeth Hervey), B.'s letters to, **5**, 270; **8**, 154, 161; mentioned, **3**, 145n, *174n*; **7**, 95, 188 and n; **4**, 309n; London, house 278–9, 283n, 285; wife of 5th Duke, **5**, 23, 270 and n, 278; B. commends the Gambas to, **8**, 154–5, 159 and n, 161, 170, 204

Devonshire, Georgiana, Duchess of, **2**, 283; **3**, 42 and n, 74, 97n, 174 and n

Devonshire, Georgiana, Duke's sister, **4**, 128n

Devonshire, William George Spencer Cavendish, 6th Duke of, **1**, 55n, 125n; **2**, 96 and n, 160; **3**, 174n; **4**, 128 and n; at Chatsworth, 263 and n, 267 and n, 269

Devonshire Place, **10**, 30 and n

De Witt, John (Jean), **3**, 212n; torn in pieces, **9**, 197 and n

Diana, **5**, 203

Dibdin, Thomas J., B.'s letters to, **4**, 304(2), 316, 335; mentioned, **8**, 68 and n, 133; **9**, 36; joint manager, Drury Lane, **4**, 304–5, 305n, 306, 311, 315n, 319, 334; **5**, *135 and n*, 140, 143; *The British Raft*, 136n;

Dibdin, Thomas—*continued*
The Grinders, **6**, 28n; 'The Maid of
Lodi', **5**, 135n and n; 'tight little
island', **1**, 2; **5**, 136 and n, **7**, 50
Dick, **7**, 230
Dickens, Charles, *Pickwick Papers*, **1**,
197n
Diderot, Denis, **7**, 103; *Jacques le
Fataliste*, **11**, 222
Diego, adjutant, **7**, 246, 247, 248
D'Herbelot, **3**, 164
d'Herbois, Collot, **5**, 168 and n
Dillon, Lord, **10**, 102
Dillon, Madame, **10**, 157
Diocletian, **3**, 256
Diodati (family), **5**, 80
Diodati (villa), **5**, 80, 81, 82, 94, 96,
97, 104, 114, 118, 121, 124, 132,
206, 243, 296, 297; **6**, 114n, 125n,
126n
Diodorus Siculus, **8**, 26, 27, 128–9,
129n
Diogenes, **9**, 11
Dionysius, **3**, 256; **11**, 165
Disraeli, Benjamin, Earl of Beacons-
field, **7**, 39n; *Coningsby*, **3**, 71n, 94n;
5, 109n
D'Israeli, Isaac, B.'s letter to, **9**, 171;
mentioned, **3**, 79; **6**, 30; **7**, 39n, 223,
253; **8**, 77, 145, 237; printed B.'s
MS notes, **9**, 172n; *Quarterly Review*
article, **7**, 217 and n; *Curiosities of
Literature*, **3**, 50 and n; **4**, 44; *The
Literary Character*, **6**, 83 and n, 84;
9, 136 and n, 171, 172; *Quarrels of
Authors*, **3**, 251 and n; **4**, 297
D'Ivernois, Sir François, **9**, *22 and n*
Djezzar Pasha, at Acre, **2**, 181 and n
Doberan, Mecklenburg-Schwerin, **3**,
86n
Doctor ——, B.'s letter to, **1**, 247 and
n
Doctor's Commons, **4**, 245; **5**, 33 and
n; **9**, 177
Dodd, John, stranded sailor, **6**, 184–5
Dodd, Rev. William, **9**, 99 and n
Dodona, **2**, 134n
Dodsley, Robert, *Cleone*, **7**, 191n;
Collection of Poems, **4**, *164 and n*
Dogherty, Dan, bout with Belcher, **1**,
162n; **7**, 233
Domenichino, **6**, 148
Donat and Orsi, **10**, 131
Doncaster, **3**, 117, 118, 120, 122, 123
Donegal, Lady (née Anna May), **3**,
247 and n
Don Juan (Shelley's boat), **10**, 11, 39,
44
Don Juan, tradition in Spain, **8**, 78
Donzelli, **7**, 131, 135
Dorant, Mr., **2**, 154; **11**, 156n

Dorant's Hotel, B. at, **1**, 142–66; **2**,
49, 53, 55, 57, 127, 154
Dorchester, Lady, **1**, 24
Dorchester Gaol, **6**, 240n
Dormer, Caroline, **3**, 213n
D'Orsay, Count Alfred, B.'s letter to,
10, 156; mentioned, 141, 142, 146,
157, 172, 175, 183; arrived in
Genoa, 135n, 229; a Cupidon
déchaîné, 136–7, 138; his journal,
138 and n, 139–41, 146, 156; drawing
of B., 167 and n; **11**, 235; B. on, **10**,
174; parting gift from B., 192; and
Lady Blessington, 197
Dorset, **2**, 93, 108n, 138, 216n
Dorset, George John Frederick, 4th
Duke of, **4**, *274 and n*, 279
Dorsetshire, **1**, 110n
Dorville (D'Orville), Henry, B.'s
letters to, **6**, 198, 203, 218; **7**, 125;
8, 142; **11**, 192; mentioned, **7**, 80,
104, 118; tends to B.'s affairs in
Venice, **6**, 174 and n, 175, 183, 191,
203, 204, 213, 229, 238; **7**, 27; to
send Allegro to Bologna, **11**, 192 and n
Douglas, Hon. Frederick Sylvester
North, **6**, *243 and n*; Essay on
Greeks, **8**, 225 and n; **11**, 184 and n
Douglas, Sir John and Lady, accusation
against Princess of Wales, **3**, 25 and
n, 26, 27 and n, 197n
Dove, printer, **4**, 316
Dovedale, **5**, 201
Dover, **1**, 276; **2**, 64; **5**, 64n, 69 and n,
71n, 295; **6**, 9
Dover St., **3**, 13
Dowden, Wilfred S., **11**, 196n
Downing College, Cambridge, **1**, 277;
7, 225n, 230
Downing Fellowship, **7**, 225
Downshire, Marquis of, **2**, 160
Downton, **7**, 154n
Dowton, William, actor, **4**, 316 and n
Doyle, Col. Francis Hastings, **5**, 61 and
n
Doyle, Selina, B.'s letter to, **5**, 62;
mentioned, 61n, 62
Drachenfels Castle, **5**, 160
Dragomestri (Astakos), **11**, 88, 90,
92, 102
Dragonetti, Domenico, **8**, 241
Drako, George, **11**, 31, 41, 87
Draper, Mr., **2**, 116
Dresden, **3**, 125n, 182
Drew, J. P., **3**, 198n
Drontheim, **8**, 146; **9**, 24
Drummond, Charles, **8**, 228
Drummond, Sir William, **1**, 254n; **2**,
125n; **6**, 11, 125, 132; **9**, 103;
Oedipus Judaicus, **2**, 140 and n, 142,
147, 151; **11**, 179

Drury, Byron, **4**, 270
Drury, Benjamin Heath, **1**, 182 and n, 183
Drury, Henry Joseph, B.'s letters to, **1**, 144, 153, 208, 237, 245; **2**, 58; **3**, 202; **4**, 214, 270; mentioned, **2**, 20, 38, 109, 113, 155, 162n; **3**, 7, 50 and n, 187 and n; **4**, 213n, 301n; **7**, 253; **9**, 164, 189; **10**, 65; and B. at Harrow, **1**, *41 and n*, 42, 49, *144n*, 150, 152, 216, 217, 240, 241, 242; marriage, 144n, 173 and n, 245; reconciles B. to Butler, 145n; at Harrow, 151; B. to dine with, 164, 166; B. sent game, 176; urged to buy B.'s satire, 177; in a row, 178; 'of facetious memory', 182; 'that matrimonial man,' 254; at Montem, 247 and n; spoiled by matrimony, **2**, 27, 54, 95 and n; good Latinist, 112; B.'s letters to, offered to Murray, **8**, 228
Drury, Dr. Joseph, **1**, 41n, *42n*, 73–4; relations with B., 43, 49, 53, 56, 58; retirement, *53 and n*, 54, 59, 62, 63; thought B. might become an orator, **9**, 16, 43
Drury, Mark, **1**, 49 and n, 50, 64n
Drury Lane, **7**, 217; **10**, 96 97, 99
Drury Lane Theatre, **2**, 210n, 212; **3**, 73, 215, 230n, 232n; **4**, 115n, 118n, 133n, 153n, 254n, 285n, 293n, 311n, 312, 313n, 315 and n, 316n, 328n, 330, 336n; **5**, 29n, 30 and n, 37n, 72n, 77, 82n, 85n, 107 and n, 135n, 136n, 140, 143, 168, 170, 182n, 195 and n, 198, 208, 261n; **6**, 18, 35; **8**, 61, 66n, 68n, 185n; **11**, 165 and n; burned, **2**, 20 and n, 191 and n, 210, 221; new theatre opened, 191n, 192, 221n; Whitbread as manager, 211n, 212n, 213–14; B. sent tickets to Hunt, **4**, 294; rebuilt, 296n; Whitbread's death, 302; Dibdin and Rae managers, 305n; fallow dramas on shelves, 319; Coleridge promised tragedy, 322 and n; Address, **2**, 191n, 192, 193, 197, 204n, 205 and n, 206, 207, 209–11, 212 and n, 213–14, 219, 220–22, 223–4, 225–6, 235, 249–50, 252, 281; **3**, 7n, 20n, 54n, 121; Address, B.'s apology for, **11**, 181–2 and n; Sub-Committee, **2**, 282; **3**, 54n; **4**, 285n, 296 and n, 301n, 302, 306n, 309n, 311–12, 319, 322–3, 334, 336–7; **5**, 67 and n, 135n, 150, 158–9 and n, 172, 196, 205n, 206, 253, 267; **6**, 24; **9**, 16n, 35–6, 36–7; B. reads plays, 35–6
Druses, **2**, 181
Dryden, John, **3**, 168; **6**, 85, 166, 168, 181, 234, 253; **7**, 83, 252; **8**, 21, 101;

9, 11; in Johnson's *Lives*, **8**, 115 and n; Hobhouse compared to, **11**, 158; *Absalom and Achitophel*, **8**, 164 and n; *All for Love*, **3**, 207n; *Annus Mirabilis*, **2**, 207 and n; *Aurung-Zebe*, **8**, 40 and n; *Conquest of Granada*, **2**, 168n; **11**, 226; 'Huntsman's Ghost', **8**, 48; trns, Juvenal *Satires*, **7**, 153 and n; 'Theodore and Honoria', **7**, 39; **8**, 48n
Dublin, **2**, 132n, 144n, 284; **3**, 95n; **4**, 253n, 296n; **7**, 68, 69, 106, 117, 122; **8**, 16n, 240; **9**, 21, 35
Dublin Theatre, **5**, 72
Dubois, Edward, **1**, 190 and n
Duck Puddle, **2**, 58
Dudley, John William Ward, 1st Earl of, *Letters to 'Ivy' from the First Earl of Dudley*, **1**, 214n
Duels, *see also* Byron, Duels; Moore and Jeffrey, **2**, 118 and n, 119; and assassination, **7**, 184; between French and Germans, **10**, 181; famous duels, **7**, 178 and n
Duff, Helen, sister of Mary, **3**, 222; **4**, 261
Duff, Mary, **4**, 260 and n, 261; **9**, 102n; B.'s early passion, **3**, 210, 221–2, 258; marriage to Robert Cockburn, **1**, 116n; **3**, 222 and n
Duffie, Lt. Col. John, B.'s letters to, **11**, 43, 51; mentioned, 18 and n, 30, 95, gave B. military coat, 43 and n
Duke St., **3**, 216n
Dulwich, **1**, 41 and n; **8**, 227
Dumergue, dentist, **10**, 111
Duncan, Adam, 1st Viscount, **5**, 132n
Duncan, Mr. writing master, **8**, 108
Duncan-Jones, Mrs. E. E., **7**, 252n
Dundas, Rear-Admiral, **6**, 172n
Dundee, **9**, 35
Dunedin, **4**, 275
Dunlap, W., *Memoirs of George Frederick Cooke*, **3**, 95 and n, 230n
Dunn, Henry, B.'s letters to, **9**, 75, 105; **10**, 31, 51; mentioned, 11, 25, 31–2, 194, 201, 203n, 204, 206, 214; B.'s agent, **9**, 75, 105, 135n, 202 and n, 204; shipment of Allegra's body to England, 163 and n, 193; B.'s orders from, **10**, 51; and B.'s lawsuit with Dupuy, **11**, 140, 150
Dupont, General, defeat at Baylen, **1**, 221n
Duppa, Richard, *Life of Raffaele*, **5**, 221 and n
Dupuy, Francesco, **9**, 161 and n; **10**, 152 and n; **11**, 140 and n
Dupuy, Villa, **9**, 135n, 161n, 173; **10**, 152n; **11**, 140n
Durham, **2**, 175n, 284; **4**, 149, 192,

Durham—*continued*
193, 195, 196, 208, 210, 211, 212,
213, 216, 217, 218, 227, 228, 230,
238, 261, 262, 263; **5**, 104; **6**, 81
D'Ussières, Henrietta, B.'s letter to,
4, 122; mentioned, **1**, 9; **4**, 122 and
n; **10**, 29 and n
Dutch, The, **3**, 187; **8**, 34, 47, 48
Dutch courage, **7**, 169
Dutch Legation, Constantinople, **11**,
216
Dutens, Louis, *Memoirs of a Traveller*,
6, 11 and n
Dwyer, **1**, 216, 239, 247; **3**, 130
Dyer, Sir Edward, *Gronger Hill*, **8**, 94
Dyke, Miss, future wife of Moore, **7**,
117n
Dysart, Earl of, **7**, 178n
d'Ysone, Contessa Borgarelli, B.'s
letter to, **10**, 190; mentioned, 83 and
n, 108 and n, 191n, 192n

Eagles, Rev. John, ed. *The Journal of
Llewellin Penrose*, **3**, 176 and n, 182,
186n, 189; **4**, 160
Eardley, Sampson (formerly Gideon)
(later Baron Eardley of Spalding), **3**,
69 and n; **4**, 122
Earthquakes, Lisbon, Lima, and
Calabria, **9**, 30; Missolonghi, **11**,
106, 119, 120, 124, 125
East India, **5**, 235
East India Company, **1**, 175 and n, 177,
179n
Eastern Journey, B. raising money for,
1, 202, 204, 205 and n
Eastern tales, **4**, 12–13
Eastlake, (Sir) Charles Lock, **6**, 172n;
'Byron's Dream', *173 and n*
Eaton, Daniel Isaac, imprisonment, **3**,
185n, 186; *Ecce Homo*, 185 and n;
Politics for the People, 185n
Eccelino da Romano, **3**, 253 and n
Eclectic Review, The, **1**, 147 and n,
167n; **2**, 124; **11**, 174
Eden, George (later Earl of Auckland),
2, 202 and n, 217, 222; **4**, 155 and n
Edgecombe, clerk, **6**, *143 and n*, 144,
147, 163, 174, 175, 183, 235, 237;
7, 28; to bring Allegra to Bologna,
6, 198, 213, 218; **11**, 192; imputed
peculations, **6**, 229–30, 231, 233–4;
237; B.'s messages to, 177, 191,
203–4
Edgecombe, Mrs., **6**, 144, 213
Edgeworth, Maria, **4**, 24; **8**, 29 and n;
9, 33–4; to meet B., **3**, 44 and n, 48
and n; B. on, **7**, 217–18, 229; at Sir
Humphry Davy's, **11**, 180n; *The
Absentee*, **3**, 48n; *Belinda*, **2**, 194 and
n; **3**, 48n; *Ennui*, **3**, 48n; **9**, 34 and n;

The Modern Griselda, 48n; *Patronage*,
3, 204 and n, 247; reviewed by
Edinburgh, 252 and n; B. hates
Patronage, **4**, 146 and n; B. on, 25
and n; **11**, 225: *Tales of Fashionable
Life*, **9**, 34 and n
Edgeworth, Richard Lovell, f. of Maria,
7, 217; **8**, 30 and n; **9**, 33–4;
described by B., **4**, 25 and n; *Memoirs*,
8, 29 and n, 42
Edgeworth, Mrs. R. L. (née Beaufort),
7, 217; **8**, 30 and n; **9**, 33
Edinburgh, **1**, 112; **2**, 46, 131, 177;
3, 109n, 238; **4**, 273, 303; **5**, 295; **8**,
38n; **10**, 18n; B. planned trip to, **1**,
131–2
Edinburgh Annual Register, **2**, 112
Edinburgh mail, **1**, 50
Edinburgh Review, The, **2**, 37, 102,
104, 106, 118n, 125, 156, 174 and n,
190; **3**, 94, 96, 118n, 203n, 213,
214n, 224 and n, 225, 226n, 232n,
239n, 252, 273; **4**, 87 and n, 142 and
n, 146, 147, 148, 149, 150, 152,
154, 156, 201, 209n, 250, 252n,
266n, 271n, 324; **5**, 35, 38 and n, 111
and n, 150, 153, 170 and n, 177, 183n,
185, 192n, 194, 198, 204, 262, 268
and n, 269, 277; **6**, 66, 86n, 123,
137, 207n; **7**, 114n, 131, 172, 196,
200, 202, 217, 229; **8**, 164, 178; **9**,
42, 75, 78, 160; **10**, 40, 135; review
of *Childe Harold*, **1**, 11; **11**, 188n;
review of *Hours of Idleness*, **1**, 137n,
157 and n, 158n, 159 and n, 162–3,
167n; **8**, 103, 219; Southey invited to
contribute, **1**, 177 and n; B. believed
Jeffrey author of review, 178n;
Hyperborean, 239; Brougham one of
founders, 255n; severe on B. and
Hodgson, 276; review of Canto 4 of
Childe Harold, **9**, 11; attacked B's
plays, 158, 159, 161, 166, 167–8,
170, 173
Edinburgh, University of, **11**, 216
Editor of Venice newspaper, B.'s letter
to, **5**, 201
Edleston, John, B.'s letter to, **11**, 173;
B.'s *pure* love and passion', **1**, *88n*,
110n, 117n, 118n, 124–5, 232n; **8**,
24 and n; did not recognize B., **1**,
122; the Cornelian, 123 and n; **2**,
119 and n; appearance, **1**, 123;
parting from B., 124; verses addressed
to, 129n; accused of indecency, 257n;
death, **2**, 110 and n, 114, 116 and n,
117 and n, 119–20, 121, 141 and n;
poems to 'Thyrza', 116n, 139 and n,
163–4 and n; **4**, 308 and n; stanzas in
Childe Harold to, **2**, 121 and n; B.'s
note to in cypher, **11**, 173; B.'s poem

in memory of, 178; B.'s attachment to, 213

Edmonton, **7**, 16

Edward IV, **3**, 209n

Egremont, 3rd Earl of, **3**, *4 and n*; **11**, 183; and Lady Melbourne, **4**, 289 and n

Egypt, **1**, 227n, 230; **2**, 5n, 7, 9, 38, 40, 41; **6**, 99

Ehrenbreitstein, **5**, 77

Ehrsam, Theodore G., *Major Byron*, **1**, 26

Eiger, Kleiner and Grosser, **5**, 101, 106

Elba, **3**, 256; **4**, 90n, 91, 100, 126n; **9**, 173; **11**, 29

Eldon, John Scott, 1st Earl of, Lord Chancellor, **1**, 191 and n; **2**, 167; **3**, 90n; **9**, 28, 97; judgment against Shelley, **6**, 252 and n; against Southey, 253n; antagonistic towards B., **9**, 188–9, 191, 206

Eleanora, **6**, 92

Electra, **5**, 198; **6**, 150

Elemore, **4**, 211 and n

Elephant, **6**, 108, 132

Elgin, Thomas Bruce, 8th Earl of, **2**, 12n, 27n, 47 and n, 134; attacked in *Childe Harold*, 63n, 106, 156–7, 172 and n; in *Curse of Minerva*, 131; wanted to see B., 65 and n; **3**, 58; in *Horace in London*, 20 and n

Elgin Marbles, **2**, 5n, 47n, 66 and n

Ekenhead, Lt., swims the Hellespont, **8**, 80, 81, 82, 83

Elijah, **5**, 179

Elise, see Foggi, Elise

Elisei, Lt. Giovanni Battista, **7**, 26, 131, 156, *157 and n*, 216; **8**, 36 and n; riding accident, **7**, 134, 140; offended with B., 147–8

Elizabeth I, Queen, **3**, 62n; **7**, 204n

Ellenborough, Edward Law, 1st Baron, **1**, 139n; **3**, 31; sentences Eaton, 185n; idealized as 'Lord Oldborough', **4**, 25 and n; not 'Lord Oldborough', **11**, 225

Ellice, Alexander, **1**, 209n

Ellice, Edward, B.'s letters to, **1**, 209, 254; **9**, 173; mentioned, **1**, *209 n*, 254; **2**, 131; **6**, 225 and n; **11**, 158; and B.'s interest in S. America, **9**, 173 and n, 174; on B.'s standing in England, **11**, 172

Elliot, Sir Gilbert, 1st Earl of Minto, **9**, *15n*

Ellis, George, **3**, 208 and n; reviews *The Corsair and Lara* in the *Quarterly*, **4**, 145n

Ellis, George Agar (later Baron Dover), *The True History of the Iron Mask*, **11**, 224

Ellis, Mr. and Mrs., **5**, 30 and n

Ellison, **4**, 271 and n

Elliston, Robert William, **2**, 53n, 204 and n, 211, 214, 223; and *Marino Faliero*, **8**, 60 and n, 64, 66 and n, 67, 68, 112, 116, 119, 120, 129, 132, 135, 136, 139, 141

Elmò, Teresa's dog, **6**, 203 and n

Elphinstone, Margaret Mercer (later Comtesse de Flahault), B.'s letters to, **2**, 183, 186; **4**, 112; **5**, 64; mentioned, **4**, 182–3; **5**, 14n, 64; B. gave her Albanian dress, **1**, 231n; **4**, 112 and n; invited B. to Tunbridge Wells, **2**, *183 and n*, 186–7; B. sends her a book, **5**, 64 and n

Elwin, Malcolm, *Lord Byron's Family*, **11**, 230; *Lord Byron's Wife*, **2**, 256n; **4**, 300n, 317n; **9**, 207n

Emmanuel College, Cambridge, **1**, 167n

Encyclopaedia Britannica, **3**, 239n

Encyclopédie, **8**, 42n

England, **2**, 3, 7, 8, 16, 17, 39, 41, 46, 85, 92, 96, 105, 244, 245, 255; **4**, 113; **7**, 20; **8**, 78, 92; **9**, 41; B. will never live in again, **1**, 232; **5**, 135, 226, 227, 252; B.'s reluctance to return, **1**, 232n; **5**, 230–1, 236, 237; **6**, 242, 243; **7**, 40, 50, 100, 115, 122, 153–4; **8**, 100; **11**, 167; B. dislikes, **1**, 234; **8**, 89; Adair to return to, **1**, 236, 254; B. hears nothing from, 242; B. thinks of returning to, 246; **5**, 165, 177, 184–5; Hobhouse's return to, **1**, 247, 249, 253, 254–5; **3**, 243 and n; B.'s affairs in, **1**, 251; B. fifteen months from, **2**, 18; Hobhouse in, 18, 19, 22, 31, 42; B. may have to return to, 19, 23, 26, 32; **11**, 169; compared to other countries, 2, 35, 41; B. year and a half out of, 38; B. returning to, 44, 48, 51, 52–3, 54; B. arrived in, 59–60; B. urges Hobhouse to return from Ireland, 125, 136; Caroline back in, 245, 247; B. intends to leave, **3**, 38; B.'s last absence from, 76; French invasion threatened, 249n; Madame de Staël in, 272–3; that 'tight little island', **5**, 136; **7**, 50; B. contemplates returning on business, **6**, 6, 7, 67, 212, 228–9, 230, 240, 241; B. has no desire to visit it again, 17, 25, 26, 32; B. hates the country, 53; Allegra's illness prevents return, 245; B.'s intended voyage, 245–6, 249, 250–1, 252, 254–6; B. put off voyage again, 255–6, 259; possible revolution in, **7**, 14–15, 237; B. lost all local feeling for, 86; B. on way to in 1798, 204, 212; will not go to war,

England—*continued*
244; weather, **8**, 11; society in, 113; attacks on B. in, **9**, 52; Don Juan in, **10**, 12, 23, 116; B. back in, **11**, 159; rumours about B. in, 169; B.'s leaving, 190; Leoni wished to reprint *Childe Harold* translation in, 194 and n

Englefield, Sir Henry Charles, **5**, 58 and n

English, The, hospitable to B., **11**, 15, 16, 18, 21, 22, 30, 45; B. met in Greece, **2**, 9; in Athens, 23, 31, 42, 43, 46; know nothing of sculpture, 66n; in Italy, **5**, 124, 132, 146, 191, 210; few in Venice, **6**, 43, 44, 65; English courage, **7**, 169; ignorant of Italy, 256–7; B. avoids, **8**, 141 and n, 149, 179, 214; gossip by, 204–5; B.'s associates in Pisa, **9**, 61; B. calumniated by, **10**, 23, 109, 120, 123; arriving in Greece, **11**, 66; in the Greek service, 143, 146; Phil-hellenes, 59n, 108; in Ionian Islands, 100; gossip about B. at Rome and Florence, 165

English Language, **2**, 208; **5**, 235; **6**, 17; **7**, 252; **9**, 31; **10**, 156, 190; **11**, 215; B. continues to write in, **8**, 210; language of birds, **11**, 137

English Revolution, **9**, 30

Enniscorthy, **2**, 108, 109, 125, 126, 131

Ennius, **8**, 201

Epaminondas, **2**, 16n; **9**, 48

Ephesus, **1**, 235, 236, 240, 247, 250, 251, 254n, 255; **2**, 183, 262; **10**, 142; **11**, 157

Epictetus, **9**, 45

Epicureans, **7**, 115

Epicurus, **3**, 188, 210; **4**, 82, 168

Epidaurus, **11**, 22n; National Assembly at, 215

Epimenides, **11**, 33 and n

Epinay, Madame, **7**, 167

Epirus, **1**, 226 and n, 228, 233, 234, 237, 238; **2**, 134; **4**, 172; **8**, 15

Epistle of St. James, **9**, 96 and n

Epping, **6**, 243

Epping Forest, **3**, 80

Erivan, Persia, **5**, 104

Erizzo, Andrea, **6**, 19

Erneis, **4**, 220

Erskine, Henry David, **1**, 121 and n; **4**, 144n, 151

Erskine, Thomas, 1st Baron, B.'s letter to, **1**, 59; mentioned, **1**, 121 and n; **2**, *32 and n*; **3**, 227, *247n*, 251; **9**, 15, 96; Hobhouse's pamphlet against, **6**, 187 and n; defends the Whigs, **7**, 16n; B. on, **9**, 44; 'A Letter to the Earl of Liverpool . . .', 42, 59n; 'On the Causes and Consequences of the War with France,' **3**, 248 and n, 253

Eskimaux, **9**, 47

Esmeralda, **8**, 126 and n

Essex, George, 5th Earl of, **4**, 133 and n; **5**, 159 and n; Drury Lane Committee member, **4**, 296 and n, 297

Este, **5**, 264 and n, 269, 295; B.'s villa, **6**, 16–17, 43, 60, 69

Este, House of, **6**, 182

Esterre, Mrs., **4**, 296 and n

Eton, **1**, 184n, 276; **2**, 162 and n, 282; **11**, 83; cricket match with Harrow, **1**, 71; **2**, 163; **9**, 12

Etonian, The, **8**, 193 and n

Etruscan, **8**, 228

Euganean Hills, **5**, 264n; **6**, 16, 43, 69

Eugene, Viceroy, **5**, 191

Eunuchs, **7**, 153

Euphrates, **4**, 55

Euripides, **2**, 127, 140; **11**, 179; ed. by Porson, **2**, 124n; B. compared to, **9**, 11; *Medea*, **1**, 245–6

Europe, **1**, 237, 251; **2**, 4, 17; **3**, 236; **5**, 202, 204; **6**, 66, 180, 212, 227; **7**, 235n; **8**, 20, 36, 78, 80, 82, 83; **9**, 17, 215; **10**, 209, 230; **11**, 37, 69, 71; B.'s popularity in, **10**, 36

Eusebius, **6**, 9, 29, 38

Eustace, Rev. John Chetwode, *A Classical Tour Through Italy*, **3**, 51 and n; **5**, 263 and n

Euterpe, **4**, 156

Euxine, **3**, 205

Evangelicals, **1**, 114; **2**, 181n; **6**, 96n, 97

Evans, Mr., **1**, 42 and n, 49

Evans, R. H., auctioneer, sale of B.'s books, **5**, 42n; **11**, 185 and n

Eve, **2**, 112; **9**, 46, 53, 54

Everett, coachman to B., **5**, 75

Examiner, The, **2**, 233, 281; **3**, 41; **4**, 307 and n, 332n; **5**, 15n, 15–16, 19n, 58n; **8**, 83; **9**, 110n, 209, 216, 234; **10**, 123, 162; Parry, **11**, 217

Execution, **5**, 229–30

Exeter 'Change, **3**, 206; **4**, 278n, **5**, 214

Exmouth, Sir Edward Pellew, 1st Bt. and 1st Viscount, **5**, 107 and n

Eyre, Mr., the trunk-maker, **2**, 81

Eywood, Presteign, **2**, 233, 234, 235, 245, 251, 254, 286; **3**, 5, 13, 29n, 32, 33, 34, 45; B. happy at, 36, 210; **11**, 182n

Ezzelin, **3**, 253

Fabbri, Mrs. Santino, **8**, 168

Faber, George Stanley, *Great Gods of Phoenicia*, **8**, 237 and n

Fabre (Fabri?), **5**, 197

Fabre, François, **8**, 14n

Faenza, **6**, 165, 167, 176, 190, 214; **7** 27, 131, 138, 216; **8**, 11, 12, 36, 43

Fagnani, Emma, *The Art Life of a XIXth Century Portrait Painter, Joseph Fagnani*, **5**, 191n

Fagnani, Joseph, portrait of B., **5**, 191n

Falcieri, Giovanni Battista (Tita), B.'s servant, **7**, *39 and n*, 48, 242, 245, 247, 248; **8**, 46, 126; arrested, 140 and n, 142, and n, 156; and Masi affray, **9**, 139 and n, 142, 144 and n, 150, 158, 160, 161; in exile with the Shelleys, 147 and n, 148–9, 178 and n; with B. till poet's death, 147n; B. bought his exemption from conscription, 148; B.'s praise of, **11**, 81; and B.'s convulsive attack, 113

Faliero, Marino, Doge, **5**, 203, 233; B.'s model, **7**, 131 and n, 132, 141–2

Falkland, Capt. Charles John Cary, 9th Lord, **1**, 192 and n, *195 and n*; **3**, 17n

Falkland, Christina, Lady, **1**, *195 and n*; **3**, *17 and n*, 24 and n

Falkner, Dr. T., B.'s letter to, **1**, 102; mentioned, **1**, 102 and n

Falmouth, **1**, 207, 209, 210, B. at, 205–14, 254; **2**, 14; and female peculator, **11**, 156; handsome youths 156

Falstaff, **1**, 4; **2**, 44; **9**, 95

Fane, Lady Sarah Sophia (later Lady Jersey), **4**, 120 and n

Fanny, B.'s dog, **1**, 126 and n

Fano, **7**, 177

Farebrother, (Fairbrother); auctioneer, **4**, 299 and n; **6**, 114 and n, 222; **7**, 73, 85; **9**, 82; **10**, 86

Farleigh, **1**, 64 and n, 76 and n; **2**, 36, 146, 234; **3**, 158 and n; **4**, 230, 235, 238

Farquhar, George, **3**, 149; *The Beaux' Stratagem*, 151 and n, 235 and n, 242; **6**, 46 and n; **8**, 17 and n, 50 and n; **10**, 136; *The Constant Couple*, **7**, 220 and n, 224 and n; *The Recruiting Officer*, **6**, 114; **8**, 134 and n; **11**, 230

Farquhar, James, **5**, 26 and n

Farquhar, Sir W., **2**, 260

Farrell, Orson, **7**, 230, 232

Farrer, T., **1**, 73 and n

Faulkner, George, **2**, *144 and n*; **7**, 72

Fauvel, Louis François Sebastian, **2**, *11 and n*, 12, 14, 27 and n; **4**, 299n

Fawcet, Sir William, **1**, 47 and n

Fawcett, John, **8**, 55 and n

Fawkes (Faux), Guy, **7**, 75, 76

Fawkes, Mr., **10**, 174

Fazakerly, John Nicholas, **2**, *5 and n*

Fearman, (Fairman?), publisher, and

Don Juan, **8**, 90 and n, 91–2; **10**, 53 and n

Fellowes, Hon. Newton, and lunacy trial of his brother, **4**, 186 and n, 189, 235, *254 and n*, 259, 265, 292 and n; **10**, *119n*; B.'s statement on Portsmouth marriage, **4**, 236–7

Fenice Theatre, **5**, 142 and n, 143n, 148, 151, 152, 160, 171, 176, 181, 197

Ferdinand, King of Naples, **8**, 12 and n, 20

Fernes, Bishop of, **2**, 132

Ferney, **5**, 277n

Ferrara, **5**, 211, 214; **6**, 132, 144, 154, 165, 182, 191, 236–7; **7**, 192; Certosa Cemetery, **1**, 15; **6**, 146–9, 150; Ariosto and Tasso, **5**, 217, 255; **6**, 8n, 145; and Parisina's story, **5**, 217, 255; **6**, 59; visited by B., **11**, 190

Fersen, Count Axel, **5**, 147 and n, 148

Field Place, **9**, 234

Fielding, Henry, **1**, 13; **2**, 217; **6**, 91, 94, 253; **8**, 11–12 and n, 13; **10**, 68; works compared to *Don Juan*, **1**, 13; his Jacobinism, **9**, 50–1; *Amelia*, **2**, 259; **9**, 124 and n; *Jonathan Wild*, **3**, 7 and n, 202 and n; **7**, 49 and n; **9**, 50; *Joseph Andrews*, **3**, 13 and n; **4**, 100 and n, 109 and n, 275 and n; **6**, 40 and n, 124; **7**, 115; **9**, 50 and n, 124 and n; **10**, 98 and n; **11**, 220; 'Journey from this World to the Next', **9**, 62; *Tom Jones*, **3**, 134 and n, 171 and n; **4**, 85, 111 and n; **6**, 80 and n, 82, 108 and n, 234, 253; **7**, 132 and n; **10**, 52 and n, 98 and n; *The Tragedy of Tragedies, or The Life and Death of Tom Thumb the Great*, **1**, 177, 186, 208 and n; **4**, 247–8, 248n; **5**, 238 and n; **6**, 90, 214 and n; **9**, 28; **11**, 159, 220, 230; *The Wedding Day*, **9**, 67–8 and n

Filetto, **7**, 128n, 143n, 155, 176n, 185n, 226, 228, 235n, 240n

Finch, Col. Robert, **5**, *136 and n*

Finden, William, **7**, 165n

Fingal, Lord, **2**, 125

Finlay, George, at Missolonghi, **11**, 134 and n; *History of Greece*, **10**, 169n; **11**, 126n, 134n, 143n

Fiott, John, **2**, *33 and n*, 37

Firdausi, Abdul Kásim, *The Sháh Námeh*, **3**, 101 and n

Firenze (Florence), **5**, 216–17

Fitzgerald, Col., **5**, 147 and n, 181

Fitzgerald, Lord Edward, **3**, *249 and n*; **6**, 209

Fitzgerald, William Thomas, **4**, 19 and n, 72, 100n; 126; **5**, 45; **6**, 27, 47 and n, 209 and n; **7**, 84, 205, 236

87

Fitzgibbon, Richard Hobart (later 3rd Earl of Clare), **10**, *57*; **11**, *66*, 148 and n
Fitzpatrick, Gen. Richard, **3**, 219; **8**, 29 and n
Fitzwilliam, Earl of, **2**, 160
Fitzwilliam Museum, **2**, *66*n
Flack (Slack?), Mr. and Mrs., **11**, 64
Flahault, August Charles Joseph, Comte de, **2**, 183n; **5**, *14 and n*; **10**, 41
Flahau[l]t (née Mercer), Mme, (*see also*, Elphinstone, Margaret Mercer), **6**, 146; **8**, 54 and n
Flanders, **5**, 78, 81, 117, 213
Fleet Street, **2**, 105, 235n, 285; **3**, 21; **4**, 117, 260, 337; **6**, 79, 101; **8**, 74
Flemish School, **5**, 116
Fletcher, John, **6**, 95
Fletcher, J. and Massinger, P., *The Beggar's Bush*, **4**, 319 and n; *see also* Beaumont and Fletcher
Fletcher, William, B.'s letters to, **5**, 105; **11**, 20; mentioned, **1**, 43n, 161 and n, 163, 188 and n; **2**, 9, 43, 56, 103; **3**, 20, 120; **4**, 67, 124n, 226; **6**, 74, 108, 145, 171, 181, 213, 229, 235; **7**, 79, 119; **8**, 46; **11**, 86n; 'lamentations after beef and beer', **1**, 10, **2**, 34; unhappiness abroad, **1**, 10, 229–31, 235, 250; **2**, 18; threat to send him home, **1**, 10, 244 and n, 249, 252; death of his father, 188; involved with prostitutes, 203–4; continued in B.'s service, 206; on Lisbon Packet, 212; in storm at sea, 229; **11**, 158; refractory, **1**, 244 and n; an incumbrance, 249, 250; B. keeping him, 252; butt of B.'s jests, **2**, 4; his wife Sally, 4, 18; disgusted by Eustathius, 6: scalded foot, 6; a walking cinder, 7; has a Greek mistress, 13; Hanson to pay his wages, 25; sent home, 25, 26, 27, 29, 30, 31, 34, 35, 37, 39–40, 42, 49; to be given the mill, 52, 71; fat and facetious, 130; and Dutch widow's maid, 218; frightened in Epping Forest, **3**, 80; does not read Caroline's letters, 83; alarmed by B.'s drinking, 145; compared to 'Ursine Sloth', 206; and B.'s wounded eye, 247–8; the 'learned', **4**, 308; **6**, 62; **8**, 64; **9**, 64; marriage to Ann Rood, **4**, 309n; **5**, 23n, 63n, 70; abroad with B., 71, 73, 76, 97, 105, 144, 216; Bluecoat School application for his son, 170–1; indigestion, **6**, 19–20; his supposed letter to Hobhouse, 44–5; amorous adventure with Tiretta, 45 and n, 255; sent to

care for Basil Hall, 64n; frightened by Fornarina, 70; witnesses B.'s conveyances, 87; his malapropism, 138; disarmed Fornarina, 197; to be breeding beast of burden, 212; sobbing at B.'s illness, 239; eager to return to England, 249; and Hobhouse's bail, **7**, 50; read Hobhouse's speeches, 154; illness, 179, 227; Commandant died in Fletcher's bed, 247, 249, 251; **8**, 125; to copy Bacon's apothegms, 14; trusted by B., 46; 'that illustrious man of letters!', 74; facetious about Hobhouse, 100, 123; **9**, 65; money lender, **8**, 149; and ghosts of Casa Lanfranchi, **9**, 74; witness, **10**, 97; with B. on trip to Morea, **11**, 157
Fletcher, 2nd Mrs. William (née Ann Rood), **5**, 23 and n, 63n, 70; refused a character by Lady Byron, **6**, 171, 181
Flood, Henry, **9**, *13 and n*, 27; silenced by Courteney, 12–13
Florence (Firenze), **4**, 93; **5**, 121, 124, 146, 191, 210, 211, 214, 215, 220, 229, 231, 233, 244, 294; **6**, 38, 39, 43, 65, 91, 142 and n; **7**, 13, 20, 47, 54, 75, 257; **8**, 14n, 20, 54, 79n, 151n, 157, 159n, 161 and n, 168, 169, 176n, 184, 190, 205; **9**, 53, 80, 131, 142n, 143, 144, 147, 148, 149, 157, 158, 162, 180, 193, 201, 210, 211n, 217, 235, 236; **10**, 48, 50, 56 and n, 103, 107n, 113, 131, 162 and n, 179; **11**, 163, 165; B. in, **5**, 216–18, 227–8; **9**, 50; Hobhouse gone to, **11**, 197
Florida, The (English vessel), carried B.'s body to England, **11**, 146n
Foggi, Elise, **8**, 97n; nurse to Allegra, **6**, 39n; story of Shelley, **7**, 80, 191 and n
Foley, Thomas, 3rd Baron, **3**, 86n, 93, 95; **4**, 164 and n
Foligno, **5**, 233
Fontenelle, Bernard le Bouvier, Sieur de, **3**, 184 and n
Fontenoy, **3**, 213n
Fonthill Abbey, **6**, 17
Foote, Mrs. Maria, **4**, *118 and n*; **9**, 83n
Foote, Samuel, *Mayor of Garratt*, **2**, 95 and n; **3**, 100n; **4**, 256 and n, 269 and n, 271; **6**, 141 and n, 187 and n; **7**, 205 and n, 222 and n, 223; **11**, 108 and n; *The Orators*, **2**, 144 and n
Foppington, Lord, **2**, 227 and n; **11**, 222
Forbes, Lady Adelaide, **4**, 119 and n; **5**, 227 and n; B.'s attachment to, **3**, *75 and n*; a possible match for B., **4**, 120 and n, 121, 126 and n

Forbes, Lady Elizabeth, **4**, 113 and n

Ford, Jack, pugilist, **3**, 94n

Ford, John, dramatist, **3**, 199; **6**, 95

Ford, John, lawyer, **10**, 113, 114 and n, 115, 119

Foreign Quarterly Review, **3**, 217n

Forgeries, **1**, 26–7

Forlì, **6**, 188, 198n, 201, 202, 220; **7**, 27, 112, 143, 213; **8**, 12, 16, 17

Fornarina, The, *see* Cogni, Margarita

Forresti, George, B.'s letter to, **2**, 262; met B. at Malta, 10 and n, *262n*

Forresti, Spiridion, **2**, 262n

Forster, H. B., **10**, 173n

Forster, John, *Life of Goldsmith*, **3**, 79n

Forsyth, Joseph, *Remarks on Antiquities, Arts*, etc., **5**, 233 and n, 234; **7**, 182 and n, 183; **11**, 229

Forteguerri, Niccolò, *Ricciardetto*, **7**, 113 and n; **8**, 224n

Fortune (Goddess), **5**, 164–5; **9**, 41

Fosbroke, Thomas Dudley, **2**, 128 and n

Foscarini family, La Mira, **6**, 204 and n

Foscarini Villa, **5**, 237n; **6**, 204

Foscolo, Ugo, **5**, 293; **7**, 54, 222; **8**, 69, 76, 79, 151; **9**, 90; added to Hobhouse's notes on *Childe Harold*, **6**, 51 and n, 72n, 90n; wants B. to undertake a great work, 105; B. on, **7**, 194, 195, 201; and *Marino Faliero*, 205, 238; on Italian literature, **11**, 170n; *Ricciarda, Tragedia*, **7**, 150 and n, 195–6; *Ultime Lettere di Jacopo Ortis*, **6**, 51n, 105

Fossati, advocate, **7**, 174; **11**, 194

Foster, Lady Elizabeth, **3**, 145n, 174n

Foster, John, B.'s letter to, **2**, 24; mentioned, *24n*, 30, 37 and n

Foster, John Thomas, **3**, 174n; **5**, 270n

Fowke, artisan, **11**, 111 and n

Fox & Co., **1**, 207

Fox, Charles James, **1**, 67n, 113, 236n; **3**, 219, 239n, 247n; **4**, 105n, 112n, 262n; **5**, 95n, 221n; **6**, 12n, 47, 48, 86, 89; **8**, 29n; **9**, 14, 155; criticized in *Quarterly*, **3**, 126 and n, 239, 242 and n; East India Bill, 232n; **9**, 13n; best speech, 13

Fox, Henry, 1st Baron Holland, *see* Holland, Lord

Fox, Henry Edward, s. of Lord Holland, B.'s letters to, **2**, 257; **3**, 78, 82, 85; **10**, 131 and n; mentioned, **2**, 257 and n; **3**, 15, 78 and n; **6**, 278; **10**, 145; his Toledo swords, **3**, 78, 82 and n; goes to *Nourjahad* with B., 224 and n, 226; B. fond of, 232; **10**, 131n, 135, 174; a halting angel, 136

Fox, Henry Stephen, **5**, 221 and n

Fozard, **10**, 74, 147

Frame Bill, **1**, 16; **2**, 165 and n, 166 and n; **7**, 205n

Frampton, Mary, *Journal*, **5**, 276n

France, Mr., B.'s letter to, **4**, 89; mentioned, 89 and n, 227

France, **2**, 11n, 28n, 41, 71, 127; **3**, 210, 218, 248n; **4**, 37, 93, 157n, 282, 283n, 284, 285, 306n; **5**, 78, 95, 187, 197, 202, 294; **6**, 33, 43, 174, 240, 241; **7**, 244; **8**, 36, 41, 98, 113, 240n; **9**, 41, 114; **10**, 109; **11**, 104n, 216; unrest in, **7**, 77; copyright, **8**, 74; prose translations of B. in, **9**, 52; B. popular in, **10**, 153

Francesca of Rimini, (*see also* under Byron, Works), **6**, 181, 182, 189; **7**, 112n; **8**, 39

Francesconi, **6**, 8

Francis I, **8**, 118

Francis, Sir Philip (Junius), **6**, 18, 19, 35

Franciscan (Capuchin) Convent, Athens, **2**, 18, 27

Frankfort, **7**, 125

Frankfort Gazette, **2**, 30

Frankfort Lottery, **9**, 126

Franklin, Benjamin, **3**, 218; **9**, 174, 197; **10**, 52

Frascati, **5**, 221, 233

Fraser, Commander and Mrs., **2**, 126 and n, 132 and n

Frederick Augustus, Duke of York, *see* York and Albany, Frederick Augustus, Duke of

Frederick II (the Great), **5**, 216n; **7**, 113; **9**, 121 and n

Freeling, Sir Francis, B.'s letters to, **4**, 237, 307; mentioned, 237 and n, 307 and n

Frejus, **11**, 84n

Fremont (?), Julia, **6**, 140

French, the, **2**, 198; **3**, 187, 249n; **8**, 165; army in Portugal, **1**, 218n; in Athens, **2**, 35, 37, 43, 46; threatened invasion of England, **7**, 184n

French-Armenian professorship, **5**, 130–1

French courage, **7**, 169

French Government, **11**, 53n

French language, (*see also* Byron, languages), **2**, 185n; **5**, 100, 235, 262n; **6**, 3, 17, 35, 60; **7**, 38, 104, 197; **10**, 168, 207; **11**, 31n, 215

French life, **7**, 42

French papers, **5**, 137; **9**, 11

French Revolution, **1**, 16; **2**, 286; **3**, 247n; **5**, 220n; **7**, 80; **8**, 78 and n, 240; **9**, 30, 97n; **10**, 140

Frere, John Hookham, **3**, 170, 175, 187, *216 and n*; **5**, 59 and n, 134 and

Frere, John—*continued*
n, 174, 259, 260, 263; **6**, 78; against
publication of *Don Juan*, 98; **11**, 171
and n; **7**, 46, 54, 57, 180; *Anti-
Jacobin*, **5**, 59n, 260n; *Whistlecraft*, **3**,
80 and n, 216 and n; **5**, 59n, 267 and
n, 269; **6**, 4 and n, 24, 61; **7**, 42, 113
and n; **8**, 193n, 229

Freytag, **5**, 199

Frezzeria, **5**, 129n

Fribourg Canton, **5**, 99, 103, 104

Fricker sisters, **9**, 207 and n

Friedel, Adam, 'Baron', **11**, 127–8 and
n

Friedland, **9**, 48

Friese, German servant, **1**, 206 and n,
208

Frimont, Marshall, **8**, 122 and n

Friuli, **2**, 198

Frome, **9**, 75n

Frost (employed on *Bolivar*), **10**, 12
and n, 37, 40 and n, 43–4, 45, 75

Fry, Mrs. Elizabeth, **1**, 23; **9**, *74 and
n*; **11**, 32, 40

Fulham, **8**, 68n

Fuller, Mr., **9**, 177

Funds, The, **6**, 102, 103, 143 and n,
228, 232, 247, 252n; **7**, 14–15, 44,
167, 202, 210, 213, 220–1, 248, 249,
252, 255, 257; **8**, 62, 89, 91, 135,
137, 139, 143, 149, 152, 158, 171,
176, 180–1, 182, 209, 239, 240; **9**,
62, 73, 101, 112, 124, 128, 152, 186,
187, 195, 196, 199, 209, 211; **10**,
53, 59, 87, 113; **11**, 135, 136, 144;
not to be sold if too low, **10**, 38, 94,
95

Furnival's Inn, **8**, 101

Fuseli, Henry, **3**, 253–4, 255; **4**, 161n;
11, 224; 'Ezzelin', **4**, 161n

Fusina, **5**, 237n; **6**, 54, 72, 231; **8**, 66,
68, 81

Fust, Johann, **10**, 117 and n

Fyler, Capt., **6**, 188; **7**, 41

Gaels, **7**, 61

Gaetano (groom), **10**, 12 and n, 43,
45, 75; **11**, 81

Gail, Jean Baptiste, **7**, 104n, 127

Gail, Madame, **7**, 104 and n, 206

Galeazzo, Giovanni, **3**, 253

Galiffe, James A., *Italy and Its Inhabitants*, **7**, 184 and n

Galignani, Jean Antoine, B.'s letters
to: **6**, 33, 118; mentioned, **8**, 28, 56,
60, 65, 70, 72, 105, 191; **10**, 95, 145,
146; Paris publisher, **7**, 127, 179,
203, 256; and B.'s French editions,
117 and n, 216 and n, 218, 225; **9**,
216; and B.'s French copyrights, **8**,
72, 74; **9**, 84; **10**, 134, 179, 204; supposed death, **8**, 84; requests a
memoir of B., **9**, 79 and n; B. considers as possible publisher, 92, 93,
94, 100; *Literary Gazette*, **8**, 84

Galignani's Messenger, **6**, 33, 89, 114n,
118–19, 131, 166, 187, 205, 223–4,
233, 262; **7**, 15, 17, 75, 131, 154, 171,
179, 205; **8**, 11, 56, 118, 120, 121,
124; **9**, 74, 110, 117, 126, 157, 167,
170, 190, 193, 198, 216; **10**, 40, 67,
105, 138, 148

Galileans, **3**, 164

Galilee, **2**, 89

Galilei, Galileo, **5**, 218; **8**, 53

Galliani, Angelica, **6**, 276

Gallina, Vincenzo, **8**, 17–18

Gallo, Marzio Mastrilli, duce di, **7**,
255 and n

Galt, John, B.'s letters to: **2**, 158; **3**,
57, 195, 196; mentioned, **2**, 23, 33,
and n, 156; present to B., **3**, 57;
describes Romaika, 58 and n; **11**,
223; and *Bride of Abydos*, **3**, 195 and
n, 237, 238; and *Giaour*, 230, 238;
Annals of the Parish, **2**, *22n*; *Letters
from the Levant*, **3**, 57n, 58n; **11**,
223; *Life of Lord Byron*, **2**, 22n; **3**,
195n; *Voyages and Travels . . .*, **2**,
164n

Galvanism, **5**, 257

Galway, Viscount, **4**, 278n

Gamba, Count (Teresa's grandfather),
10, 176

Gamba Ghiselli, Countess, *see* Guiccioli,
Countess Teresa

Gamba, Giulia, **11**, 79, 137

Gamba, Laurina, **11**, 79, 137

Gamba, Olimpia, **11**, 79, 137

Gamba Ghiselli, Count Pietro, B.'s
letters to: **8**, 167, 170, 173, 183;
biog. sketch, **7**, 273; mentioned, 33,
148, 152, 185, 210, 216, 221, 227,
235; **8**, 12, 14, 15, 160, 170, 180, 188,
190, 205, 212, 213, 214, 242, 243,
247, 249; **9**, 56, 107, 161n, 175, 181;
10, 19, 30, 69, 161–2, 181, 195; **11**,
43, 138, 154; at school in Rome, **6**,
180; **7**, 160n, 165; **9**, 42; warned
Guiccioli against B., **7**, 126, 197 and
n; a revolutionary, 146, 155, 273;
his opinion of Fanny Silvestrini, 209;
and the revolution, **8**, 16–17, 17–18,
20, 40, 43; returns arms to B., 45–6,
47; exiled, 105n, 151n, 152, 154,
157; wants to go to Switzerland, 175,
178, 179; wild about liberty, 214;
and Masi affair, **9**, 168–9 and n;
ordered to leave Tuscany, 179 and n,
180; asylum in Lucca, 184 and n, 185;
eager to go to Greece with B., **10**,
143, 176; recalled from exile, 191;

on the *Hercules*, 210n; sent news to Teresa, **11**, 15, 18, 21, 42, 51, 56, 66, 121; trip to Ithaca, 18, 19; a fine fellow, 23; his opinion of the Greeks, 43; illness, 52, 79, 106; occupied with Greek business, 78; B.'s praise of, 82; captured by Turks, 86 and n, 87 and n, 89; released by Turks, 90, 91 and n, 96, 98; and red cloth, 93, 96–7; Suliotes placed under his command, 115 and n; and *Telegrafo Greco*, 134; *Narrative of Byron's Last Journey to Greece*, **7**, 273; **11**, 20n, 52n, 100n, 106n, 115n, 125n, 130n, 149n

Gamba Ghiselli, Count Ruggero, B.'s letters to: **8**, 150, 202, 243; biog. sketch, **7**, 272; mentioned, **6**, 180, 245, 247, 259, 275–6, 277; **7**, 29 and n, 30, 33, 55, 88, 129, 146, 147, 148, 152, 155, 166, 172, 177, 193, 210, 216, 221, 227, 240n, 243; **8**, 12, 14, 18, 169, 175, 180, 183, 184, 188, 190, 199, 212, 213, 242, 247; **9**, 56, 107, 151, 175, 181; **10**, 107n; **11**, 21, 79, 137; drew Byron into Carbonari, **7**, 272; and B.'s liaison with his daughter, 18, 88, 135, 147, 164, 166, 235, 272; exiled, **8**, 105n, 151n, 154, 157, 160, 161, 168, 214; B. hopes for his recall, 154–5, 170, 175, 179, 180, 184, 205; and Masi affray, **9**, 135, 139 and n, 161n, 168–9, 169n; ordered to leave Tuscany, 179 and n, 180; asylum in Lucca, 184 and n, 185; with B. in Genoa, **10**, 14, 30, 55, 69; and Marchesa Sagrati, 56; recalled from exile, 176, 178, 191

Gamba family, **5**, 297; at Villa Dupuy, **11**, 140n

Ganymede, **1**, 238

Garcilaso de la Vega, **11**, 84 and n

Gardel, **1**, 159n

Garden of Heroes, **11**, 79n

Gardner, bookseller, **3**, 67n

Garrick, David, **2**, 210 and n, 220, 225n; **4**, 290 and n; **6**, 30, 166 and n; on Johnson and Beauclerk, **7**, 16 and n; *A Miss in Her Teens*, **10**, 56 and n

Garrick, David, and Colman, the Elder, *The Clandestine Marriage*, **3**, 137 and n, 216 and n; **5**, 274n; **6**, 32; *The Country Girl*, **3**, 42 and n

Garrow, Sir William, **4**, 76 and n

Gassendi, Pierre, **4**, 82 find n

Gastouni, **11**, 128n

Gates, Payson G., **10**, 25n

Gauls, **5**, 14

Gay, John, **2**, 114; **8**, 148n; *Beggar's Opera*, **2**, 259; **3**, 8, 239; **5**, 182n; **7**,

72 and n, 103 and n; **8**, 85, 110 and n; **11**, 228; *The What d'ye call't*, **3**, 167 and n

Gay, Mme. Sophie, **7**, 104 and n, 206

Gazette de France, **8**, 123

Gegdes, **2**, 21

Gehnis, **11**, 192

Gell, Sir William, B.'s letter to: **4**, 105; mentioned, **3**, 234 and n; **4**, 103 and n, 105; *Narrative of a Journey in the Morea*, **10**, 171 and n; *The Topography of Troy, Itinerary in Greece*, **1**, *238 and n*, 239; **3**, 234n; **4**, 97 and n

Genesis, **7**, 196; **11**, 179

Geneva, **5**, 53, 70, 71 and n, 73, 74, 77, 78, 80, 81, 90, 93, 94, 114, 126, 129, 162, 207, 209n, 297; **6**, 26, 238; **8**, 98, 114, 157, 159, 170, 171, 175, 176, 179, 214; **9**, 201, 236; **10**, 169n, 203; Byron at 1, 276; B.'s address, **5**, 107, 111, 114, 117, 118, 119, 120; B. refuses to go there to sign papers, **6**, 31–2, 33, 34, 39, 40, 48, 50, 53, 56, 60–1, 71, 72–3, 77; gossip in about B., **11**, 165

Geneva, Lake of, **8**, 157

Genoa, **4**, 161; **5**, 210, 296; **6**, 191; **7**, 132, 184; **9**, 87, 148, 161n, 175 and n, 178, 179, 184, 186, 201, 202, 203 and n, 204, 209, 212; **10**, 12n, 30n, 36, 57, 66, 77, 79, 86, 97, 102, 104n, 107n, 108n, 112, 114, 122, 128, 130, 131n, 132, 139n, 140, 160, 179, 180, 186, 190, 192, 195, 199, 201, 203, 204, 205, 210, 211, 213 and n; **11**, 16, 18, 20, 24, 26, 29, 76, 81, 107, 148, 152; B.'s banker in, **1**, 17 B.'s boat being built at, **9**, 113, 116; B.'s proposed move, 201, 202, 203n, 209, 211, 214, 217; Villa Saluzzo, 214, 219; B. arrived in, **10**, 13, 14, 25n; B. at, 15, 16, 18, 28, 52; deluge in, 28–9; B. sailed from, 212; **11**, 29; B.'s address, 47

Genoa Gazette, **10**, 50

Gentile, **2**, 89, 98

Gentleman's Magazine, **1**, 63n; **3**, 62n, **11**, 226

Geoffrey of Monmouth, *History of British Kings*, **1**, 178

George, dragoman, **1**, 235n

George II, **3**, 215

George III, **1**, 113n, 236n; **2**, 80 and n, 142n, 170n, 219, 221n; **3**, 109n, 117, 215, 232n; **5**, 209n, 210n; **10**, 208; **11**, 155; death, **7**, 40, 41, 44 and n, 50; insanity, 192; as Prince of Wales, **8**, 71n; Southey's apotheosis, 229 and n, 230, 236; **10**, 13n

George IV (*see also* Wales, Prince of, and Prince Regent), **2**, 219; **4**, 112n;

George IV—*continued*
8, 126, 187n; 9, 72n; coronation, 7, 41–2, 50, 65, 72, 86, 95, 98, 119, 120n; 8, 92, 143 and n, 144, 153, 162, 187n; in Ireland, 213n; anecdote, 225n

Georgiou, Eustathius, 2, *6 and n*, 7, 10

Geramb, François Ferdinand, Baron de, 2, *144 and n*; 9, 96 and n

German Barons, 11, 108

German courage, 7, 169

German Greek Committees, 11, 71

German journals, 9, 11

German language (*see also* Byron, languages), 5, 100, 252; 6, 4; 7, 106, 113, 203; 8, 25–6

German life, 7, 42

Germans, 5, 147, 205, 221; 6, 180; 8, 173; in Greece, 2, 35, 37; in Greek service, 10, 179–81; 11, 66, 142, 145, 147, 150

Germany, 3, 176, 237; 4, 26; 5, 270; 6, 223; 7, 138; 8, 78, 167; 9, 162; 10, 180n; 11, 134n, 216; B.'s works popular in, 9, 52, 163, 164; 10, 153, 225n

Gerostati, C., 11, 109, 133

Ghent, 5, 71–4

Ghigi, Pellegrino, B.'s letter to: 8, 71; mentioned, 71; B.'s banker, 86

Giaffer Pasha, 2, 114, 125

Giavella, Nicola, 11, 31, 41

Gibbon, Edward, 2, 136; 3, 174n; 4, 95 and n, 161, 168, 248; 5, 22, 217, 263, 269, 270n; 6, 189; 8, 155; 9, 76, 100, 103, 116; read by B., 1, 148, 242; house near Lausanne, 5, 81; *Decline and Fall of the Roman Empire*, 9, 117; 11, 45 and n; *Miscellaneous Works*, 4, 251 and n

Gibbs, Messrs., 10, 101

Gibbs, money lender, 10, 146, 147

Gibbs, Sir Vicary, 2, 67n

Gibraltar, 1, 187n, 202n; 2, 37, 164n; 3, 57n, 115; 5, 14; 10, 114n; B. leaving for, 1, 203, 208, 210, 214, 215; B. sent back servants from, 206, 222; B. arrived on *Hyperion* frigate, 216, 221, 225; B. at, 216–23, 230; 2, 4n; servants sent by sea, 1, 219; B.'s funds sent to, 247; climate, 2, 3

Gibraltar, Strait of, 2, 50, 58, 74, 261; 4, 151 and n, 152

Gifford, William, B.'s letters to: 3, 63, 161; biog. sketch, 271; mentioned, 1, 194n; 2, 249; 3, 97, 100n, 156n, 170, 206, 209; 4, 14, 16, 18, 20, 24, 32, 299n; 5, 111, 138, 153, 174, 185, 259; 6, 11, 13, 15, 16, 20–1, 26, 59, 123, 206; 7, 234; 8, 182, 193, 198, 204, 207, 219; 9, 53, 54, 64, 181; no

nonsense, 1, 14; wrote comment on B.'s work, 177, 179; to inspect *Childe Harold*, 2, 78, 80 and n, 91–2, 98–9, 101, 109, 130; member of Alfred Club, 125n; ed. of *Quarterly Review*, 285; 3, 161, 271; 4, 90n; B.'s literary advisor, 3, 62n, 63–4, 165, 271; 5, 22, 58, 90, 113, 157–8, 183, 193, 196, 219, 263, 268; 7, 57, 168, 170, 172, 176, 179–80, 181, 182, 238; 8, 61, 70, 74, 94, 99, 111, 128, 129, 206; B.'s regard for, 3, 64, 271; 4, 15, 25, 37, 38, 45, 94, 103, 146; contributor to *Anti-Jacobin*, 3, 271; delighted with 3rd canto of *Childe Harold*, 5, 105 and n; B.'s gratitude, 106, 108, 115, 209; B.'s differences with, 169; attacked by Webster, 169n; 11, 163 and n; B.'s friendship for, 5, 169, 176, 192; disapproves of third act of *Manfred*, 211–12; ridicules Della Cruscans, 234 and n; unwell, 255, 269; on B.'s judgment of Pope, 265n; liked *Marino Faliero*, 7, 175, 194, 205; B. wishes he would write life of Pope, 8, 110; praised B.'s diction in *Marino Faliero*, 114; and B.'s 'majestic march', 136; approves of *Sardanapalus*, 156, 158; dislikes new dramas, 218; and *Cain*, 9, 103, 104; edits B.'s work, 10, 42; B. his prodigal son, 11, 117, 123; to judge *Lament of Tasso*, 190 and n; *Baviad, Maeviad*, 1, 276; 2, 86, 87n; 3, 64; 5, 234n; 7, 175 and n; 9, 70; *Epistle to Peter Pindar*, 1, 174 and n; Juvenal, translation, 2, 80n; Massinger edition, 2, 249; 3, 64

Gigante, Giuseppe, 8, 124 and n, 131

Gight (Mrs. Byron's estate), 2, 72n, 156n; 8, 73

Gilchrist, Octavius Graham, B.'s letters to: 8, 199, 203; in Pope controversy, 111 and n, 199 and n, 201; B.'s defense of, 116, 197; three pamphlets, 199 and n, 200

Gillies, John, *History of Greece*, 8, 238 and n

Gillies, Robert Pearse, *Childe Alarique*, 3, *217 and n*; ed. *Foreign Quarterly Review*, 217n

Ginguené, Pierre Louis, 8, 41, 53 and n; *Histoire Littéraire d'Italie*, 7, 54 and n; 8, 14 and n

Ginnasi, Count, 8, 184n

Giordani, Pietro, 9, 30 and n

Giorgi, Countess, 6, 109

Giorgi, Signor, 11, 191

Giorgione, 1, 94n; *Famiglia di Giorgione*, 5, 213 and n; *Judgment of Solomon*, 7, 45; *La Tempesta*, 11, 228

Giovanni, Don, priest at Filetto, **7**, 185 and n, 186

Giraud, Nicolo, **2**, *10 and n*, 12 and n, 13, 21, 29; **3**, 120; bathing with B., **1**, 207n; **2**, 14; nurses Byron, 16; at school, 46; in B.'s will, 71

Girgenti, **1**, 224

Giuliani, B.'s letter to, **9**, 215; mentioned, **9**, 215 and n, 217; **10**, 103, 107 and n, 152

Giulietta, **6**, 92

Giuseppe (student), **2**, 12

Giuseppe (Hobhouse's servant), **5**, 142

Glasse, Hannah, *The Art of Cookery*, **3**, 238 and n

Glenbervie, Sylvester Douglas, Lord, **2**, *170 and n*; **3**, 234 and n, 235; **6**, 243n; trns. *First Canto of Ricciardetto*, **8**, 224 and n; **9**, 146 and n

Glendower, Owen, **3**, 10

Glennie, Dr., **1**, 41 and n

Glettenheimer, **6**, 92

Globe, The, **3**, 204; **4**, 258

Globe Hotel, Livorno, **9**, 167n

Gloucester, **8**, 140n

Gloucester, Duke of, **2**, 92n

Gloucester Cathedral, **8**, 201

Gloucestershire, **1**, 184n; **11**, 155

Glover, Mrs. Julia, **9**, 35

Glover, Richard, **1**, 113

Gnoatto, Mr., **6**, 255; **7**, 65, 79

Godolphin, Lord Francis, **1**, 60n

Godwin, Mary (*see also* Shelley, Mary), **5**, 162, 293–4, 296; **6**, 76, 82, 125n; *Frankenstein*, 126

Godwin, William, **5**, 293, 294; **6**, 76, 82, 126; **9**, 27, 205; in financial straits, **5**, 16 and n, 17, 18; and Shelley's will, **10**, 16, 158; B.'s financial aid to, **10**, 18

Godwin, Mrs. William, **9**, 205

Goethe, Johann Wolfgang von, B.'s letter to: **10**, 213; mentioned, **8**, 25, 198 and n; definition of architecture, **3**, 211 and n; review of *Manfred*, **7**, 106 and n, 113, 220 and n; *Marino Faliero* dedicated to, 206 and n; **8**, 66; *Edinburgh* review of, 164; B. compared, to **9**, 11; his story of murder by B., 80n; *Sardanapalus* dedication, 91, 93, 163, 167, 179; **10**, 64; *Werner* dedicated to, **9**, 163, 179; **10**, 60, 64 and n, 65, 73; admirer of B., **9**, 164, 165; B.'s admiration of, **10**, 73, 213 and n; letter about B., 77, 99, 109; lines to B., **10**, 213, 214; visited by Millingen, **11**, 216; *Aus meinem Leben, Dichtung und Wahrheit*, **5**, 111n; *Faust*, **9**, 81, 118; *Faust* translated for B., **5**, 206, 268; **7**, 113; *Faust* and *Manfred*, **5**, 270; **9**,

165; *Faust* illustrations, 75, 162; *Werther*, **8**, 78 and n

Goetz, Countess, **5**, 132 and n, 142, 146, 206, 279; **6**, 41

Golden Horn, **1**, 251

Goldoni, Carlo, **2**, 60, 104; **7**, 43; **8**, 15n; the 'Italian Molière', **5**, 274 and n; comedies in Venice, **11**, 189 and n; *La Vedova Scaltra*, **5**, 238

Goldsmith, Oliver, **1**, 2; **2**, 210; **3**, 79 and n; **7**, 83; his indigence, **6**, 85; *Citizen of the World*, **11**, 230; *The Good Natured Man*, **1**, 50; **4**, 260 and n; **6**, 106n, 244 and n; **8**, 239 and n; 'Retaliation', **7**, 63 and n; 'Serious Reflections on the Life and Death of the late TC', **2**, 64 and n; *She Stoops to Conquer*, **1**, 94; **2**, 113 and n; **3**, 123 and n; **6**, 207 and n; **9**, 123 and n; *The Traveller*, **1**, 239–40n; **10**, 92 and n; **11**, 219, 229; *Vicar of Wakefield*, **2**, 11 and n, 59 and n, 185n, 192 and n; **3**, 10 and n, 15 and n, 213 and n; **5**, 172 and n, 177 and n, 215 and n; **6**, 63, 123 and n; **8**, 38 and n, 40, 92, 239 and n; **9**, 50 and n, 124 and n; **11**, 60 and n, 85 and n, 163 and n

Gomorrah, **6**, 143

Gondolas, **6**, 44, 54, 65, 66

Gonorrhea, **2**, 46, 56, 58; **6**, 14, 19, 25, 207; **11**, 159

Goodall (? Godsall), and a vis à vis carriage for B., **2**, 62, 64n

Goodall, Mrs., **4**, 138

Gordon, Lord Alexander, **1**, 130

Gordon, Charles David, B.'s letters to: **1**, 70, 74; mentioned, 70 and n, 75; **3**, 85n; B.'s letters to offered to Murray, **8**, 227

Gordon, David, of Abergeldie, **1**, 70n

Gordon, George, 12th laird of Gight, **1**, 274

Gordon, Lord George, **7**, 45 and n

Gordon, Jane, Duchess of Gordon, **1**, 130 and n, 132; **3**, 37n

Gordon, Joanna, **2**, 108n

Gordon, Sir John, of Gight, **7**, 204, 212

Gordon, Pryse Lockhart, B.'s letter to, **5**, 80; mentioned, 76, 80 and n; *Personal Memoirs*, **6**, 24n, **11**, 190n, 229

Gordon, Thomas, **11**, *39 and n*; aided Greeks, 50; and the London Greek Committee, **11**, 108; *History of the Greek Revolution*, **6**, 4n; **11**, 39n, 130n, 213

Gordon, Mr., wine merchant, **1**, 220

Gordons, **7**, 204

Gordon's Hotel, **1**, 124

Gorgon, **11**, 198

Göttingen, University of, **2**, 64; **8**, 146

Goulburn, Edward, **9**, 19 and n
Gower, Lord, **4**, 127n
Gracchi, **4**, 177; **8**, 107
'Gradus ad Parnassum', **3**, 220
Grafton, George Henry Fitzroy, 4th Duke of, **9**, 27
Graham, Mr., **7**, 193
Graham, Sir B., **1**, 165; **2**, 28 and n
Graham, General, **2**, 57
Graham, Mrs. Maria (*see also* Callcott), B.'s letter to, **6**, 172; her history, 172n; *Indian Journal, Letters on India*, 172n
Graham, Sandford, **2**, *29 and n*, 30, 31, 33, and n, 37, 43
Graham, Capt. Thomas, RN, **6**, 172n
Graham, Sir Thomas, **3**, 180 and n
Grammar School, Aberdeen, **8**, 108
Gramont, Duc de, **2**, 185n
Gramont, Philibert, Comte de, **8**, 148; **10**, 156 and n; Mlle de Saint-Germain and Mme de Sénantes episode, **3**, 147n; *Mémoires*, **3**, 146 and n, 148n; **7**, 202
Grampian Hills, Scotland, **4**, 20
Granada, Archbishop of, **11**, 125 and n
Granard, George Forbes, 6th Earl of, **3**, 71n, 75n; **4**, 113n, 119n
Gran Bretagna (Grande Bretagne), Hotel, Venice, **6**, 74 and n; **7**, 28
Granby, John Manners, Marquis of, **4**, 127 and n
Grand Canal, **5**, 179, 251; **6**, 25 and n, 40, 43, 48, 54–5, 60, 64, 65, 133, 196, 238; **8**, 81
Grant, David, B.'s letter to: **11**, 62; mentioned, 26n
Grant & Co., **11**, 61
Grant, Rev. Johnstone, preaches against *Cain*, **9**, 100 and n
Grant, Sir William, **10**, 75
Grantley, Lord, **1**, 40n; **10**, 119n
Granville, Harriet Countess of, *Letters*, **3**, 211n
Granville, Lord, **4**, 127n
Grassetti, Dr. Gaetano, **11**, 78 and n
Grattan, Henry (? Jr.), **3**, 157 and n; **6**, 86; **8**, 214, 219, 246, 251; **9**, 13 and n, 21, 26; oratory, 27
Grattan, Mr. **10**, 179
Grattan (young), **2**, 256n
Gravesend, **3**, 91
[Gravot?], Monsieur, **10**, 171
Gray, May, **1**, *40 and n*
Gray, Thomas, **2**, 67 and n; **3**, 141; **4**, 50, 332; **5**, 86 and n, 87; **6**, 30, 85; **8**, 21; *The Bard*, **2**, 211 and n; **3**, 256 and n; **4**, 62 and n; **5**, 142 and n; *Elegy*, **8**, 53n; additional stanzas, 50–1; *Odes*, **4**, 164; 'Progress of Poesy', **11**, 234

Greathead, Bertie, **5**, 233
Grecian Coffee House, **4**, 89, 272, 273
Greece, **2**, 5n, 24n, 35, 53, 55, 58, 71, 88, 134, 156n, 162, 190; **3**, 58, 179, 218, 224n; **4**, 97, 172, 269; **5**, 48, 99, 126, 201, 205, 263, 296; **6**, 98, 150, 173; **7**, 219, 236; **8**, 36, 221; **9**, 17, 23, 147n, 198, 205n, 236; **10**, 48n, 56n; B.'s first voyage, **1**, 10; Fletcher uncomfortable in, 10; B.'s letters from, 17, 249; B. to sail from Malta for, 223; B. first reached, 225; Climate, 229, 235, 248; **2**, 3, 92, 181; B. to pass year in, **1**, 232; B.'s travels in, 234, 255; ancient and modern, 237; classical regions, 238; ruins of, 242; B.'s intention to return to, 243, 244, 250, 254; **2**, 190, 258; **3**, 35, 40; Aberdeen's explorations, **1**, 254n; B. has seen much of, **2**, 9; antiquities, 29n; B. sorry to leave, 54; *Childe Harold* written in, 78; B.'s nostalgia for, 85, 95, 137, 163, 181; bigotry in, **3**, 119; B. finds Rome finer, **5**, 221; travel books, **8**, 219; B.'s desire to go to, **10**, 86, 142, 143, 144, 149, 157, 172, 173, 177; B. going to, 133, 134, 154, 190, 193–4, 195–6, 197, 199, 200, 204, 206, 209, 210; B. would prefer to be buried there, 157; supplies for, 162n, 186–7, 188, 195, 196–7, 202, 210n; foreign officers in, 170; commercial relations with England, 170; cheapness in, 171; B. sailing for, 210n, 211, 212, 213; printing press for, 211; uncertainties of situation in, **11**, 15; B. left for, 29; B. willing to serve but for dissensions, 38, 44; B. thought of purchasing land in, 49; three courses for, 71; its meaning to B., 103; national wealth pledged for loan, 146n
Greek army, **11**, 216
Greek cause, B. to stick by, **1**, 17; **11**, 21, 22, 35, 40, 42, 76, 81, 83, 84–5, 91, 95–6, 97, 100, 110, 116, 126, 131, 147; B.'s loan of £4000, 34, 59n, 61–2, 65, 69, 73, 74, 75, 77, 80, 94, 117, 140, 144, 153, 215–16; B.'s expenditures on, 74, 130–1, 142, 144, 146, 152
Greek Committee, *see* London Greek Committee
Greek Corps, **11**, 149
Greek dance, **3**, 58 and n; **11**, 223
Greek Deputies, **11**, 41, 52, 59 and n, 61–2, 64, 72, 73, 75, 80, 110, 117, 125, 130 and n, 131, 140, 144, 145 and n, 147, 148, 149, 150, 154; not yet sent to London, 45, 50, 54; arrived in Cephalonia, 52n, 59 and n

Greek fleet, **11**, 22, 30, 34, 40, 43, 52n, 54, 72, 75, 76, 80, 81, 87, 88, 140; aid to Missolonghi, 62, 65; beat the Turks, 65, 66; activated by B.'s loan, 65, 69, 216; B. to pay, 91, 93

Greek Government, B.'s letter to: **11**, 66; mentioned, 16, 27, 29, 31, 32, 33, 38, 39, 40, 41, 43, 45, 53, 57, 71, 72, 75, 88, 90, 93, 135; B. sent message to, 23 and n; agents peculating, 28, 32; sent emissaries to B., 52 and n, 53; B.'s letter to on dissension, 69; B.'s advances to, 96, 102; and Ionian Government, 100; seeking loan in islands, 142, 152; B. invited to head Western Greece, 141, 144–5

Greek language (*see also* Romaic), 2, 102n, 104; **5**, 130, 156; **6**, 12, 68; **9**, 97n; **11**, 132n, 157

Greek loan, **11**, 27, 41, 50, 52n, 54, 59n, 60–1, 65, 72n, 73, 75, 77, 80, 82, 83, 104n, 117, 130n, 140, 141, 142, 144, 146 and n, 151, 152, 153; B. recommends to Committee, **10**, 210; Commission named, **11**, 146n; and Barff, 146n

Greek monogram, 2, 152 and n

Greek mythology, **1**, 15

Greek National Library, **11**, 68n

Greek nationalism, **2**, 32n

Greek Navy, **3**, 249n

Greek Orthodox Church, **1**, 228n

Greek Privateers, B.'s letter to, **11**, 99; mentioned, 100 and n, 102

Greek Provisional Government, **10**, 142, 147, 151, 171, 184, 202; asks Committee for money, 210

Greek Revolution, **1**, 242n; **6**, 4n; **8**, 122, 135, 198, 239; **9**, 23; **10**, 169n; 171n, 180n; **11**, 22n, 38, 128n; B. thinks of joining, **8**, 211, 214; treatment of prisoners, **10**, 152; Garden of Heroes, **11**, 79n; portraits of heroes by Friedel, **11**, 128n

Greeks, 2, 9, 12, 26, 29, 30, 31, 35, 36, 37, 43, 134, 216; **5**, 157n, 293; **6**, 226; **7**, 138, 194; **8**, 15, 48, 106, 152; **9**, 208; none know problem from poker, **1**, 17; **11**, 83; dissension among them, **1**, 17, 23; **10**, 213; **11**, 16, 21, 22, 23, 24, 26, 27, 30, 32, 38, 39, 40, 41, 44, 45, 50, 53, 54, 65, 71, 72 and n, 73, 75, 80, 84, 128 and n, 130 and n, 132, 135, 138 and n, 146–7; B. likes, **1**, 238; better than Spaniards, 250; B.'s servants, 2, 4, 48, 51, 59, 60, 94; their 'national depravity', 11n; bathing habits, 14; 'boy love', 29 and n; notes on modern Greeks, 102, 103, 115; B. has not

made up his mind about, 125; moral axioms of, **3**, 120; incest theme, 196 and n; do not welcome strangers, **10**, 144; their needs for the war, 169–70, 181; treated foreign allies well, 180; abused by B. in journal, **11**, 29n; character moulded by slavery, 32–3; capacity for lying, 33; B. on character of, 15, 16–17, 40, 43; successes, 54, 72, 75, 76; might influence B. by intrigue, 54–5; not much war activity, 58; Erskine's letter on, 59n; ignorant of mathematics and music, 77; as soldiers, 79n; and Capt. Yorke, 100 and n; offered loan by Knights of Malta, 104 and n; money advanced by B., 135; demands on B.'s purse, 107–8, 117, 118–19; taken into Patras, 129

Greek sculpture, 2, 45 and n

Greek Testaments, **11**, 126

Greek University (Corfu), **11**, 138n

Greek tragedy, **8**, 57

Greek women, 2, 46

Green, David Bonnell, **6**, 123n

Gregson, Bob, **1**, 162n, 182 and n; **3**, 216n

Grenville, William Wyndham Grenville, Lord, **1**, 62n, 67n, 113n, *186 and n*; 2, 167 and n; **4**, 60, 217, 287n; **6**, 79; **9**, 14, 27, 73 and n

Gretry, André Ernest, **8**, 41

Greville, Lady Charlotte (née Cavendish), **1**, 19; **3**, 254 and n

Greville, Col., B.'s letter to: 2, 168; and Argyle Institution, 168 and n, 169

Greville, Fulke, **4**, 105n

Grey, Charles, 2nd Earl, **1**, 209n; 2, 167n, 171n, 211n; **3**, 70, 174; **4**, 60, 105, 117n, 126 and n, 290, 296n; **6**, 18, 79; **8**, 27, 28, 120n; **9**, 14, 27, 30, 73, 105, 106; **11**, 184; on *Moniteur*, **3**, 254 and n

Grey, Lord and Lady, B.'s letter to: **11**, 184

Grey, Lady, 2, 171 and n; **11**, 184

Grey de Ruthyn, Henry Edward, 19th Lord, B.'s letter to: **1**, 168; leased Newstead Abbey, 45 and n, 60, 163, 168; offended B., *45 and n*, 46; detested by B., 49–50, 54, 55, 59, 60, 168n; Mrs. B. in love with, 54; marriage and death, 222 and n

Griffith[s] (creditor), **10**, 96, 113

Griffiths, George Edward, publisher, *Monthly Review*, 2, 164 and n, 167; **5**, 176 and n; **11**, 230

Griffiths, Ralph, founder, *Monthly Review*, **6**, 32n

Grillparzer, Franz, *Sappho*, **8**, 25 and n, 26

Grimaldi, Joseph, **1**, 152 and n; **3**, 9; **4**, 153 and n

Grimm, Friedrich Melchior, reviews of, **3**, 96 and n, 118n, 247 and n; epitaph on Voltaire, 117–18; story of Comte de Caylus, **6**, 205 and n; *Correspondance Littéraire et Philosophique*, **3**, 195 and n; **4**, 284n; **6**, 205 and n; **7**, 103 and n; **8**, 30, 31, 41 and n, 46

Grindelwald, **5**, 94, 102, 106, 205

Gritti, Count, **6**, 25n

Gritti, Palace, **6**, 25n, 37

Grosser Eiger, **5**, 101, 106

Grossius, agent of Lord Aberdeen, **2**, 156

Grub-street, **5**, 252; **7**, 39 and n

Gruter, Jan, *Corpus Inscriptionum*, **2**, 145 and n

Guardian, The, **4**, 11

Guarini, Giovanni Battista, *Il Pastor Fido*, **5**, 217; **6**, 118 and n

Guatimozin, Aztec chief, **6**, 216 and n

Guelph, George, **2**, 49

Guelphs, **6**, 171

Guernsey, **1**, 176n; **8**, 220

Guicciardini, Francesco, **4**, 161 and n

Guiccioli, Count Alessandro, B.'s letters to: **6**, 201; **7**, 159; biog. sketch, **6**, 276–7; mentioned, 128 and n, 184, 202, 213, 242, 247, 255, 259; **8**, 34, 233, 234; **9**, 11n, 181; old and rich, **6**, 107, 114, 164, 168, 173, 186, 276; his reputation, 130, 144, 164; father of the foetus, 141; cuckolded in his own palace, 144, 163; at the theatre, 152; friendship with B., 157, 168, 176, 276–7; took B. riding in coach and six, 163, 168, 276–7; wish to be British Vice-Consul, 164 and n, 208, 235, 277; tricked into buying ring, 203 and n; due in Venice, 225, 237; lays down conditions for Teresa, 239, 244; quarrels with Teresa over B., 241, 248; first wife, 276; attitude to wife's liaison, 277; B.'s relations with, **7**, 12 and n, 13, 17, 18, 24, 29, 30, 36, 46–7, 52 and n, 87, 89, 90, 118; B.'s opinion of, 13, 20–1, 67, 94, 128 and n, 140; and his wife's liaison with B., 67, 88, 94, 112, 146, 147, 160 and n; and Ravenna Theatre, 26n, 52n; and Teresa (maid), 29, 30, 32–3, 33n, 34, 36; borrows money from B., 92 and n, 163 and n; 'a fit of discovery', 101; on the eve of divorce, 101, 102–3; Papal decree, 125 and n, 126 and n, 136, 165; a Cavaliere di San Stefano, 128 and n; conversation with Cardinal and Alborghetti, 134; a threat to B.,

136–7, 143, 155; unpopularity, 149, 165; and Teresa's allowance, 151–2, 152n, 156, 215, 235n; his strange proposals to B., 163; temporary alliance with Revolution, 272; separation from wife, **10**, 30; would forgive Teresa, 176, 178

Guiccioli, Attilia, **7**, 163 and n

Guiccioli, Ferdinando, **6**, 177 and n, 201; **7**, 29, 30, 172, 174; Lega on his death, 176 and n

Guiccioli, Countess Teresa (née Gamba Ghiselli), B.'s letters to: **6**, 109, 115, 120, 128, 134, 139, 141, 151 (2), 153, 155, 156, 157, 159, 160, 161, 168, 169, 171, 198, 199, 202, 215, 220, 246, 249, 250, 254, 255, 258; **7**, 11 (2), 12 (2), 13 (2), 18, 21, 23 (2), 26 (2), 29, 30, 31, 32, 33, 35, 36, 37 (2), 38, 52, 53, 54, 55, 56 (2), 66, 67, 86, 88 (2), 89, 90, 91, 92 (2), 93, 107, 108, 109 (2), 110, 128, 129, 133, 139, 140, 142, 145, 147, 148, 149, 150, 154, 156 (2), 157, 161, 162, 164, 166, 171, 173, 175, 185, 186, 189, 193, 196, 198, 209, 214, 221, 226, 227, 234, 240, 241 (3), 242 (2), 243; **8**, 63, 158, 160, 169, 177, 178, 182, 184, 187, 190, 195, 199, 204, 212, 213, 221, 235, 241, 243, 246, 249; **9**, 107; **10**, 93 (2), 100, 104, 107, 212; **11**, 15 (2), 18 (3), 21, 42, 48, 51, 56, 66, 78, 101, 111, 121, 137; biog. sketch, **6**, 277–8; mentioned, **1**, 79n; **5**, 295, 297–8; **6**, 189, 213; **7**, 47, 245, 247; **8**, 33, 51, 138; **10**, 69, 76, 81, 121n, 165n, 191; no ear for B.'s style, **1**, 1; alleged abduction, 8; **6**, 237; B.'s love for after three years, **1**, 9; **8**, 234; dislike of *Don Juan*, **1**, 13; **7**, 202; **8**, 145 and n, 147, 148, 198, 235; B.'s meetings with, **1**, 20; B. joined her in Pisa, 21;; **6**, 275, 277, 278; B.'s letters in Italian to her, **1**, 24; Prepiani's portraits of B., **5**, 191n; B.'s first mention of, **6**, 107 and n; beginning of liaison with B., 107 and n, 108, 114–15, 276, 277; B.'s love for, 151, 168, 199–200, 203; **7**, 30–1, 33, 34, 92, 140; **8**, 160, 170, 177–8; Italian Caroline Lamb, **6**, 115, 248; B. wonders if she received his letters, 120; miscarriage, 121, 130, 141, 165, 167; B.'s formal letter to, 128 and n; instructions to B., 144; illness, 151, 163, 165, 167–8, 173, 175, 176; keeps B.'s handkerchief, 154n; refused to elope with B., 156 and n, 157; popularity, 162–3; improves in health, 177, 198; gossip about her

and B. in Venice, 178–80, 190; writes to Scott, 182–3, 183n; described by B., 185–6, 248–9; rides with B., 186, 188; to join B. in Bologna, 199, 204, 206, 278; loses B.'s ring, 201 and n, 203 and n; B. laments his attachment, 214, 216; contemplated elopement, 230 and n, 240, 241, 248, 277; no expense to B., 231–2, 241; in Venice, 237; refused her husband's conditions, 239, 240; to consult Dr. Aglietti, 241; choice between husband and lover, 241, 244–5, 248; to return with her husband to Ravenna, 241–2, 244, 248; B.'s assurances of love, 247, 251; B. goes to her in Ravenna, 255, 256, 258–9, 278; paraded her foreign lover, 262; separation decree from Pope, 277, 278; after B.'s death, 278; marriage to Count de Boissy, 278; relations with B. and her husband, 7, 17, 18, 20 and n, 24, 30, 92, 102–3; ill at Ravenna, 18; jealousy, 20 and n, 26n, 151, 186; B. on their relationship, 22, 88, 105, 107; amico ed amante in eterno, 26 and n; 11, 15 and n; and Allegra, 7, 35, 36, 66, 80; read *Glenarvon*, 37 and n; refuses to see B., 53 and n, 55–6; her miniature, 59; and B.'s letters, 67 and n; separation from her husband, 67, 102, 110 and n, 112, 136; 8, 34, 41, 117, 214, 233; B. urged her to stay with her husband, 7, 87, 88, 89, 105; Guiccioli's knowledge of liaison with B., 89, 90–1; B.'s wish to marry her, 91 and n, 109 and n; ill with erysipelas, 93 and n; her terms for staying with Guiccioli, 105; on Queen Caroline, 122; papal decree on separation, 125 and n, 126 and n, 127; joins her father at Filetto, 128 and n, 143n; fears for B.'s safety, 134–5; concerned about gossip, 134n; urges B. to visit her, 143 and n and *passim*; and Elisei, 156, 157; hurt at receiving *Adolphe*, 163 and n; to meet B. again, 174, 176; Ferdinando's death, 176n, 185; B. calls her Gaspara, 193 and n, 197; date of birth, 193n; B. urges prudence, 235 and n; menaced with convent, 236–7; 8, 157, 159n, 160, 161, 168, 175, 214, 233; 9, 181; 10, 30; returns to Ravenna, 7, 240 and n; opposed to B.'s going to Greece, 273; 9, 198; 10, 143, 176, 178, 183; B. visited, 8, 12, 13–14, 16, 18, 23, 36, 51; age, 16 and n; quarrels with B. over love in drama, 26; appearance, 95; B. wants Holmes to

paint her picture, 95; refuses to leave Ravenna, 150–1 and n; in Bologna, 161, 168, 175; goes to Florence, 161, 168, 169, 184; B. on her future home, 177–8, 184; 'gossip', 190 and n, 199, 212, 213, 222; proposed Shelley as tutor, 204–5; her numerous letters to B., 213; wanted to write to Augusta, 217, 235; B. asks her to punish Lega, 243; bust by Bartolini, 9, 58n, 121–2, 121n, 136 and n, 217; 10, 18; retains B.'s letter to *Courier*, 9, 100n; her servant arrested, 132, 139n; at Villa Dupuy with B., 161n, 169; arrangements for Allegra's body, 163; 'Stanzas to the Po', 167; urged to appeal to Grand Duchess, 180; gave B. permission to continue *Don Juan*, 182, 187–8 and n, 198; with B. at Casa Lanfranchi, 184n, 202; refuses B.'s legacy, 193n; 10, 55, 162; saved B.'s skin as relic, 9, 197n; wished to go to Greece with B., 198; 10, 178, 198; portrait by West, 9, 211; 10, 18; liaison with B., 30, 197; frightened by lightning, 52; suit for separation, 56; sister's death, 100; delighted with D'Orsay's journal, 140; jealous of Lady Blessington, 175, 177; wants to stay with Countess d'Ysone, 191 and n, 192; may retire to convent, 198; B. wrote to in English, 11, 18; B. left his heart in Italy, 55; Barry to tell her of B.'s leaving for Missolonghi, 82; at Villa Dupuy, 140n; *Lord Byron, Jugé par les Témoins de sa Vie*, 6, 278; *My Recollections of Lord Byron*, 5, 64n; 'Vie de Lord Byron en Italie', 6, 156n, 278

Guiccioli Palace, 1, 21; 7, 13n, 33n, 92, 134n

Guido, 5, 216; 6, 148

Guido di Polenta, 6, 261; 7, 112 and n

Guilford, Francis North, 4th Earl, 5, 210 and n, 212, 241; 11, 164

Guilford, Frederick North, 5th Earl, B.'s letter to: 9, 79; mentioned, 5, *199 and n*, 210, 212, 215, 241; 9, 79 and n; 11, 50, 138, 164

Gully, John, 1, 162n, 182n

Gustavus III, King of Sweden, 4, 284

Guy Faux, 7, 75, 76; 11, 182

Guyana, 3, 66n

Habeas Corpus, 5, 208; 6, 16 and n; 7, 49 and n; 11, 166 and n

Haddington, Thomas Hamilton, 6th Earl of, 3, 61 and n

Hafod, 5, 89

Hagar, 5, 116

Hague, The, **3**, 212
Hales, **1**, 139
Halford, Sir Henry, Bt., **9**, 72 and n, 73
Halicarnassus, **11**, 165
Hall, Capt. Basil, B.'s letter to, **6**, 64n
Hall, Rev. Thomas, B.'s letter to, **9**, 193; chaplain at Leghorn, 193 and n, 197
Haller, von Hallerstein, Karl Freiherr, **2**, 27n, *30 and n*, 33 and n, 37n
Halnaby, **2**, 283; **4**, 230 and n, 239, 261, **5**, 66, 97; **9**, 194, 195, 209, 212; honeymoon, **4**, 249–57
Halsband, Robert, ed., *Letters of Mary Wortley Montagu*, **1**, 251n
Hamburg, **9**, 24
Hamilton, Lady Anne, **4**, 104 and n
Hamilton, Anthony, *Mémoires de la vie du Comte de Gramont*, **3**, 148 and n; **10**, 156 and n
Hamilton, Lord Archibald, **11**, 64 and n
Hamilton, Sir Hew Dalrymple, **6**, 127n
Hamilton, (née Duncan), Lady Dalrymple, **6**, 127 and n
Hamilton, Sir Hew and Lady, Dalrymple, **5**, 132 and n
Hamilton, 9th Duke of, **4**, 128n; **11**, 185n
Hamilton, William Richard, **2**, 12n; **5**, 260, 269
Hamlet, Mr., **10**, 162
Hammersley's Bank, **1**, 202, 205 and n, 214n, 223, 225, 233, 245; **4**, 108, 115, 130n, 131, 171, 270; **5**, 171; **6**, 7; **10**, 97, 99
Hammond, George, **4**, 287 and n; **5**, *260 and n*; **6**, 62
Hampden, **3**, 228
Hampden Club, **6**, 166, 211n; **9**, 23
Hampshire, **1**, 71, 72 and n, 76n; **4**, 230n; **7**, 236
Hampstead, **5**, 61, 97; **10**, 105
Hancock, Charles, B.'s letters to, **11**, 89, 91, 94, 95, 106, 133; biog. sketch, 214; mentioned, 96, 97, 111; B.'s banker on Cephalonia, 16n, 63n, 65n, 75, 88, 89n, 131; Barff's partner, 213
Handel, George Frederick, **6**, 19; *Messiah*, **1**, 124
Hannibal, **2**, 138 and n; **4**, 302; **8**, 69 and n; **9**, 48, 210; **10**, 142
Hanover, House of, **4**, 317
Hanson family, **1**, *51n*, 61, 207, 275; country house (Farleigh), 64 and n, 72n, 76 and n
Hanson, Charles, B.'s letters to, **2**, 204, 219, 226; **3**, 5, 28, 29, 33; **4**, 87, 106, 108, 125, 140, 141 (2), 148, 335; **6**, 31, 42, 50, 54, 57; **7**, 101, 116, 119, 146; **9**, 212; **10**, 46, 75; **11**, 183;

mentioned, **1**, 51n, 186, 243; **2**, 25, 68; **3**, 29n; **4**, 24, 30, 142, 143, 147, 225, 227, 272, 279; **5**, 70, 189, 236, 279; **6**, 77 and n; **7**, 240; **9**, 107, 191, 205, 211; **10**, 47, 48, 72, 78, 90; death of his mother, **4**, 87 and n; sale of Newstead, 140; contemplated marriage, 335 and n; to manage Noel estates for B., **9**, 176, 177, 212; bought B.'s bond to Claughton, 217
Hanson, Hargreaves, B.'s letters to, **1**, 63, 64, 76, 77 (2), 78, 80, 167; mentioned, 43, 60, 69, 77n, 78, 81 and n, 128 and n, 129 and n, 142, 169, 186, 243; **2**, 25, 36; at Harrow with B., **1**, 51n, 62; apprentice to his father, *64 and n*, death, 64n
Hanson, Harriet, **1**, 51n, 107, 182; **2**, 25
Hanson, Capt. James, **1**, *40 and n*
Hanson, John, B.'s letters to, **1**, 40, 50, 51, 59, 62, 68, 70, 78, 81, 82, 84, 85, 90 (2), 91 (2), 92, 101, 113, 116, 119, 120, 128 (2), 134, 137, 142, 143, 144, 148, 149, 151, 169 (2), 170, 174, 175, 181, 183 (2), 184, 185 (2), 188, 191 (2), 192, 195, 199 (3), 200, 201, 202, 203, 204 (2), 205 (2), 207, 213, 214 (2), 217, 222, 223, 225, 231, 233, 234, 236, 243, 245, 252; **2**, 18, 25 (2), 35, 38 (2), 41, 56, 62 (2), 66 (2), 67, 68, 96, 99, 122, 133, 134, 139, 144, 146, 147, 152, 153 (2), 154, 166, 167, 189 (3), 201, 231, 233, 238 (2), 241, 248, 255 (2); **3**, 6, 13, 17, 22, 23, 25, 38, 39 (2), 55, 56, 76, 138 (2); **4**, 24, 30, 31, 38, 40, 43, 118, 121, 142, 143, 145, 147, 150, 155, 160, 163, 166, 170, 174, 180, 186, 188, 194, 195, 203, 206, 211, 220, 222, 223, 225, 227, 232, 244, 247 (2), 248, 251, 253, 254 (2), 257, 258, 261, 264, 272, 273, 276, 279, 281 (3), 282, 283, 288, 291, 292 (2), 293, 298, 300 (2), 303, 306, 307, 311, 317, 318, 333, 336, 337; **5**, 26, 34, 42, 46, 65, 69, 70, 89, 128, 150, 189, 236, 261; **6**, 71, 73, 74, 103; **7**, 69, 101 (2), 116, 145, 168, 202, 240; **8**, 62; **9**, 106, 112, 115, 126, 155, 177, 191; **10**, 16 (2), 38; biog. sketch, **1**, 275; mentioned, 40n, 43, 49, 51n; **2**, 51, 61, 103, 146n; **3**, 76, 243; **4**, 230n, 329; **5**, 26n, 30, 266, 270; **6**, 6, 13, 31, 32, 33, 39, 40, 42, 48, 49, 50, 51, 52, 53, 56, 58, 59–60, 61, 72–3, 80, 81, 100, 105, 109, 114, 201, 228; **7**, 14, 94, 95, 110, 116, 120, 136, 155, 156, 191, 213, 220, 235, 239; **9**, 56, 107, 124, 176, 195

205, 212; **10**, 35n, 59, 65, 97, 127, 143, 147, 150, 153, 158; no wit in B.'s letters to, **1**, 12; B. plotted to spend holiday with, 56–59, 61; B. seeks invitation from, 58–60; solicitor to stamp office, 62 and n, 113 and n; **4**, 217 and n; recommended Cambridge to B., **1**, 63; B.'s Court of Chancery allowance, 74n, 78n, 82n, 83, 90 and n, 128 and n; B.'s Rochdale property, 76 and n, 163, 181, 233–4; **2**, 39, 40, 41, 57, 201; on way to Lancashire, **1**, 77; supplied B.'s furniture and cellar, 78, 80; B.'s Cambridge expenses, 82, 83, 88, 91, 116, 119–20; excuses B.'s mother's behaviour, 85; B.'s mother's pension arrears, 89 and n; feud with B., 101–2, 113; Health, 107, 113, 175; to be B.'s trustee, 175; gathering affidavits for B., 191n, 195n; attempt to mortgage Newstead, 199 and n; Wymondham copyholds, 199, 203n, 205 and n, 233; B.'s will, 202 and n; **2**, 71–3; **4**, 298 and n, 303; **11**, 156; no letters from, **1**, 234, 235; **2**, 4, 8, 16–17, 18, 23; B. had no remittance from, **1**, 244; B.'s creditors, 256 and n; **11**, 160–1; suggests sale of Newstead, **2**, 25, 26, 28, 32, 35, 41, 45, 52; Wymondham purchase money, 39; account of B.'s affairs, 42–3, 44; with B., to Lancashire, 60, 84, 88, 94, 114–15, 156; Newstead rents, 153 and n; **5**, 226; Newstead sale, **2**, 188n, 189; **6**, 25; and Newstead affairs, **3**, 22, 24, 29, 39, 56; **11**, 189 and n; at Farleigh, **3**, 158 and n; marriage of his daughter, 248n, 249; death of his wife, **4**, 87 and n, 118 and n; urged to sell Rochdale, 142, 143, 150, 186, 253; B.'s marriage settlement, 186 and n, 193, 196, 199, 202, 204, 206, 210–11, 222n, 232, 233, 238, 239, 241, 245, 270, 300n; **9**, 108; his delays, **4**, 210–11, 212, 213, 215, 216, 217, 219, 220, 222, 223, 226; **6**, 63, 72; **7**, 40, 167, 168, 198, 202, 210, 212, 240; B. on his talents, **4**, 217–18; his neglect of B.'s affairs, 223–5, 270, 271 and n, 272–3, 275–6, 276–7, 278, 292, 300; and Portsmouth affair, 235, 236–7; **10**, 119n, 124–5, 129; Hobhouse to see, **4**, 251, 253; called 'Spooney', 255 and n, 259, 271; **5**, 77; **6**, 14 and *passim*; his son's engagement, **4**, 335n; and separation business, **5**, 51; urged to sell Newstead, 74, 140, 230, 231, 236–7, 257–8, 261, 271–2, 273; to prevent

removal of Ada from England, 128–9, 145, 150–1, 153, 154, 160, 180, 189, 199; B. defended, 161, 199; on B.'s debts, 246–7; **6**, 221; B. insists on his bill, 6; **7**, 198, 202; **9**, 73, 109, 165, 219; **10**, 27, 46, 47–8, 51, 60, 75, 78, 84–5, 86, 90, 91, 99, 110, 113, 125, 129, 155; **11**, 24, 28; B.'s opinion of **6**, 59–60, 63; goes to Venice, 74n; leaves B.'s books in London, 77, 82, 105; and customs officials, 77–8; money owing to, 78–9, 101, 102, 103, 113–14; B.'s suspicions of him, 87–8; statement of account of sale of Newstead, 222 and n; ambition to become a peer, 232; objects to Irish mortgage, **7**, 40, 44, 50, 64, 68, 69, 70, 71, 75, 82, 85, 94, 167; **8**, 61–2, 152 and n; scolded by B., 62, 63; B.'s dissatisfaction with, 72, 87, 89, 208; B.'s relationship with, 74–5, 87; Portsmouth estates, 208; softened by Sheridan, **9**, 32; and Rochdale tolls, 106, 108, 114; and Noel estate, 111, 112, 113, 177; his accounts to be audited, 188; and sale of stocks, **10**, 38; B. to communicate with only through Kinnaird, 96; Rochdale appeal, 99, 110; **11**, 25; and Rochdale sale, 49; and Mountnorris mortgage, 50; delayed trip to Rochdale, 159; to deal with B.'s creditors, 160–1; to bring Newstead to sale, 167; business agent, 176, 185; borrowed from B., 226

Hanson, Mrs. John, B.'s letter to, **1**, 107; mentioned, 40, 50, 60, 62, 82, 84, 85, 142, 143, 174, 175, 182, 184, 223, 225, 233, 236; **2**, 67, 68, 162, 201; **3**, 22, 39, 139, 158; always been a mother to B., **1**, 51n; **2**, 25; death, **4**, 87 and n, 118 and n

Hanson, Laura, **10**, 124n

Hanson, Mary Anne, marriage to Earl of Portsmouth, **1**, 51n; **3**, 248 and n, 249; **4**, 236–7; **10**, 119n, 124–5, 129

Hanson, Newton, unpublished memoir of B., **1**, 51n; sent to Eton, **2**, 162, 164; pupil of Hodgson, **4**, 175 and n, 180, 217 and n, 220, 291; saw B. in Venice, **6**, 74n, 78n, 87

Hanson and Birch, **1**, 128 and n, 205n; **2**, 3

Harcourt, General William (later Earl Harcourt), **1**, 46 and n; **9**, 25 and n

Harcourt, Mrs., **1**, 46, 47, 48

Hardstaff, Newstead tenant, **1**, 183 and n

Hardwicke, Elizabeth, Countess of (née Lindsay), **3**, 252 and n; **4**, 103 and n, 105

Hardwicke, Philip Yorke, 3rd Earl of, **3**, 252n; **4**, 103 and n

Hardy, Admiral Sir Thomas Masterman, **10**, 30n, 31

Hardy, Lady (née Louise Emily Berkeley), B.'s letters to, **10**, 30, 31, 49, 101, 173, 197; distantly related to B., *30 and n*, 31, 130n; met B. in London and Genoa, 30 and n, 31, 57; to Leghorn, 31–2, 51; and Webster, 49–50, 101, 102, 129, 130, 131, 174, 198; defended B., 173–4

Hare, Naylor, **2**, 87 and n

Harley, Lady Charlotte (later Lady Bacon), 'To Ianthe' in *Childe Harold*, **2**, 258n; **3**, 33n, 201n; portrait by Westall, 33 and n; B. considered as future wife, 36, 42 and n

Harley, Lady Jane, Hobhouse's romantic interest in, **2**, 258 and n; **3**, 6; **11**, 182 and n; resembles Miss Smith, **4**, 330n; **9**, 36

Harleian Miscellany, **2**, 249 and n, 258 and n, 286

Harlequin, **9**, 11

Harlequin's Misfortunes, **8**, 117 and n

Harlow, George Henry, portraits of B. and La Fornarina, **6**, 192 and n; drawing of B. with long hair, 259 and n

Harmer, Harry, 'the coppersmith', **3**, 94n

Harness, William, B.'s letters to, **1**, 154, 155, 163, 166, 193, 197; **2**, 137, 142, 148; **11**, 174, 176; sentimental attachment to B., **1**, *154n*; favourite of B. at Harrow, 154, 155–6; Speech Day recitation, 166 and n; correspondence with B., **2**, 136, 141; **8**, 228; **11**, 179; Newstead visit, **2**, 140, 142, 145, 148, 155; **11**, 179

Harrington, Barnaby, *Drunken Barnaby's Journal*, **3**, 95 and n

Harrington, Charles Stanhope, 4th Earl of, **4**, 118n

Harrington, Mr., **9**, 83

Harrington, Major-General, **11**, 71

Harris, Harry, **8**, 60 and n, 64, 66, 67, 68

Harris, Thomas, **4**, 326 and n

Harrogate, **1**, 77, 100n; **2**, 76, 84, 95, 127; **11**, 159

'Harroviensis', **9**, 142 and n, 145n, 151 and n, 152, 167

Harrow, **2**, 95, 126n, 133, 137, 145, 148, 155, 163, 215n; **3**, 190n, 210; **4**, 75, 144n, 274n, 293; **5**, 211, 277n; **7**, 229, 230, 253; **8**, 23, 25, 56n; **9**, 14, 27, 35n, 37, 42, 43, 49, 164n, 166, 170; **11**, 83; B. at **1**, 41–3, 49–60, 68–70, 274; B. in scrapes, 41–2, 49–50; Drury, headmaster, 41n, *42 and n*, 43, 49, 53–4, 56, 58, 59, 62, 63; B. reluctant to return, 43 and n; B. placed in higher form, 43; B. preparing to leave for, 46 and n, 48; speech days, 48, 63 and n, 69 and n, 119, 166 and n, 170n; **5**, 188n; B.'s quarrel with Butler, **1**, 64n, 111 and n, 133n, 145n, 146, 153; Butler headmaster, 64 and n, 69, 111; Cricket match with Eton, 71; **2**, 163; **9**, 12; B.'s debts, **1**, 88; Long's brother at, 119 and n; B.'s schoolfellows, 121n, 154 and n, 176 and n, 197n; view of in B.'s poems, 138; men at Cambridge, 139; B. to visit Drury at, 145, 152, 153, 164; B. proposed duel near, 150; lost its charm for B., 151; B.'s reconciliation with Butler, 155n; B. obsolete among Harrow men, 193; **11**, 177; B. dined with Drury, **1**, 196; Bland at, 246–7n; B. visited, **2**, 61; Sheridan at, **6**, 68; Wildman at, 81; B. and Clare at, **11**, 148

Harrow church, **9**, 146, 163; **10**, 54–5, 64, 65; **11**, 224

Harrow Club, **9**, 23

Harrowby, Dudley Ryder, 1st Earl of, **2**, 167 and n, 227 and n, 231; **4**, 267 and n; **7**, 62 and n

Harrowby, Earl and Countess of, **3**, 80

Harrowby, Lady, **4**, 19, 20

Hartington, Wiliam Spencer, Marquis of (*see also* Devonshire, Duke of), **1**, 55 and n, 125 and n, 139 and n

Harvard College, **10**, 131n

Harvey, Isabel, B.'s letter to, **10**, 175; asked for B.'s picture, 175 and n

Harvey, William, **10**, 125

Hastings, **2**, 162n; **4**, 137–8, 139, 142n, 143, 144, 156, 228, 259

Hastings, Francis Rawdon, Marquis of, **10**, *196 and n*, 197

Hastings, Frank Abney, and his armoured steamboat, **11**, 79 and n

Hastings, Warren, **3**, 219n; **4**, 253n; **9**, 13

Hastings House, **4**, 139, 143, 228

Hatagée, Turkish girl, **11**, 111 and n, 120–1, 124, 126, 127, 132, 215

Hatfield, **3**, 117

Hawke, Mr., marriage bet, **4**, 222 and n, 256–7, 260

Hawkesworth, John, *Voyages*, **6**, 212n

Hay, Capt. John, B.'s letters to, **4**, 256, 260; **9**, 102, 128, 135, 139, 140, 158; mentioned, **3**, 182; marriage bet, **4**, 222 and n, 223, 256 and n, 260; **9**, *102n*; and Masi affray, 128n, 135 and n, 139–40, 143, 151, 154; in leghorn, 135 and n

Haydn, Franz Joseph, **6**, 19; **10**, 189
Haydock Lodge, **4**, 165, 271–2
Haydon, Benjamin Robert, **6**, 83
Hayes, **5**, 97
Haygarth, William, **2**, 33 and n, 37
Haymarket Theatre, **2**, 143n, 149
Hayreddin, **3**, 213 and n
Hayward, Joshua Henslow, B.'s letter to, **10**, 131; mentioned, *131n*
Hazlitt, William, **5**, 112 and n; **6**, 83; *Conversations of James Northcote*, **5**, 64n; B.'s note in answer to, **6**, 100 and n; 'talks pimples', **8**, 38; *Table Talk*, **9**, 216 and n
Hazlitt, William Carew, *Memoirs of William Hazlitt*, **9**, 216n
Headford, Marquis and Marchioness, **1**, 132 and n
Heath, Charles, engraver, **7**, 165n
Heath, Rev. Robert, **2**, 82n; **3**, 45n
Heathcote, Lady (Katherine Sophia Manners), **3**, 36, 49, 50, 252, 254; **4**, 86n; **5**, 198, 204; Caroline incident, **3**, 71–2, 74, 84n, **4**, 86n, 330n
Heathcote, Sir Gilbert, **4**, 326, 330
Heber, Reginald, accuses B. of Manicheism, **7**, 132 and n; reviewer of *Sardanapalus*, **10**, *68 and n*
Heber, Richard, **3**, 170, 187, 202; **8**, 207 and n; to review Lord Brooke's book, **3**, 62 and n
Hebrew, **2**, 151; **7**, 138
Hebrews, Epistle to the, **7**, 144 and n
Hebrides, **4**, 151n; B.'s planned trip to, **1**, 73, 132 and n
Hecla, **1**, 132; **7**, 98
Hegira, **4**, 101
Heidelberg, Mrs., **4**, 259; **6**, 41
Helen of Troy, **7**, 31, 34
Hell, **8**, 78
Hellenic helmet (Byron's), **11**, 128n
Hellenica Chronica (Greek Chronicle), **11**, 132n, 139 and n, 218
Hellespont, **3**, 160; **4**, 325; B.'s swimming of, **1**, 215n, 237, 242, 243–4, 247; **2**, 30, 34, 200; **8**, 80–3, 162
Hell-Fire-Club, **1**, 161n; **9**, 186n
Helvetius, Claude Adrien, *Encyclopédie*, **8**, 42n
Hemans, Mrs. Felicia, B. speaks disparagingly of, **7**, 158 and n, 182, 183, 201; **8**, 236 and n; *Modern Greece, a Poem*, **5**, 262 and n, 263; *Restoration of the Works of Art in Italy*, 108 and n; *The Sceptic*, **7**, 113 and n
Henderson, John ('Bath Roscius'), **3**, 250 and n
Hengo, **6**, 26
Henley, John, 'Orator', ridiculed by Pope, **5**, 267 and n; compared to

'Orator' Hunt, **7**, 81; *Oratory Transactions*, **1**, 210 and n
Henry VI, **3**, 209n
Henry VIII, **3**, 38 and n; **4**, 80n; B. compared to, **9**, 11
Henry, Patrick, **9**, 174
Hentsch, Charles, B.'s letter to, **5**, 112; B.'s banker in Geneva, **5**, 93, 94, 107, 110, 112 and n, 113, 114, 118, 121, 124, 155, 163; **6**, 39; **8**, 157 and n, 158; **10**, 228
Hera, **8**, 189n
Heraclitus, **3**, 103; **4**, 208; **9**, 47
Herald, The, **3**, 25, 55; **4**, 51
Herbert, Baron, **1**, 224
Herbert, the Hon, William, *Helga, Hedin*, **7**, 114 and n
Hercules, **9**, 47
Hercules, brig, **10**, 194, 201, 203, 210n, 228; **11**, 15, 20n, 21, 27, 29, 39
Herefordshire, **2**, 84, 95, 230, 234, 250; **3**, 7n, 15, 29, 32, 34
Hermogenes, **11**, 232
Hero, priestess of Aphrodite, **1**, 237n
Herod, **1**, 6; **2**, 84
Herodes Atticus, **3**, 213 and n
Herodotus, **1**, 148; **8**, 189 and n; **9**, 153 and n; **10**, 116n
Herschel, Sir William, **9**, 46
Hertford, Marchioness of, **10**, 29n
Hertfordshire, **1**, 277 (second printing), **2**, 237
Hervey, Elizabeth, **11**, 230
Hervey, Lady Elizabeth (later Duchess of Devonshire), **3**, 174n; **5**, 270 and n
Hervey, John, Baron Hervey of Ickworth, **6**, 30, 31
Hervey, Mrs., novelist, **6**, 127 and n
Herzfeld, Ricki B., **8**, 52n, 71n; **9**, 58n, 107n, 215n; **10**, 21n, 107n 165n, 192n; **11**, 62n, 64n, 70n, 72n, 106n
Hesketh, Capt. Henry, **11**, 149, 150
Hetairia, **11**, 104n
Hexham, **2**, 215
'Hibernicus', submits a play to B., **4**, 323
Hicks Spring and Thorpe, **5**, 278
Highet, Gilbert, **1**, 207n
Highgate, **5**, 97; **7**, 232
Highgate Hill, **5**, 297
Hill, Capt., **11**, 47 and n
Hill, Dr., **2**, 36
Hill, Aaron, 'Progress of Wit', **8**, 11 and n
Hill, William Noel, British Minister, **9**, 175 and n, 184; **10**, 69, 108n, 126, 127, 128, 135, 137, 156–7, 174, 191n, 196, 197
Hinde, **11**, 179
Hippocrates, **10**, 56
Hiron, **7**, 234

101

Hoadly, Benjamin, *The Suspicious Husband*, **8**, 14 and n
Hoar, William, B.'s letter to, **4**, 293; agent to Sir R. Milbanke, 202 and n, 203, 206, 210, 212, 218, 224, 225, 226, 228, 230, 232, 233, 245, 293 and n, 300 and n, 317
Hoare, banker, **3**, 6, 21, 39, 139; **4**, 86, 108, 115, 117, 171, 260, 270, 293, 299, 337; **5**, 73–4, 78; **6**, 79, 101; **11**, 162
Hoare, 'Pug', **1**, 109 and n
Hobbes, Thomas, **8**, 244
Hobhouse, Sir Benjamin, M.P., **1**, 275; **2**, 252; **4**, 148n, 194; **6**, 75
Hobhouse, John Cam (later 1st Baron Broughton de Gyfford), B.'s letters to, **1**, 150, 158, 159, 160, 161, 164, 187; **2**, 5, 9, 11, 14, 21, 26, 27, 31, 39, 41, 43, 44, 48, 55, 59, 61, 64, 69, 83, 102, 113, 114, 117, 123, 124, 128, 129, 130, 135, 143, 147, 150, 151, 155, 161, 251; **3**, 6, 14; **4**, 96, 143, 170, 213, 253, 255, 259, 266, 270, 271, 272, 275 (2), 278, 283, 308; **5**, 24, 51, 60, 61, 71, 72, 75, 76, 78, 79, 80, 132, 142, 181, 197, 214, 216, 243; **6**, 8, 14, 16, 19, 20, 25, 31, 37, 39 (2), 40, 44, 49, 50, 51, 54, 56 (2), 63, 72, 76, 78, 79, 81, 88, 91, 93 (2), 95, 97, 106, 130, 138, 142, 145, 165, 187, 200, 211, 213, 225, 244; **7**, 49, 62, 70, 80, 99, 114, 121, 122, 153, 177, 180, 204, 216, 221; **8**, 83, 99, 121, 148, 224, 239; **9**, 67, 69, 81, 88, 123, 138, 201, 216; **10**, 55, 81, 121, 124, 142, 149, 151, 163, 168, 176, 179, 184, 188, 200, 203; **11**, 21, 26, 27, 39, 50, 60, 85, 149, 182; biog. sketch, **1**, 275–6; mentioned, 4, 11, 20, 104n, 121 and n, 241, 242, 274; **2**, 34, 152n, 167, 173, 262n, 263, 282, 287; **3**, 44, 57, 201; **4**, 61, 69, 73, 146, 164, 194; **5**, 52, 56, 60n, 70, 91, 136; **6**, 13, 24, 26, 31, 58, 61, 74, 75, 79, 80, 82, 86n, 90, 94, 100, 101, 133, 148, 192, 224, 227, 228, 232, 236, 242, 256; **7**, 46, 54, 60, 114, 120, 156, 165, 168, 181, 190, 238, 243; **8**, 22, 73, 81, 83, 91, 101, 128, 130, 132, 136, 145, 151, 153, 176, 185, 191, 197, 209, 233, 237, 250; **9**, 18, 19, 56, 112, 151, 152, 153, 194; **10**, 22, 26, 54 and n, 61, 63, 73, 90, 111, 126, 169, 170, 171, 189n; **11**, 116; character of B.'s letters to him **1**, 4, 24; his radical associates in Parliament, 16; Cambridge Whig Club, 139n, 159–60; **7**, 230–1; joint publication with B., **1**, 141 and n, 239 and n, 248; with B. at Brighton, 167n; Newstead theatricals, 170; dines at Annesley Hall, 173 and n; **11**, 176n; with B. at Newstead, **1**, 177, 179; lines on Bowles, 188 and n; **8**, 126 and n, 130, 134, 143, 239; in B.'s will, **1**, 202n; **2**, 72; on B.'s swimming feats, **1**, 215n; in Cintra, 218n; on Strané, 229–30n; scribbles, 235; returning to England, 239, 241, 245, 246, 249, 253, 254; **2**, 4, 8–9, 26; **5**, 91, 279, 295; **6**, 3, 6, 8; **11**, 157; as traveller, **1**, 240; **3**, 97; **7**, 221–2, 223–4; reviews of his poems, **1**, 248, 253; and Matthews, 277 (2nd printing); **7**, 138n, 225, 230, 231 and n, 232–3, 234; **8**, 24, **9**, 89; on *Pylades*, **2**, 7n; in England, 18, 19, 36, 39; and Lady Hester Stanhope, 21; his notes seized by the French, 36; specimens of Greek sculpture, 45 and n, 47 and n, 48, 56, 59, 60; projected society, 46; quarrels with his father, 46–7, 47n; indebtedness to B., 47n, 48, 161 and n; uncertain future, 32–3, 49, 54–5, 56; in Ireland with his regiment, 64 and n, 76, 80, 96, 108, 155; views on Elgin Marbles, 66 and n; affected by Matthews's death, 69, 70, 74, 77, 93; urged to write memorial to Matthews, 83; assisted by Demetrius, 102, 103, 113, 155; notes by B., 125 and n, 135; tale from Boccace, 127; and Lady Jane Harley, 258n; **11**, 182n; to get Lady Oxford's picture for B., **3**, 6; his travel plans, 28; his stepmother, 44; a cynic, 47; B.'s 'guide philosopher & friend', 51–2, continental tour, 51, 197 and n; left B. alone in Levant, 156, 168, 250; his debt to B., 212; returned from European tour, 243 and n; **4**, 67 and n; calls B. a *loup garou*, **3**, 246; began a poem, 248; to theatre with B., 249; B.'s regard for, **4**, 57, 171–2, 213, 226, 250; **11**, 169; B. recommended to Lady Holland, **4**, 57; on Phillips portrait of B., 79; B. to inscribe Napoleon Ode to, 94; to go to Paris with B., 96 and n; left for Paris without B., 98 and n, 100; with B., at masquerade, 135; on name of *Lara*, 143–4, 146, 154 and n; well reviewed, 163–4; B. wants to go to Italy with, 171–2, 191, 207; to accompany B. to Seaham, 238, 246, 247; and Hanson, 251, 253, 254, 257, 272, 273; and Jeffrey, 265, 266 and n, 269, 275, 276, 277, 278; reviews Leake's book, 266n, 269, 271 and n; gives Annabella De Ligne's autograph, 283 and n; and Napoleon's escape, 283 and n; his letters from

Paris, 287n, 294 and n, 298, 306; his brother killed, 302; and B.'s separation, **5**, 48, 51, 62n, 69, 92; dined with B. and Hunt, 61; relics brought from Paris, 65 and n; to join B. in Geneva, 71 and n; letter from B. carried by Mrs. Rawdon, 79, 226; carries letters and messages to Augusta, 91, 94, 95; B. conceals feelings from, 94; on Alpine journey with B., **1**, 25; **5**, 96–104, 106, 107, 109, 205; and B.'s boat accident, 108, 110; in Italy with B., 115, 121, 123, 134; and Polidori, 122, 127, 295; in Rome, 137–8, 140, 141, 158, 168, 173, 174, 181–2, 224, 225; **11**, 163, 165; mishap on road to Rome, **5**, 142; quarrel with *Quarterly*, 169 and n, 172, 176, 201, 208; to Naples, 227, 229, 230; **11**, 166; and B.'s bust, **5**, 235, 243 and n; at La Mira, 254–66, 256, 268, 274; notes for *Childe Harold* IV, 263 and n, 265, 269 and n, 272; **6**, 7, 8n, 14 and n, 19, 20, 75 and n; on Countess Albrizzi, **5**, 293; carried MS of Canto IV of *Childe Harold* to England, **6**, 3, 8, 9; to correct B.'s proof, 15, 215; and Sotheby's letter, 24, 33, 35; his wig, 26; **8**, 96; stands for Parliament, **6**, 26, 34, 39, 49, 52, 88–9, 92, 93 and n, 106–7, 109, 211; **11**, 168n; and Di Breme, **6**, 51, 63, 90 and n, 91, 93, 96; and Foscolo, 51 and n; B. affected by his neglect, 54; *Childe Harold* IV dedicated to, 69 and n, 75n; as orator, 76; **11**, 170; B. on his talents, **6**, 88–9; **7**, 78, 111, 222; on indelicacy of *Don Juan*, **6**, 103, 125, 137, 138; has separation documents, 127; challenged to a duel, 165 and n, 168, 187, 211–12; in Newgate, 187n; **7**, 16 and n, 25, 57, 59n, 102, 191n, 223; **9**, 88n; **11**, 59n; against publication of *Don Juan*, **6**, 206; **11**, 171 and n; genteel reformer, **6**, 233, 247; **8**, 240; his radical pamphlet, **7**, 15–16 and n, 49; election to Westminster seat, 16n, 44, 49, 70 and n, 75, 78, 85, 154; and B.'s bust, 44; **9**, 21, 55, 63, 67, 69–70, 71, 88, 122 and n; and reformers, **7**, 44–5, 49; and the Radicals, 49, 63, 80–1, 99, 223, 252; released from Newgate, 49 and n, 70 and n; B.'s lampoon on, 59 and n, 62, 73, 75, 78, 102; offended at B.'s lampoon, 59n, 99, 104, 224; to check B.'s Italian proofs, 83; and 'Orator' Hunt, 86, 99; opposed to B.'s reply to *Blackwood's*, 201; his age, 212; accuses B. of indolence,

221–2, 223; B. on, 223–4, 252 at; Cambridge with B., 230–1; and the Queen, 243 and n; wants no life of B., **8**, 11n; epigrams on Long, 24; to correct B.'s Italian, 76–7; witness of B.'s swimming, 81, 83; to entertain Curioni and Taruscelli, 84–5; to check B.'s *Hints*, 88; defender of Queen Caroline, 100n, 148n; acting of *Marino Faliero*, 120 and n; attacks Parliament, 120n, 121n; and Canning, 120 and n, 121, 149; **9**, 101, 138; B. to omit stanza on Queen, **8**, 147, 148 and n, 194; to read *Don Juan* proofs, 192, 194; B.'s letters in his care, 216, 226; preface to *Rimini*, 218; B.'s alter ego, 220; B.'s letters to offered to Murray, 228; parody on Savage, 239; and *a* Mr. Tulk, **9**, 25; his prologue, 36; stabbed Scrope Davies, 39; calls eagles vultures, 41; on *Cain*, 67, 70, 101 and n, 103, 124; scurrilous letter to B., 67, 70, 72, 74, 82, 101 and n; on sale of B.'s Memoirs, 70, 72, 74, 88 and n; B.'s ballad to, 88n, 101 and n; insurance on Lady Byron's life, 158, 166; B. declined seeing his friend, 177; saw B. at Pisa, 209, 210, 211; **10**, 14; on Portsmouth trial, 124n, 127; and Greek affairs, 143, 144, 147, 150, 170, 171, 172, 179, 184, 186, 196, 202, 229; **11**, 45, 50, 53, 57, 72, 73, 80, 146; power of attorney for B., **10**, 154, 168, 196; quoted B. to his electors, 196; B. sought his advice on mortgage, **11**, 50; and Greek Deputies, 60; pamphlet attacking Erskine, 59n; with Londos in 1809, 104n; a 'Sow's Ear', 157; in storm at sea, 158; gone to Ireland, 159; with B. and Davies at Cocoa Tree, 162; and the *Quarterly*, 163, 165; diminutive size, 165 and n; compared to Gulliver, 168; B. cannot help his electioneering, 168–9; and B.'s business, 170; travelling plans with B., 182; his knowledge of the East, 183; Moore on, 197; *Francesca*, **6**, 41 and n, 56; *Historical Illustrations of the Fourth Canto of Childe Harold*, **5**, 263 and n, 269 and n; **6**, 14n, 51n, 54, 72, 90n; **7**, 182; **11**, 170 and n; *Imitations and Translations* (Miscellany), **1**, 141n, 208, 210, 239n, 241, 251, 255; **2**, 11, 16, 19, 22, 26 and n, 29, 32, 42, 43, 44, 45, 49, 50, 53, 55, 59; **3**, 213 and n; **7**, 232; **11**, 158, 176n; B.'s poems in 'Miscellany', **2**, 26n, 75; *Journey through Albania*, **1**, 276; **2**, 26, 61, 81, 101, 103, 104 and n, 106,

Hobhouse, John Cam—*continued*
109, 111, 113n, 131, 132, 134, 135,
136, 141, 155 and n; **3**, 41 and n, 51,
and n, 60, 61, 201n; **4**, 32, 33 and n;
5, 37; **11**, 179, 182n; *Letters by an
Englishman Resident at Paris . . .*, **5**,
77 and n, 215 and n; criticised by
Croker, 169 and n; **11**, 163n; 'Weeks
at Bath', **2**, 65 and n, 81
Hobhouse diary, **2**, 4n
Hoby, Mr., bootmaker, **7**, 159, 171; **9**,
124
Hoche, General, **5**, 77
Hockthorn, **5**, 100
Hodges, John M. **11**, 111 and n, 119,
128 and n, 132n 139
Hodgskin, Thomas, **11**, 218
Hodgson, Miss, B.'s letter to, **2**, 122;
mentioned, 122 and n
Hodgson, Francis, B.'s letters to, **1**,
173, 176, 178, 182, 196, 198, 210,
211, 215, 216, 240, 253; **2**, 18, 26,
36, 54, 77, 88, 95, 97, 105, 109, 111,
127, 129, 132, 136, 139, 145, 159,
160, 163, 164, 167; **3**, 6, 57, 59, 130,
150, 187; **4**, 74, 137, 139, 142, 213,
216, 291; **7**, 252; **8**, 114; **11**, 175,
178; biog. sketch, **1**, 276; mentioned,
88n, 178n, 239, 247, 274; **2**, 29, 58,
59, 61, 84, 103, 114, 131, 142, 143,
151, 156, 157, 167n; **3**, 7 and n, 50n,
59; **4**, 223, 301n; **5**, 141, 149, 177;
6, 33; **8**, 116, 234; **11**, 176n; argues
with B. on religion, **1**, 14–15; **2**,
88–9, 97–8, 136; marriage, **1**, 144n;
his father a friend of Gifford, 174n;
loans from B., 196 and n, 198; **2**, 27n;
3, 130n, 187n, 210n, 228 and n; **4**,
213 and n, 259; on reviews of
Hobhouse, **1**, 248; his father's death,
2, 27 and n; capable Latinist, 83; his
'Alterative', 86, 87n; his songs, 97;
to be ordained, 113; retains Moore's
challenge to B., 118n, 120–1, 129
and n; addiction to wine, 124, 129,
141, 145–6; **11**, 179; annoyed by
Webster, **2**, 124; dined with Moore,
Rogers, and B., 127, 128, 129;
enamoured of a strumpet, 130, 148,
149, 150; to correct B.'s Greek, 136;
asked to review Galt's *Voyages*, 164
and n; at Newstead, 136, 145, 148,
155; and *Monthly Review*, **3**, 57 and
n, 59; and *The Gaiour*, 100, 168;
engagement, 187n, 202n, 206; **4**,
213n, 214, 233; recommended to Dr.
Butler, **3**, 150 and n; likes *Bride of
Abydos*, 166, 168, 208; reviewed
Safie, **4**, 74 and n; at Hastings, 137–8,
139, 144, 148, 151, 214; to tutor
Newton Hanson, 175, 180, 220, 291;

possible chaplain to Lord Portsmouth,
216–17, 220; note to Annabella, 234,
235 and n; appointed to Bakewell, **5**,
131 and n, 235; wants news of B., **7**,
252; takes up Pope, **8**, 88, 112n;
indebtedness to B., 156; B.'s letters
to offered to Murray, 228; astonish-
ing memory, **9**, 12; to visit B. at
Newstead, **11**, 179, 180; diuretic
letter, 166; *Charlemagne*, translation,
2, 197n; **3**, 97 and n, 130n, 150 and
n; *Childe Harold's Monitor*, **8**, 112
and n, 114 and n; *The Friends*, **6**, 134;
7, 253; *Lady Jane Grey*, **1**, 178n; **2**,
87 and n, 95 and n; *Memoir*, **1**, 184n;
7, 252n; *Saeculo-Mastix*, **8**, 112 and
n; *Sir Edgar*, **1**, 246n; **2**, 20 and n,
55, 145 and n; *Translation of Juvenal*,
1, 191n; **2**, 95 and n, 101n, 104; **3**,
150
Hogg, James, B.'s letters to, **4**, 84; **5**,
13, 37; mentioned, **4**, 11, 84 and n,
154; **8**, 219; B. recommends him to
Murray, **4**, 151, 152, 162, 164, 167;
asks B. for a poem, **5**, 37 and n; *Pil-
grims of the Sun*, 38 and n; 'The Poetic
Mirror', **4**, 84 and n, 151n, 164n, 268;
5, 37n; *Winter Evening Tales*, **7**, 200
and n
Hohen, Princess Biron, Duchess of, **4**,
128 and n
Hohenhausen, Baroness of, **6**, 180
Hohenzollern, Prince of, **6**, 178;
Holbach, Paul Heinrich Dietrich
Baron d', and Rousseau, **11**, 228;
Histoire critique de Jésus-Christ, **3**,
185n
Holcroft, Thomas, *Memoirs*, **5**, 112 and
n; *The Road to Ruin*, 140n; 'Tale of
Mystery', 140, 143
Holderness, Mary Doublet, Countess
of, **1**, 273; **8**, 229; **9**, 77; Augusta's
grandmother, **1**, 46n, 52n, 60n
Holford, Margaret, *Margaret of Anjou*,
5, 112 and n, 185 and n, 187, 193,
194, 199; **6**, 27n; *Warbeck of Wolfen-
stein*, **7**, 200 and n
Holland, **2**, 109n, 112 and n; **3**, 232,
235, 237; **4**, 54; **8**, 36, 44 and n; **11**,
85, 107; expulsion of French, **3**,
171–2, 180 and n, 211, 212 and n,
218; B.'s planned trip, 176 and n,
180, 184, 187, 212–13, 218, 223,
231, 234, 235
Holland, Lady (née Elizabeth Vassall),
B.'s letters to, **4**, 57, 338; **5**, 53;
mentioned, **2**, 180, 204, 205, 206, 220,
223, 226, 230, 251; **3**, 35, 37, 131,
147, 168, 206, 215; **4**, 57, 61, 64–5,
73, 320; **5**, 87, 206; **8**, 164 and n;
10, 122, 174; **11**, 59; taunted

Caroline Lamb, **2**, 253; not pleased with B.'s liaison with Lady Oxford, 265; divorced Sir Godfrey Webster, 281; ill-natured, **3**, 90, 128; *Journal,* 97n; B. gets on well with, 171, 231; liked *Bride of Abydos,* 175, 208; B. sent *Bride* to, 176, 189; her fire screen, 226

Holland, Henry Fox, 3rd Baron, B.'s letters to, **2**, 165, 168, 180, 191, 203, 204, 205, 206 (2), 207, 209, 212, 213, 219 (2), 220 , 221, 223 (2), 224 (2), 225; **3**, 30, 34, 155, 166, 167, 189, 193; **4**, 59, **5**, 30, 39, 40; **10**, 122; **11**, 59; biog. sketch, **2**, 281; mentioned, **1**, 157 and n; **2**, 195, 215; **3**, 223, 225, 230, 231, 236, 238; **4**, 14, 18, 61, 64–5, 73, 144n, 320 and n, 321; **5**, 241, 269; **6**, 25, 39, 60; **7**, 201 and n; **8**, 66; **9**, 13, 14, 26; **10**, 122, 131n, 135; B. deferred to **11**, 16; overture to B., **2**, 128; and Nottingham weavers, 161n, 165–6; and B.'s maiden speech, 167 and n; presented with *Childe Harold,* 168; attacked in *English Bards,* 168n; leader of Whig opposition, 180n; asks B. to write Drury Lane Address, 191 and n, 193, 197, 204n, 211n, 212; at Bowood, 223 and n; likes *Giaour,* **3**, 34; wants to meet Hodgson, 130; B. sent Sligo's letter to, 155–6, 155n; *Bride of Abydos,* 163 and n, 166, 170, 175, 208; Baldwin's petition, 165n, 193 and n; Junius, 215; B. likes his society, 226; on Sheridan's sentimentality, 239; and B.'s separation, **5**, 30 and n, 31, 39–40, 53, 56; and Greek Deputies, **11**, 59; *Life and Writings of Lope Felix de Vega Carpio,* **5**, 206 and n; **8**, 14

Holland, Lord and Lady, **6**, 18

Holland, Dr. (afterwards Sir) Henry, **2**, 124n; **3**, 111; **4**, 299; *Travels in the Ionian Islands,* **3**, 110 and n; **5**, *241 and n*

Holland Chapel, **9**, 100n

Holland House, **1**, 19; **2**, 211; **3**, 122, 127, 130, 208, 211, 239n, 245, 272; **4**, 133; **9**, 20

Holmes, James, B.'s letter to, **10**, 176; mentioned, **7**, 62; portrait of B., **3**, 170, 224 and n; miniatures of B., **5**, 190 and n, 212, 242; **6**, 26; miniature of Augusta, 223; B. wants Holmes to come to Italy, **8**, 95 and n, 135, 136, 139, 181; B. thought his portrait the best, **10**, 175, 176

Holstein, **6**, 180; **9**, 24;

Holton, Mrs. **11**, 222

Holy Alliance, **7**, 188; **11**, 58

Holyhead, **2**, 247

Holy Roman Empire, **2**, 144n

Home, John, **3**, *109 and n*; *Douglas,* 109n; **8**, 143 and n

Homer, **1**, 109; **2**, 182; **4**, 85, 256; **7**, 31; **8**, 11, 22; **9**, 77; **10**, 63 and n; **11**, 30, *Iliad,* **3**, 239; **4**, 153 and n, 325 and n; translations, **8**, 25n, 93, 148n

Homer Travestie, **8**, 22 and n

Homosexuality, **10**, 98n; Lord Grey, **1**, 45n, 46, 54, 55, 168 and n; Edleston, 88n, 122–7, 257n; **2**, 110 and n, 114, 116 and n, 117; **8**, 24 and n; Beckford, **1**, 210 and n; boy-love, 207n, 232; **2**, 29 and n; Eustathius, 6; Veli Pasha, 10; Sgricci, **7**, 51–2; Lukas, **11**, 213–14

Hone, William, *Don Juan Canto the third* (piracy of B.), **6**, 236 and n, 237

Hood, Jane, **4**, 68n

Hood, Thomas, **4**, 68n

Hookham, Edward, **2**, 16n

Hookham, Thomas, jr., **2**, 16 and n, 45

Hookham, T. and E. T., printers, **4**, 74n

Hope, Thomas, **4**, 110 and n; **5**, 116 and n, 117, 210, 215, 241; **11**, 164; *Anastasius,* **3**, 27n; **4**, 110n; *Anastasius* admired by B., **7**, 138 and n, 182

Hope, Mrs. Thomas, **3**, 27 and n; **4**, 110 and n, 111, 116; **9**, 29

Hopkinson of Southwell, **6**, 222

Hoppner, John, R. A., **5**, 294

Hoppner, Richard Belgrave, B.'s letters to, **5**, 264, 274, 275, 279; **6**, 15, 84, 143, 146, 163, 164, 174, 229, 230, 233, 236, 254, 262; **7**, 24, 27, 65, 78, 79, 103, 106, 118, 135, 174, 191, 203, 214; **8**, 70, 75, 97 (2), 112, 118, 123, 124, 130, 157, 226; **10**, 76, 82, 112, 128; **11**, 191 (2), 194 (2); biog. sketch, **5**, 294–5; mentioned, **6**, 26, 35, 75, 142, 150, 151, 162, 174n, 177, 204, 238, 240; **7**, 125, 226; **8**, 81, 139, 142, 145; **9**, 55, 150; **11**, 194n; and B.'s liaison with Teresa, **1**, 8; **6**, 178n, 179–80, 190–1 229, 230; sublets Villa d'Este to B., **5**, 264n, 269, 274 and n; **6**, 16; B. on his elegy, **5**, 279; B. sought his help, 275; kept Allegra for B., **6**, 39n, 175n; swimming with B., 51, 237, 278–9; asked to provide vice-consulship, 164; birth of his son, 13, 16, 19; **11**, 191 and n; asked to arbitrate, **6**, 229, 230, 233–4, 237; to disburse B.'s debts, 254–5; translates Goethe review, **7**, 106, 113, 119; furnishes evidence for the Queen, 180, 204–5, 222; and Shelley and

Hoppner, Richard—*continued*
Claire, **7**, 191 and n; **8**, 97 and n; to sell articles for B., **10**, 76, 82–3, 112, 122 and n
Hoppner, Mrs. R. B., **6**, 144, 150, 164, 165, 175, 230, 234, 238, 262; **7**, 25, 28, 78, 80, 104, 119, 136, 203; **8**, 70, 75, 98, 113, 118, 158; **10**, 76, 77, 83, 112; **11**, 195; birth of son, **6**, 9, 13, 15, 19; **11**, 191; B.'s opinion of, **6**, 254
Hoppner, Rizzo, **11**, 191
Horace, **2**, 11, 13 and n; **5**, 265; **6**, 102 and n, 139; imitation of *Ars Poetica*, **2**, 42 and n, 43 and n, 45, 49, 53, 59, 80, 81, 90, 103, 112; **4**, 77 and n, 78, 320 and n; **6**, 46 and n, 96 and n; **7** 179 and n; **8**, 59 and n; **9**, 122 and n; **11**, 220, 225, 226; *Carmina*, **2**, 96 and n; **8**, 31 and n; *Epistles*, **4**, 263 and n, 301 and n; **9**, 114 and n, 166 and n; *Epistulae*, **1**, 145 and n; **6**, 118n; *Epist. ad Pison.*, **11**, 171n; *Odes*, **2**, 14 and n, 47 and n; **7**, 123n, 144 and n, 153; **9**, 39 and n; **10**, 29n; *Odes and Epodes*, **3**, 101n, 215 and n, 218 and n, 236 and n, 244 and n; *Satires*, **9**, 29 and n; **11**, 232
Horn, Mrs., in *Nourjahad*, **3**, 226 and n
Horner, Francis, **3**, 225–6, *226n*; **11**, 164; mentioned, **5**, 192 and n; death, 210, 215, 241
Hornby, Capt. of *Volage* frigate, **2**, 50, 55
Hornsey, **5**, 186 and n, 200n, 211 and n
Horse Guards, **7**, 16n
Horsham, **9**, 234–5
Horsley, **1**, 184n; **11**, 155
Horsley, Master, **2**, 142
Horton, Anne (later Wilmot), **5**, 47n
Horton, Wilmot (?), **5**, 224 and n
Hoste, Commodore, **8**, 54n
Hottentot, **10**, 11
Hounslow, **5**, 51; **6**, 75; **10**, 202
Houson, Anne, **1**, 94 and n, 104 and n, 126 and n
Howard, money-lender, **2**, 60, 154, 255 and n; **4**, 24; **10**, 146, 147
Howard, Lady Caroline Isabella (Lady Cawdor), **1**, 52 and n; **4**, 191n
Howard, Lady Elizabeth (Duchess of Rutland), **1**, 52 and n
Howard, the Hon. Frederick, **1**, 61 and n; **2**, 75 and n; death at Waterloo, **4**, 302 and n; **5**, 70 and n, 71
Howard, Lady Georgiana, **4**, 128 and n
Howard, Lady Gertrude, **3**, 68 and n; **4**, 127n; friendship with Augusta, **1**, 52 and n, 55, 61 and n, 66–7, 68, 69
Hudson, **3**, 83
Humboldt, Baron Friedrich Heinrich, von, **6**, 243

Hume, David, **4**, 161; **6**, 30, 59; **8**, 58; **9**, 100, 103, 116; on miracles, **2**, 97; *History of England*, **8**, 75 and n; *Philosophical Essays*, '*Essay on Miracles*', **1**, 14, 15
Hume, Joseph, **11**, 108 and n
Humphreys, William H., **11**, 138 and n
Hungarians, **7**, 132
Hungary, **2**, 199; **5**, 235
Hunt, stage boxer, **2**, 214 and n
Hunt, Henry, 'Orator', **6**, 187n, 211 and n, 229; **7**, 44, 50, 99; **8**, 240n; **10**, *57 and n*; 'Manchester Massacre', **7**, 63 and n, 80–1, 82, 86
Hunt, Henry, B.'s letter to, **10**, 24; mentioned, 24 and n, 32, 62, 66, 72
Hunt, James Henry Leigh, B.'s letters to, **3**, 188, 203; **4**, 49, 294, 295, 306, 316, 318, 319, 324, 332; **5**, 15, 18, 50, 58; **9**, 208; 216; **10**, 21, 25, 32, 39, 81, 83, 88, 89, 205; biog. sketch, **2**, 281–2; mentioned, **3**, 79, 188–9, 203n; **4**, 49 and n; **5**, 79, 81, 196; **8**, 173; **10**, 22, 24, 108, 116, 117, 121; wrote 'upon system', **1**, 10; **6**, 46 and n; his children like Yahoos, **1**, 10; **10**, 11, 32; 'a clever man', **2**, 233; imprisonment, **3**, 49n; **4**, 210 and n; B. on, **3**, 228; released from prison, **4**, 294 and n; B. sent theatre tickets, 294; **5**, 50; saw Hobhouse's Paris letters, **4**, 294 and n, 306; praises Wordsworth, 317n, 324; and *The Examiner*, 332n; **5**, 15n, 16, 19n, 58n; relations with Murray, 13, 19, 208 and n; complimented B. in *Examiner*, 19 and n; dedicatory letter to B., 32 and n; dined with B., 61; row with the *Quarterly*, 201, 211, 234; and Mary Shelley, 296; B. visits him in jail, **3**, 49 and n; **7**, 184n; stood by B. in separation, **9**, 86; invited to Italy by Shelley and B., 95n, 110 and n, 161 and n, 179n, 183, 185; B. warned of collaboration with, 110n; B.'s financial assistance, 113–14, 208, 218; **10**, 13, 60, 66, 105, 114, 138; on B.'s new signature (N.B.), **9**, 171n; at Casa Lanfranchi, 179n, 182; at cremation of Shelley, 192 and n; quarrels with B., 202n; with Mary Shelley in Genoa, 205n; and Hazlitt, 216n; left adrift by Shelley's death, **10**, 13; B.'s comments to Murray on, 25 and n, 36, 57, 68–9; B.'s delicacy in dealing with, 34; B. will not abandon, 36, 68–9; not living with B., 52, 55, 77;; B. on his character, 69, 105, 138; *Autobiography*, **5**, 182n; *Correspondence*, **10**, 25n; *Descent of Liberty*, **4**, 167 and n, 295

and n; 'The Dogs', **10**, 39 and n, 133n; *Feast of the Poets*, **4**, 49n, 50, 295 and n, 317 and n, 324 and n; *Foliage*, **6**, 46 and n, 47 and n; reviewed in the *Quarterly*, 83 and n; *The Liberal*, **9**, 95n, 182, 183, 197, 234; **10**, 66; *Lord Byron and Some of His Contemporaries*, **9**, 171n; 'Ode for the Spring of 1814', **4**, 98; *The Story of Rimini*, **1**, 10; **2**, 281; **4**, 295 and n, 317 and n, 319 and n, 320,326, 330 and n, 331n; **5**, 18–19, 19n, 35, 58–9, 208 and n, 211, 214, 234; **6**, 46, 122 and n, 181, 189

Hunt, Mrs. James Henry Leigh, **10**, 37n

Hunt, John, B.'s letters to, **9**, 216; **10**, 23, 47, 79, 117, 120, 122, 133, 145, 150, 158, 160, 166, 181, 201, 206, 212; biog. sketch, **9**, 234; mentioned, **10**, 65, 87, 118, 134, 178; B.'s publisher after Murray, **2**, 281, 286; **10**, 90n, 200; prosecuted for publishing *Vision*, **8**, 181n; **10**, 39n, 47 and n, 57, 67n, 68; publisher of *Don Juan*, **8**, 225n; **9**, 183n; **11**, 24, 75, 110 and n; and the *Vision of Judgment*, **9**, 179, 181–2; **10**, 13 and n, 16, 21, 66n; confrontation with Murray, **9**, 213; *The Examiner*, 234; and *The Liberal*, **10**, 18n, 72–3, 80, 110, 115, 116, 117, 120, 121, 123; B.'s praise of, 13, 105, 138; annoyed B. with advertisement, 13 and n, 32; and Murray, 13, 16, 17, 18, 21, 22, 26, 28, 33, 36, 41, 116; possible future publisher of B., 23 and n, 42, 58–59, 62, 66, 69, 72–3, 80; to deal with Kinnaird, 23 and n, 24, 27, 33, 145; B. to provide legal defence, 53, 66, 72, 73, 76, 79–80, 98, 162; **11**, 49, 136; can't buy copyright, **10**, 53, 70; not advisable to publish with, 58, 59; published *Age of Bronze*, 81, 150 and n, 151, 154; B.'s financial assistance, 97–8; and pirates, 98, 104, 150; to correct *Don Juan* through press, 158; to publish B. for 15% of profit, 182, 201; his accounts, **11**, 117; convicted of libel, 135–6

Hunter, **9**, 42

Hunter, Capt., **2**, 126

Huntingdon, Lord, **7**, 196 and n, 200 and n

Huntingdon Castle, **7**, 200 and n

Huntly, George Gordon, 8th Marquess of, **3**, 253

Huntly, George Gordon, 2nd Earl of, **1**, 273; **2**, 68 and n; **7**, 212

Hurtsbourne, **4**, 170 and n, 175, 189, 194, 216–17

Hurt, Rev. —, 'sports' on Newstead Manor, **4**, 311

Hussein Bey, **1**, 231 and n

Hutton, William, *The Battle of Bosworth Field*, **1**, 131 and n

Hyacinth, L'Abbé, **2**, 14

Hyacinth and Apollo, **1**, 207 and n; **2**, 124 and n

Hyde Park, **6**, 186

Hyde Park Corner, **5**, 179

Hydra, **4**, 46

Hydra (Idra), (island), **10**, 169, 173; **11**, 22n, 30, 38, 43, 72n, 126n, 215

Hymettus, **1**, 3; **2**, 37, 137

Hyperion frigate, **1**, 216

Hypsilantes (Ipsilanti), Prince Alexander, **6**, 4n; **11**, 39n

Iambelli, **6**, 231

Ibrahim Pasha, **1**, 226; **2**, 21, 22, 114, 125; **11**, 216

I Cappucini (Villa d'Este), **5**, 264n, 274 and n

Iceland, **7**, 98

Ida, Mount, **4**, 325

Iden, Alexander, **7**, 81 and n

Ignatius, Metropolitan of Arta, **11**, 23n

Ilfracombe, Devon, **4**, 222n

Illyric, **2**, 123

Illusion, or the Trances of Nourjahad, Drury Lane performance, **3**, 175 and n, 224n, 226 and n

Illissus, **1**, 238

Illyria, **1**, 235, 237, 238

Illyricum, **1**, 226

Immortality, **2**, 88–9; **9**, 45–6

Imola, **8**, 249; **9**, 49, 53, 167n

Imola, Count and Countess of, **8**, 184 and n

Incest, **1**, 273; **3**, 87 and n, 96 and n, 102 and n, 102 and n, 196 and n, 199; **5**, 13n, 68 and n; **7**, 174 and n

Inchbald, Mrs. Elizabeth (née Simpson), **3**, 236 and n; **6**, 11; *A Child of Nature*, **4**, 118 and n; *Lover's Vows*, 311n; *Nature and Art*, **3**, 236 and n; *A Simple Story*, 236 and n

Inchbald, Joseph, **3**, 236n

Inchiquen the Jesuit's Letters during a Late Residence in the United States, **4**, 93 and n

Incledon, Charles, opera singer, **5**, *182 and n*; **8**, 97

India, **1**, 172 and n; **3**, 104, 232n; **4**, 45, 147n; **5**, 81, 171n, 235; **6**, 18; **8**, 27; **9**, 235, 237; **10**, 63, 197; **11**, 20n, 218

Indians, **3**, 249n

Ingilby, Sir William, **2**, 131 and n, 148

Ingram, I., B.'s letters to, **10**, 83, 122; mentioned, **6**, 81; **10**, 76, 82, 130

Ingram, Mrs., **10**, 82

Ingram family, **8**, 113 and n

Innes, Catherine (later Gordon), **1**, 274

Insom, Christoforo, banker, **6**, 200 and n, **205**, 210, 213

Interlachen, **5**, 100, 103

Ionia, **1**, 242; **2**, 164

Ionian Islands, **1**, 226n; **2**, 5n, 111n; **10**, 143n; **11**, 20n, 30, 34n, 63, 89n, 90, 100n, 142, 214

Ionian merchants, **11**, 65 and n

Ionian Sea, **1**, 246n

Ionian University, **2**, 5n; **3**, 199n; **5**, 199n

Ionian vessel, **11**, 129; captured by Greeks, 100 and n, 102

Ipsara, **11**, 30

Ipsilanti, Prince Alexander, *see* Hypsilantes

Ipswich, Lord, **1**, 71 and n, 75; **7**, 229

Ireland, **2**, 217; **3**, 128n, 194n, 232n; **4**, 12, 18n, 32, 45, 144n, 165, 260, 274n, 297, 323; **6**, 205; **7**, 98; **8**, 100, 189, 251; **9**, 13, 34, 63, 183, 197; **10**, 105, 138; **11**, 46, 66; Hobhouse in, **2**, 64n, 76, 132, 155; **11**, 159; Caroline Lamb in, **2**, 192n, 194, 200, 216, 217, 222, 237, 239, 244, 245, 255; reception of George IV, **8**, 213n

Ireland, William Henry, B. reviewed *Neglected Genius*, **2**, 156n; **3**, 7n; **9**, 42n

Irish Committee, **9**, 183 and n, 193, 196-7

Irish mortgage, **6**, 252 and n, 256, 260; **7**, 15, 64, 68, 69, 71, 75, 82, 85, 94, 101, 106, 115, 116, 119, 122, 123, 136, 145, 169, 190, 210, 214; **8**, 34, 61-2, 117

Irish parliament, **9**, 13 and n

Irving, Washington, **8**, 219; admired by B., 146; admires *Don Juan*, **9**, 55; *Bracebridge Hall*, **10**, 83; *A History of New York*, **8**, 53 and n, 173 and n; *The Sketch Book*, **7**, 200 and n; **8**, 53 and n, 145

Isadas, **5**, 238n

Ishmael, **3**, 119, 213; **5**, 116

Ismael, battle of, **11**, 111n

Isaiah, **7**, 57

Isle of Man, **2**, 55

Isle of Wight, **11**, 46

Isola Bella, **5**, 125

Israel, Ten tribes of, **11**, 58

Italian courage, **7**, 169

Italian girls, **11**, 44

Italian journals, **9**, 11

Italian language, **2**, 59, 135, 178, 208; **3**, 240; **5**, 115, 116, 166, 235; **6**, 3, 8 and n, 32-3, 35, 42; **7**, 83, 180, 252; **8**, 14, 25, 35, 77; **10**, 18-19, 93n, 168, 170, 211; **11**, 31n, 50, 68n, 132n,

215; B. intended to write his best work in, **6**, 105; B.'s letters in, 111n; the word *love* most beautiful in, 215; B.'s fluency in, **8**, 91, 210, 228; B. writes in to English and Greeks, **11**, 137

Italian literature, **5**, 207, 255; **6**, 18n, 51n; **11**, 170n

Italian poetry, **7**, 42

Italian tragedy, **8**, 240-1

Italian uprising, failure of, **8**, 49, 50, 91, 102, 104, 116

Italians, **7**, 126, 194; return to operas and maccaroni, **1**, 17; **8**, 105; B. met in Greece, **2**, 9, 35, 37; agreeable, **5**, 117; B. did not write for, **6**, 15; complain of English neglect, 38, 59; speak ill of each other, 230; detest the English, **7**, 184; lacking in unity, 239; **8**, 102, 211; worse than English, **10**, 107; in Greek service, **11**, 150

Italy, **2**, 28n, 285, 287; **3**, 176, 217; **4**, 88n, 93, 101, 161, 171, 172, 178, 191, 269; **5**, 53, 76; **6**, 15, 86; **8**, 78, 158, 176; **10**, 180; B.'s letters from, **1**, 9; the English in, **5**, 124, 132, 146, 187, 194, 210, 227, 229; beauty of, 202; B.'s reaction to, **6**, 216, 232; B. knows manners of, **7**, 42-3, 83, 126, 138, 165, 170-1, 180; **8**, 189; trouble brewing in, 45, 76, 77, 82, 84-5, 98, 137, 138, 154, 158, 169, 172, 207, 221; failure of uprising, 190, 235, 237; disturbed state, 208, 210, 212, 213, 217; war imminent, **7***, 236, 245, 249, 255, 256; **8***, 27, 43, 46, 48-9, 84, 87, 89, 95; revolutionary unrest in, 13, 15, 17, 19; society in, 113; B.'s knowledge of, 189; travel books, 219, 220; B. expects to return to, **11**, 21, 56-7; B. thought of purchasing land in, 49; servile condition of, 71

Ithaca, **1**, 225; B. thinks of buying, **2**, 23; B.'s journey to, **11**, 16n, 18 and n, 19, 22, 30, 46; Greek refugees in, 23, 32, 213; Greek violation of neutrality of, 34, 90, 102

Jackman, Isaac, *All the World's a Stage*, **2**, 192n; **6**, 207 and n

Jackson, John ('Gentleman'), B.'s letters to, **1**, 169, 170, 171, 180; **4**, 153; mentioned, **1**, 92n, *162 and n*, 169 and n; **2**, 8; **3**, 94, 221; **4**, 90, 91, 214; **5**, 80, 179 and n; **6**, 20; **7**, 99, 123, 224; **9**, 12; **11**, 159, 166; B. sparring with, **3**, 251, 253, 255, 257; his portrait, 115 and n; Pugilistic Club, 216 and n

Jacob, (Jacobsen), Mr., **6**, 180

108

Jacob, Sir, *see* Milbanke (Noel), Sir Ralph
Jacobins, **6**, 13; **8**, 240; **9**, 96, 97n
Jacobinism, **9**, 50
Jacobsen, Mr., **9**, 24
Jamaica, **1**, 274; **4**, 330; **9**, 18; **11**, 215
James (? B.'s servant), **1**, 65 and n
James I, King of Scotland, **1**, 273–4; **2**, 68 and n, 182
James II, **1**, 178; **3**, 37
James, Henry, *Aspern Papers*, **5**, 294
Janina (Yanina, Ioannina), **2**, 10n, 11, 18, 102, 134, 261, 262 and n; **10**, 180n; B. to visit, **1**, 224, 225; B. in, 226 and n; 227n, 231; B. met grandson of Ali, 249–50
Jansenists, **5**, 216n
Japan, **10**, 230
Jason, **11**, 156n
Java Gazette, **4**, 117 and n; **8**, 27; **9**, 30
Jefferson, Thomas, **8**, 53
Jeffrey, Francis, B.'s letter to, **11**, 188; mentioned, **1**, 3–4, 193n; **7**, 178; **8**, 61, 102, 178; **9**, 64; **10**, 166; reviews 3rd canto of *Childe Harold*, **1**, 11; **2**, 174n, 178 and n; **5**, 170 and n, 183 and n, 185–6, 198, 204; thought to have reviewed *Hours of Idleness*, **1**, 177n, 178n, 255n; review by, 193n; to review Hobhouse's 'Miscellany', **2**, 45, 50; in *English Bards*, 118n, 174n; **9**, 86 and n; **11**, 188n; aborted duel with Moore, **2**, 118–19, 123–4 and n; to marry an American, **3**, 94; a monarch-maker in literature, 209; B.'s praise of, 252–3; reviews *Corsair* and *Bride of Abydos*, **4**, 87 and n, 92 and n, 142n, 152, 156; suggests B. should write a tragedy, 157–8, 158n; ed. *Edinburgh Review*, 201, 265–6, 266n, 269, 270, 274, 275, 276, 277, 278, 324; **5**, 268n, 269; likes *Hebrew Melodies*, **4**, 330; attacks Coleridge, **5**, 150, 177; in *Hints from Horace*, **8**, 88; reviews B.'s dramas in *Edinburgh*, **9**, 158, 159 and n, 170, 173, 176; praised *Childe Harold* in *Edinburgh*, **11**, 188n
Jeffreys, Judge George, **2**, 174n; **11**, 49n; 'Bloody Assizes', **1**, 178n
Jeffries, James St. John, **4**, 114n
Jehovah, **8**, 53
Jekyll, horse-dealer, **1**, 170, 171
Jena, **9**, 48
Jena Gazette, **5**, 198, 201–2, 204
Jennings, Sam, **2**, 8
Jeremiah, **3**, 208 and n, 209; **4**, 126
Jericho, **1**, 17; **11**, 83
Jersey, George Childe-Villiers, 5th Earl of, **2**, *173n*, 224; **3**, 271–2; **4**, 116, 120n, 129, 196, 290; **6**, 38; **9**,

44, 45; **11**, 149; B. at his country house, **2**, 209, 215, 219, 221, 246; his hospitality, 252; invites B. to Middleton, **3**, 207, 209
Jersey, Lady (née Lady Sarah Sophia Fane), B.'s letters to, **4**, 120, 195, 300; **6**, 38; **11**, 149; biog. sketch, **3**, 271–2; mentioned, 67, 70, 90, 197n, 234, 273; **4**, 105, 110, 111, 117, 120n, 131, 144 and n, 290; **5**, 64n, 133; **7**, 239; **9**, 44; **10**, 31, 103; reigning beauty and wit, **2**, *173n*; B. at country house, 173 and n, 215n; her hospitality, 252; Prince Regent returns her picture, **4**, 152 and n, 154; B. recommends a gentleman to her society, **6**, 38, 39
Jersey, Lord and Lady, **5**, 94, 110, 114, 130, 218, 222, 224
Jerusalem, **2**, 38, 42; **3**, 213n; **5**, 138–9
Jervis, Sir John (later Earl St. Vincent), **1**, 220n, 244n
Jervoise, Capt., **10**, 165
Jesuits, **10**, 105; *Memoires de Trevoux*, **8**, 140 and n
Jesus College, Cambridge, **2**, 117
Jews, **2**, 98, 147; **5**, 157n, 278; **6**, 45
Joao, V., **1**, 218–19n
Job, **3**, 52, 208, 209, 224; **4**, 132, 220; **5**, 84–5n
Jocelyn, Hon. Percy, Bishop of Clogher, **9**, 191 and n; **10**, 13
Jocelyn, Lord, **3**, 106 and n
John, (King), **5**, 14, 127
John Bull, **3**, 131; **5**, 277
John Bull (periodical), **1**, 67 and n; **10**, 135
Johnson, Miss, **2**, 180n
Johnson, Dr. Samuel, **1**, 111, 163n; **3**, 67n, 214n, 228, 247n, 256; **4**, 19, 69, 74 and n, 93, 278n, 314, 315n; **5**, 131n; **7**, 175; **8**, 29n, 74, 164; **9**, 68, 86, 208; **11**, 233; a good hater, like B., **1**, 11; certain to hear truth from his bookseller, **2**, 90; Anna Seward friend of, 132n; and Madame D'Arblay, 143, 146; his Drury Lane Prologue, 205, and n, 206, 210 and n, 212 and n, 214; morbid melancholy, **6**, 85; and Beauclerk, 166 and n; **7**, 16n; defends Prior, **6**, 208 and n; and Langton, **7**, 191 and n, 205; Boswell and, **9**, 86, 89 and n; on Dr. Dodd, 99 and n; Life of Edmund Smith, 69 and n; on Chesterfield, **10**, 171n; companion in a postchaise, **11**, 227; *Life of Savage*, **6**, 47; *Lives of the English Poets*, **6**, 47, 72; **7**, 224 and n; Dryden, **8**, 115; *London*, **6**, 253; **11**, 171–2; *Rasselas*, **10**, 22,

Johnson, Dr. Samuel—*continued*
102; *Vanity of Human Wishes*, **2**, 179 and n; **7**, 100 and n; **8**, 19, 103 and n; **9**, 32 and n, 180 and n; **10**, 180 and n

Johnston, James, attributes poems to B., **5**, 84–5, 138 and n, 139, 143–4, 150, 151, 158, 159; **9**, 44; 'Lord Byron's Pilgrimage to the Holy Land', **5**, 138n, 139; defended by Leach, **9**, 44

Jones, Mr., **10**, 146, 147

Jones, Frederick L., ed., *Maria Gisborne & Edward E. Williams, Shelley's Friends, Their Journals and Letters*, **5**, 110n

Jones, Gale, **2**, 22

Jones, Jacob, Commodore of frigate *Constitution*, **9**, 161 and n, 162n, 164, 165 171

Jones, Richard (?), actor, **3**, 249

Jones, Rev. Thomas, B.'s letters to, **1**, 100, 108; mentioned, *79 and n*, 80, 100 and n; B. paid debt to, 90, 116; Cambridge tutor, **7**, 232

Jones, Sir William, **2**, 91 and n

Jonson, Ben, **8**, 57, 110

Jordan, Mrs. Dorothea, as Miss Hoyden, **3**, 249 and n

Josepha, Donna, gives B. a lock of hair, **1**, 219 and n

Josephine de Beauharnais, **3**, 210n

Joshua, **11**, 179

Journal of the Byron Society, **3**, 15n

Journals (Byron's), *see also under* Byron, Journals; scope of, **1**, 18–23; text and MSS, 25–6

Jouy, Victor Joseph Etienne de, *L'Hermite de la Chaussée d'Antin*, **10**, 207 and n; *Sylla*, 207n; **11**, 76

Jove, Temple of, **1**, 3; **2**, 37

Judaea, **2**, 89

Judges, **11**, 166

Jugurtha, King of Numidia, **8**, 14n

Julian (Emperor), **9**, 150; **11**, 45

Julian Calendar, **11**, 61n

Julius Caesar, *see* Caesar, Julius

Jungfrau, **5**, 94, 101, 106, 188, 205, 206, 268; **7**, 113; **9**, 96

Junius (Sir Philip Francis), **3**, 215; **6**, 18, 19, 35

Junot, Andoche, **1**, 218n

Jupiter, **8**, 35

Jura (Mt.), **5**, 80, 99, 104; **8**, 157

Justamond, **2**, 211n

Justinian, Emperor, **1**, 150

Juvenal, **3**, 150; **4**, 80; **6**, 12n; imitations by B. and Hobhouse, **1**, 141 and n; *Satires*, 194 and n; **2**, 45, 80, 95 and n; **3**, 256 and n; **7**, 153 and n; **8**, 128 and n

Kalamos, **11**, 89 and n

Kames, Henry Home, Lord, **1**, 112; **9**, 47

Kara-Deniz ('Black Sea'), **11**, 224

Karaiskakis, George, **11**, 150 and n, 151 and n

Karteria, armoured steam boat, **11**, 79n

Karvellas, Francis, **10**, 169n

Karvellas, Nicolas, B.'s letter to, **10**, 172; mentioned, 169 and n, 171, 203; refuses information and asks for money, 184, 185, 185–6

Kean, Edmund, **4**, 67, 117, 119, 212, 216, 279, 286, 294, 334; **5**, 50, 82n, 172, 195n, 259n; **8**, 60, 112, 181; **9**, 11, 31; **11**, 165n; Bertram, **4**, 337; Iago, 115 and n, 118; Ian, 290; Ivan, 311, 323; Macbeth, 235; *de Montfort*, **8**, 208, 210; Richard III, **3**, 244; **4**, 57, 110, 111, 334; objects to *Saul*, **5**, 205 and n; as Sir Giles Overreach, **6**, 206; **7**, 194; and Sotheby, **6**, 24; **9**, 35

Keats, John, **4**, 68n; **10**, 69; B. sorry for criticism of, **1**, 11; his attack on Pope, 11; poetic philosophy in letters, 12; *p-ss a bed poetry*, **7**, 200; drivelling idiotism, 202; *Onanism* of poetry, 217, 225; praised in *Edinburgh*, 229; killed by the *Quarterly*, **8**, 102, 103, 104, 117, 119, 162, 166, 172, 173; Shelley's elegy, 162; B. suppressed his criticism of, 166, 172; *Endymion*, 103, 163 and n; *Hyperion*, 163 and n; *Lamia, Isabella . . . and Other Poems*, **7**, 200n; *Lamia*, found in Shelley's pocket, **9**, 185 and n, 186, 198; *Sleep and Poetry*, **8**, 104 and n, 163

Keats-Shelley Journal, **5**, 297; **6**, 123n; **9**, 100n; **10**, 25n; **11**, 218, 220

Keepsake, The, **8**, 97n; **9**, 102n

Keith, Lady (née Hester Maria Thrale), **3**, 247 and n, 249

Kelham, William, **1**, 222n

Kelly, Capt., marriage bet, **4**, 222 and n, 257

Kelly, Frances Maria (Fanny), **5**, 135 and n, 158 and n; in *The Magpie*, **4**, 316 and n

Kelly, Michael, *Reminiscences*, **4**, 115n

Kelso, **9**, 102n

Kemble, Charles, **9**, 83n

Kemble, John Philip, **1**, 63n; **2**, 147 and n; **3**, 244; **4**, 67; **8**, 60; **9**, 16n, 31; in *Coriolanus*, **2**, 149; asks B. to write a tragedy, **4**, 37; 'O. P.' riots, 297 and n

Kemmis, James, **1**, 176 and n

Kenney, James, *Raising the Wind*, **2**, 191 and n; **6**, 226 and n

Kennedy, Dr. James, B.'s letters to, **11**, 84, 126, 131; biog. sketch, 214–15; tries to make converts to Christianity, **11**, 46; tried to convert B., 56, 87n, 215; rumours, 84 and n; possible departure, 106; and Hatagée, 111 and n, 127; and motto of *Telegrafo Greco*, 131–2 and n, 134; *Conversations on Religion with Lord Byron*, 215

Kennedy, Capt. Moses, **2**, 36

Kensington, **2**, 281; **3**, 9

Kensington Palace, **7**, 237

Kent (County), **7**, 81n; **9**, 186

Kent, Duke of, **6**, 18n

Kent, Elizabeth, **10**, 25n, 37 and n

Kentish Town, **9**, 100 and n, 111

Keppel, Lady Anne Amelia, **10**, 88 and n

Keppel, Maria, singer (called Mrs. Kinnaird), **5**, 75, 81, 83, 136, 140, 163, 168, 172, 274; **6**, 7; went back to stage, **5**, 107 and n, 197, 198 and n, 231; Kinnaird breaks with, **6**, 33–4; told Kinnaird B. made love to her, 34, 37; Kinnaird's late mistress, 40; and Kinnaird, **11**, 228

Keratia, **2**, 5, 31

Kerr, Robert, **8**, 216n

Keswick, **3**, 16n

Kidd, Capt., **1**, 208, 211, 212

Kidderminster, **4**, 164n

Kilkenny, **4**, 302

Killeen, **1**, 176n

King, John, money-lender, **1**, 89n; **2**, 154; **11**, 232

'King of Bohemy', **6**, 63

King's Arms, **3**, 216n

King's Bench prison, **3**, 164n, 206n, 228

King's College, Cambridge, **1**, 184n, 276; **2**, 84, 95; **7**, 224n

Kingston Lacy, **1**, 110n

Kington, **3**, 8 and n

Kinnaird, Charles, 8th Lord, B.'s letters to, **6**, 124, 140, 176; **8**, 231; **9**, 66; mentioned, **4**, *157n*, 212, 220; **5**, 264, 267; **8**, 83, 84; expulsion from France, **4**, 157 and n; and Taruscelli, **6**, 39–40, 124 and n; his mistress, 165, 168, 176 and n, 190; Marinet affair, *165 and n*; at Rome, **9**, 66; visited B. at Genoa, **10**, 195, 196 197 198

Kinnaird, Hon. Douglas, B.'s letters to, **4**, 249; **5**, 82, 83, 106, 134, 139, 158, 160, 167, 171, 194, 195 (2), 225, 230, 245, 246, 273; **6**, 6, 33, 41, 48, 49, 52, 59, 72, 78, 79, 87, 91, 93, 97, 100, 101, 102, 109, 113, 136, 142, 210, 217, 221, 222, 228, 231, 240,

252, 255, 260; **7**, 15, 74, 85, 94, 101, 110, 116 (2), 120, 136, 144, 167, 190, 198, 213, 220, 235, 239, 255; **8**, 57, 63, 71, 73, 76, 86, 91, 95, 101, 127, 129, 131, 135, 137, 143, 152, 158, 171, 176, 180, 185, 191, 194, 195, 198, 205, 208, 211, 221, 222, 230, 232, 238; **9**, 55, 60, 61 (2), 71, 72, 73 (2), 81, 82, 84, 89, 91, 92, 93, 94, 100, 105, 107, 111, 113, 114, 127, 130, 134, 137, 141, 144, 151, 152, 158, 162, 165, 176, 185, 186, 187, 188, 189, 192, 193, 194, 195, 198, 199, 201, 203, 204 (2), 205, 207, 208, 209, 211 (2), 213, 215, 217; **10**, 19, 24, 26, 27, 33, 35 (2), 37, 38, 41, 46, 47, 51, 52, 58, 59, 61, 65, 67, 70, 72 (2), 75, 77, 84, 87, 88, 89, 90, 91, 94, 96, 97, 98, 104, 108, 110, 112, 114, 117, 121, 126, 134, 135, 144, 146, 150, 152, 154, 158, 162, 184, 187, 195, 196, 200, 211; **11**, 51, 57, 58, 74, 80, 85, 110, 116, 135, 136, 143, 189, 191; biog. sketch, **2**, 282; mentioned, **1**, 275; **4**, 157n, 195, 198, 212, 264, 278, 279; **5**, 72, 75, 79, 81, 182; **6**, 8, 13, 14, 19, 20, 21, 26, 45, 51, 58, 72, 76, 77, 78, 90, 93, 94, 95, 103, 131, 132, 138, 142, 145, 166, 168, 244, 245, 247, 256; **7**, 97, 99, 123, 153, 156, 168, 178, 181, 202, 224, 240, 248, 256, 257; **8**, 56, 58, 61, 66, 75, 88, 100, 102, 120, 122, 124, 127, 131, 136, 149, 162, 210, 218, 220, 240; **9**, 16 and n, 55, 58, 59, 74, 77, 90, 91, 118, 122, 125, 136, 137, 138, 139, 141, 142, 155, 156, 159, 177, 179, 191, 192, 206, 212; **10**, 58, 80, 176, 203; **11**, 24, 82, 123, 149, 165; cynical toughness of B.'s letters to, **1**, 4; B.'s buffooneries in letters to, 12; B.'s letters to published with omissions, 24; member of Cambridge Whig Club, 139n; and Maria Keppel his mistress, **2**, 129 and n; his 'wife' a singer, **5**, 107 and n, 198; break with Maria Keppel, **6**, 33–4, 40; kept his piece nine years, **7**, 179; his common law wife, **11**, 228; told B. he looked ill, **2**, 141; and *Hebrew Melodies*, **4**, 187n, 220, 250, 260, 274, 280; as banker, 270; **11**, 153, 155; and Drury Lane Theatre, **4**, 296 and n, 297, 301n, 309n, 322, 326–7, 330, 334; **6**, 24, 97; **11**, 165 and n; B.'s business agent, **5**, 68, 77, 90, 137, 139, 204; **10**, 17, 19–20, 38, 46, 47–9, 59–96 *passim*, 65, 71, 75 and n, 78, 84–5, 113–14, 123, 124, 126, 143, 144, 149; **11**, 170; to urge sale

Kinnaird, Hon. Douglas—*continued*
of Newstead, **5**, 74, 236–7, 242, 261;
11, 167; and B.'s 'Monody on the
death of Sheridan', **5**, 82 and n, 106;
as translator, 143; Drury Lane Committee, 158–9, 159n, 168; M.P. for
Bishop's Castle, 168 and n, 172n; **7**,
75, 95; going to Italy, **5**, 209, 219,
222, 243, 258, 262, 266; **11**, 166;
visited B. in Venice, **5**, 267, 268; **6**,
124n; returning to England, **5**, 270,
272, 278; B. hopes he will marry, **6**,
42; B. annoyed at his not writing,
52; Parliamentary election, 59n, 61,
63, 200 and n, 210–11, 212; with
Hobhouse to handle B.'s affairs, 78–
80, 88; against publishing *Don Juan*,
101, 107; **11**, 171 and n; and B.'s
financial affairs, **6**, 210, 221, 228, 231,
240–1; **8**, 91, 95–6, 122, 135, 143,
152–3, 171, 176, 180–1, 185–6,
230–1; **9**, 73, 92, 108; 187–8, 193ff;
proposes an Irish mortgage, **6**, 252
and n, 256; **7**, 15, 40, 41, 50–1, 64,
69, 70 and n, 82, 94, 190; genteel
reformer, 44, 49, 62, 63; on
Davies, 50, 86; B. sent 'Lines to the
Po', 97, 150; B.'s willingness to take
mortgage, 101, 115, 116, 136; no
longer in Parliament, 205; and the
staging of *Marino Faliero*, **8**, 63, 119,
126; liked *Don Juan*, 65; to entertain
Curioni and Taruscelli, 86, 129 and n,
130; garbled letters in *The Keepsake*,
97n; brusque to Murray, 101; to
answer Murray in mercantile matters,
187; to read *Don Juan* proofs, 194;
gave B. contradictory advice, 224,
239; and *Vision of Judgment*, 233; on
stage with B., **9**, 36–7; thinks *Cain* a
puzzler, 61; B.'s trust in his integrity,
62; and B.'s challenge to Southey, 62,
95n, 102 and n, 109–10, 114–15, 117,
160 and n; B. confided quarrel with
Hobhouse, 69; to find publisher for
Vision, 88, 89, 100; to insure Lady
Byron's life, 105–8 *passim*, 112, 113,
115, 124, 188, 211, 214; B. sent
documents on Masi affray, 133, 135,
146, 151; power of attorney for B.,
165; **11**, 48, 51; B.'s budget, **9**, 206,
207, 209, 213, 214; B.'s literary
agent, **10**, 12, 13, 18, 19–20, 39, 41,
47, 51, 52, 53, 58, 59, 64, 66, 70, 72,
88, 117, 127, 132, 135, 151, 158,
181–2, 201, 228; Murray to deliver
B.'s MSS to, 22, 26; and John Hunt,
23 and n, 24, 27, 39, 120, 121, 160;
to obtain B.'s MSS from Murray, 23
and n, 24, 28; fall from horse, 33 and
n, 35, 41; another fall from horse,

57, 61; fears publication of *Don Juan*,
126, 127; alarmed about new cantos,
134–5, 145, 146, 149; Queen's
banker, 135; to supply credits for
Greek adventure, 143, 145, 147, 151,
153, 154, 168, 177–8, 186, 200; **11**,
17, 28, 42, 76, 77, 80, 82, 83, 85, 93,
101, 110, 135, 139, 144; and London
Greek Committee, **10**, 157; B.'s
friend, trustee, and literary agent,
228; sale of Rochdale, **11**, 47, 48, 51,
55, 57, 76, 78, 82, 83, 85, 86, 116,
117; and B.'s mortgage proposal,
116; to present B.'s bills to Greek
Committee, 129; B.'s regard for, 169
Kinsham Court, **2**, 239, 240, 251, 258;
3, 8, 13, 59
Kirkby, Mr., **4**, 165
Kirkby Mallory, **5**, 15, 23, 65, 66; **7**,
207, 214; **9**, 145, 195, 199, 203, 205,
206, 212, 214, 218; **10**, 47, 59, 60,
85, 90, 91, 96, 99, 111, 114, 149,
150, 159; **11**, 42 50, 57, church
living at, **10**, 14–15, 54 and n, 203 and
n, 204; money due to B., **11**, 75,
117, 144
Kiveton, **1**, 60 and n
Kleiner Eiger, **5**, 101, 106
Kleist, Ewald Christian von, **11**, 84
and n
Kleist, Heinrich von, **3**, 221
Kletsgerberg (Gletscherberg?), **5**, 100
Klopstock, Friedrich, **9**, 24
Knapp, **3**, 187
Knight, Henry Gally, B.'s letters to,
11, 183, 188; Eastern tales, **4**, 80 and
n; B. ridicules his verses, **6**, 3 and n,
27 and n, 28; B. on, **7**, 132–3, 168–9,
180, 183, 230; *Alashtar*, **5**, 262 and
n; **6**, 3 and n; **7**, 35 and n; **11**, 188;
Ilderim, **2**, 5n; **3**, 191 and n; **5**, 111
and n, 112 and n, 185 and n, 187, 193,
194, 199, 205, 249, 250, 263;
Ilderim, *Phrosyne*, *Alashtar*, **11**, 183
and n; *Phrosyne*, **2**, 5n; **5**, 262 and n;
6, 3 and n; **7**, 35 and n
Knight, Richard Payne, **1**, 158; **3**, 33,
247 and n; **6**, 68 and n; **10**, 142 and
n; **11**, 222
Knighton, Sir William, **4**, 182, *189 and
n*
Knowles, Mr., **6**, 90
Knox, Capt. Wright, B.'s letter to, **11**,
19; mentioned, 18 and n, 19n, 30
Knox, Mrs. Wright, **11**, 19
Koës, H. C., **2**, 27n
Kolokotrones, Theodore, **11**, 22n, 30,
45n, 52n, 143, 151n, 213; head of
Executive body, 72n
Kondouriottes, **11**, 72n
Koran, **3**, 169

Körner, Earl Theodor, *Schwert-lied*, **11,** 85 and n

Kosciusko, Thaddeus, **8,** 40 and n; **11,** 44, 84

Kotzebue, August von, **10,** 180n; assassinated, **6,** 104n; **7,** 113 and n; *Spaniards in Peru,* 184n

Kozlovsky, Prince Feodor, **11,** 223

Kozlovsky, Prince Peter, **3,** *45 and n,* 50, 69 and n, 76, 83; **4,** 45 and n; **11,** 223

Kranidi, **11,** 72n

Lacedaemon, **11,** 70n

Kunnersdorff, **11,** 84n

Kurshid Pasha, **10,** 180 and n

Labbia, Countess, **5,** 239

Lacedaemon, **11,** 70n

Lacedaemonians, **2,** 36

Lachin y gair, **1,** 75 and n

Laclos, Choderlos de, **11,** 224; *Les Liaisons Dangereuses,* **3,** 220 and n

Lafayette, Marie-Joseph, Marquis de, **1,** 16; **7,** 80

La Fontaine, Jean de, **6,** 76, 95; 'Le Roi Candaule et le Maître en Droit,' **7,** 126 and n

Lago di Garda (Benacus), **5,** 123 and n, 126, 132

Lago Maggiore, **5,** 114, 115, 117; **9,** 210

Laibach, Congress of, **8,** 12n, 21, 27, 33

Laius, **6,** 173

Lake, J. W., ed., B.'s letter to, **10,** 204; *British Prose Writers,* 204; *Complete Works of Lord Byron,* 204 and n

Lake Leman (Geneva), **5,** 80 and n, 81, 99, 104, 124

Lake Poets (Lakers), **6,** 10; **8,** 201; **9,** 117

Lamartine, Alphonse Marie Louis de, **6,** 278; 'L'Homme—à Lord Byron', **7,** 111 and n, 112, 127 and n; *Méditations Poétiques,* 111 and n

Lamb, Lady Caroline (née Caroline Ponsonby), B.'s letters to; **2,** 170, 175, 176, 185, 222, 242(2); **3,** 43; biog. sketch; **2,** 283; mentioned; **1,** 4–5, 221n; **2,** 174 and n; **3,** 19, 28, 32 and n, 59, 67, 142, 143; **4,** 17, 19, 20, 27, 28, 32, 54, 65, 90, 103, 104, 123, 158, 179, 210, 212, 239, 242, 250, 258; **5,** 162; **6,** 93; **7,** 174; **9,** 16; B.'s attachment ceased; **1,** 5; anonymous letter to B.; **2,** 169n; 'a little volcano', 170; her tempestuous conduct, 170–1, 176 and n, 177, 183n, 184 and n, 185 and n, 193–4, 195, 198, 225n, 226, 239, 240–1, 243–4, 248, 264, 283, 284, 286; her fascination, 170–1; parentage, 174

and n; sent B. Annabella's poems, 175–6 and n; **4,** 56 and n; near elopement, **2,** 184n, 186; B.'s parting letter, 185–6; runs away, 187 and n, 188; leaves for Ireland, 189n, 192 and n; her letters from Ireland, 194, 200–1, 208, 209, 217, 218, 230, 232, 233, 235–6, 237, 239, 241, 246, 247; B.'s strategems for dealing with, 198, 227, 230, 232–3; B. tries to pacify, 200–1; B. ceases to write, 202–3; B. no longer in love with, 222 and n, 242; wants conference with B., 243, 246, 247, 249, 250, 253; **3,** 3 and n, 4, 21–2, 23, 26, 27, 35, 36, 42; returns to England, **2,** 240, 245, 247, 248; B. tells her he is attached to another, 242, 246; threatens revenge, 243, 246; writes to Lady Oxford, 243–4, 245, 247, 253, 265; threatens to visit Eywood, 245, 246; at Brocket Hall, 250 and n, 260; affair broken off, 251; B. to return her letters, 252, 254, 256 and n; wants return of gifts, 252–3, 255 and n, 257; burns effigies of B.'s picture and letters, 260 and n, 264; B. considers her mad, 265; continues to plague B., **3,** 3 and n, 4, 7, 8, 16, 28, 35–6, 37, 42, 43, 46, 65, 67, 69, 70, 83, 85, 87, 90, 91, 93, 98, 128, 129, 139, 152, 154, 158, 171, 174, 214; B. wished to keep her quiet, 3 and n, 8, 157; her letter half in rhyme, 4; 'Agnus', 7, 46 and n; signs herself 'Phryne', 8 and n, 23; runs away, 9; Ne 'Crede Byron' on her livery buttons, 9; seized B.'s picture, 10–11, 12, 14, 15, 17, 25, 26, 31, 35, 36–7, 42 and n, 46, 173; broke all but 6th and 9th Commandments, 12; called Medea, 15, 16; affair of the necklace, 16; B. out of scrape with, 32; B. abhors her conduct, 35–6; B. sent her Lady Oxford's hair, 37 and n, 40, 140 and n; her bonfire, 40; **11,** 182; *The Giaour,* **3,** 40, 51 and n, 102 and n; B. agrees to see her, 43, 45, 46, 47; abuses Rogers, 47; platonic speculations, 48; B. on her character, 52; incident at Lady Heathcote's, 71, 72, 74, 84n, 170; **4,** 86n, 87, 330n; defended by De Staël, **3,** 76; a mirror of quiet, 91; guesses at B.'s new attachment, 125 and n, 126; 'cold' letter from B., 139, 143–4; and Mme de Staël, 237; B.'s utter detestation, **4,** 21, 132–3; continues to write to B., 23, 26, 34–5, 123–4, 132; wants B.'s picture, 26, 119; a foolish wicked woman, 116; puzzled about

Lamb, Lady Caroline—*continued*
B., 124; B. tries to keep her out, 134; B. on her character, 135, 204–5; B. thinks her mind disordered, 135; accosts B. at masquerade, 135–7; and B.'s engagement and marriage, 178–9, 180, 185, 188, 192, 199, 200, 203 and n, 251; forged B.'s handwriting, 193 and n; suspected of contradicting B.'s engagement, 193, 194–5, 196–7; at Paris, 310, 312 and n; at Chatsworth, 263n; rumour of separation from husband, 266–7; mad and malignant, 310, 312–13; at Brussels, 5, 28n; and B.'s poems to Augusta, 67–8, 68n; Augusta distressed by, 88–9, 93; 8, 217; in correspondence with Lady Byron, 5, 93; her novels, 232, 258; letter to B.' 266; her electioneering, 6, 107 and n; Teresa resembles, 115, 248; masquerades as Don Juan, 7, 169 and n; B.'s letters to offered to Murray, 8, 227; *Glenarvon*, 2, 242n, 283; 5, 81; 7, 37 and n; 10, 178; motto for, 5, 85 and n; B.'s opinion of, 85, 86, 131; B.'s verse comment, 187, 193, 199; reviewed in Jena paper, 198, 204; Italian translation, 255

Lamb, Charles, 2, 138, 178n; 4, 97n; 6, 83

Lamb, Frederick, 3, 70 and n, 86 and n

Lamb, Hon. George, 2, 45 and n, 147, 232n; 3, 126, 145n, 232 *and n*; 4, 234, 250; 5, 83, 159 and n; 6, 88n, 106n, 107 and n; Drury Lane Committee, 4, 295, 309, 314, 334, 336; quarrels with Scrope Davies, 6, 138

Lamb, Mrs. George (née Rosalie St. Jules), B.'s letter to, 4, 309; mentioned, 2, 183, 184, 186, 187n, 217, 232 and n, 240, 259 and n, 264; 3, 31, 37, 90; 4, 250 and n, 251, *309 and n*; 5, 215, 223

Lamb, Peniston, 3, 46n; death, 4, 250n

Lamb, Sir Peniston, *see* Melbourne, Lord

Lamb, William (later 2nd Viscount Melbourne), 2, 175n, 185n, 188, 196, 209, 236, 241n, 244, 257; 4, 21, 204, 238, 250 and n; 9, 89, 107; angry with B., 3, 65; rumoured separation from Caroline, 4, 266–7; prologue to *Ian*, 290n; B. on, 312–13

Lamberti (composer), 'La Biondina in Gondoletta', 6, 276

Lambton, John George (later 1st Earl of Durham), 6, 89; 8, 121n

La Mettrie, Julien Offray de, 5, *216 and n*

Lanarkshire, 11, 64n

Lancashire, 2, 48, 59, 60, 61, 67, 77, 84, 85, 91, 93, 99, 104, 107, 108, 109, 110, 115, 127, 156; 3, 21, 24n, 226n; 11, 231

Lancashire estate, *see* Rochdale

Lancaster, 10, 84

Lancetti, 6, 45n, 255

Lander, 2, 45

Landor, Walter Savage, *Count Julian*, 3, 36 and n

Lanesborough, Lady, 11, 232

Lanfranchi Casa, 5, 298; 8, 189n, 246; 9, 74 and n, 75, 179n, 184n, 237; Hunt's children in, 1, 10

Lanfranchi family, 9, 74

Langhorne, Rev. John, trns. Plutarch's *Lives*, 8, 127 and n

Langle [Longhi?], 7, 65, 100

Langton, Bennett, 7, 191 and n; 9, 89n

Lansdowne, Sir Henry Petty-Fitzmaurice, 3rd Marquis of, 1, 19, 231n; 2, 223 and n; 3, 244, 254; 4, 61; 5, 222, 224; 8, 111, 251n; 9, 14, 64; 10, 140 and n; Bowood estate, 5, 200n; 6, 24 and n

Lansdowne, Lady, 3, 252; 4, 65

Laplace, Pierre Simon, Marquis de, *Essai . . . sur les Probabilités*, 4, 201 and n

Lapland, 11, 78

Laplanders, 9, 47

Lardner, Dionysius, *Cabinet Cyclopaedia*, 3, 253n

Larissa, 2, 9, 10, 11, 22; 11, 124

La Roche, 5, 100

La Rochefoucauld, François, Duc de, 3, 210, 229; 7, 78; 9, 117, 124; 10, 128; *Maximes*, 2, 16 and n, 177 and n; 3, 102 and n; 6, 106 and n; *Réflexions Morales*, 8, 41 and n

Las Cases, *Memorial . . .*, 11, 34n

Lateran Museum, 4, 93n

Latin language, 1, 215; 2, 32 and n, 43, 83, 90, 112–13, 178; 5, 126, 156; 7, 231; 8, 61, 88

La Trappe, Nuns of, 5, 104

Latro, Porcius, 5, 221n

Lauderdale, James Maitland, 8th Earl of, 1, 158; 3, 242; 4, 60; 9, 14; in Venice, 6, 76 and n, 78; carried B.'s poetry to England, 81, 82, 85, 87, 89; 11, 170 and n; gossips about B., 6, 92, 93; on Hobhouse's oratory, 11, 170

Laugier, 7, 132

Laurence (surgeon), 11, 46

Laurie, Dr., and B.'s club foot, 1, 41n

Lausanne, 3, 118n; 5, 86, 96, 97; 6, 18; 10, 101, 106, 129

Lauterbrunen, 5, 205

Lavater, Johann Kaspar, 3, 253; 4, 167

Lavender, Nottingham (quack), **1**, 39n

Lawrence, Sir Thomas, **5**, 294; **8**, 28; portrait of Lady Blessington, **10**, 174–5, 229

Leach, defends J. Johnston, **9**, 44 and n

Leacroft, Capt. John, B.'s letters to, **1**, 104, 105(2); mentioned, **1**, 104 and n, 127 and n, 131n

Leacroft, Julia, **1**, *51 and n, 94n*, 98, 104 and n, 116

Leacroft, Mr. and Mrs., **1**, 104–5, 106, 131n

Leake, William Martin, **1**, 237; **2**, 102 and n, 125, 134, 261 and n, 262n, 263; **4**, 269, 274; Resident at court of Ali Pasha, **1**, *227 and n*; *Researches in Greece*, reviewed by Hobhouse, **4**, 266n, 271n, 276

Lean, E. Tangye, *The Napoleonists*, **10**, 119n; **11**, 228–9

Leander, swam the Hellespont, **1**, 237 and n, 242–3, 243–4, 250; **2**, 34; **8**, 80, 81, 82, 162

Learmont of Ercildoune, Thomas ('the Rhymer'), **3**, 122 and n

Leckie, G. F., **2**, 168n, 169

Ledbury, **1**, 71, 74; **3**, 15

Le Despenser, Lord, **9**, 186 and n, 187, mortgage, **10**, 38, 59

Le Despenser, Lady, **3**, 102 and n

Lee, Harriet, *Kruitzner, or The German's Tale*, **10**, 40 and n, 55

Lee, Harriet and Sophia, *The Canterbury Tales*, **8**, 224 and n, 237

Lee, Nathaniel, **2**, *207 and n*; **6**, 27; Bedlam tragedy, **5**, 179 and n; madness, 238 and n

Leeds, Francis Osborne, 5th Duke of, **1**, 45n, 46n, 60n, 273; **8**, 34 and n; **6**, 62n

Lefkas, Island of, **1**, 246 and n

Lega, *see* Zambelli

Leghorn, **3**, 251n; **8**, 111, 149; **9**, 82, 83, 89, 95n, 135n, 140, 147, 148, 149, 156, 157, 158, 161n, 167, 173, 178, 179, 181, 184n, 185, 187, 188, 189, 193 and n, 202n, 203, 204, 206, 217; **10**, 26, 31, 32, 42, 50, 66, 71, 74, 92, 102, 113, 128, 152, 154, 162n, 179, 185n, 187, 194, 200, 201, 203, 204, 205, 206, 213; **11**, 16, 29, 107, 140, 152; Villa Dupuy, **9**, 135n, 156, 157, 161–9, 161n; Tuscan authorities and the *Bolivar*, 178 and n, 192 and n; B. arrives in, **10**, 210n; Browne joined B. at, **11**, 15n

Leghorn, Governor of, B.'s letter to, **9**, 178

Legnani, Luigi, **7**, 242 and n; **8**, 138 and n

Leicestershire, **4**, 289; **6**, 217; **9**, 19n, 106, 112, 115

Leigh, Hon. Augusta (née Byron), *see also* Byron, Hon. Augusta; B.'s letters to, **1**, 165, 179, 180; **2**, 74, 84, 85, 88, 93; **3**, 32, 67, 68(2), 114, 158; **4**, 17, 25(2), 115, 126, 130; **5**, 44, 61, 67, 69, 70, 74, 88, 91, 92, 94, 109, 113, 114, 118, 119, 122(2), 126, 128, 140, 144, 153, 159, 170, 175, 190, 223, 224, 227, 231, 236, 242; **6**, 62, 69, 129, 171, 185, 222, 228, 247, 251, 259; **7**, 14(2), 153, 159, 166, 207, 227, 239, 243, 251, 257; **8**, 139, 209, 233; **9**, 56, 120; **10**, 14, 15, 28, 54, 111, 203; **11**, 44, 120; biog. sketch, **1**, 273; mentioned, **2**, 84 and n, 283, 284; **4**, 19, 22, 26n, 77 and n, 91, 94, 124, 127 and n, 145–6, 147, 167, 200, 204, 211, 215, 220, 226, 228, 232, 233, 262 and n; **5**, 55, 79, 111, 115, 120, 163, 294; **6**, 26, 62n, 106, 134, 258; **7**, 44; **8**, 34n, 128, 135, 136, 229; **9**, 21, 83; **10**, 176; B.'s playful letters to, **1**, 4; her fecundity, 6; **7**, 208, 227; conflict of B.'s relation with, **1**, 19; married cousin, **1**, 165n; birth of a daughter, 179 and n; distressed by B.'s attack on Carlisle, 251; in B.'s will, **2**, 73; **3**, 126 and n; **4**, 298 and n; **5**, 66; invited to Newstead, **2**, 86, 88; financial difficulties, **3**, 32 and n, 210n; B. put off Lady Oxford for her, 68, 69; at London parties with B.' 68, 70, 73; at Six Mile Bottom, 83 and n, 112 and n; meant to go abroad with B., 85, 89, 93, 114–15, 153n; B. trying to overcome attachment, 87 and n, 123 and n, 142; liaison with B., 87 and n, 88, 96 and n, 102 and n, 113 and n, 124n, 125n, 142, 174, 205n; invited to Aston, 126n, 127n; B. neglected for Lady Frances, 143; to visit Farleigh with B., 158, B.'s passion for her deepest, 174; as Zuleika, 195n; seal of herself and B., 206, 208; only one who cares for B., 218, 236; Carlisle–B. quarrel, 255 and n; B.'s 'summer adventure', **4**, 16 and n; her shyness, 22, 40, 222; subsequent relations with B., 23n, 24n, 27–8, 54n, 66n, 110–11; with B. to Newstead, 25, 40, 45–6, 167, 176; B.'s financial assistance, 25–6, 115–16 and n, 130–1, 227–8, 259, 298 and n; her pregnancy, 44, 96n, 104n; urged B. to see Mary Chaworth, 48; dearest in B.'s heart, 69; her marriage, 112; B.'s poem to, 114 and n; and her friend Lady Charlotte, 127–8, 187–8, 191–2, 195, 198 and n; accompanies B. to Hastings, 137–8,

Leigh, Hon. Augusta—*continued*
140, 142 and n; B.'s symbol for, 187
and n, 191n; and B.'s forthcoming
marriage, 179, 191–2, 197, 219; B.'s
visits to, 227, 232–3, 247, 309–10;
visit of B. and wife, 280–5; wrote to
Hodgson for B., 291; death of her
father-in-law, 308n; go-between in
separation, 5, 23, 24, 25, 27, 34, 42,
44, 46; at Lady Jersey's ball, 64n;
parting from B., 65, 66; B. urged
Lady Byron to be kind to, 66; 7, 41,
212, 256–7; rumoured affair with B.,
5, 68n; and B.'s daughter Ada, 69
and n, 93, 120, 127; distress at
gossip, 88–9, 93, 242–3; B. sends
presents to her children, 91, 93;
objects to publication of 'Epistle to
Augusta', 91n, 106, 110; sends B.
lock of hair, 92–3; B. invites her to
France, 95; B.'s love for, 96, 119; 7,
159, 257; Alpine journal for, 5, 96–
105, 108, 109, 114, 188, 268; 8,
11, 176, 217; love symbol, 5, 114 and
n; letters incomprehensible, 137, 273;
friendship with Bentincks, 171;
Prepiani miniatures of B., 191, 212,
242; 6, 74; worried about B.'s illness,
5, 222; full of woes, 231–2, 255; B.'s
wish to provide for, 6, 6, 247–8, 251;
9, 120; invited abroad by B., 6, 185;
10, 15, 30 and n, 55; on Scrope
Davies, 6, 187; her miniature by
Holmes, 223; and Lady Byron, 7, 14,
41, 212, 239 and n, 251, 256–7; and
B.'s loan, 155, 159; on B.'s supposed
arrival in England, 177; moralizes
over Queen Caroline, 243 and n;
thought *Don Juan* execreble, 8, 65;
financial future, 89, never sends
agreeable news, 123; full of mysteries
and miseries, 217; gave B. a Bible,
238; observed B.'s change of disposition, 9, 25 and n; and Margaret
Parker, 40; an only child, 52, 77;
invited to Pisa by B., 56–7; received
game from Lady Byron, 10, 14;
passed B.'s letters to Lady Byron,
111n; B. wants annuity for her, 133;
asked B. not to leave legacy, 162; her
birth, 208; on B. and Mary Chaworth,
209; told B. of Ada's illness, 11, 33;
stood by B. in separation, 169; and
Gertrude Howard, 225
Leigh, Mr. Chandos, 3, 77; 4, *43 and n*,
44
Leigh, Gen. Charles, 1, 44n, 60n; 4,
131 and n; his son's marriage to
Augusta, 1, 52 and n, 86; death, 4,
307; contest over his will, 308n
Leigh, Frances, 1, 60n

Leigh, Col. George, 1, 60n; 4, 247,
259, 280, 281; 5, 232, 255; 7, 155
and n, 159, 207, 240; 10, 15, 208;
marriage to Augusta, 1, *44n*, 165n,
273; 4, 112; of 10th Dragoons, 1,
47n; obstacles to his marriage, 52 and
n; Equerry to Prince of Wales, 165
and n; B. saw at Brighton, 180,
quarrel with Prince of Wales, 2, 85
and n, 86; 4, 131 and n; in debt, 25,
116n; on betting on B.'s marriage,
200; doesn't admire B.'s marriage,
227–8; his helplessness, 308n; 5, 96
Leigh, Elizabeth Medora, 4, 17n, 104n;
5, 67 and n
Leigh, Georgiana, 1, 179 and n; 3,
205; 4, 131; 5, 67, 89, 91, 127; 8,
235; 9, 120
Leinster, 1st Duke of, 3, 249n
Leinster, 3rd Duke of, 1, 125 and n
Leipsic, 9, 164
Leith, 3, 94
Le Mann, Francis, (physician), 5, 81,
191; 8, 42
Le Mesurier, Edward, B.'s letter to,
10, 164; mentioned, 164 and n
Lempriere's dictionary, 1, 17; 8, 102;
11, 147
Leominster, 3, 34; 4, 157n
Leoni, Michele, B.'s letters to, 6, 42;
11, 192; translator of *Childe Harold*,
6, *42n*; 7, 97 and n; 9, 157 and n;
11, 194n; wished B.'s permission to
translate, 11, 193 and n, 194 and n
Leonidas, 9, 48
Leonidas, Greek brig of war, 11, 92
Lepanto (Navpactos), attack on plan-
ned, 11, 94 and n, 102, 107, 110, 115,
139; attack postponed, 112n, 123;
Suliotes refuse to march against, 91n,
143
Lepanto, Gulf of, 1, 237; 3, 253; 11,
50, 148
Lerici, 9, 147n, 184n, 203n; 10, 56,
102; B.'s illness at, 11, 12–13, 14, 19,
28, 56; 11, 196
Le Sage, Alain René, *Gil Blas*, 1, 111
and n; 2, 63 and n; 3, 61; 4, 327; 5,
211; 6, 61, 212 and n; 7, 168; 8, 88
and n, 148; 9, 175; 11, 125 and n
Leslie, Charles, *Short and Easie
Method with Deists*, 8, 238 and n
Lethe, 3, 224
Leuctra, 9, 48
Levant, the, 3, 29, 60, 90, 213, 250;
10, 76, 83, 134, 142, 143, 145, 151,
153, 154, 168, 177, 178, 186, 188,
199, 212
Leveson-Gower, Lady Charlotte, 3,
254 and n; Augusta wanted B. to
marry, 4, 127n, 187–8, 191–2, 217;

116

relationship to Carlisles, 127n, 134n; B.'s meeting with, 127–8, 131 and n; marriage to Earl of Surrey, 198 and n, 212 and n

Leveson-Gower, Lord Granville (later Earl of Granville), **3**, *232 and n*, 237 and n; **4**, 191n

Leveson-Gower, Harriet, Countess of Granville, *Letters*, **3**, 211 n

Levi, money changer, **5**, 72

Levis, M. de, *Souvenirs et Portraits*, reviewed in *Edinburgh Review*, **4**, 92 and n

Levy, Miss Catherine, B.'s letter to, **4**, 313; mentioned, **4**, 313 and n

Lewellyn, **11**, 160 and n

Lewis, Benjamin, black servant, **11**, 31 and n

Lewis, Matthew Gregory ('Monk'), B.'s letters to, **3**, 4; **4**, 295; **11**, 183; mentioned, **3**, 207, 227, 230 and n, 233; **5**, 244 and n, 251, 254, 255, 257; **6**, 243; **7**, 113; **8**, 54; anecdotes of in 'Detached Thoughts', **1**, 21; and de Staël, **3**, 240–1, 4, 33; to meet Rogers, 295; going to Jamaica, 330; translated *Faust* for B., **5**, 206, 268; and Sheridan, **9**, 17–18; a bore, 18; B. on his character, 18–19; mystified by Dandies, 22; *Ambrosio or the Monk*, **3**, 205 and n, 234; *Castle Spectre*, **9**, 17; 'Pleasure and Desire', **3**, 151–2; *Timour the Tartar*, **2**, 212n

Liberal, The, **2**, 282; **3**, 102n; **7**, 35n; **8**, 172n; **9**, 58n; **10**, 18n, 23, 25, 32, 33, 42, 72–3, 80, 81, 87, 89n, 94, 105n, 117, 122n, 133n, 173 and n; publishes B.'s 'Letter', **6**, 214n; *Vision of Judgment* published in, **9**, 183, 234; **10**, 13n, 39 and n, 47n, 66; B.'s connection with, 34; outcry against, 108, 116–17; B. to collect poems for volume from, 109; B. wishes to retire from, 110, 114, 120, 121, 123; paid expenses, 134; Kinnaird considers a failure, 136; 4th number, 151

Liberals, **8**, 16, 17, 18, 33, 45, 117, 118, 155

Libochabo, **2**, 125, 129; **5**, 76

Licenza, **5**, 233

Lido (Venice), **5**, 130n, 295; **6**, 7, 10, 17, 20, 51, 52, 54, 60, 77, 89, 92, 118, 144, 147, 149, 196, 205, 237; **7**, 63; **8**, 81, 141n

Liege, **8**, 170

Ligne, Prince de, **4**, 283 and n

Lima earthquake, **9**, 30

Limerick, **1**, 134

Linckh, Jacob, **2**, 27n, *37 and n*

Lincoln, Bishop of, **3**, 22n; **9**, 53; **11**, 222

Lincolnshire, **1**, 82n

Lincoln's Inn, **4**, 271n; **10**, 67n

Lingua Franca, **2**, 37

Lintot, Barnaby Bernard, publisher, **2**, 30, 114, 131; **5**, 28; **6**, 29

Lionardo, B.'s courier, **6**, 166 and n

Lipari Islands, **11**, 29

Lisbon (Lisboa), **2**, 37, 104; **4**, 161; **5**, 210; **8**, 23; B. at, **1**, 214–16, 217, 236, 248; compared to Gibraltar, 218

Lisbon earthquake, **9**, 30

Lisbon Packet, **1**, 208, 210, 211–13, 214

Lisle, **10**, 174

Lismore, **2**, 132n

Lissa, **8**, 54 and n; victory, **2**, 48

Liston, John, (actor), **2**, 160 and n, 192n; **6**, 229, 230; **7**, 179; **9**, 71 and n

Liston, Robert, successor to Adair, **2**, 262 and n

Litchfield, inn-keeper in Cambridge, **1**, 122 and n

The Literary Club (Johnson's), **9**, 99n

Literary Fund, **10**, 23, 64, 70

Literary Gazette, **7**, 201n; **8**, 84, 166n

Little, Thomas, *see* Moore, Thomas

Little Pidlington, **6**, 215

Livadia, **1**, 250; **6**, 173

Liverpool, **2**, 67; **6**, 227

Liverpool, Earl of, **1**, 186n; **3**, 66, 206; **7**, 183 and n; Erskine's letter to, **11**, 59n

Livy, **5**, 152 and n

Lizard, The, **9**, 95

Ljubljana, **8**, 12n

Llandaff, Bishop of, **2**, 136n

Lloyd, Charles, **2**, 138

Loch Leven, **7**, 204, 212

Locke, John, **4**, 60, 82

Locke, William, **3**, 243, 255; **11**, 224, 226

Locke, Mrs. (unidentified), **4**, 240 and n

Lockhart, G., **11**, 235; *The Lockhart Papers*, **9**, 156 and n

Lockhart, John Gibson, **8**, 99n; *John Bull's Letter*, 145 and n; and Scott's daughter, **9**, 87

Lodi, **3**, 256; **9**, 48

Loeb Classical Library, **2**, 14n

Lofft, Capell, **2**, 76 and n, 179 and n

Lo-Kristi, **5**, 73, 76

Lombard Street, **4**, 260, 337

Lombardy, **5**, 126, 127, 221, 227, 230; **6**, 91, 167, 190; **7**, 82, 127, 135, 206, 211; **8**, 119; **9**, 149; **11**, 166

London, **2**, 28, 37, 47, 56, 59, 69, 78, 108, 155, 163, 192, 194, 231, 237, 239, 241, 242, 284; **3**, 89, 118, 242;

London—*continued*

4, 15, 34, 67, 69, 159, 161, 169, 172, 174, 176, 177; **5**, 14n, 15; **7**, 193, 230, 237, 253; **10**, 122; 'year of revelry 1814', **1**, 3; B. in, 86–91, 93–9, 126–33; **3**, 45; **4**, 178; less familiar to B. than Stamboul, **1**, 250; B.'s years of fame in, 276; B. saw Matthews in, 277; B. returning from abroad, **2**, 49; Sunday described in *Childe Harold*, 75 and n; B. going to, 110, 116, 118, 120, 148, 177, 247, 251, 259; **3**, 13, 15; B. to be incog. in, 39, 40; Whig Society, 128n; Madame de Staël in, 273; high society in, **4**, 25; B.'s joy at leaving, 36; B. returned to, 49, 149, 283n, 285; 'glorious London', 86; only place to take conceit out of a man, 152; the place for fun, **5**, 38; B.'s nostalgia for, 201; **9**, 170; the walls are privileged, **7**, 84; B. contemplates return to, 254; balls in, **8**, 43; Sligo saw Davies in, **11**, 157; B. left year before, 190

London Chronicle, The, **4**, 14 and n

London Greek Committee, B.'s letters to, **1**, 17; **10**, 179; **11**, 79, 127; mentioned, **10**, 157, 162 and n, 163, 177, 196, 200, 202, 203, 229, 230; **11**, 15, 20n, 22, 24, 27, 29, 31n, 37, 39, 50, 53, 54, 55, 59n, 79 and n, 83, 85, 86, 94, 101, 108, 110, 127n, 133, 146 and n, 147, 216, 217, 218; Blaquiere one of founders, **10**, 139n, 229; B.'s membership, 142–3, 151–2, 168, 169, 170, 171, 172, 173, 179, 183, 184, 187–8, 210, 211, 212; **11**, 44, 45; should increase funds for Greeks, 55; Stanhope agent of, 64n, 65, 66, 68; sent Drs. Millingen and Tindall, 72 and n; supplies not practical, 77, 83; stores, 88, 106–7; sent arms laboratory to Greece, 105–6; to name commission for Loan, 142

London Hotel, **4**, 142

London Magazine, **8**, 99n, 111n

London plague, **9**, 30

London University, **1**, 255n

Londos, Andreas, B.'s letters to, **11**, 103, 122; mentioned, 141, 143n; Cogia Basha, **2**, 6n; **11**, 104n

Longhi, banker, **6**, 260; **7**, 104

Long, Catherine, **2**, 142 and n

Long, E. B., B.'s letter to, **1**, 200; mentioned, 95n; **8**, 25, 227; death of his son, **1**, 200 and n

Long, E. N., B.'s letters to, **1**, 95, 109, 114, 116, 117, 118, 121, 139, 150, 152; mentioned, 73 and n, 109n, 119; **2**, 133n; **7**, 224, 230; **8**, 23 and n,

24–5; B. to visit at Little Hampton, **1**, 95 and n, 97n; in the Guards, 114 and n, 115n, 151, *200n*; to dine at the Pantheon, 152 and n; death, 200 and n; **8**, 24; B.'s letters to offered to Murray, 227

Long, Henry, **1**, 119 and n, 151

Long, Sir James Tylney, **2**, 142; **4**, 79n

Long, (?Kion) (unidentified), **4**, 236 and n

Long, Mr., **4**, 288, 328–9

Longman, Thomas Norton, publisher, B.'s letters to, **2**, 181; **11**, 181; mentioned, **2**, 181; **4**, 280 and n; **6**, 55, 56, 140; **7**, 120, 121, 244; **8**, 141, 251 and n; **9**, 89, 91; **11**, 187; *Lalla Rookh*, **3**, 112n; **5**, 131, 165 and n, 251 and n; to publish Moore, **4**, 285n, 323n

Longman, Hurst, Rees and Orme, **1**, 132n, 141n; **2**, 23, 53, 143n

Lonsdale, William Lowther, 1st Earl of, **2**, 215 and n

Loo-Choo Islands, **6**, 59n, 60, 63, 64n

Lope de Vega, *see* Vega Carpio, Lope Félix de

Loratelli, Marquess, **7**, 65

Lords, House of, **2**, 155, 158 and n, 160, 161n, 165 and n, 281; **3**, 22n 31, 55 and n, 165n, 232n, 242, 255n; **4**, 62, 128n, 144n, 238, 244n; **5**, 19n, **6**, 25 and n, 165n; **7**, 130, 188, 205 and n; **9**, 27, 112; **10**, 46; B. taking seat, **1**, 16, 67n, 195 and n, 196 and n

Lotti, **6**, 92

Louch, **1**, 170

Loudoun, Countess of, **2**, 215n

Loughborough, **7**, 231

Loughborough, Alexander Wedderburn, 1st Baron, **6**, 11; **9**, 28

Loughnan, Son, and O'Brien, agents for Greek Loan, **11**, 146n

Louis, Prince of Bavaria, **2**, 30n

Louis, King of Etruria, **6**, 178n

Louis XII, **4**, 43

Louis XIV, **7**, 131; apocryphal story, **8**, 119 and n

Louis XV, **9**, 20n

Louis XVI, **5**, 147; **11**, 227

Louis XVIII, **4**, 100 and n, 101; **5**, 34n; **7**, 50n

Louth, **9**, 236

Louvel, Pierre Louis, assassin, **7**, 50 and n, 113 and n

Love, Mr., jeweller, sells B. silver-gilt for gold, **5**, 173, 203; to frame B.'s miniatures, 212

Lovelace, Earl of, *Astarte*, **4**, 105n

Lovelace Papers, **5**, 228n; **11**, 173n

Lovell, Ernest J., Jr., **5**, 297; **7**, 165n; Blessington, *Conversations*, **3**, 128n;

Medwin's *Conversations of Lord Byron*, 157n
Low Countries, B. on, **5**, 75
Lowe, Sir Hudson, **11**, 228–9; custodian of Napoleon, **5**, 215 and n; Governor of St. Helena, **9**, 26
Lowe, Rev. Robert, B.'s letter to, **1**, 203; mentioned, 203 and n
Lower Grosvenor St., **8**, 25
Lowth, Dr. Robert, **2**, 104 and n
Lowther, **1**, 139
Lowther, William, **2**, 215n
Lucan, *Pharsalia*, **2**, 14 and n
Lucca, **6**, 69; **9**, 78, 79, 81, 148, 179, 180, 181, 184, 185, 236; **10**, 56n
Lucian, **9**, 62; **10**, 149
Lucifer, **2**, 112; **7**, 204; **9**, 53
Lucilius, **8**, 201
Lucretia, **2**, 250
Lucretius, **3**, 7, 73, 210; **4**, 81; *De Rerum Natura*, **1**, 216 and n; **6**, 67 and n; **7**, 192 and n, 200 and n; **9**, 126 and n; **11**, 226
Lucrezia of Imola, **8**, 184 and n
Lucy (Lucinda), **1**, 187, *189 and n*, 191, 232n; **2**, 105 and n, 106, 131, 155 and n
Ludd, King, **5**, 165
Luddites, **1**, 186n; **5**, 149; **7**, 236
Ludgate Hill, **4**, 171
Ludlow, General Edmund, **5**, 97 and n; **9**, 41 and n
Ludwig, John Frederick, of Ratisbon, **1**, 219n
Lugano Gazette, **6**, 187; **7**, 36, 50, 130, 196; **8**, 36
Lugo, **8**, 247
Luigi, servant, **7**, 11, 56, 128, 139–40, 149, 197; **8**, 12n
Luigi, Martini, **1**, 15; **6**, 147, 149
Luigi da Porto, **5**, 132n
Luigia, **6**, 92
Lung' Arno, **9**, 129, 133
Lunghi [Longhi], bankers, **7**, 167
Luriottis, Andreas, **10**, 139n, 142, 147; **11**, 38, 59n, 62, 69, 129, 130n, 131, 144, 146n, 147
Lushington, Dr. Stephen, **10**, 99, 110, 113; Lady B.'s counsellor, **5**, 30n, 33 and n, 40, 180; **9**, 145 and n, 176, 177, 186, 187, 188, 194, 198, 205, 207, 211, 213
Lushington and Colborne, Lady Byron's trustees, **9**, 207 and n
Lusieri, Giovanni Battista, **2**, 10, *12 and n*, 16, 27n, 29, 33; with B. at Cape Colonna, 13, 30–1; with B. at Malta, 46; and Lord Elgin, 65n, 134, 156, 172n
Lutheran, (B.'s servant), **2**, 4
Lutherans, **7**, 73; **8**, 48

Luttrell, Henry, **3**, 85n, **97** *and n*; **4**, 119n; B. on, **7**, *165 and n*, 182 and n; **9**, 19, 156, 207; *Advice to Julia*, **3**, 97n; **7**, 165 and n, 182 and n; **9**, 136 and n
Lutzerode, Baron, translator of B., **9**, 165 and n
Lyceum Theatre, **2**, 214; **4**, 296n
Lycophron, *Cassandra*, **6**, 235
Lyon, Newfoundland dog, **11**, 86n
Lyons, **4**, 284
Lysander, **9**, 47
Lysicrates, monument to, **2**, 11n, 12n
Lyttelton, Lord, **1**, 113
Lyttelton, George, 1st Baron, **1**, 146 and n; *Dialogues of the Dead*, **7**, 256 and n
Lyttelton, Thomas, 2nd Baron, **1**, 146 and n
Lyttelton, William Henry Lyttelton, 3rd Baron, **9**, *15n*; Sheridan on, 15

Maby, Mr., **11**, 189
MacCarthy, Dr. J. W., B.'s letter to, **10**, 206
Macaulay, Zachary, B.'s letter to, **3**, 189; ed. *Christian Observer, 189 and n*
Macdiarmid, John, *Lives of British Statesmen*, **1**, 141 and n
Macdonald, Dudley, **9**, 43
Macedonia, **1**, 226
Macgill, Thomas, *Dominus*, **2**, 16, 29 and n, 30; **11**, 220
Machiavelli, Niccolo, **5**, 216, 218; **6**, 18; *Il Principe*, **4**, 161–2; *Opere*, **3**, 252 and n
Machinidas, **11**, 70n
Machinnes (Macchinnis), **6**, 86
Machirelli (Macchiarelli) Giordani Countess Cecelia, gm of Teresa, **7**, 153, 174 and n, 177 and n, 215 and n
Mackay, George Eric, *Lord Byron and the Armenian Convent*, **5**, 157n
Mackenzie, Sir Alexander, *Voyages from Montreal . . .*, **1**, 256 and n
Mackenzie, Henry, *The Man of Feeling*, **1**, 111 and n, 112, 113
Mackintosh, Sir James, B.'s letter to, **3**, 121; mentioned, **2**, 125n; **3**, *80 and n*, 111, 127, 130, 131, 227, 228, 244, 247, 248, 250; **4**, 290; **6**, 11; **9**, 19, 20; essay on Burke, **3**, 80n, 224–5; B.'s admiration for, 80n, 104, 121, 241; reviewed Staël's *Germany*, 96n, 224 and n; and *Bride of Abydos*, 177, 226; defended B. in *Morning Chronicle*, 251; suggests help for Godwin, **5**, 16 and n, 18; *History of England*, **3**, 253n; *History of the Revolution in England in 1688*, 253n

Mackintosh, Lady, **3**, 121, 228, 232, 236
Macleod, Col., **2**, 216, 217
Macmahon, Col., **10**, 22
McMillan, B. *Rejected Addresses . . . for Drury Lane*, **2**, 204n; 'Dejected Addresses', 249 and n, 252
Macnamara, **7**, 230
Macneil, Hector, **1**, 194
Macpherson, James, *Ossian*, **1**, 115, 130n, 132 and n, 163 and n; **2**, 84; **3**, 109n; **4**, 315n
Macready, William Charles, **9**, 83n
Macri, Mrs. Tarsia and daughters, **1**, 240 and n; **2**, 11n, 13 and n, 46
Macri, Theresa ('Maid of Athens'), **2**, 13, 46
Maddison, creditor, **10**, 27, 41, 96
Madison, James, **8**, 53
Madras, **1**, 172; **5**, 235
Madrid, **1**, 217, 221; **2**, 216n; **3**, 153; **8**, 12n
Mafra, **1**, 218–19 and n
Magdalen Asylum, **2**, 265 and n
Magellan, Straits of, **6**, 212n
Magliabecchi, Antonio, **3**, *239 and n*
Mahmoud [Mahmout] II, Sultan, **1**, 242 and n, 243, 244; **2**, 3, 8, 9, 18, 22; **3**, 58n; **4**, 100; **11**, 157
Mahmout Pasha, **1**, 231 and n, 249–50, 254
Mahomet, **2**, 97; **3**, 213, 215; **6**, 5, 122; **11**, 41, 125, 132
Mahomet, rope-dancer, **2**, 214 and n
Mahon (unidentified), **1**, 165
Mahoney, Miss, **7**, 104 and n, 127
Mahratta War, **11**, 218
Maida Vale, **4**, 294n; **5**, 15
Maiden Lane, **3**, 107n; **5**, 15
Maidenhead, **3**, 56
Mainote pirates, **2**, 30, 31, 36; **10**, 180
Maintenon, Madame de, **7**, 38
Mainvielle, Mme Fodor, **6**, 105n
Maitland, Sir Thomas, **1**, 239n; **11**, 20n, 34 and n; and neutrality of Ionian Islands, 90
Mala, Venetian playwright, **5**, 150
Malamocco, **6**, 10; **8**, 77
Malaprop, Mrs., **11**, 229
Malatesta, Launcelot, of Rimini, **5**, 214; **6**, 182
Malcolm, **5**, 260n, 269
Malcolm, Sir John, **4**, *147 and n*, 150; *History of Persia*, 147n, 148 and n
Malcolm-Smith, E. F., *Life of Stratford Canning*, **3**, 160n
Mallet (Malloch), David, **2**, *180 and n*
Malmaison, **5**, 65
Malone, Edmond, ed. of Shakespeare, **3**, 80 and n; notes to Spence's *Observations*, **6**, 4n

Malta, **2**, 3, 7, 8, 11, 28, 33, 38, 49, 51, 53, 56, 57, 58, 71, 262n; **3**, 57n, 75; **4**, 321n; **8**, 26n; **9**, 31; **10**, 196n; **11**, 26n, 62, 65, 94, 110, 157, 158, 159, 220; B. to sail for, **1**, 203, 208, 210, 214; credit sent to, 207, 245; B.'s address abroad, 215, 218, 234, 235, 236, 240, 241, 243, 244, 247, 248, 249, 250, 253, 254, 255; **2**, 4, 9, 17, 18, 19, 29, 33, 38, 39, 40, 45n, 198n; B. at, **1**, 223–5, 255; **2**, 44–8; B.'s affair with Mrs. Spencer Smith, **1**, 224, 239, 240; B. challenged officer at, 224 and n, 225, 239 and n, 240; B. well received by governor, 225, 239; B. left on *Spider*, 226; B. left for, **2**, 4n; vases carried to, 11; Hobhouse at, 21, 28, 31, 42; B.'s ague at, 44, 46, 51, 53, 56, 58; **11**, 159; B.'s farewell to, **2**, 126 and n
Malta, Knights of, **11**, 104 and n
Malta Mercury, **11**, 156
Malta packet, **1**, 199, 208, 221
Maltby, Harriet, **1**, 127 and n
Malthus, Thomas Robert, **1**, 6; **2**, 74, 98; **9**, 19
Malucceli, Antonio, Teresa's servant, **9**, 139 and n, 158, 160–1
Malvasia, Alessandro, Cardinal Legate, **6**, 172, 174, 176, 177–8, 181, 189; **7**, *47 and n*
Malvasiana Academy, The, **7**, 47n
Malvern Mercury, **8**, 215
Manchester, **6**, 232; Peterloo Massacre, **7**, 80, 81; **9**, 134 and n; **10**, 57n
Manchester (servant?), **2**, 36
Manchester, Duchess of, elopement, **3**, 37 and n
Manchester, William Mantagu, 5th Duke of, **3**, 37n
Manfrini Palace, **5**, 213 and n, 215
Manicheism, **8**, 89, 142; **7**, 132; **8**, 237
Mann, Horace, **6**, 30
Manners, Miss, **2**, 108n
Manners, John, **3**, 85n
Manners, Lady R., **10**, 113, 114, 115, 119
Manners-Sutton, Charles, Archbishop of Canterbury, B.'s letter to, **4**, 244; mentioned, **5**, 179; member of Alfred Club, **2**, 125; B. applied for special marriage license, **4**, *243–4n*, 245
Mannheim, **5**, 77; **6**, 104n
Manning, Peter J., **5**, 82n
Mansel, William Lort, Master of Trinity, **1**, *81 and n*, 92 and n; Bishop of Bristol, **7**, 154; Matthews and, 234
Mansfield, **1**, 171; **4**, 108
Mansfield, William Murray, 1st Earl of, **6**, 89

Mansion House, **1**, 3; **2**, 37

Mantinea, **2**, 16 and n; **9**, 48

Manton, Joe, gunsmith, **4**, 260; **5**, 71; **6**, 90, 140; **7**, 78; **8**, 31; **9**, 63, 75

Manton's pistols, **3**, 82, 209

Mantua, **5**, 211 and n, **8**, 40

Marat, Jean-Paul, **1**, 16; **7**, 45, 80

Marathon, **1**, 237; **2**, 36; **5**, 76; **9**, 48

Marceau, General François, Sévérin Desgravins, **5**, 77; **10**, 165 and n; **11**, 55, 76

Marchand, Leslie A., *Byron: A. Biography*, **1**, 40n, 88n, 100n, 104n, 117n, 167n, 170n, 257n; **2**, 200n; **3**, 17n; **5**, 15n, 267n, **8**, 24n, 185n; **9**, 74n; **10**, 35n, 124n; **11**, 177n

Marciana Library, **5**, 182n

Marcus Aurelius, *see* Aurelius

Mardyn, Mrs., actress, in *Lover's Vows*, **4**, 311 and n, 312; rumoured affair with B., **5**, 30n

Maremma, **9**, 102n

Marengo, **5**, 125; **9**, 48

Margarot, Maurice, member of Corresponding Society, **5**, 15n

Margarot, Mrs., Elizabeth, subscriptions for, **5**, 15 and n

Margate, **3**, 94; **5**, 179, 210

Maria-Louisa, Grand Duchess, **6**, 178 and n, 221n

Maria Theresa, Empress, **3**, 110; **10**, 185n

Marie-Antoine, Electress, **9**, 121n

Marie Antoinette, **5**, 147; **11**, 227

Marietta, housemaid, **6**, 20

Marinet, Kinnaird's informant, **6**, 165 and n

Marini, **7**, 94

Marischalchi Gallery, Bologna, **7**, 11, 45

Marius, Caius, **6**, 25 and n

Marlborough, **9**, 32

Marlow, **6**, 7

Marlowe, Christopher, *Faustus* compared with *Manfred*, **5**, 268 and n, 270; *Tamburlaine*, **1**, 216 and n

Marmarotouri, **2**, 32n

Marmont, Marshal, defeated by Wellington, **2**, 216n

Marmontel, Jean François, **5**, 147; 'Mme. Tencin', **2**, 236 and n; *Mémoires d'un Père*, **7**, 63 and n

Marsyas-Apollo contest, **6**, 145n

Martial, *Ad Julium Cerealem*, **2**, 145 and n

Martigny, **5**, 115

Martin Marprelate, **8**, 127

Martineau, Harriet, *Cent-Soisante Quatorze Lettres a Stendhal*, **10**, 190n

Martinetti, Mme., **8**, 154

Martini, **8**, 168

Mary Magdalen, **2**, *263*

Mary Queen of Scots, **1**, 178 and n; **7**, 204, 212

Masi, Sergeant-Major Stefani, affray with B. and party, **9**, 128 and n, 128–35, 138–40, 151–9, *passim*, 171–2, 186; **11**, 194n, 195n; and Shelley, **9**, 128n, 160 and n; Taaffe's statement, 133 and n, 140, 236; stabbed by Papi, 139n, 172n; far-reaching effects of affray, 168–9, 169n, 175–6

Mason, Mrs. (Lady Mount Cashell), **9**, 205 and n

Mason, William, **6**, 30

Massena, Marshal, the scalp of, **1**, 118; retreats into Spain, **2**, 91 and n

Massingberd, Mrs. Elizabeth (née Waterhouse), B.'s letters to, **1**, 84, 93, 100, 166, 167; **2**, 60; **11**, 173, 176; mentioned, **1**, *82 and n*, 122 and n; **2**, 154; **4**, 259 and n; guarantor of B.'s loan, **1**, 87n, 93 and n, 166 and n, 182, 183 and n, 214; annuities, **2**, 60, 62, 122–3, 139, 147, 152, 153; **5**, 247, 278; **6**, 6, 42; death, **2**, 231 and n; go-between with money lenders, **11**, 176 and n

Massingberd, Mrs. and Miss, **11**, 156 and n

Massingberd, Miss, **2**, 234 and n; **10**, 16–17, 65–6, 74, 146–7

Massingberd, Capt. Thomas, R.N., **1**, 82n

Massinger, Philip, **3**, 61, 64; **4**, 319n; **6**, 95; *A New Way to Pay Old Debts*, 192 and n, 206 and n; **7**, 194 and n

Materialism, **9**, 45, 46

Mathematics, **2**, 158, 231, 284; Cocker's arithmetic, **10**, 61 and n

Mathias, Thomas James, B.'s letter to, **2**, 176; and *Childe Harold*, 171 and n, 178; *Pursuits of Literature*, 86–7, 87n, 171n, 176, *The Shade of Alexander Pope*, 171n

Matlock, **3**, 107, 122

Matlock, Mrs. **10**, 61

Matta, Charles de Bourdeille, Compte de, **3**, 147 and n, 148 and n

Matthew, Gospel of, **11**, 222

Matthews, Charles Skinner, B.'s letters to, **1**, 206; **11**, 159; biog. sketch (2nd printing), **1**, 277; mentioned, **1**, 81n; **2**, 26, 32, 42, 46, 47, 50, 80; **9**, 60n, 89; **11**, 155; Hobhouse's closest friend, **2**, 70, 77, 83–4; drowned in Cam, **2**, 68 and n, 69, 120 and n; **8**, 24; **11**, 159n, 221; B. hints to him of his amours, **2**, 7, 10, 14, 16, 23, 29, 49; nicknamed 'Citoyen' by B., 13, 14, 16 and n, 49; B. suggested joint literary periodical, 33, 43, 56; con-

Matthews, Charles Skinner—*continued*
tributor to *Miscellany*, 45, 49, 50,
55; last letter to B., 69–70; B. on his
character and abilities, 76, 77, 81,
83–4, 92–3, 95, 157; a most decided
atheist, 76; and Hobhouse, **7**, 138n,
225, 230, 231 and n, 232–3, 234;
possible memoir, 224, 230; correspondence with B., 224, 225; Fellow
of Downing, 225 and n, 230; B.'s
recollections of, 230–4; Newstead
visit, 231 and n, 232; interest in
pugilism, 233; at the Opera, 233–4
Matthews, Henry, **2**, 143; **9**, 60 and n,
61, 67; **11**, 161 and n, 221 **7**, 172,
183, 224, 233; *Diary of an Invalid*,
138 and n, 182, 183
Matthews, John, **1**, 277
Matthisson, Friedrich von, **5**, 85 and n,
86
Maturin, Rev. Charles Robert, B.'s
letter to, **4**, 336 and n; mentioned, **5**,
37n, 77, 83; **9**, 80; play accepted by
Dury Lane, **4**, 336–7; gift of £50
from B., 337; B.'s intended aid, **5**,
16n; B. on, 237–8; published by
Murray, 251n, 252, 259 and n;
reviewed by Coleridge, 267 and n;
Bertram, **4**, 336 and n; **5**, 77, 79,
82n, 85 and n, 201; **6**, 124 and n; **9**,
35; **11**, 165n; *Manuel*, its failure, **5**,
195 and n, 196, 198, 203–4, 205, 210,
237; **11**, 165n; *Melmoth the Wanderer*,
4, 336n
Maupertuis, Pierre Louis, **8**, 46 and n;
9, 76
Mavrocordatos, Prince Alexander, B.'s
letters to, **11**, 36, 70, 104; biog.
sketch, 22n, 215–16; mentioned, 34,
41, 65 and n, 73, 87, 89n, 102, 115,
127, 128, 129, 130, 134, 135, 138,
140, 141; only civilized Greek, 22;
out of office, 22, 28, 30, 43, 44, 54;
with the Greek fleet, 34; asked B. for
loan of £4000, 52n; asked B. to come
to Missolonghi, 65n; B. to join, 75,
76–7, 78, 80, 81, 84; arrived with
Greek Fleet, 77; says B. will
'electrify' the troops, 85; letters to
Maitland, 90; invited to England,
104 and n; to Anatoliko with B., 106
and n; commissioned B. commander,
115 and n; B.'s opinion of, 124; will
go to Salona, 137 and n, 139, 140–1,
142, 144; invited to Morea, 141; and
Karaiskakis, 150 and n, 151
Mawman, J. bookseller, B.'s letter to,
8, 195, 196; mentioned, **9**, 54, 91;
sold copies of *Hours of Idleness*, **8**,
195n; called on B. in Ravenna, 195,
197, 207, 217, 223; and errors in

Don Juan, 196; carried B.'s Memoirs
and prose story to Moore, 196 and n,
198, 217, 245; and Roscoe's *Pope*,
201
Maxwell, Capt. Sir Murray, **6**, 59 and
n, 60, 93
May, Sir Edward, **3**, 247n
Mayence (Mainz), **5**, 76, 78
Mayer, Messrs., **9**, 203
Mayer, Mr., B.'s letter to, **11**, 118;
mentioned, 118n
Mayfield, Mr. B.'s letter to, **1**, 194;
Birthday Ode to B., 188, 194
Mayfield Cottage, **3**, 73n, 81; **4**, 100,
157, 253n, 270; **5**, 200n
Mayo, Dr., **11**, 46
Mazzoni, [Manzoni?,] **6**, 130, 188
Mealey, Owen, **2**, 153, 157 and n; **6**,
222; **9**, 55; **10**, 27, 47 and n, 91;
Steward of Newstead Abbey, **1**, *43
and n*, 121 and n, 204; **4**, 108, 150,
163, 166, 170, 248, 265 and n, 293
and n, his delinquencies, **1**, 168 and n,
189; B. orders discharge, **4**, 317
Mecca, **2**, 187; **3**, 53, 190–1
Mechlin, **5**, 72, 73, 74, 76
Medea, **1**, 245–6; **3**, 15, 16; **11**, 156n,
197
Medici Chapel and Gallery, **5**, 218
Medina, **3**, 190–1
Mediterranean, **1**, 135, 221, 239; **2**,
198, 218; **3**, 76, 93, 176; **4**, 151, 152;
8, 54, 111, 214; **9**, 173; **10**, 137,
170, 187; **11**, 65, 124, 186n, 214,
224
Medmenham Abbey, **1**, 161 and n, **9**,
186n
Meduna, **3**, 254
Medusa, **3**, 40
Medwin, Thomas, B.'s letter to, **9**, 95;
biog. sketch, 234–6; mentioned, **2**,
185n, 256n; **3**, 157n; **5**, 298; **11**,
231; brought report of auto-da-fé, **9**,
78n; riding with B., 80; left Pisa, 83
and n; and Southey's letter to *The
Courier*, 95n; in Shelley and B.'s
circle, 234–5, 237; plan for Greek
Committee, **10**, 163; *Conversations
of Lord Byron*, **1**, 1, 15; **9**, 235; **10**,
190n; *The Life of Percy Bysshe
Shelley* **9**, 235; *Oswald and Edwin*,
235
Mee, Mrs. **3**, 6, 14; **4**, 120n
Megara, **2**, 6, 8
Mehmet III, Sultan, **1**, 250–1n
Meillerei, **5**, 81, 82, 92; **6**, 126
Mekhitar, Peter, **5**, 130n
Melandri, **6**, 62
Melbourne, Lady (née Elizabeth Mil-
banke), B.'s letters to, **2**, 171 (2)
181, 184 (2), 187, 188, 192, 193,

198, 199, 202 (2), 208, 216, 222, 226, 229, 232, 235, 236, 239, 240, 242, 243, 245 (2), 247, 248, 250, 252, 253, 254, 255, 257, 258, 260, 263, 264; **3**, 3 (3), 8, 10, 11 (2), 12, 13, 15, 16, 17, 18, 21, 23, 25, 26, 27 (2), 31, 35, 36, 40, 42, 44, 46, 47 (2), 50, 51, 53, 59, 65, 69, 70, 71, 72, 74, 77, 83, 85, 86, 87, 90, 91, 92, 97, 102, 108, 110, 112 (2), 115, 123, 125, 127, 132, 133, 136, 139, 141, 144, 145, 148 (2), 151, 152, 154, 157, 170, 173; **4**, 19, 21, 23, 26, 27, 31, 33, 39, 47, 53, 64, 69, 75, 86, 90, 99, 103, 104, 108, 110, 111, 116, 119 123 129, 132, 134, 135, 137, 158, 175, 178, 180, 185, 187, 191, 194, 198, 199, 204, 205 (2), 211, 217 (2), 227, 228, 229, 231, 249, 251, 258, 262, 266, 267, 289; biog. sketch, **2**, 283–4; mentioned, **1**, 6–7; **2**, 199, 215; **3**, 37n, 86n, 109, 131, 221, 234, 248; **4**, 17, 43n, 107n, 130, 196, 202, 219, 239, 240, 242, 244, 245, 254, 260, 262n; **5**, 89, 128; **8**, 155, 246; **9**, 20; **10**, 140n; B.'s chief confidante, **1**, 4–5; **3**, 141–3; **4**, 34, 35, 135, 136, 178, 179, 200, 204; her letters the most delightful, **1**, 19; **3**, 37, 153, 219, 221; B.'s letters to her, **1**, 24; **8**, 226; B. gives account of Mrs. Smith, **1**, 224n; asks B. to leave town, **2**, 184 and n; and B.'s affair with Caroline Lamb, 198; and B.'s wish to marry Annabella, 202, 226 and n, 229, 232; B.'s regard for, **3**, 3, 4, 179, 209, 219, 272; **4**, 56–7, 203, 258; her influence on B., **3**, 3, 4, 93; and Lord Egremont, 4n; **4**, 289 and n; **11**, 183; intermediary between B. and Caroline, **3**, 8–9, 16, 23, 40, 52, 143, 152, 153n; early marriage, 46n; her conversation, 48, 93; and Caroline-B. at Lady Heathcote's, 72 and n, 74; and B.'s liaison with Augusta, 83, 87 and n, 93, 102 and n, 113n, 124n, 125 and n; **4**, 21n, 66 and n, 110, 111, 198, 262; and Annabella, **3**, 98, 103, 108 and n; saved B. from two fatal liaisons, 153; and *Bride of Abydos*, 170, 175 and n; residence in Whitehall, **4**, 87n; intermediary for B. with Annabella, 99 and n, 111, 179, 181, 183, 199; B. to call her aunt, 199, 229, 258, 262; her amusing comments, 230; very unwell, **6**, 23; death, 34, 243; compared with Countess Benzoni, 40, 97

Melbourne, 1st Viscount (Sir Peniston Lamb), **2**, 45n, 187n, 233; **3**, 45, 46n, 66, 232n; **4**, 90, 204, 211–12, 218,

250, 258, 336; paid visit to B., 205

Melbourne, Lord and Lady, **9**, 16

Melbourne House, **2**, 183n, 241 and n; **3**, 45, 271; **4**, 238n, 239

Meletius of Janina, **3**, 61 and n; Archbishop of Athens, **2**, 114 and n, 125, 134, 190; *Ancient and Modern Geography*, 59 and n, 60, 114 and n

Mellon, Harriet, **9**, 138n

Melpomene, **4**, 158 and n

Melville, Henry Dundas, Viscount, **1**, 66 and n

Memoirs (Byron's), *see* Byron, *Memoirs*

Menelaus (ship), **4**, 198n

Mengaldo, Cavaliere Angelo, **6**, 96, 144 and n, 177, 179, 180; **7**, 79; **8**, 81, 82, 131; **11**, 194; swimming matches with B., **6**, *51 and n*, 60, 191, 279; and Dr. Aglietti's daughter, 190 and n; B. on, 190–1

Mercati, Count, **11**, 138 and n, 141, 143

Mercer Elphinstone, Margaret, *see* Elphinstone, Margaret Mercer

Mercure du Dixneuvième Siècle, **10**, 207n

Merivale, John Herman, B.'s letters to, **3**, 50; **4**, 12, 293, 301; mentioned, **2**, 55; **3**, 7 and n, 50 and n, 170; **4**, 94; **7**, 54; reviews Grimm's *Correspondance Littéraire*, **3**, 247 and n; *see also*, Bland, Robert; well reviewed, **4**, 163–4; submitted play to Drury Lane, *301 and n*; *Orlando in Roncesvalles*, 12 and n

Merry, Robert, Della Cruscan school, **5**, 233 and n

Merryweather, Francis, **6**, 213 and n, 233–4; **7**, 79, 103; imprisoned for a day, 106 and n; B.'s lawsuit against, **11**, 194–5 and n.

Merton College, Oxford, **11**, 155

Meryon, Charles Lewis, **2**, 21n

Messina, cobbler of **6**, 12 and n

Messina, Straits of, **11**, 29

Mestri, **6**, 54, 72, 74; **8**, 66, 68

Metastasio, **2**, 60; **3**, 110, 195

Metaxa, Count Constantine, **11**, 25 and n, 26, 32

Metaxata, **11**, 20 and n, 45, 58, 134n; B. in village of, **1**, 23; B.'s house destroyed by earthquake, **11**, 43

Metcalf (referee), **10**, 84–5

Methodism, **2**, 77, 112; **3**, 66; **4**, 87, 164n; **6**, 101; **10**, 128; **11**, 87n

Methodists, **1**, 115; **4**, 332 and n; **9**, 17

Metternich, Prince, **4**, 131–2

Meyer, Jean Jacques, **11**, 132 and n, 139 and n

Meyer Davis Collection, U. of Penn., **1**, 168n; **6**, 83n; **9**, 172n

Meyler, Richard, 'Dick the Dandy-killer', **9**, *21 and n*
Mezzofanti, Giuseppe (later Cardinal), **9**, 30–1
Michelangelo, **5**, 216, 218, 221; **9**, 11, 74
Michelli, Conte, **6**, 15
Michelli, Contessa, **6**, 32, 96, 114; **8**, 241; **10**, 130
Middleton, Jersey estate, **2**, 209, 215n, 218, 229, 237, 239, 240, 241, 246; **3**, 9, 13, 123, 135, 153, 170, 207, 213, 231, 271; **4**, 32; **9**, 44
Middleton, Dr., **5**, 67
Milan, **4**, 93; **5**, 93, 111, 126, 127, 128, 129, 132, 181, 197, 200; **6**, 15, 39n, 91, 124 and n, 165, 213n, 240; **7**, 95; **8**, 41n, 116, 124, 232; **9**, 66, 149, 210; **10**, 189; B. at, **5**, 113–22, 137, 147, 197, 206; Ambrosian Library, 114, 116, 123; Society at, 117, 119, 120, 125; Polidori banished, 121, 122, 124, 126; **11**, 163
Milan Gazette, **7**, 173; **8**, 123
Milan papers, **8**, 117, 118, 119
Milbanke, Anne Isabella (Annabella), *see also* Byron, Lady; B.'s letters to, **3**, 98, 103, 108, 118, 119, 158, 178; **4**, 54, 60, 65, 71, 78, 82, 101, 130, 148, 155, 158, 161, 168, 169, 173, 176, 177, 180, 182, 189, 193, 196, 202, 203, 206, 207, 210 (2), 215, 219, 221, 223, 226, 232 (2), 233, 234, 235, 236, 238, 239 (2), 240 (2), 241 (2), 242, 243, 244, 245 (2), 246, 247; biog. sketch, **2**, 284; mentioned, **3**, 48n, 78, 110, 153; **4**, 75, 77 and n, 134n, 135, 200, 211, 223, 225, 227, 235n; 'encumbered with virtue', **1**, 5; **4**, 109; 'a *cold collation*', **1**, 5; **2**, 246; 'Princess of Parallelograms', **1**, 5; **2**, 231, 261; **4**, 48; thought she could reform B., **1**, 5; B.'s un-censored candour, 5; B.'s 'Guide, Philosopher, and friend', 5–6; **4**, 177; 'all the cardinal virtues', **1**, 7; **2**, 208; conflict of B.'s relation with, **1**, 19; friendship with Augusta; 273; patron of Blacket, **2**, 53n, 80, 132, 175; B. on her poems, 175–6; **4**, 56 and n; saw B. at Melbourne House, **2**, 183n, B. wishes to marry, 195, 202, 218; B.'s admiration for, 195, 199, 202, 217, 230, 232; **4**, 109, 174, 183–4, 202, 207; supposed engagement to Eden, **2**, 202 and n, 217, 222; B.'s marriage proposal, 202, 217, 218, 226 and n, 229, 232, 283; **3**, 12, 98, 103; rejected B.'s proposal, **2**, 226 and n, 227, 229; B. not offended by her refusal, 226, 227, 229, 230, 232;

Lady Melbourne's interest in match with B., 226 and n, 229, 232, 237, 240, 245, 261; B. never was en-amoured, 227, 236, 246; her 'character' of B., 229 and n, 233; B.'s marriage intentions, **3**, 18–19, 53, 98–9, 103; B. rejoices in her escape from him, 53; her requirements for a husband, 108 and n; **4**, 230; on B.'s despondency, **3**, 109, 113; mathe-matician, 124, 159, 160, 227; 'your A.', 124n; her indiscretion in writing to B., 124–5; and Miss Montgomery, 136 and n, 159; B. believed her attached to another, 160 and n, 178n; **4**, 149; to retain B. as a friend, **3**, 178 and n, 179, 227; separation pro-ceedings, 225n; B. will be in love with her again, 251 and n; B. thinking of proposal, **4**, 55–6, 99, 111, 155; her story about previous attachment, 66, 216; rumour she refused B. a second time, 79, 83; on religion, 101, 109; prudish and prim, 123, 129; her correspondence with B., 130; B. declared his love, 155; her convoluted style, 158n; her consistency, 168; B.'s tentative second proposal, 169–70, 171 and n, 174; her acceptance of B., 174–6, 180ff., 195; Moore thinks her too straight-laced, 177; first meet-ing with B., 182–3; marriage settle-ment, 186, 196, 199, 201, 202–3, 204, 208, 223, 225, 229–30; to be heir of Lord Wentworth, 186, 187; honey-moon prospects, 204, 215, 230 and n, 239; her virtues, 209, 217; her first letter to B., 210 and n, 221; B.'s first visit to Seaham, 228–31; most silent woman, 228; passions stronger than supposed, 229; her fine feelings, 231; Hodgson's note to, 235 and n; marriage arrangements, 239, 243–7; her doubts and questions, 246; formed for B.'s destruction, **5**, 119; 'that virtuous monster', 141; B.'s 'funeral' with, **11**, 167
Milbanke, Lady Judith, *see also* Noel, Lady, **2**, 217, 218 and n, 284; **3**, 121; **4**, 67, 130, 159, 174, 189, 197, 203, 206, 207, 208, 211, 216, 227, 230, 238, 247, 249, 256, 262; B. doesn't like her at all, 228; B. gets on pretty well with, 231; passion for business, 232; her longevity, 260; came to London, 288 and n
Milbanke, Sir Ralph, *see also* Noel, Sir Ralph, **2**, 218 and n, 283, 284; **3**, 121; **4**, 67, 101, 130, 149, 159, 162, 174, 180, 192, 196, 197, 199, 203, 211, 212, 216, 218, 222n, 224, 225,

226, 230, 247, 258, 261, 271; in debt, 179, 208; B. pleased with, 228, 231; called Sir Jacob, 256 and n; Baronet is eternal, 260; repeats his speeches, 262, 263; possible death, 265; played fiddle, 279

Mildmay, Sir Henry, 3, 170; 9, 22n; 10, 141; elopement with Lady Rosebery, 4, 225 and n, 227, 242

Miller, Joseph (Joe), 3, 223 and n

Miller, William, B.'s letters to, 2, 3, 63; mentioned, 2, 136, 137, 141, 142, 146; 11, 179; B.'s debt to, 2, 22, 57, 62, 66; *Childe Harold*, 63 and n; at Albemarle St., 235n, 286

Millingen, Julius, biog. sketch, 11, 72n, 216; mentioned, 151, 146n and Hatagée, 111n, 127; and B.'s last illness, 216; *Memoirs of the Affairs of Greece*, 54n, 150n, 216

Milman, Henry Hart, Dean of St. Paul's 8, 163, 193 and n, 207, 228; reviewed by Heber, 7, 132 and n, 168; *Fall of Jerusalem*, 138 and n; 9, 53 and n; *Fazio*, 6, 18 and n; *History of Christianity*, 18n; *History of the Jews*, 18n

Milnes, Robert Pemberton, (Mills), 6, 89; 7, 154 and n, 168, 225 and n, 230; 9, 14

Milo, 10, 180

Milo, Greek athlete, 3, 256

Milo, Titus Annus, 7, 81 and n

Miltiades, 9, 48

Miltitz, Baroness, 7, 146

Milton, John, 2, 82; 3, 37, 141; 4, 50, 278n, 332, 358; 5, 66; 6, 42, 85; 7, 83; 8, 40, 109; B. thought Pope his equal, 200; B. compared to, 9, 11; his Satan as impious as Cain, 53, 60, 89, 103, 118; *Comus*, 2, 219; 3, 63 and n; 8, 23 and n; 11, 157 and n; *Il Penseroso*, 8, 19 and n; *Paradise Lost*, 4, 13; 8, 68 and n, 115, 208 and n, 250 and n; 10, 116 and n; *The Reason of Church Government*, 9, 161 and n; *Samson Agonistes*, 2, 83 and n; 9, 60 and n

Mimnermus, 4, 51 and n

Minerva, 2, 157; 3, 20n

Minerva, Paris paper, 6, 262

Minorca, 3, 115

Mira, la, 5, 237n, 238, 243, 273; 6, 59n, 183, 204n, 230, 237, 238, 245; 7, 63, 67

Mirabeau, Honoré-Gabriel, Comte de, 1, 16; 3, 218; 7, 80; B. compared to, 9, 11; his eloquence, 14; 'words are things', 3, 207 and n; 4, 74 and n; 11, 224

Miracles, 2, 97

Missiaglia, Giovanni Battista, B.'s letters to, 8, 98, 135; mentioned, 6, 179, 183–4, 204, 205, 213, 218; 7, 28, 174, 191, 203; 8, 70–1, 75, 84; 10, 76n; proprietor of Apollo Library, Venice, 6, 30, *177 and n*; B. recommended to Murray, 59, 122; B. unable to assist, 224–5; to send B. *Minerva*, 262

Missolonghi, 5, 74n; 10, 179n, 180; 11, 20n, 26, 32, 34, 41, 72n, 79n, 80, 87 and n, 88, 92n, 96, 100n, 106n, 111n, 127n, 134n, 138n, 146n; B. left for, 1, 26; B. going to, 229, 233; Hobhouse intended to join B. at, 276; B.'s death in, 4, 189n; 10, 35n; 11, 19n; B. invited to by Metaxa, 25, 26; attacked by Turks, 40; siege of, 65; Greek fleet to aid, 52n, 62, blockaded by Turkish fleet, 54, 102, 150 and n; B.'s loan to aid, 59 and n; Stanhope left for, 64n; safe for present, 72; B. leaving for, 81, 82, 84, 85; B. prevented from reaching, 87; B. landed at, 92 and n, 101, 102; marshy situation, 107; arms laboratory in, 105–6; B.'s financial aid to, 130; plague rumoured, 135, 136; false alarm, 137n, 140; weather, 137, 141, 142, 151; Parry arrived in, 106, 108

Mistico, 11, 86n

Mitchell, Mr., saddler, 1, 144 and n, 148

Mitchell, Thomas, trns. *Comedies of Aristophanes*, 7, 184 and n; 8, 132 and n

Mitford, Mary Russell, 1, 154n

Mitford, William, *History of Greece*, 1, 20–1; 8, 13, 14, 15, 18, 26, 27, 129n, 238

Mithridates, 4, 23

Mitylene Island, 6, 119, 132; 8, 150 and n

Mocenigo, Madame, 6, 93, 174, 183, 254; 7, 65, 79, 103, 119

Mocenigo Palace, 5, 296; 6, 25n, 39n, 40, 43, 196, 204, 234; 7, 39n; 200 Louis a year, 6, 48–9, 65; B. giving up lease, 7, 119, 125, 135; 11, 194n

Modena, 5, 211; 8, 41n

Mohammed, 3, 191

Moira, John Hastings, 1st Earl of, 3, 71n, 75n; 4, 119n; 7, 200

Moira, Francis Rawdon Hastings, 2nd Earl of, 2, 215n; 9, 27; 10, 153

Moldavia, 11, 215

Molière, 8, 31; disparaged by Schlegel, 165 and n; *L'Avare*, 1, 52 and n

Monaco [Munich?], 7, 146

Monbron, Fougeret de, *Le Cosmopolite*, 2, 100 and n, 105; 5, 37

Moncada, Marquis, 5, 272–3

Monckton, Hon. Mary, **4**, *278n*
Moniteur, **3**, 254
Monselice, **5**, 264
Montagu, Edward Wortley, **3**, *213 and
n*; **4**, 11; **5**, 276n
Montagu, Lady Mary Wortley, **1**,
189–90, 250 and n; **5**, 275–6; **6**, 30,
64; **7**, 184; *Letters*, **1**, 250; **5**, 275
and n, 276; and Pope, **2**, 130; **8**, 85
and n; and Algarotti, **6**, 30, 60
Montaigne, Michel de, *Essays*, **10**, 150
Montanari, Maria, **8**, 35–6, 38–9
Mont Blanc, **1**, 115; **3**, 233; **5**, 78, 89,
91, 93, 96, 97, 106, 115, 120, 127,
188
Montbovon, **5**, 98, 99, 205
Mont Cenis, **6**, 73
Mont Davant, **5**, 98
Montecchi, **5**, 132, 206
Montem, **1**, 166 and n, 247 and n
Montenero, **9**, 135n, 161n, 164n, 179n;
10, 152n; **11**, 140n
Montesquieu, Baron, *The Spirit of the
Laws*, **1**, 148 and n
Montgomery, Hugh, **3**, 136n
Montgomery, James, **4**, 50n
Montgomery, Mary Millicent, **3**, 136
and n, 159
Monthly Literary Recreations, **1**, 129
and n; **9**, 42 and n
Monthly Mirror, **1**, 150n, 167n
Monthly Magazine, **8**, 83n
Monthly Review, **1**, 141 and n, 147; **2**,
156 and n, 167n; **3**, 7 and n, 57 and n;
59; **5**, 176 and n; **6**, 32n; **7**, 196; **8**,
156, 186n, 219; **9**, 42; **11**, 174n, 230
Monti, Count, *see also* Mosti, Count, **7**,
192; **11**, 233
Monti, Vincenzo, **3**, 245 and n; **5**, 119,
124, 154, 206; **6**, 91 and n, 96;
translator of Homer, **7**, 31; political
turncoat, 152 and n; *Aristodemo*; **3**,
245; *Mascheroniana*, **5**, 117 and n
Mont St. Jean, **5**, 76
Monza, **5**, 125 and n
Monzoni [Mazzoni?], **7**, 112
Moore, Barbara, d. of Thomas, death,
6, 9–10
Moore, Doris Langley, Museum of
Costume, **1**, 231n; *The Late Lord
Byron*, **6**, 235n; **7**, 244n; **8**, 11n; **10**,
189n, 190n; **11**, 214; *Lord Byron:
Accounts Rendered*, **10**, 74n, 104n,
119n; **11**, 31n, 162n
Moore, Dr. John, *View of Society and
Manners in Italy*, **5**, 174 and n, 233,
237; **7**, 131 and n, 142; *Zeluco*, **3**, 37;
5, 174n; **7**, 131n
Moore, Sir John, **1**, 239n; **11**, 25
Moore, John, f. of Thomas, **5**, 164 and
n

Moore, Olivia Byron, B.'s god-
daughter, **4**, 173; death, 153 and n,
284 and n
Moore, Peter, Drury Lane Committee,
4, 296 and n; **5**, 159 and n; **9**, 36
Moore, Thomas, B.'s letters to, **2**, 118,
120, 121, 122, 145, 159, 169, 170,
173, 176, 177; **3**, 49, 54, 66, 72, 75,
78, 81, 82, 94, 100, 104, 106, 111,
112, 122, 130, 183, 193; **4**, 12, 16,
18 (2), 30, 51, 62, 72, 76, 79, 91,
113, 114 (2), 115 (2), 117 (2), 118,
120, 125, 138 (2), 151, 156, 157, 172,
173, 177, 208, 243, 252, 255, 263,
265, 269, 273, 277, 279, 284, 289,
296, 301, 322, 326, 329; **5**, 14, 35,
44, 129, 146, 164, 176, 185, 186,
200, 210, 227, 249; **6**, 9, 23, 45, 66;
7, 16, 104, 111, 117, 125, 170, 206,
218, 244, 245; **8**, 54, 67, 84, 104,
108, 116, 123, 133, 140, 146, 164,
188, 196, 213, 214, 219, 225, 228 (2),
236, 250; **9**, 63, 79, 81, 109, 110,
115, 116, 118, 120, 122, 160, 170,
182, 190, 196; **10**, 105, 136; **11**, 84,
125; biog. sketch, **2**, 284–5; mentioned, **1**, 3, 158, 277; **3**, 33, 54n,
79n, 97, 203, 208, 217, 230, 272; **4**,
45, 61, 91, 100n, 102, 113n, 138n,
140, 149, 154, 164, 198, 255 and n,
262, 266 and n, 270, 271, 273, 295,
326; **5**, 87, 90, 111, 147n, 194, 197,
206; **6**, 6, 18, 78, 83, 192; **7**, 14, 17n,
69, 83, 102, 104n, 131, 139, 175,
178, 184n, 245n, 246n; **8**, 29n, 30 and
n, 46, 56, 61, 172, 207, 219, 224,
235, 238; **9**, 35, 142, 158, 190n; **10**,
26, 59, 64, 174; **11**, 179; B.'s letter
to on poetry, **1**, 2; bowdlerizes B.'s
letters, 4; B.'s letters to among best,
4; no affections, 14; not a strict
Catholic, 15; B.'s journal of 1813–14
given to, 25; **4**, 126 and n; **8**, 11; B.
gave him his Memoirs, **1**, 25–6; **6**,
59n, 232, 235, 261; **7**, 169, 244 and n;
copy of B.'s Memoirs, 207n; on the
Newstead ghost, **1**, 39n; abortive
duel with Jeffrey, **2**, 118n, 123 and n;
near duel with B., 118–19, 120–1,
123 and n, 152 and n; offence at
English Bards, 118 and n, 119, 120,
121, 123 and n; friendship with B.,
121, 122, 123, 127, 128, 129, 131,
145, 146, 147, 168n, 169, 170, 173–4,
176, 177; entré into Whig society,
123n; Alfred Club, 145 and n; on
Campbell, 147, 149; invited to meet
Caroline Lamb, 169–70; his wife's
beauty, 177, 178; **6**, 237–8; B.'s
affair with Caroline, **2**, 177; with B.
to see Leigh Hunt, 281; his pseudo-

nyms, **3**, 49 and n; asked to be editor of a periodical, 66–7; at Mayfield Cottage, 73n; Moira his patron, 75n; attack on Prince Regent, 75n; his songs, 79 and n; at Ashbourne, 81 and n; underrates himself, 111, 194; visited Hunt in prison, 189; his many talents, 215, 220, 232, 236, 245; referred to in *Edinburgh Review*, 224 and n; Lord John Russell his executor, 226n; national lyricist of Ireland, **4**, 12–13, 114n, 262, 297–8; dedication of *Corsair*, 12–14 and n, 16, 17, 18 and n, 20, 59; advises B. to marry, 21; urged B. to enter parliamentary debates, 63 and n; B. urged him to write drama, 115; cut up in *Champion*, 115 and n; in *Java Gazette*, 117 and n; **8**, 27, 28; **9**, 30; promoted match between B. and Lady Adelaide Forbes, **4**, 120 and n; death of daughter Olivia, 153n; **5**, 14n; reviews Thurlow's poems, **4**, 156 and n, 172 and n, 209 and n; in London, 240; **8**, 245, 246, 247; **9**, 156; asks B. for coat pattern, **4**, 243 and n; post in Bermuda, 243 and n; on Boyd's *Chrysostom*, 252 and n; at Chatsworth, 263 and n, 267; lines to Lady Jersey, 269 and n; dislike of 'Lord of the Iseles', 280n; to publish with Longmans, 285n; epilogue to *Ian*, 290n; Drury Lane Committee, 296 and n, 302; B. asks him to write opera, 302, 322; B. asks him to review Coleridge, 324; 'Sacred Melodies', **5**, 14n; on Lady Frances Webster, 28n; B.'s verses to, 148–9, 176; **8**, 85; *Corsair* dedicated to, **5**, 154; B. on his misfortunes, 164n, 165; moves to Hornsey, 186n, 200n, 211 and n; B.'s liking for, 192, 239, 265; **10**, 34; leaves Mayfield cottage, **5**, 200 and n, 201; proposed dedication to B., **6**, 10; cottage at Sloperton, 24n; B. to ask Moore to approach Longman for him, 55, 56; Registrar to the Admiralty, Bermuda, 67n; visit to Ireland, 67 and n; embezzlement by his deputy, 67n, 205 and n, 209; **8**, 251 and n; with B. in Venice, **6**, 230, 232, 236, 238; **8**, 66; sold B.'s *Memoirs* to Murray, **6**, 235n; **7**, 244n; **10**, 22, 33; death of daughter Barbara, **6**, 9n, 13, 16; at Paris, **7**, 28, 34, 106; **8**, 219; **9**, 93, 94, 101, 160 and n; French edition of works, **7**, 117 and n; marriage, 117n; and B.'s birthday, 170 and n; and Rogers, 181; **8**, 132–3; and Mulock's lectures, **7**, 244n; B. proposes joint journal,

254–5; **8**, 55, 147, 166; and B.'s Ravenna Journal, 11n; story of French husband, 55n; thought B. would be popular in Paris, 91; lines on the Neapolitans, 105 and n, 108n, 109, 131; and Bowles affair, 109 and n, 134 and n, 146; told story about Bowles, 111–12; urged by B. to sell *Memoirs*, 141; B.'s *Memoirs*, 164 and n, 176 and n, 182, 188, 217, 226, 227 and n, 250 and n, 251; **9**, 57, 68–9, 70, 74, 85 and n, 88, 168, 182; has B.'s correspondence with Lady Byron, **8**, 177; at home in high life, 207; sums received for poems, 211; to edit B.'s *Memoirs*, 216, 226; B. sent him *The Irish Avatar*, 236 and n; member of Watier's Club, **9**, 22 and n, 23; and quip about Edgeworth, 34; likes *Don Juan*, 55; opinion of *Cain*, 60, 61, 64, 67, 111 and n, 119n; and Southey, 62; Lord Lansdowne's offer to pay debts, 64; and *Irish Avatar*, 71; suggests 'bemonstered' biography of B., 79–80 and n; B.'s MSS to be sent to Moore, 93, 101; *Werner* sent to, 93, 94, 100, 112, 115, 116–17, 118, 125, 136; warned B. about Hunt association, 110n; effect of his being in society, 119; on Shelley's influence on B., 119n, 121, 122n; singing duets, 170; and *The Liberal*, 183, 197; changed angels into muslims, **10**, 105 and n, 116, 137, 160; friend of Blessingtons, 174, 175; thought B. continuing *Don Juan*, **11**, 125 and n; MS journal, 196 and n, 229; information about B. from Hancock, 214; Anacreon's *Odes* (translation), **2**, 123 and n; **4**, 274 and n; 'Come rest in this bosom', **7**, 246 and n; *Epistles, Odes, and other Poems*, **8**, 24 and n; **10**, 29 and n; 'Epistle from Tom Cribb to Big Ben', **9**, 116 and n; *The Fudge Family in Paris*, **6**, 46 and n; **8**, 78n; *Fudges* (in Paris and England, and possibly Italy), **7**, 106 and n, 117; *Irish Melodies*, **3**, 113n, 114, 131n, 193–4, 220; **4**, 114n, 298n, 330 and n; **6**, 67n, 206 and n; **7**, 117, 218–19; **8**, 230 and n; **9**, 117 and n; **11**, 85 and n; *Lalla Rookh*, **3**, 101n, 112n, 194n; **4**, 12–13, 157 and n, 209 and n, 323 and n, 330 and n; **5**, 124 and n, 131, 134, 150, 177, 186 and n, 192, 195, 206, 222, 227, 248; **9**, 171; published by Longman, **5**, 165 and n, 251n; B. on, 249 and n, 250, 251–2, 262, 265; received £3000 for, 263; success of poem, 239; **6**, 11, 46, 232; **8**, 140,

127

Moore, Thomas—*continued*
164 and n; *Letters and Journals of Lord Byron with Notices of his Life*, **1**, 4, 24, 39n, 111n, 120n, 136n, 148n, 158n, 176n, 195n; **2**, 177n; **3**, 33n, 101n, 102n, 112n, 130n, 164n, 194n, 240n, 258; **4**, 156n; **5**, 14n, 91n; **6**, 15n; **7**, 39n, 58n, 60, 125n, 188n; **8**, 11n, 134n, 196n, 228n; **9**, 64n, 80n; **10**, 213n; **11**, 68n, 83 and n, 89n, 104n, 186n; passages omitted, 196 and n; *Life of Sheridan*, **3**, 54n; **5**, 201 and n, 207; **6**, 47–8, 68 and n; *Loves of the Angels*, **3**, 102n, 104; **8**, 140 and n, **10**, 105 and n, 116, 137 and n, 160; *Memoirs*, **2**, 162n; **4**, 330n; *M.P. or the Bluestocking*, **2**, 97 and n; 'Oh breathe not his name', **7**, 218–19; 'One dear smile', **4**, 125 and n; *Poetical Works of the Late Thomas Little*, **1**, 13, 103 and n, 132 and n, 137, 141 and n; **2**, 97n; **3**, 96 and n; **5**, 126n; **6**, 91, 94, 234; **7**, 117 and n; 207; **8**, 200; **10**, 68; *Twopenny Postbag*, **3**, 73 and n, 75n, 194–5, 215; **4**, 73; **11**, 180 and n
Moore, Mrs. Thomas, **2**, 177, 178; **4**, 158, 253, 284, 303; **5**, 14; **8**, 228
Morandi, **7**, 131
Morat, **5**, 78, 86, 99, 104, 111, 112, 163; **8**, 20 and n; **11**, 227
More, Hannah, **3**, 238
Morea, **2**, 24, 30, 31, 33, 34, 37, 114, 262; **3**, 206; **4**, 26, 321; **5**, 214; **7**, 236; **10**, 180 and n, 181, 203; **11**, 16, 19n, 27, 29, 30, 38, 45 and n, 50, 55, 65, 69, 72, 80, 90, 128, 135, 138n, 141, 143, 146, 185 and n, 213; B. landed in, **1**, 225; Veli Pasha governs, 226, 231; B. leaving for, 229, 232; B. passed some time in, 233, 237, 250; B. to visit, 243, 244, 246; **2**, 3; Fletcher to accompany B. to, **1**, 252; Aberdeen's explorations, 254n; B. in, **2**, 5–11, 14–23, 27; B. with fever in, 14–16, 18–19, 29, 42; Greek Government in, **11**, 94
Moreau, Jean Victor Marie, at Dresden, **3**, 125 and n
Morelli, Abbé, **6**, 35; custodian of Marciana Library, **5**, 182n, 293
Moreri, Louis, **4**, 104, 106; *Grand Dictionnaire Historique*, 102 and n
Moretto, B.'s bulldog, **6**, 235 and n
Morgan, Major, **4**, 257
Morgan, Sir Thomas Charles (Dr.), **6**, 13
Morgan, Sydney Owenson, Lady, **6**, 12; attacked in *Quarterly Review*, 12n, 13; *France*, 12n; *Italy*, **7**, 165 and n, 170; **8**, 186 and n, 189; **10**, 55–6 and

n, 61n; *Memoirs*, **3**, 214n; *The Mohawks*, **10**, 61 and n; *O'Donnel*, **4**, 146 and n
Morghen, Raphael, engraver, **3**, 248n; **8**, 79 and n; **9**, 211 and n, 214
Morillo, Gen. Pablo, **8**, 126 and n
Morland, banker, **9**, 116
Morland and Ransom, bankers, **5**, 107, 196, 236, 254 and n, 262, 266, 270, 272; **6**, 6–7, 26, 43, 54, 58; **11**, 155
Morning Chronicle, B.'s letter to, **11**, 181; mentioned, **2**, 125, 166n, 183n, 225 and n, 228 and n, 250n, 254; **3**, 55, 60n, 182n, 251; **4**, 37n, 45, 152 and n, 242, 252n, 291, 302; **5**, 34n, 52n, 58n, 138n, 165, 169n, 172, 176, 184n, 197; **8**, 67; **9**, 19; **11**, 182n; published B.'s lines on Prince Regent, **4**, 42; defended B.'s lines, 52 and n; praised B.'s Ode on Napoleon, 102 and n; contradicted B.'s engagement announcement, 192–3, 194, 195, 197–8, 200; announces B.'s arrival in England, **7**, 172, 173–4, 176, 177; Webster's reply to *Quarterly*, **11**, 163 and n
Morning Herald, The, **1**, 144 and n; **2**, 166; **4**, 19, 240
Morning Post, **2**, 125, 167, 197, 235, 254; **3**, 25n, 65, 90n, 107, 218, 224 and n, 236, 240n, 242; **4**, 45, 49, 50, 51, 53, 62, 63, 64n, 71n, 208, 258, 269; **5**, 45, 59, 194, 277; **7**, 205, 214n; **11**, 170; announced B.'s engagement, **4**, 192, 219, 252, 269 and n
Morosini, **3**, 248
Morpurgo, J. E., ed. Hunt's *Autobiography*, **5**, 182n
Morris, Charles, laureate, **3**, *79 and n*
Morris, Gouverneur, **8**, 53n
Mortlake, **2**, 84
Mortlock, Mr., Mayor of Cambridge, **1**, 92 and n
Morton, Thomas, 'The Knight of Snowdon', **2**, 160 and n
Moscow, **9**, 48
Moses, **3**, 164; **4**, 302
Moslems, **11**, 35
Mosques, **1**, 240, 242, 243, 250, 251; **2**, 3, 8, 18
Mosti, Count, **6**, 144, 146, 148; **11**, 233
Mottley, John, *Joe Miller's Jests*, **3**, 223n
Mouctar Pasha, **1**, 231n; **2**, 22
Mount Athos, **1**, 115; **2**, 33; **8**, 82
Mount Caucasus, **1**, 177, 217; **3**, 233
Mt. Ida, **1**, 238
Mount Sion, **1**, 217; **2**, 39
Mount Temeret (Tomerit), **1**, 237
Mountjoy, *see* Blessington, Lord

Mountnorris, George Annesley, Viscount Valentia, Earl of, **3**, 216 and n; **4**, 67 and n; **10**, 113 and n; proposed mortgage, **11**, 24, 50

Mountnorris, Lady, **4**, 22 and n

Mouros, **3**, 85

Moverly, **9**, 191n

Mozart, Wolfgang Amadeus, **10**, 189; *Barber of Seville*, **7**, 25

Mudie, Miss, **2**, 214 and n

Muggleton, Lodowicke, **2**, 82 and n

Muggletonian sect, **2**, 82 and n

Muir, Henry, B.'s letter to, **11**, 87; mentioned, 29, 87 and n, 89, 93, 95, 96, 106, 107, 134, 215

Mule, Mrs., B.'s firelighter, **3**, 246

Muley Moloch of Morocco, **7**, 49

Müller, Johann von, *History of the Helvetic Confederation*, **5**, 86 and n

Müllner, Adolf, *Die Schuld*, **8**, 25 and n

Mulock, Thomas, lectures in Paris, **7**, 244 and n, 245, *Answer Given by the Gospel to the Atheism of All Ages*, 49 and n; eulogizes B.'s poetry, 49

Munda, **9**, 48

Munich, **6**, 124

Munichia (Turcolimano), **2**, 37

Münster Mercury, **2**, 65

Murad III, Sultan, **1**, 251 n

Murad, IV, **3**, 256 and n

Murat, Joachim, King of Naples, death, **4**, 330 and n, 331

Muratori, Ludovico Antonio, **8**, 41 and n, 59n; *Antiquitates Italicae*, **6**, 188n

Murillo, Bartolomé Esteban, **5**, 213

Murphy, Arthur, **9**, 67 and n; *The Citizen*, **6**, 48 and n; *The Way to Keep Him*, **3**, 136 and n, 145

Murray, Archibald, of HMS *Rochfort*, **9**, 212 and n, 213, 218

Murray, Charles, **8**, 181 and n; **10**, 67 and n

Murray, Joseph (Joe), B.'s letter to, **1**, 204; mentioned, 142, 143, 176; **2**, 4, 71, 74, 85, 88, 94, 148, 232; **3**, 21, 105–6; **4**, 121; **5**, 52 and n; **7**, 70; **9**, 20; servant of 5th Lord B., **1**, 45n, 138 and n; honest fellow, 181; must live in clover, 189; B. regrets leaving him, 206; on Lisbon Packet, 212; sent home from Gibraltar, 221, 222, 225, 235, 244; to be paid board and wages, **5**, 89, 151, 189; to be looked after, **6**, 41, 43; death, **7**, 208

Murray, John I, **2**, 285

Murray, John II, B.'s letters to, **2**, 78, 90, 98, 100, 174 (2), 175, 190, 196, 211, 224, 227, 228, 234, 249; **3**, 4, 10, 20, 28, 33, 41, 48, 49, 50, 51, 54 (2), 55, 60 (2), 61, 64, 65, 66, 68,

69, 78, 83, 84, 87, 100, 115, 125, 131, 132 (2), 141, 156 (2), 157, 162 (2), 163 (2), 164, 165 (2), 166 (2), 169 (3), 170, 172, 173, 175, 176, 177 (3), 181 (2), 182, 183 (2), 185, 186 (2), 188, 190 (2), 191 (3), 192 (2), 197 (2), 201 (3), 203; **4**, 11 (3), 14 (2), 15, 16, 17, 18, 20, 22, 24, 32, 33, 36, 41, 44, 46, 47, 48, 49, 52 (2), 57 (2), 58, 59, 64, 65, 70, 71, 76 (2), 81, 83, 89, 91, 94 (3), 95 (3), 96 (2), 98 (2), 102 (2), 103 (2), 106 (2), 107, 112, 117, 126, 129, 132 (2), 134 (2), 140 (2), 142, 144, 145 (2), 146 (2), 147 (2), 149, 150, 153, 154, 160, 162, 163, 167, 248, 250 (2), 264, 287 (3), 292, 294, 307, 308, 315 (2), 331 (2), 333, 337; **5**, 13, 17 (2), 18, 22, 28 (2), 36, 37, 42, 52, 57, 58 (2), 59, 60 (3), 62, 67, 81, 84, 90, 105, 107, 110, 111, 113, 115, 121, 132, 137, 138, 151, 154, 163, 169, 173, 174, 177, 178, 183, 191, 203, 207, 211, 212, 214, 217, 219, 220, 222, 229, 232, 235, 237, 239, 241, 244, 247, 249, 251, 253, 254, 256, 257, 262, 264, 266, 267, 269, 272, 275; **6**, 3, 7, 9, 11, 15, 21, 22, 24, 26, 30, 31, 32, 34, 38, 52, 53, 55 (2), 57, 58, 60, 62, 63, 70, 82, 85, 90, 94 (2), 98, 99, 104 (2), 105 (2), 122, 125, 133, 138, 139, 148, 167, 192, 205, 206, 215, 216, 218, 223, 224, 227, 235, 238, 252, 256; **7**, 14, 34, 41, 45, 47, 54, 57, 58 (2), 59, 60 (2), 73, 74, 76, 82, 96, 101, 102, 113, 114, 124, 131, 137, 141, 142, 146, 150, 158 (2), 161, 162 (2), 164, 165 (2), 168, 169, 172, 173, 175, 176 (2), 179, 181, 182, 188, 191, 194, 199, 203, 204, 206, 212, 216, 223, 228, 230, 238, 247, 250 (2), 256, 257; **8**, 53 (2), 56, 58, 59, 60, 61, 64, 66, 67, 69, 73, 76, 77, 80, 85, 87, 89, 90, 92 (2), 99, 102, 109, 111, 116, 118, 126, 127, 128, 136, 144, 145, 147, 149 (2), 151, 155, 161, 166, 172 (2), 176, 178, 181, 186, 192, 194, 197 (2), 201, 203, 205, 206, 216, 219, 224, 226, 232, 235, 236, 244, 247, 248 (3), 251; **9**, 53 (2), 57, 58 (2), 59, 69, 74, 77, 90 (2), 91, 103, 121, 125, 132, 136, 141, 146 (2), 151, 155, 156, 159, 163, 166, 167, 178, 179, 181, 182, 189, 192, 206, 212; **10**, 12, 16, 17, 21, 22, 28, 36, 40, 52, 63, 67; **11**, 123, 184 (2), 185, 186, 187 (2), 190 (2), 192; biog. sketch, **2**, 285–6; mentioned, **1**, 248; **2**, 185n; **3**, 3n, 5n, 6, 20n, 69n, 131, 189, 208, 234, 251, 253, 273; **4**, 15, 50, 57n, 81n, 98, 104n, 117, 147n,

Murray, John II—*continued*
153, 157, 159–60, 243, 249, 252, 275, 287n, 289, 305, 316; **5**, 43, 77, 81, 83, 87, 131, 139, 141, 153, 161, 171, 178n, 182, 185, 186, 187, 195, 198; **6**, 4n, 10, 14, 19, 76, 90, 91, 172n, 213, 232, 259; **7**, 39, 51, 62, 75, 94, 95, 99, 111, 120, 127, 178, 179, 184n, 190, 205, 211, 213, 239, 251, 253, 255; **8**, 13, 18, 23, 27, 34, 87, 92, 100, 105, 128, 129, 137, 141, 142, 149, 158, 181, 198, 199, 205, 221, 231, 232, 239, 240; **9**, 30, 81, 83, 118, 141, 151, 154, 170, 195, 201, 203, 204, 205, 206; **10**, 27, 33, 42, 53, 67, 68, 73, 96, 123; **11**, 117, 126, 194, 229–30; literary coterie, **1**, 3; B.'s letters to among his best, 4; B.'s verses to, 6; **5**, 193–4, 258–60; **6**, 3–6, 27–9; B.'s quarrels with, **1**, 11; B. on bargain and barter, 12; **8**, 153, 244–5; **9**, 62; relationship with B. **1**, 13; might publish B.'s poems, 248; published *Childe Harold*, 274; **2**, 63n, 76, 81, 83n, 84, 90–1 and n, 113, 224n, 228; B.'s letter on Matthews, **1**, 277 (2nd printing); **7**, 230–4; received Attic Hemlock from B., **2**, 59n; submits MS to Gifford, 78, 80, 98–9, 101, 109, 130; asks B. to moderate some passages, 91 and n, 99, 107; arouses B.'s anger, 101, 105, 107, 111; has MS of *Childe Harold*, 150; publisher of Bernard Barton, 178 and n; and Scott, 182 and n; publisher of Lucien Buonaparte, 197; **3**, 78n; and the Drury Lane Address, **2**, 220, 221; removal to Albemarle Street, 235 and n; **3**, 7; published Hunt's *Rimini*, **2**, 281; **4**, 331 and n; **5**, 19, 32 and n, 208n; and Caroline Lamb, **2**, 283; **3**, 17; publisher of *Quarterly Review*, 5n, 11 and n, 51n, 62 and n; 'Anax of publishers', 66; and Caroline's forged letter, 10–11 and n, 36n; and Hobhouse, 15; saw Lady Charlotte Harley, 33; not publisher of *Waltz*, 41 and n; and *Giaour*, 44n, 51 and n, 59, 62, 63; friend of D'Israeli, 50n; B.'s books to, 56; B. and Gifford, 64, 161; publisher of Moore's life of B., 112n; and Phillips engraving, 113; *Curse of Minerva*, private printing, 132 and n; *Bride of Abydos*, 164 and n, 232, 237; given Phillips portrait of B., 167; **5**, 28n, 106; publisher of Penrose journal, **3**, 176 and n; offered 1,000 gns. for *Giaour* and *Bride*, 187–8, 212; **4**, 63, 71n; and *Satirist*, **3**, 197 and n; associated with Blackwood,

238 and n; **6**, 3n, 126; and *Corsair*, **3**, 243; objects to dedication to *Corsair*, **4**, 14n, 17, 18 and n, 32 and n; sold 10,000 copies of *Corsair* in one day, 44 and n; omitted B.'s lines on Regent, 52, 54; 'intercepted letters', 57 and n; payment for B.'s poems, 63–4, 64n, 71n, 71–2; B. recommends Hogg to him, 151, 152, 164; publishes Coleridge, 285n, 321n, 331n; brings B. and Scott together, **2**, 286; **4**, 287 and n, 358; attacked by robbers, 294 and n, 297; gave drawings to Lady Byron, 292 and n; *Five Tragedies* (Sotheby), 315 and n; *La Pie Voleuse*, 315 and n; offers B. financial assistance, 333 and n; offers B. 1,000 gns. for *Corinth* and *Parisina*, **5**, 13 and n, 16, 17, 18; *Siege of Corinth*, 13n, 16 and n; B.'s complaint about, 17, 18, 19; **6**, 52, 53, 55, 56, 57, 100, 102–3, 131, 138, 166, 205; **10**, 116; *Parisina* **5**, 18, 22n; praised by B., 19; concerned about B. in separation, 29 and n; and B.'s books, 36–7, 42 and n, 57–8, 62, 66; showed B.'s verses to C. Lamb, 67–8, 68n; relics of Waterloo sent to, 76; publishes *Bertram*, 85n; takes *Childe Harold* III to Gifford, 105n; amounts paid to B. for *Childe Harold* III, 105–6, 106–7, 167, 171, 239, 246, 263, 266; to publish new journal, 108 and n; **6**, 3 and n, 4, 9, 29; and Frere, **5**, 134 and n; published Monody on death of Sheridan, 136n; and 'indelicacy' in *Don Juan*, **6**, 138; and imposter, **5**, 143, 145, 150, 158, 159; and omissions from B.'s MSS, 159, 160, 169 and n, 257 and n; *Manfred*, 183 and n, 225, 239, 246, 254; and Croker, 184 and n; and B.'s Alpine journal, 188; B. urged him to publish de Staël, 205; wishes to publish Hobhouse, 216; published *Life of Raffaele*, 221n; *Tasso*, 225–6, 239, 246, 254; Armenian friars introduced to, 235; published Maturin's *Manuel*, 251n; and Polidori's tragedy, 258 and n, 260–1; his drawing room, 260n; money due to B., 263, 266, 274; **6**, 34–5, 39, 40, 41, 42, 48, 49, 50, 51, 52, 55, 59, 92, 102, 145, 221; **10**, 20, 153; published Hobhouse's *Historical Illustrations*, **5**, 269n; Polidori's diary, 295; and Knight, **6**, 3 and n, 27, 28; 4th Canto of *Harold*, 3 and n, 32, 36, 45–6, 53, 105; his authors, 3–4; his friends, 5; called coxcomb of booksellers, 11 and n, 102; financial dealings with B., 26, 39, 46, 52, 56, 77, 109, 132, 136–7,

138, 143, 145, 187; **8**, 71–7 *passim*, 96 and n, 153, 171, 218, 250 and n; **9**, 62, 63, 71, 72, 73, 82, 84, 89, 91, 93; books for B., **6**, 77, 78n, 83–4; **8**, 135, 144, 219–21; sent kaleidoscope to B., **6**, 77n, 82; and Isaac D'Israeli, 83n; and publication of *Don Juan*, 91, 200 and n, 210, 234; 'Vampyre' story sent to him, 126 and n; his reaction to *Don Juan*, 200 and n, 205; **10**, 35 and n, 60; B. asks him to get vice-consulship for Guiccioli, **6**, 208–9; buys B.'s *Memoirs* from Moore, 235n; **7**, 244n; **10**, 22; and pirates, **6**, 252 and n, 256; **9**, 99, 187, 200, 207, 209, 211, 218; publishes *Don Juan*, Cantos, 3, 4, and 5, 7, 250n; 1832–3 edition of B.'s works, 17n, 60n; to send bulldogs to B., 41; abuses *Edinburgh Magazine*, 49; failure to acknowledge packets and letters, 76, 77, 121–2, 257; need not publish B.'s works, 85–6, 96, 114, 116; B. to leave him as publisher, 121–2; **9**, 90, 93–4, 101, 104, 110, 116n, 120; **10**, 23, 28, 36; scolded by B., **7**, 124; **8**, 126, 192–4; **10**, 12, 16, 17, 28; and *Marino Faliero* acting, **8**, 22, 59, 66n, 68 and n, 73, 78; B.'s letter to on Bowles, 44, 50, 53, and n, 79, 85 and n, 90, 92, 94, 102, 109 and n, 113, 114, 122, 239; failure to write to B., 56, 57–8, 58–9, 72, 126, 127, 143, 209; and Galignani copyrights, 72, 74; **10**, 134; to pay in guineas, **8**, 74, 132, 189; omitted stanza of *Don Juan*, 87n; as B.'s publisher, 92, 109–10, 137, 149, 158; asked to send Holmes to B., 95 and n, 135, 136, 181; B.'s 2nd letter on Bowles, 99 and n, 111 and n, 134, 166 and n, 172; complains that Kinnaird is brusque, 101; B.'s poetry disparaged by, 117; publisher to the Admiralty, 126 and n; **10**, 22; his offers to B. for poetry, **8**, 185–9 *passim*, 191, 208, 211–12, 222–3, 244–5; mercantile matters, 187; B. declined his offer for poems, 191; upbraided for printer's errors, 197; B. thinks him shuffling, 206; Arimaspian, 208 and n, 250; B. offers terms of future correspondence, 219–21, 224; B. threatened a new *English Bards*, 224; and B.'s *Memoirs*, 228–9, 250 and n, 251; **9**, 70, 84–5 and n, 88n; bill for books, **8**, 232, 239; B. considering withdrawal of MSS, 233; treatment of *Don Juan*, **9**, 54, 55, 82, 84, 104, 200; financial difficulties, 56, 218; sharp letters from B., 60; B.'s request not to send

him gossip, 61; and B.'s bust, 67, 69, 70, 71; threatened for publishing *Cain*, 88, 103, 104, 120, 122, 125 and n, 137 and n, 152; omitted dedication to Goethe, 91, 93, 163, 167, 182; **10**, 64; B. to extract MSS from Murray, **9**, 93, 94, 112, 116n; B.'s works in 17 volumes, 100n; to publish *Werner*, 116–17n, 120, 121, 142, 151, 155, 159, 166, 167, 199; B. relented and returned MSS to, 120, 124; Taaffe's *Commentary*, 123, 126, 236; gave MS of *Beppo* to Ada, 127n; accused of dawdling over MSS, 146, 153, 155–6, 168; wrote B. discouragingly, 161; asked to turn over *Vision* to John Hunt, 182; Stanzas on Wellington, 182–3; never writes to B., 188; and Davison, 199, 200; and John Hunt, **10**, 13, 32, 36, 41, 42, 57, 58, 67, 70; gave wrong copy of *Vision* to J. Hunt, 16, 17, 18, 21, 24, 25, 27, 158; his losses, 19, 24, 27, 52; offered B. 1,000 guineas per canto, 19, 58; showed B.'s letter about Hunt, 25 and n, 32, 33, 36, 57, 68; a curious riddle, 26; B.'s comments on, 27; refusal to see J. Hunt, 32; and Allegra's funeral, 54–5; B. suspicious of, 58, 62, 70, 98, 104, 108, 110, 123, 135, 145, 149; on new cantos of *Childe Harold*, 69, 108, 126, 127, 135; declines publishing *Don Juan*, 70; ledger account of *Werner* sale, 70–1n; money due for *Werner*, 85, 153, 154–5, 159; **11**, 24, 42, 50, 74; B.'s account for books, **10**, 86; one-eyed, 116n; sent supplies to B., **11**, 24; B. sent poetry to, 170 and n; B. sent *Manfred*, 164 and n; to send B. the *Quarterly*, 182; publisher of Knight, 183 and n; published *Lament of Tasso*, 190 and n; errors in *Childe Harold*, Canto III, 190 and n; tradesman or gentleman, 197; sought injunction for B., 227

Murray, Mrs. John, II, **6**, 206; **8**, 207
Murray, John IV, **1**, 24; *Lord Byron's Correspondence*, **3**, 28n; **4**, 262n
Murray MSS, **1**, 205n, 206n, 214n
Murphy, Arthur, *Zenobia*, **11**, 233
Museum of Costume, Bath, **1**, 231n
Mustapha, **3**, 58n
Mustani, Countess, **5**, 183
Musters, John (Chaworth-Musters), **4**, 48, 226–7, 228
Mustoxidi, learned Greek, **5**, *182 and n*; **11**, 228
Mutz, B.'s dog, **5**, 103–4, 127, 144, 217; **6**, 108, 235 and n
Mycenae, **6**, 150

'My Dictionary' journal, **8**, 105 and n, 106–8

Mykonos, **2**, 23 and n, 33 and n

Nagle, Sir, E., anecdote, **8**, 225n

Nairn, **3**, 80n

Naldi, Giuseppi, baritone, **1**, 195 and n

Nancy, Mrs. Byron's maid, **3**, 222

Nantes, **6**, 176, 177

Napier, Lt. Col. Charles James, B.'s letter to: **11**, 20; biog. sketch, 20n; mentioned, 22, 25, 31, 45, 55, 64, 83; favourable to Greek cause, 15n; wished to serve Greek Committee, 25; his hospitality to B., 27; B. dined with, 58; B. recommends to Bowring, 73, 74, 77; B. recommended to Kinnaird, 74; approves Hastings' plan, 79 and n; on Greek Loan Commission, 146n; recommended Mavrocordatos, 216

Naples, **4**, 93; **5**, 191, 197, 210, 221, 263n; **6**, 35, 65, 69, 148; **7**, 54, 192; **8**, 79, 95, 97 and n, 98, 232; **10**, 108, 126, 127, 151; Constitutional Government, **7**, 188n; King of, **6**, 92; **7**, 256; **8**, 12, 20; Pontifical Government, **7**, 188n; Queen of, **2**, 199; Revolution, **7**, 127, 136, 137, 138, 154, 172, 210, 211, 218, 255n

Napoleon, *see* Buonaparte, Napoleon.

Napoleonic War, **2**, 215n; **10**, 196n; **11**, 20n

Nauplia (Napoli di Romania), **2**, 16; **11**, 45n, 53, 57, 65, 72n

Nathan, Isaac, B.'s letters to, **4**, 187, 249; **5**, 68; presented matsos to B., **5**, 68–9; music for *Hebrew Melodies*, **2**, 282; **3**, 209n; **4**, *187n*, 220, 249 and n, 280; *Reminiscences of Lord Byron*, 187n

National Gallery, **3**, 214n; **6**, 173n

National Portrait Gallery, Scotland, **10**, 18n

Navagero, **7**, 132

Navarino, **10**, 180; **11**, 30

Navpactos, *see* Lepanto

Naxos, **3**, 31

Naylor, **10**, 113

Nazareth, **6**, 81

Neale, Mr., **2**, 153 and n

Neapolitans, B.'s letter to: **7**, 187; mentioned, **7**, 187, 236; **8**, 18, 36, 43, 44, 46, 48, 84, 124, 131; **9**, 150; treachery of, **8**, 99–100, 102, 104, 105 and n, 106, 108 and n, 109 and n, 115, 116, 122, 127, 211, 219

Neapolitan revolution, **8**, 12n

Neapolitan territory, **10**, 169

Necker, Jacques, **3**, 272

Negris, Theodore, **10**, *169 and n*

Neipperg, Adam Albert, Comte de, **6**, 219 and n

Nelson, Lord Horatio, **1**, 135, 230n; **9**, 48; **10**, 30n

Nemesis, **2**, 157; **5**, 165, 168, 181, 220, 232, 243, 246; **6**, 21, 70, 81, 82, 84, 90, 209

Nero, **6**, 12n

Nerva, **8**, 107

Nestor, **8**, 100n

Netherlands (Low Countries), **2**, 7; **5**, 86

Nettle, B.'s poodle, **3**, 118 and n, 122, 126, 127

Neufchâtel, **5**, 99, 104; **9**, 121n

Neuhause, **5**, 100

Nevile's Court, **1**, 79n

Newark, **1**, 133; **4**, 46; **11**, 173n

New Bond Street, **8**, 91

Newfoundland, **1**, 176n

Newfoundland dog, **10**, 164 and n

Newgate Prison, **2**, 177n; **7**, 45n, 70n; Mrs. Fry, **1**, 23; **9**, 74 and n, **11**, 32, 40; Eaton in, **3**, 185n; Hobhouse in, **6**, 187n; **7**, 16n, 49, 50, 57, 59 and n, 70n, 75, 102, 191n, 223, 224; **9**, 74, 88n; Erskine and Hobhouse, **11**, 59n

Newgate Monthly Magazine, **3**, 185n

Newington Butts, **11**, 166

Newmarket, **1**, 17, 135; **2**, 124; **3**, 32, 83n, 85; **4**, 200, 224, 276, 281; **9**, 19; **11**, 80, 156 and n

New Monthly Magazine, **6**, 119n, 131n

New Road, **8**, 207n

New South Wales, **11**, 221

Newstead Abbey, **2**, 20, 52, 99, 107, 126, 146, 158, 232; **3**, 38, 39, 114, 205; **4**, 41, 52n, 54, 124, 125, 148 and n, 157, 158, 171, 191, 212, 224, 228, 230, 238, 274, 311, 317; **5**, 26n, 52, 200; **7**, 204n, 208, 222, 225; B. at, **1**, 39–40; **2**, 68–116, 161; Horses to go to, **1**, 40; Mealey as steward, 43n, 121n; **10**, 47n; B. with Mealey at, **1**, 43–4; leased to Lord Grey, 44n, 45n; B. invites Gordon to, 72; Joe Murray at, 138 and n; view of suggested for frontispiece, 138; Lord Grey leaving in April, 163; Lord Grey invited to, 168; amateur theatricals, 170; **11**, 175 and n; Mrs. Byron to live at, **1**, 175; Boatswain's tomb, 176n, 178; B. will not sell, 179, 195–6, 202, 223; **2**, 25, 26, 28, 32, 35, 40, 41, 42, 45, 56, 94, 195; B. refurbishing, **1**, 180, 181, 199; tenants, 183; tenants celebrate B.'s birthday, 185 and n, 188; Hanson going to, 185–6; **4**, 309; maids at, **1**, 187, 189 and n, 191, 232n; **2**, 105–6, 131, 155, 162, 163; proposed mort-

gage, **1**, 199 and n; **8**, 87; **9**, 209, 211; **11**, 160; remittances from, **1**, 234; garden walls like Seraglio's, 251; Hanson manager of estate, 275; Hobhouse and Matthews at, 277 (2nd printing); B.'s mother at, **2**, 4; sold to Claughton, 28n, 188n, 189–90 and n, 215, 218, 238 and n, 248; **3**, 22, 24, 25, 28n, 29, 30, 70, 77, 81; **9**, 108; **11**, 185; Claughton's down payment, **2**, 28n; B. to return to, 46, 49, 51; **4**, 157, 158, 160, 206, 207, 208, 211, 216, 220, 232; **11**, 159; B. invites Hodgson there, **2**, 54; Mrs. Byron's home, 61; to be entailed in will, 71; B. to be buried in garden, 72; as matrimonial mansion, 86, 95, 109; **4**, 204, 215; 3,800 acres, **2**, 115; rents, 115, 133, 145, 156; **4**, 171, 247, 248, 264, 292, 293, 299, 300; **5**, 226, 236, 262, 272; **6**, 7, 39, 41, 54; Hodgson and Harness, **2**, 140, 141, 142, 143, 155; **11**, 179; contents to be sold, **2**, 162; **3**, 56 and n; auction of 1812, **2**, 184n, 188n; **4**, 299n; Hanson has gone to, **2**, 204; party in 1809, 287; contracts, **3**, 3; B. happy at, 36; B. regrets leaving, 96; Webster enamoured of maid, 116; B. and Webster at, 136–8, 145–8; **4**, 29, 31–2; B. regrets sale, **3**, 209; delayed sale prevented trip abroad, **4**, 21; B. and Augusta at, 40, 44, 45–6, 49, 161–78; Mary Chaworth wants B. to keep, 40; B.'s liking for, 40; Claughton at, 45, 47; Taxes, 108, 163, 166, 227; Claughton forfeited £25,000 and returned estate, 150 and n, 152, 155, 156, 168, 172, 216, 218, 299n; B. resolved to sell again, 165, 166, 179, 186, 188, 189–90, 199, 254, 255, 257, 259, 262, 291; Claughton wants to renew purchase, 264–5; preparing for auction 1815, 291, 292, 299 and n; acquired by Byrons, **5**, 19 and n; B.'s inheritance, 26n; earthquake at, 52 and n, 53; B. urges sale, 70, 134, 135, 139–40, 151, 161, 222, 226, 230, 236–7, 242, 245–6, 247, 257, 261, 271–2; **11**, 167; sale to Wildman, **5**, 70n, 277 and n, 278; **6**, 13, 34, 48, 65, 74 and n, 173; **10**, 46, 78; disposal of purchase money, **6**, 6, 39, 41, 79, 143n, 222n; purchase price, 13, 52, 222n; Wildman at, 81; produce of sale invested in funds, 143n; Matthews at, **7**, 231 and n; Irish mortgage, **8**, 61–2, 65; Mr. Walker's interest in, **11**, 189 and n

New Testament, **2**, 104; **7**, 125 and n, 144 and n, 172 and n

New Times, The, **3**, 21n

Newton, Isaac, **3**, 63n, 236

New York, **3**, 95n; **8**, 40n, 53 and n

New York Academy, **9**, 198, 211; **10**, 18

New York Public Library, **9**, 43n

Nice, **10**, 15, 55

Nichols, **2**, 67n

Nicholson (carpenter), **1**, 170

Nicopolis, **1**, 225, 229

Niger, **4**, 316n; **6**, 244n

Nile, Battle of, **4**, 154n

Niobe, **10**, 94

Noah, **3**, 164

Nodier, Charles, **10**, 207n, 209

Noel, Hon. Elizabeth, **4**, 288n

Noel (formerly Milbanke), Lady Judith, B.'s letter to: **5**, 34; mentioned, **5**, 26n, 46, 224, 228, 256; **6**, 65, 79, 91, 114, 138, 171, 228; 232; **7**, 172 and n, 179, 196, 208, 214, 239; **8**, 92; **10**, 47, 113, 115, 119, 126, 149, 150, 153, 163; legatee of Lord Wentworth, **4**, 288 and n, 289; becomes Noel, 288n, 289, 297, 303, 327–8, 337; at Kirkby, **5**, 15; and Mrs. Clermont, 31n; account of Ada to Augusta, 34; and Ada, 36, 109; B.'s mother-in-law jest, 165, 208, 231; illness and recovery, **8**, 96, 101, 102, 105, 123, 126, 128, 133, 139, 149, 181, 229, 232; 'she is immortal', **9**, 72, 73; contingency of her death, 82; death, 105 and n, 109, 111, 120 and n, 123–4, 198; **10**, 85; and B.'s portrait, **9**, 127 and n, 145, 164; and Wentworth estates, 152, 155, 165–6, 177, 196

Noel (formerly Milbanke), Sir Ralph (Sir Jacob), B.'s letters to: **5**, 20, 23; mentioned, **4**, 186, 196, 201, 208, 262, 263–4, 265, 279, 317n, 327–8, 336, 337; **5**, 224, 228, 256; **6**, 102, 103 **8**, 208; **10**, 19, 114n; becomes Noel, **4**, 288n, 289, 297, 302–3; Annabella's marriage settlement, 300n; proposed separation of B. from wife, **5**, 20 and n, 21, 23–4, 31; B. sorry for, 36; owes B. money, 52, 57, 189, 226, 236, 262; **6**, 7, 34, 41, 43, 48, 54, 221; equivocal letter about Ada's going abroad, **5**, 150, 154, 161–2; Chancery bill against B., 180, 190, 198–9; 'Sir Jacob', 246 and n; **6**, 101; mentioned, **9**, 105, 120, 209, 212; owes B., 55, 56, 62–3, 73, 82, 92, 108, 195, 199, 201; use of Kirkby Mallory, 111, 113, 145; payment of Annabella's dowry, **10**, 91

Noel, Rev. Thomas, **10**, 14–15, 54 and n, 203 and n, 204

Noel, estate, **9**, 105–6, 109, 111–12,

Noel—*continued*
114, 117, 127, 128, 138 and n, 141–2, 144–5 and n, 176, 186, 187, 198, 199, 201, 211, 212; **10**, 42, 110, 113, 119, 126, 132–3, 153, 155, 168; **11**, 42

Nore, The, **2**, 52; **9**, 95

Norfolk, **2**, 72

Norfolk, Duke of, **3**, 167–8; **4**, 198n; **6**, 47; **9**, 27

Norfolk copyholds, **1**, 203 and n, 214, 234, 235

Normandy, **5**, 104

Normandy, 1st Duke of, **6**, 26 and n

Norman-Ehrenfels, Count of, **10**, 179 and n, 180

Normans, **7**, 61

North, Catherine, **2**, 170 and n

North, Francis, *see* Guilford, 4th Earl of

North, Frederick (2nd Earl of Guilford), **2**, 170n

North, Frederick, Lord (later 5th Earl of Guilford), **2**, 5 and n, 10; **3**, 199 and n; *see also* Guilford, 5th Earl of

North British Magazine, **2**, 175

Norton, Honorable Grace, **1**, 40n

Norway, **8**, 146; **9**, 24

Norwegians, **8**, 95

Norwich, **2**, 139; **3**, 219n; **5**, 272; **7**, 168n; **9**, 97

Norwich, Bishop of, **4**, 244n

Notes and Queries, **1**, 39; **3**, 185n; **11**, 87n

Nottingham, **1**, 172n, 206n, 235, 249; **2**, 9, 47, 54, 55, 56, 59, 76n, 101, 117, 118, 131, 136, 138, 145, 151, 177, 243; **4**, 39, 51, 113n, 178, 184n, 202, 209, 247, 259, 317, 320; **7**, 236; **11**, 159, 173n; B. in, **1**, 39–40 and n; Burgage Manor near, 44; B.'s loan from, 121; riots and frame breaking in, **2**, 148, 150, 155, 161 and n, 165 and n

Nottinghamshire, **3**, 9, 242; **6**, 235; **9**, 170

Nottingham Public Libraries, **3**, 16n

Nourjahad, see Illusion

Nourse, **2**, 7

Nugent, ——, friend of Luttrell, **3**, 85 and n; **4**, 119 and n; **9**, 207

Oakes, General Sir Hildebrand, Commander in Malta, **1**, 224 and n, *239 and n*; **2**, 50, 55, 126 and n, 198 and n

Oatlands, **3**, 240 and n; **4**, 33 and n; **9**, 18

Oberhasli, **5**, 102

O'Brien, Mr., **2**, 218

Obrington, Lord, **4**, 267n

Observer, The, **2**, 56

O'Callaghan, George, **1**, 139n

Ochrida, **2**, 125

O'Connell, Dan, **4**, 296n

O'Connor, Arthur, **3**, 249n

Octavia, **3**, 207

Octavius, **8**, 107

Octavius, L. Annius, **4**, 93 and n

O'Donovan, P. M., **4**, 73; satirical inscription to B., 74 and n

Odysseus (Ulysses), **9**, 237; **10**, 169n; **11**, 23n, 137 and n, 141, 142, 144, 146, 218

Œdipus, **3**, 13; **6**, 173; **10**, 22

O'Hara, Kane, adaptation of Fielding's *Tom Thumb*, **1**, 208n; **6**, 214n; **11**, 220

O'Higgins, Mr., **9**, 36

Ohio River, **3**, 229

Okeden, Mr., **5**, 96

Old Bond Street, **5**, 173

Old Burlington Street, **6**, 223n

Old Street Road, **2**, 265n; **11**, 222

Old Testament, **2**, 140 and n; **11**, 179; parody of Ten Commandments, **7**, 196 and n

Olympia, **7**, 192

Oltrocchi, Baldassare, letters of Lucretia Borgia to Cardinal Bembo, **5**, 116 and n

Olympic Theatre, **5**, 72n

Olympus, **5**, 15

O'Meara, Barry Edward, *Historical Memoirs of Napoleon*, **10**, 82 and n, 108

O'Neill, Miss Eliza, actress, **4**, 235; **5**, 261 and n

Opera, **1**, 159n, 185, 195

Opie, Mrs. Amelia, **6**, 11; **7**, 203

Orange, Prince of, **3**, 172, 180n, 211, 218

Orators, **9**, 13–14, 16–17

Orchomenos, **2**, 134

Orestes, **5**, 198; **9**, 29

Orford, Horace Walpole, 4th Earl of, *Memoirs . . . of George II*, **8**, 72 and n, 112 and n, 144, 211; **9**, 155 and n

Orford, Sir Robert Walpole, 1st Earl of, **8**, 111

Oriel College, Oxford, **1**, 214n

Origo, Iris, on Teresa's recollection of B.'s conversation, **1**, 1; *The Last Attachment*, **1**, 24; **6**, 58n, 111n, 154n, 156n, 178n, 183n; **7**, 53n, 147n, 152n, 163n, 199n; **11**, 56n, 232

Oriental languages, **11**, 215; B.'s wish to study, **3**, 217; **9**, 31

Orinoco river, **9**, 173n

Orkneys, **4**, 151 and n

Orlando, Jean, **11**, 59n, 61–2, 68, 130n, 144, 146n

Orleans, Duke of, **4**, 43

Ormond Quay, **7**, 51, 70 and n, 72

Ormonde, 17th Earl of, **1**, 125n
Orpheus, **8**, 114; **9**, 32
Orson, son of Bellisant, **11**, 233
Orthodoxy, **2**, 76, 78
Osborn, James M., **1**, 136n
Osborne, Lady Mary, **1**, 60n
Osborne, Lord Sydney Godolphin, B.'s
   letters to: **10**, 142; **11**, 90; mentioned,
   1, *45 and n*; visited B. in Venice, **6**,
   62 and n; **8**, 34 and n; B. introduced
   Blaquiere to, 142, 143 and n, 171;
   visited B. at Metaxata, **11**, 56, 58
Osborne, Thomas, **5**, 143; **10**, 28
Ossian, **1**, 130n, 132n, 163 and n; **8**, 28
Ossulston, Lord (Charles Augustus
   Bennet, Earl of Tankerville), **2**, 185n
Ossulston, Lady (née Corisande
   Armandine, d. of Duc de Gramont),
   2, 185 and n; **3**, 4, 70, 211, 236; and
   Caroline Lamb, 71, 170, 171
Ostend, **5**, 70 and n, 71 and n, 74, 75
Ostheid, Capt., sells B. a horse, **6**,
   218–19
Ostrogoths, **7**, 127
Otaheite, **2**, 89
Otranto, **2**, 19; **4**, 171; **7**, 76; **11**, 166
Otto of Bavaria, **10**, 56n
Ottoman Empire, **1**, 178, 226n
Otway, Thomas, **2**, 197 and n, 206; **3**,
   109; **5**, 131; **6**, 42, 85; **7**, 194;
   Venice Preserved, **2**, 77 and n; **3**, 256
   and n; **5**, 203 and n; **8**, 120–1 and n
Ovid, **3**, 181, 189; **11**, 156n; *Ars
   Amatoria*, **8**, 79 and n; *Metamor-
   phoses*, **6**, 206n; **9**, 77 and n; **10**, 176
   and n
Ovioli, Domenico, **9**, 51
Owenson, Sydney, *see* Morgan, Lady
Owl's Club, **9**, 23
Oxberry, William, **5**, *72 and n*
Oxford, **2**, 258; **3**, 18; **4**, 214
Oxford, University, B. preferred, **1**, 63,
   108 and n; mentioned, **1**, 176n;
   5, 110n, 156, 163, 258; **7**, 230; **8**,
   207n; **9**, 69n, 95, 111; **11**, 155
Oxford, Edward Harley, 5th Earl of, **2**,
   215, 230, 254, 286; **3**, 10, 13, 15,
   59, 65, 128, 147; invited B. to
   Eywood, **2**, 227, 231, 234, 235; B. at
   Eywood, 238, 239; to lease Kinsham
   to B., 239, 240, 251, 258; alarmed
   by Caroline's messenger, 244;
   Harleian Miscellany, 249 and n, 258
   and n; Caroline may write to, 257
Oxford, Robert, 1st Earl of, alleged
   author of *Robinson Crusoe*, **3**, 62 and n
Oxford, Countess of, (née Jane
   Elizabeth Scott), biog. sketch, **2**,
   286; mentioned, **1**, 273; **2**, 215, 216,
   223, 227 and n, 255; **3**, 14, 29, 33n,
   91, 154, 158, 174, 247; **4**, 271n; **7**,

139, 202; likened to 'Armida', **2**,
   108n, 238 and n, 250, 261; B. to play
   her off against Caroline, 233; B.'s
   attachment to, 235, 240; B. pleased
   with Eywood life, 237, 240, 246, 249,
   261; letters from Caroline, 243–4,
   245, 247, 253, 265; objects to B.
   seeing Caroline, 246, 249; children
   of uncertain paternity, 258n, sup-
   porter of Princess Caroline, 263 and
   n; liaison with B., **3**, 3 and n, 4, 27,
   32, 48, 65, 70, 142 and n; B. paid for
   her portrait, 6, 14; and B. lived like
   the gods of Lucretius, 7, 210; de-
   nounced by Caroline, 8, 9; and
   Caroline, 13, 43, 128; B. hates
   travelling with her children, 15; to
   go abroad, 19, 53, 56n, 59, 62, 65,
   69, 73; on conference with Caroline,
   42, 45; B. sends lock of her hair to
   Caroline, 37 and n, 40, 140 and n;
   false alarm pregnancy by B., 40; B.'s
   portrait for her, 41; abused Rogers,
   47; broke a blood vessel, 47; adept
   at Greek, 58, 210–11; B.'s affair
   partly to escape Caroline, 142; good
   tempered, 143; urged B. to his
   'senatorial duties', 229; and King of
   Naples, **4**, 215; and Augusta, **8**, 217;
   kept B.'s letters, 227; B. her Cavalier
   Servente, **11**, 182n
'Oxoniensis', **9**, 100n, 103n, 142 and n,
   151n

Packwood, Mr. and Mrs. George,
   Packwood's Whim, **3**, 238 and n
Paddington Canal, **2**, 101n, 113
Padua, (Padova), **5**, 211, 217, 242,
   243, 264; **6**, 8, 21, 62, 144, 163, 241;
   7, 25
Paederasty, **1**, 208, 210
Paer, General, **6**, 212
Paez, José Antonio, **11**, 231
Paine, Thomas, **3**, 247n; **7**, 17, 50;
   Age of Reason, **3**, 185n; **6**, 240n; *The
   Rights of Man*, **3**, 184n
Palatine, **5**, 227
Palavicini-Capelli, Count, **10**, 130 and n
Palermo, **2**, 7; **3**, 75
Palestine, **2**, 5n, 39, 181
Palestrina, **8**, 77
Palethorpe, tenant, **1**, 183 and n
Palgrave, Sir Francis (né Cohen), **8**,
   59 and n, 69, 161n; scholar and
   translator, **6**, *207n*; appendix to
   Marino Faliero, **7**, 238 and n
Pall Mall, **5**, 262; **6**, 210, 251; **9**, 159;
   10, 24; **11**, 26, 62, 93
Palmer, Rev. John, Professor of
   Arabic, **1**, 172 and n
Palmerston, Lord, **7**, 168; **10**, 230

Pamphleteer, The, **5,** 111 and n
Pandora, **5,** 203
Pange, V. de, **5,** 88n
Pantheism, **2,** 181
Pantheon, **1,** 152 and n; **2,** 157; **5,** 191, 227
Papadopoli, Signor, **5,** 197
Papi, Vincenzo, B.'s coachman, **7,** 78, 125, 135; and Masi affray, **9,** 139n, 172n; **11,** 81, 194 and n
Paradise Row, **8,** 207 and n
Paris, **1,** 184n; **3,** 5, 210, 232n, 256; **4,** 126, 164, 302; **5,** 53, 114, 218, 277; **6,** 33, 166, 205, 234; **7,** 50n, 104, 109, 176, 206, 227, 244n; **8,** 14n, 44n, 91, 117, 131, 141, 166, 167, 172, 191, 225, 228; **9,** 21, 64, 93, 101, 110, 118, 183n, 196, 197; **10,** 64, 95, 102, 106, 122, 153, 155, 174, 179, 204 and n, 207n, 209; **11,** 155; allies entered, **4,** 90n; **5,** 34n; English flocked to after capitulation, **4,** 93, 101, 312n, 313; Hobhouse goes to, 100, 283 and n; Lord Kinnaird exiled from, 157 and n; **6,** 165n; De Staël banished from, **4,** 158; Napoleon returned to, 284 and n; Hobhouse's letters from 287 and n, 294 and n, 298; Websters in, 310, 312n; **7,** 111; Lambs in, **4,** 310, 312 and n; B. not suited to life in, **7,** 127; young Bowles in, **8,** 111–12
Paris (abductor of Helen), **7,** 31
Paris papers, **6,** 66; **11,** 195
Park, Mungo, **6,** 244 and n; *Mission to the Interior of Africa,* **4,** 316 and n
Parker, Admiral, **9,** 40
Parker, Augusta, **9,** 40
Parker, Mrs. Charlotte Augusta (née Byron), B.'s letter to: **1,** 39; mentioned, *39n,* 175n
Parker, Christopher, **1,** 39n, 175n; **4,** 184n
Parker, H., **11,** 158
Parker, Margaret, **1,** 39n; **4,** 184n; **9,** 40
Parker, Sir Peter, **1,** *39n,* 175 and n; **4,** *184n,* death in action, 184–5, 197–8, 198n, 201–2
Parkyns, Frances (Fanny), **1,** 39 and n
Parkyns, George Augustus Henry Anne, 2nd Baron Rancliffe, **1,** 39n
Parkyns, Mrs., **1,** 39 and n
Parkyns family, **1,** *39 and n,* 149n, 196n, 206 and n; **3,** 223
Parliament, **5,** 179, 192n, 202; **6,** 171; **7,** 16n, 75, 154, 205, 223; **8,** 120n, 121n; **9,** 16–17
Parnassus, **1,** 237; **2,** 59; **3,** 253; **4,** 302; **7,** 245; **9,** 41
Parolini, **6,** 96

Parr, Dr. Samuel, **2,** 85; **6,** *68 and n*; **7,** 217; **8,** 29 and n, 30; **9,** 34; **10,** 142 and n
Parucca, Demetrius, B.'s letter to: **11,** 134; mentioned, 130 and n, 138 and n, 141, 143
Parry, Sir William Edward, *Journal of a Voyage of Discovery,* **8,** 70 and n; **11,** 103
Parry, William, firemaster, biog. sketch, **11,** 217–18; mentioned, 117, 124, 128, 137–8, 150, 152; not yet arrived, 31 and n, 41, 65, 103; arrived in Missolonghi, 106; director of laboratory for arms, 105 and n; 'a fine rough subject', 108, 110; and Hodges, 111n; and B.'s convulsive attack, 113; in command of Artillery Corps, 115; B.'s scribe, 115 and n, 129 and n, 133; his reports to Greek Committee, 125, 136, 139, 146; and artificers, 124, 142; ill, 144; *The Last Days of Lord Byron,* 217
Parsons, William, **5,** 233
Parthenon, **2,** 157, 172n; **3,** 20n; **8,** 109
Partridge, John, **5,** 176, 197
Pas de Calais, **7,** 75
Pasqual, *see* Aucher, Father Pasquale
Passy, **10,** 64, 105
Pasta, Mme., prima donna, **7,** 26 and n, 52 and n
Pasteur de Cologny, B.'s letter to: **5,** 94
Paston, George, and Quennell, Peter, *To Lord Byron,* **4,** 122n
Patagonians, **6,** 212 and n
Paternoster Row, **2,** 11, 105; **3,** 41n; **10,** 70
Paterson, Joseph, **8,** 108
Patras, **2,** 9; **4,** 45; **5,** 197; **7,** 192; **11,** 75, 80, 84, 87, 91n, 117, 123, 124, 129; B. sailing for, **1,** 224, 230n; B. at, 225, 233, 235n; **2,** 5–8; B. going to, **1,** 229, 230, 232; B. ill in, **2,** 14–16, 18–19, 44; in hands of Turks, **11,** 50; Bombard taken to, 88, 89, 90, 91n, 102
Pattieson, Patrick, **5,** 171n
Paulician, **2,** 89
Paull, James, duellist, **8,** 144n
Paul, Mr., Imperial Consul, **2,** 7 and n
Paul, Prince of Würtemberg, **5,** 276 and n
Paul Pry, **10,** 207n
Pausanias, *Description of Greece,* **5,** 74 and n; **6,** 173
Pavone, Signor, **11,** 20
Payne and Mackinlay, **2,** 101 and n, 113
Peachee (Peachey), **9,** 163

Peacock, **2**, 132
Peacock, Robert, **11**, 27 and n, 39–40, 42
Peacock, Thomas Love, **8**, 145; **11**, 225; Shelley's executor, **9**, 202n; **10**, 16
Pearce, Henry, **1**, 139n, 158 and n
Pearson, Dr., and B.'s health, **1**, 157, 158, 160
Peattie, Antony, **11**, 99n
Pedro de Cevallos, Don, **1**, 193n
Peel, Sir Robert, **2**, 128 and n, 131; **6**, 89, 145; **7**, 168, 192; **8**, 227–8; **9**, 14, 22; at Harrow with B., 43
Pegasus, **6**, 10; **8**, 22; **10**, 61
Pekin, **7**, 40
Pellegrino Inn, Bologna, **6**, 150, 162, 163, 201
Pellico, Silvio, *Francesca da Rimini*, *Il Conciliatore*, *Le Mie Prigioni*, **10**, 189n
Peloponnesus, **1**, 151; **11**, 30, 128n, 134n, 135, 139
Pendele, Monastery, **2**, 23 and n
Pendennis (fort), **1**, 210
Peninsular War, **2**, 216n
Penmanmaur, **8**, 22; **11**, 160
Penn, Mr., **4**, 187; **11**, 226
Penn, Granville, *The Bioscope*, **2**, 196 and n; *'Christian Knowledge'*, 196 and n
Penn, William, **3**, 218; **4**, 187
Pennington, Capt., duellist, **7**, 178 and n
Pennsylvania, **8**, 22; **11**, 226
Pennsylvania, University of, **6**, 83n; Library, **1**, 168n; **9**, 172n
Penton, Henry, **8**, 207n
Pentonville, **8**, 207 and n
Pera (Constantinople), **2**, 33, 39
Perceval, Lady, **1**, 185 and n
Perceval, Spencer, **3**, 232n; shot by Bellingham, **2**, 177n, 192
Perelli, Don Gaspare, **6**, 159; **7**, 130, 185n; go-between for B. and Teresa, **6**, 117n, 152, 247 and n; B.'s suspicions, 155
Perry, James, B.'s letters to, **2**, 166; **4**, 192, 197; **5**, 33; ed. *Morning Chronicle*, **1**, 190n; **2**, 166 and n 225 and n, 226, 228, 235; **4**, 46, 50, 302, 307n, 322; **5**, 34n, 52 and n, 176, 182, 184, 194; **6**, 91, 206, 225–6, 227, 232, 236; **7**, 95, 176; **8**, 61, 68, 86n; and *Bride of Abydos*, **3**, 182 and n, 188; on B.'s Ode to Napoleon, **4**, 102 and n; published B.'s lines on Lady Jersey, 152 and n; contradiction of B.'s engagement, 192–3, 194–5, 197, 198, 201; announced B.'s marriage, 252 and n; defends B., **5**, 58n; letter intended for, **8**, 89

Perry, surgeon, **3**, 34
Persia, **1**, 172 and n, 206, 208, 234, 255; **2**, 49; **3**, 27, 96 and n, 101n; **4**, 148; **5**, 157n; **6**, 98; B.'s intention to visit, **3**, 35
Persian language, **5**, 130
Persian poetry, **3**, 164
Persian Tale, **3**, 191 and n
Persius, *Satires*, **6**, 204 and n; **9**, 76 and n
Perticari, Count Giulio, *Dell'amor patrio di Dante*, **7**, 152 and n
Peru, **3**, 249n; **11**, 53n
Perugia, **5**, 216
Perugino, Pietro, **9**, 50
Peruzzi, Il Cavaliere Vincenzo, **6**, 38, 39
Pesaro, **7**, 153, 177; **8**, 131
Peter Pindar, **2**, 49
Peterborough, Charles Mordaunt, 3rd Earl of, **2**, 114
Peterhouse, Cambridge, **2**, 92n
Peterloo massacre, **6**, 227n; **7**, 63n; **9**, 134 and n; **10**, 57n
Petersham, Viscount, *see* Stanhope, Charles (later 4th Earl of Harrington)
Petrarch, **2**, 172; **3**, 240; **5**, 213, 217; **8**, 44; **9**, 90
Petrobey, Petros Mavromichales, **11**, 22n, 130n
Petronius, **5**, 36 and n; *Satyricon*, **1**, 207 and n; **2**, 14 and n
Petrotini, Signor, **5**, 255; **6**, 8, 14, 19
Petta, Battle of, **10**, 179n, 180n
Petty, Lord Henry (later Marquis of Lansdowne), **1**, 118 and n
Pforzheimer Library, **8**, 52n, 71n; **10**, 46n, 185n
Phalerum, **2**, 37
Phanariots, **11**, 22n, 215
Pharaoh, **3**, 122; **5**, 179
Pharsalia, **9**, 48
Phidias, **9**, 215
Philadelphia, **9**, 30, 164n
Philhellenes, **10**, 180, 229; **11**, 213
Philip (of Macedon), **6**, 91; **7**, 153 and n; **10**, 90 and n
Philip II, (France), **8**, 75n
Philip II, (Spain), **8**, 12n, 36
Philip V, (Spain), 213n
Philippi, **8**, 107
Philips (Bourbons) of Spain, **4**, 179
Philips, Ambrose, and Racine's, *The Distrest Mother*, **2**, 210 and n; 'Namby-Pamby', **4**, 86; *Contes Persans* (trans.), **5**, 192 and n
Philips, George, **3**, 226 and n
Philips, Thomas, **3**, 226n
Phillips, Thomas, painter, B.'s letters to: **3**, 113; **4**, 79; mentioned, **1**, 231n; **3**, 113; portraits of B., 68 and

Phillips, Thomas—*continued*
n, 70, 167 and n, 198; **4**, 43n, 79,
112 and n, 113; **5**, 28 and n, 106; **11**,
187 and n; engravings, **4**, 144 and n,
145–6, 248, 250, 287 and n
Philopoemen, **11**, 70 and n
Philosopher's Stone, **9**, 207
Philostratus, *Life* of Appolonius of
Tyana, **8**, 127 and n
Phoenix, **2**, 205 and n; **3**, 54n, 121
Phormio, **2**, 138n
Photomara, **11**, 31
Phryne (Lady Caroline Lamb), **11**,
182 and n
Piat, General, **10**, 140n
Piccadilly, **2**, 254n; **4**, 87n, 100, 283
and n, 308n; **5**, 271; **7**, 62; **9**, 88
Piccadilly Terrace, **3**, 94n; **5**, 15n, 38,
71, 92
Pichot, Amédée, essay on B., **10**, 209;
Oeuvres Complètes de Lord Byron, **8**,
114 and n; **10**, 207n
Picini, Lucrezia, **1**, 15; **6**, 147, 149
Pictet, Professor Marc-Auguste, B.'s
letter to: **5**, 207; mentioned, 207 and
n; **6**, 127 and n
Piedmont, **8**, 40
Piedmontese, **8**, 39; **10**, 181
Pierrepoint, 'Dandy', **9**, 22n; **10**, 141
Pigot, Elizabeth Bridget, B.'s letters
to, **1**, 50, 96, 100, 107, 120, 122,
124, 126, 130, 131, 135; biog. sketch,
277; mentioned, 125n, 203n; **2**,
119–20; **11**, 173n; drew Byron's
arms, **1**, 50 and n; sang *Maid of Lodi*,
51; letters to about Edleston, 88n,
124; friend of B. at Southwell, *93n*,
94 and n; B.'s letters to offered to
Murray, **8**, 227
Pigot family, **1**, *93 and n*, 94 and n,
125n, 136n; **3**, 223
Pigot, Henry, **1**, 51 and n, 136n
Pigot, John Hollis, **1**, 277
Pigot, John M.B., B.'s letters to: **1**, 93,
97 (2), 98, 99, 103, 117; **2**, 67;
mentioned, **1**, 136n, 277; friend of B.
at Southwell, *93 and n*; to send servants to B., 98–9, 136n; with B. at
Harrogate, 100 and n; medical
student in Edinburgh, 111n, 112n,
117 and n; to meet B. at Newark,
133; practices in Chester, **2**, 67 and n
Pigot, Mrs. Margaret, B.'s letter to:
2, 119; mentioned, **1**, 51; **2**, 26, 43,
44
Pigot, Richard, **1**, 136n
Pillans, James, **1**, *191 and n*
Pimlico, **10**, 29, 74
Pinacoteca, Bologna, **11**, 229
Pindemonte, Ippolito, **5**, 233 and n,
234, 241, 293

Pinto, Alessio del, **8**, 13–14, 18
Piozzi, Mrs. Hester Lynch, **1**, 53n; **5**,
233; *Anecdotes of Dr. Johnson*, **11**,
233
Piraeus, **2**, 13, 14, 37, 49; **4**, 215
Pirgos, **11**, 26
Piron, Alexis, 'Epigrammatic Machine',
9, 20 and n
Pisa, **5**, 163, 164, 179, 183, 210, 241,
296, 298; **6**, 92; **8**, 97, 171, 176n,
183, 188, 197, 202, 205, 214, 218,
219, 223, 224, 225, 228, 230, 232,
233, 234, 235, 237, 239, 241, 245,
246, 247, 248, 249, 250, 251; **9**, 49,
50, 57, 66, 80, 83n, 87, 95, 110, 128n,
148, 149, 156, 157, 161n, 165, 167n,
179n, 180, 184n, 204, 210, 211, 214,
235, 236; **10**, 11, 12, 14, 25, 31, 35,
36, 56n, 102–3, 104n, 113, 152, 160,
169; **11**, 163, 164; B. followed
Teresa to, **1**, 9, 21; B. met Clare on
road to, 22; **9**, 49–50; B.'s arrival
in, **1**, 25; **9**, 50; B. at, **1**, 276; **9**,
51–161, 179–219; B.'s intended
sojourn, **8**, 183, 184, 205, 214, 218,
225, 228; Casa Lanfranchi, 189 and
n, 190, 246; Mavrocordatos in, **11**,
215; governor of, 195
Pisan professors, **9**, 150
Pisse-Vache, **5**, 113, 206
Pistocchi, soldier, **8**, 140 and n, 142,
156
Pitt, William, **1**, 186; **2**, 21n; **3**, 79n,
120; **6**, 86, 89; **7**, 17; **9**, 14, 27
Pitt, William, the younger, **3**, 22n; **11**,
222
Pitti Palace, **5**, 218; **9**, 50
Pius VI, Pope, **10**, 56
Pius VII (Pope), **1**, 22; **5**, 210, 219,
224, 227; **7**, 229; **8**, 21, 48, 84, 214,
233; **9**, 51; **10**, 176, 177, 178; **11**,
166; his guards and B.'s liveries, **7**,
118, 127, 137; 'death to', 84; judg-
ment in Teresa's case, 123–6, 126n,
165, 235n, 272; **10**, 30
Place Vendôme, Paris, **4**, 310n
Plagiary, Dr., **2**, 228n
Plantagenet, **7**, 196
Platea, **5**, 76
Plato, **9**, 47, 117; **11**, 45; *Phaedo*, **8**, 35
and n
Platonism, **2**, 89; **3**, 135; **4**, 127, 135;
in some peril, **1**, 5; **3**, 136
Platt, Sr., **1**, 139
Pliny, *Natural History*, **5**, 221n; **7**, 258
Plunket, William Conyngham (later
Baron), **3**, *22 and n*
Plutarch, **4**, 77; **11**, 70n; Alcibiades
and his dog, **5**, 186 and n; *Lives*,
238 and n; **8**, 58, 127 and n; **9**, 47;
Morals, **8**, 238 and n

Plymouth, **2**, 184; **4**, 118n; **9**, 95n, 114

Pnyx, **1**, 254n

Po, **4**, 93; **5**, 217; **7**, 58, 76, 169, 172, 177, 180, 183, 190, 210, 211, 212, 213, 218; **8**, 33, 39n, 43; **10**, 52

Podesta, **7**, 132

Poet Laureate, **5**, 220n; **6**, 253n

Poetical Register, The, B.'s letters to: **4**, 205 and n, 268; **5**, 43n

Poland, **4**, 132n; **8**, 100

Poland, King of, **4**, 27

Pole, Sacheverell Chandos, **5**, 39 and n

Pole, William Wellesley, **4**, *79 and n*; **5**, 72 and n

Polentani family, **6**, 189

Polidori, Dr. John William, biog. sketch, **5**, 295; mentioned, 71n, 84, 142, 199, 269; B.'s personal physician, 73 and n, 161; illness at Carlsruhe, 76, 77, 78; sprained his ankle, 81, 82; B. gives him his congé, 121, 122, 124, 126, 163; quarrel in Milan, 121–2, 124, 126–7; to go to Brazil, 163, 183, 272; **11**, 163, 164; B. recommends him to Murray, **5**, 163–4, 212, 240, 241; and Pictet, 207n; **6**, 127; his patients are no more, **5**, 210, 215; **11**, 164; in Venice, **5**, 210, 212, 215; **11**, 164; B. sent pictures to Augusta by, **5**, 229; writes a tragedy, 258 and n, 260; in *New Monthly Magazine*, **6**, 119n, 131n; on Shelley, 125 and n, 126; his diary, 127; *The Vampyre*, **5**, 296; **6**, 118–19, 119n, 126 and n, 126 and n, 131n, 132, 139, 140, 198; **8**, 150n, 237

Polish uprising, **8**, 40 and n

Pollux, **3**, 221

Pompadour, Madame de, **5**, 277n

Pomponius, **3**, 213 and n

Pomposa, **6**, 130, 167

Ponsonby, Lady, **5**, 216

Ponsonby, Sarah, **1**, *125 and n*

Ponsonby, W., **1**, 139n

Pontefract, **7**, 154n, 225n

Pope, Alexander, **1**, 13, 146n; **2**, 114, 130, 168, 187, 221n; **3**, 20, 58; **4**, 53–4, 332; **6**, 77, 234, 253; **7**, 206, 233; **8**, 11n, 39, 61, 88, 115, 237; attacked by Keats, **1**, 11; **8**, 104 and n; 'more imagery in twenty lines', **1**, 14; **8**, 93–4; lines on Buckingham, **2**, 15 and n; and ruling passions, 20; criticized by Wordsworth, **4**, 325–6; and John Dennis, **5**, 28 and n; Bowles controversy, 111n; 'these be good rhymes', 219; admired by B., 265; **8**, 12, 14, 19, 21, 109–10, 200; and Mary Montagu, **5**, 275n; B.'s defence of, **6**, 31, 95, 134; **7**, 60–1, 63,

114n, 121, 179, 201, 212, 217, 229, 245, 253; his infirmities, **6**, 85; B.'s praise of, **7**, 83; Bowles-Campbell controversy, **8**, 43, 50, 76n, 85 and n, 134 and n, 199–200; B.'s letter on Bowles and, 44, 50, 53 and n, 76 and n, 77, 79, 85 and n, 90, 92, 94, 95, 100n, 101, 102 and n, 104, 109 and n, 113, 114, 121, 122, 191, 212, 239; **9**, 68, 84, 93; B.'s 2nd letter on Bowles and Pope, **8**, 54n, 99 and n, 111 and n, 134, 166 and n, 172; attack on Addison, 85n, 148 and n; Tyers' rhapsody on, 110 and n; Cibber on, 112; editors, 201 and n; B. compared to, **9**, 11; and Warburton, 145 and n, 146 and n; Warton's essay on, **10**, 83; lines to Lady Frances Shirley, 137 and n; Hobhouse compared to, **11**, 158; 'Prologue' to Addison's *Cato*, **2**, 210n; *Dunciad*, **4**, 79 and n; **5**, 267n; **6**, 31; **10**, 28 and n; **11**, 24n; 'Elegy on the Death of an Unfortunate Lady', **2**, 211; *Eloisa to Abelard*, **3**, 205 and n; **11**, 223; *Epistle to Dr, Arbuthnot*, **1**, 14; **2**, 43n; **3**, 36 and n, 161 and n, 162 and n, 233; **5**, 107 and n, 192 and n; **6**, 86 and n; **7**, 232 and n; **8**, 24 and n, 85n, 93–4; **9**, 74 and n, 197 and n; **11**, 159 and n, 221; *Essay on Criticism*, **2**, 69 and n; **4**, 92 and n; **11**, 182 and n; *Essay on Man*, **4**, 162 and n; **6**, 31; **8**, 94; **10**, 56 and n; *Iliad* (translation), **4**, 325, and n; **6**, 47n, **8**; 93, 148n; *Imitations of English Poets*, **1**, 134; *Imitations of Horace*, **3**, 96 and n; **5**, 86 and n; 'Martinus Scriblerus', **4**, 181 and n; *Memoirs of P. P., Clerk of This Parish*, **5**, 67 and n; 211 and n; **8**, 34 and n, 214 and n; *Moral Essays*, **2**, 15 and n, **3**, 91 and n, 109–10; **9**, 208 and n; **10**, 12 and n; **11**, 220; *Odyssey* translation, **11**, 46; *Rape of the Lock*, **2**, 21 and n; **3**, 214–15; **5**, 118 and n; **6**, 31; **7**, 229, 255n; **11**, 223; 'Sober advice from Horace', **8**, 200 and n; *Works*, ed. Courthope, **5**, 28n

Pope, Alexander, actor, **2**, 204 and n

Porcius Latro, Marcus, **5**, 221n

Porson, Richard, **6**, 12 and n; ed. of Euripides, **2**, 102n, *124 and n*; at Cider Cellars, **3**, 107n; *The Devil's Walk*, 240 and n; *Letters* to Archdeacon Travis, **4**, 168 and n

Porta, Luigi da, **5**, 132n

Porter, Walter, **5**, 247

Portiera, **6**, 92

Portland, William Henry Cavendish Bentinck, 3rd Duke of, B.'s letter to,

Portland, 3dr Duke of—*continued*
1, 177; mentioned, 113n, 177 and n, 192 and n; **2**, 196n; **3**, 254n; B.'s Indian proposal, **1**, 179 and n; indebtedness to B., 201 and n, 202, 203

Portland Place, **9**, 25

Portman, Edward Berkeley, **2**, 216 and n

Portman Square, **9**, 30

Portsmouth, **1**, 165; **2**, 48, 49, 51, 52, 54, 56, 57; **3**, 59, 61, 62, 84

Portsmouth, Countess of (née Mary Ann Hanson), **3**, 248 and n, 249; **4**, 142, 143, 170, 175, 180, 186n, 306, 318, 335 and n; **5**, 70

Portsmouth, Earl of, **2**, 108; **3**, 248; **4**, 142, 143, 170 and n, 175, 180, 193, 248, 306, 318, 335n; **7**, 40; marriage to Miss Norton (1799), **1**, *40 and n*; marriage to Mary Anne Hanson, 51n; **4**, 186; **10**, 119 and n, 120, 124–5, 129; commission of lunacy against, **4**, *186 and n*, 187, 189, 235, 244–5, 254 and n, 259, 261, 265, 272, 279, 292; B.'s affidavit concerning marriage, 236–7, 244 and n; **10**, 119n, 125; B.'s honeymoon plans altered by Earl's trial, **4**, 238, 239; sanity trial, **10**, 119 and n, 124–5, 127; his mad eccentricities, *119n*

Portugal, **1**, 215n, 223, 237, 247, 255; **2**, 22, 30, 53, 74, 91n, 104, 106, 146, 162, 178; **4**, 161n, 260; **5**, 71; **7**, 190; **9**, 41, 49; **11**, 157; compared to Turkey, 232

Portuguese, **2**, 215, 218; **5**, 163; **11**, 163; inferior to Spaniards, **1**, 250

Portuguese Journals, **9**, 11

Portuguese reviews, **2**, 178, 197

Pouqueville, François C. H. L., **2**, 115

Poussin, Nicolas, **1**, 94

Powell, Anthony, **1**, 82n

Powell (killed Falkland), **1**, 195n

Power, James, music publisher, **4**, 138n, 263 and n, 277n, 280, 285, 330n

Power, Mary Anne, **10**, 135n, 140, 142, 157, 172, 183, 229

Powerscourt, Richard Wingfield, Lord, **3**, 106 and n; **4**, 260; B.'s letters to offered to Murray, **8**, 227

Praidi, Mr., **11**, 38, 89 and n

Prato, **8**, 183

Pratt, Samuel Jackson, B.'s letter to: **3**, 89; mentioned, **1**, 163; **2**, *53 and n*, 76, 80, 132; **3**, 89n, 110 and n

Pratt, Willis W., *Byron at Southwell*, **1**, 125n, 196n

Prepiani, Venetian miniaturist, portraits of B., **5**, 191 and n, 212, 229, 242

Presbyterians, **8**, 108

Prescott, Mrs. **7**, 27, 28

Presteign, **2**, 234; **3**, 32, 33, 34; **11**, 182n

Prevesa, **1**, 226, 227n, 229, 230n; **11**, 75, 129; B. at, **1**, 225–33; Turkish prisoners returned to, **11**, 116, 117, 118, 120, 124

Priam, **1**, 238n

Prideaux, Humphrey, Dean of Norwich, *True Nature of Imposture . . . in the Life of Mahomet*, **7**, 168 and n

Priestley, Joseph, **8**, 29n; **9**, 100, 103, 116; Christian Materialism, 46

Prince John, **8**, 75 and n

Prince Regent (*see also* Wales, Prince of, and George IV), **2**, 80n, 263n; **3**, 25n, 38n, 41n, 50, 69, 70, 242; **4**, 32, 42, 45, 53, 66, 100n, 120n, 131n, 152, 212, 218; **5**, 109n, 277; **7**, 214n; **9**, 116 and n; **11**, 162, 223; desires to meet B., **2**, 180 and n; admiration for Scott, 180n, 182 and n, 183; refuses to call in Whig ministry, 183n; address to Parliament, 250 and n; libelled by Hunt, 281; **3**, 49n; **4**, 294n; sponsors fete, **3**, 75 and n; at Brighton, 94; his obesity, 93, 128; B.'s epigram on, 182; affected by B.'s lines, **4**, 51, 53; letter to Duke of York, 54n; attacked in 'Vault', 80 and n; B.'s engagement, 219; loans to Emperors, 298n; Lord Edward Fitzgerald's forfeiture, **6**, 209

Prince of Wales Coffee House, **9**, 28, 29

Princess of Wales, *see* Caroline, Princess of Wales

Prior, Matthew, **2**, 179 and n; **6**, 77, 91, 94; Rabelaisian tales, 253; defended by Johnson, 208 and n; *Alma*, **11**, 125 and n; *Hans Carvel*, 226

Priscianus, **8**, 215 and n

Procter, Bryan Waller (Barry Cornwall), B.'s letters to, **9**, 83, *95*; **10**, 115 and n; mentioned, **7**, 113 and n, 225; **8**, 56 and n, 207; **10**, 115 and n; *The Flood of Thessaly*, 116; *Mirandola*, **9**, 83 and n, 83–4, 120–1 and n

Propertius, **5**, 36

Prothero, R. E., ed. *The Works of Lord Byron . . . Letters and Journals*, **1**, 24, 25–6, 39n, 40n, 71n, 139n, 162n, 176n, 181n, 182n, 220n; **2**, 169n, 171n, 185n; **3**, 72n, 79n, 140n, 145n, 162n, 167n, 171n, 191n, 213n; **4**, 145n, 213n, 304n; **5**, 68n, 147n, 157n, 201n, 208n; **6**, 64n, 78n; **7**, 204n; **8**, 16n, 76n, 97n, 99n, 196n, 238n; **9**, 100n, 164n; **10**, 137n; **11**, 43n, 68n, 72n, 90n, 186n, 223

Proverbs, **9**, 86 and n; **11**, 227

Prussia, **1**, 208; **4**, 298n; **7**, 244

Prussia, King of, **2**, 124; **4**, 125n, 128n
Prussia, Prince of, **8**, 12n
Prussian Officer, B.'s letter to: **11**, 149; mentioned, 149 and n, 150
Prussians, **9**, 48
Psalms, **5**, 142; **8**, 226n
Prynne, William, **9**, 234; **10**, 69, 105
Pugilistic Club, **3**, 216 and n; **9**, 23
Pulci, Luigi, **6**, 77; *see also* Byron, Works, under *Morgante Maggiore*
Punctuation, *see under* Byron, punctuation
Purefoy, Thomas, duellist, **7**, 178 and n
Purling, Mr., **9**, 12
Purvis, Admiral, **1**, 221
Puttick and Simpson, **11**, 111n
Puységur, Mons. de, **3**, 211 and n
Pye, Henry James, **1**, *188 and n*; **2**, 180 and n; **4**, 84; *The Prior Claim*, **5**, 107n
Pygmalion, **4**, 28
Pylades (ship), **1**, 237; **2**, 7n
Pym, John, **3**, 228; **9**, 234; **10**, 69
Pyne, Mr., **6**, 82
Pyramids, **2**, 39
Pyramus, **2**, 112
Pyrrhonian, **2**, 89
Pyrrhonism, **9**, 95
Pythagoras, **2**, 208; **5**, 164

Quakers, **1**, 210; **2**, 178n
Quantana, banker, **10**, 97
Quantana, Madame, **10**, 101
Quarterly Review, **2**, 156, 197 and n, 235n, 285; **3**, 5n, 62 and n, 107 and n, 108, 126n, 161, 169n, 208n, 220, 247 and n, 250, 273; **4**, 90 and n, 93 and n, 358; **5**, 137, 169 and n, 176, 178 and n, 182, 183, 184, 185, 194, 198, 201, 204, 211 and n, 234, 259, 260n, 262, 277; **6**, 11n, 12n, 14, 18n, 29, 83 and n, 137, 207 and n; **7**, 113n, 121, 132 and n, 172, 196, 200, 201, 217, 220, 223, 253; **8**, 53 and n, 151, 199n, 237; **9**, 42, 62, 85 and n, 90, 96, 200; **11**, 182; Southey a contributor, **1**, 177n; politically inspired, 157n; scolded B., **3**, 11 and n; B. offered to review Moore in, 51 and n; edited by Gifford, 271; killed Keats, **8**, 102, 104, 117, 162, 163 and n, 172, 173; wishes to attack B., 193 and n, 250; B. does not want to see, 219; on *Cain*, **10**, 18; B. returned unopened, 40, 67; mingled praise and censure of B., 68n, 135; on Hobhouse and Webster, **11**, 163 and n, 165
Quatremer, **3**, 66n
Queen Anne, **1**, 246n
Queensbury, Catherine Douglas, Duchess of, **2**, 114

Queen's College, Oxford, **3**, 95n
Queen's Ferry, **7**, 212
Quennell, Peter, *Byron: A Self Portrait*, **1**, 24
Quinn, George, **1**, 132n
Quiroga, General, **7**, 155 and n
Quevedo y Villeges, Gomez de, B.'s pseudonym, **8**, 229 and n, 236; *Visions*, 229n; **9**, 62

Rabelais, François, **1**, 4; **8**, 35 and n
Racine, Jean Baptiste, **10**, 189; *The Distrest Mother*, **2**, 210 and n
Racket's Club (Brighton), **9**, 23; **11**, 156 and n
Radcliffe, Mrs. Ann, **5**, 145
Radford, Miss, **4**, 21, 23 and n, 29, 34
Radicalism, **9**, 50
Radicals, **1**, 16; **6**, 187n, 211 and n; **7**, 63, 80–1, 95, 99, 252; **8**, 240 and n; put Hobhouse in parliament, **1**, 275
Radzivil, Prince, **4**, 128 and n, 131–2
Rae, Alexander, B.'s letter to, **4**, 333; joint manager, Drury Lane, 305n, 306, 311; **5**, 135n; **9**, 36; as an actor, **4**, 313–14, 313n; Ordonio in Coleridge's *Remorse*, 286n, 313n
Ragusa, Duchess of, **5**, 111
Raisi, Count Pompeo, **7**, 163 and n
Raizis, M. Byron, **11**, 123n
Ralph, B.'s ancestor, **4**, 220
Rambaldi of Imola, Benvenuto, Latin commentary on Dante's *Commedia*, **6**, 181, 187–8, 188n
Ramsgate, **5**, 210
Rancliffe, George Parkyns, 2nd Baron, **1**, 39n; **3**, 71n; **4**, 111, 113 and n, 114, 118, 125; **5**, 250; **10**, 30
Rancliffe, Lady (née Forbes), **3**, 71 and n, 72; **4**, 110 and n, 119n, 120–1, 123, 127; **10**, 30
Randall, Mr. (?creditor), **4**, 118 and n, 288 and n
Randel, William, **11**, 220
Rangone, Guiseppe, ('Beppi'), **6**, 177 and n, 184, 191; Cavalier Servente to Countess Benzoni, **6**, 276; **8**, 138, 180 and n
Ransom & Co., **6**, 251; **7**, 75; **8**, 71; **9**, 106, 116, 159; **10**, 24, 37; **11**, 17, 26, 52, 62, 65, 77, 93, 94, 116, 152
Ransom and Morland, bankers, **2**, 282
Ranuzzi, **8**, 185
Raphael, **5**, 218, 221; **8**, 95; **9**, 11
Rasi, Dr., **7**, 148
Rasponi, Cristino, **7**, 24
Rasponi, Count Gabriel, **7**, 47 and n
Rasponi, Count Giulio, **6**, 184, *247 and n*; **7**, 26, 31, 143, 148; **10**, 121 and n, 122

Rasponi, Countess Spinelli, **8**, 50, 134
Ratcliffe, **4**, 41
Ravenna, **1**, 22; **5**, 211, 295, 297; **6**, 107, 114, 115, 117, 130, 132, 144, 148, 181, 184, 208, 242; **7**, 228, 240, and n; **8**, 158, 159, 180, 233; **9**, 24, 42, 51, 56, 61, 66, 87; **10**, 107n, 130, 176; B. joined Carbonari, **1**, 17; B. alone in, 21; Teresa returned to, **6**, 115, 117; B. to leave for, 124, 128, 141; B. in, 150–206; **7**, 11–258; B. delighted with, **6**, 177; B. to return to, 256, 259; B. described life in, 260–2; Guiccioli Palace, **7**, 13n, 33; Albergo Imperiale, 13n, 25; society in, 18, 25, 27–8, 35, 65–6; B. undecided about stay in, 24; bad weather, 28, 35, 39; **8**, 11, 13, 15, 16, 18, 22, 27, 28, 47, 120; uprising date settled, 14, 16, 20; Shelley in, 163n, 175, 176, 183; B. reluctant to leave, 183, 184, 188, 205, 222; B.'s preparations to leave, 205, 212, 213, 243
Ravenna Journal, *see* Byron, journals
Ravenna Theatre, **7**, 26n, 52n, 128, 130, 131
Rawdon, Bessy, admired by B., **2**, 216; drapery Miss, **10**, 129
Rawdon, Lady C., **2**, 216; death, **3**, 13
Rawdon, Francis, Baron Rawdon (later Earl of Moira), **2**, 215 and n, 216
Rawdon, Lady Selina, **3**, 75n; **4**, 119n, 313
Rawdon, Mrs., B.'s letter to, **5**, 79; to carry letter for B., 79 and n, 80, 226
Raymond, George, stage-manager, Drury Lane, **2**, 205 and n; **3**, 196 and n; 230 and n; **4**, 297 and n; sends B. a play, **5**, 67; **11**, 227
Raynal, *History of the Indies*, **2**, 211n
Reading School, **2**, 133n
Récamier, Madame de, **3**, 247
Reddish's Hotel, **2**, 49, 57
Redesdale, John Mitford, 1st Baron, Insolvent Debtors Act, **3**, 206n
Reeve, John, **2**, 82n
Reeves, Mr., **4**, 108, 163, 166
Reflector, The, **4**, 49n, 50
Reform Bill, **1**, 209n; **3**, 226n; **11**, 184n
Reformers, **7**, 16n, 44–5, 49–50, 59
Regent, Prince, *see* Prince Regent
Regent Street, **9**, 216
Reggio, **6**, 124, 141
Regillus, Lake, **8**, 108
Regnard, Jean François, **8**, 31 and n
Regnier (Regny), Madame, **10**, *56 and n*; **9**, 236
Reichenbach waterfall, **5**, 102, 205
Reiman, Donald H., ed., *The Romantics*

Reviewed, **6**, 83n; *Shelley and His Circle*, **11**, 227
Reinagle, R. R., **11**, 190n
[Reingamun?] W. H., B.'s letter to, **9**, 126
Reni, Guido, **11**, 229
Republic, A, **3**, 243, 244; **4**, 302; **8**, 240; **9**, 49
Republicanism, **7**, 84, 190
Retz, Cardinal de, *Mémoires*, **7**, 180 and n
Revelations, **7**, 125 and n, 177; **9**, 43 and n
Reynolds, John Hamilton, B.'s letter to, **4**, 68; **11**, 187; advised by B., **4**, 68–9; *Peter Bell*, 68n; **7**, 171 and n, 207; **10**, 130 and n; *Safie*, **3**, 245–6; **4**, *68 and n*, 74; reviewed in *Monthly*, 74n
Reynolds, Sir Joshua, **3**, 214n; **8**, 18–19; 'Lady Melbourne and Child', **3**, 46 and n
Rhine, (river), **3**, 124n; **4**, 37n; **5**, 74, 76, 77, 78, 82, 86, 123, 127; **8**, 26; **10**, 165
Rhode, **7**, 230
Rhodes, attorney, **4**, 333
Rhodes, **11**, 104n
Rhone, **5**, 123
Rialto, The, **5**, 203; **6**, 48, 54, 55, 66; **8**, 81
Rich, John, pantomimist, **2**, 212 and n, 214 and n; and Covent Garden theatre, **3**, 79n
Richardson, John, *Persian Dictionary*, **3**, 101n
Richardson, Samuel, **8**, 12n; pirating of his works, **2**, 144 and n; *Clarissa Harlowe*, **3**, 108, 241; *Pamela*, **2**, 250; **8**, 11 and n, 12; *Sir Charles Grandison*, **3**, 106
Richmond, **9**, 36
Ridge, John, B.'s letters to, **1**, 137, 138, 139 (2), 140, 142, 143 (2), 152, 154, 155; mentioned, **5**, 139; prints *Fugitive Pieces*, **1**, 96 and n, 97 and n, 98, 125n; and *Hours of Idleness*, **1**, 125 and n, 126n, 127, 129n, 130, 131, 132, 138; **4**, 46n, 47; prints *Poems Original and Translated*, **1**, 137 and n, 144; has not lost, 141; new edition of B.'s poems, **11**, 174 and n
Ridgway, James, B.'s letter to, **2**, 254 and n; mentioned, 16 and n, 30 and n, 47, 49, 254 and n; **4**, 98, 149; **5**, 77; **9**, 196; **10**, 42, 62, 67, 70
Ridotto, **5**, 160, 166, 171, 176, 181; **6**, 9, 11; **11**, 228
Riga (Rhiga) Constantine, **2**, 135n; **11**, 104n

Riley, money lender, **2,** 154, 155; **5,** 161 and n; **10,** 147; **11,** 161

Rima, surgeon, **7,** 131

Rimini, **5,** 211, 214; **6,** 122, 141, 145, 182, 188, 189

Rinaldo, **2,** 108n, 238n, 250

Ripon, **4,** 144n

Ripperda, Johan, Baron d', **3,** 213 and n

Ritchie, David, **5,** 171n

Rivington, Francis and Charles, publishers of *Poetical Register,* **4,** 205 and n, 268; *A Remonstrance addressed to Mr. John Murray,* **9,** 100 and n, 103 and n

Rizzato, **6,** 92

Rizzo-Patarol, Conte Francesco, **6,** 8, 40 and n, 58 and n, 91 and n, 93, 96, 180; **11,** 191n

Roberts, Capt. Daniel, B.'s letters to, **9,** 137, 184, 186; **10,** 43, 45, 75, 133, 165, 182, 211; mentioned, 25, 39, 46n; to build a boat (*Bolivar*) for B., **9,** 116, 137 and n, 236; and Shelley's drowning, 184 and n; and Shelley's boat, **10,** 11, 44 and n; and clothes for Bees and Frost, 36–7, 43–4, 45

Roberts, William, ed. *British Review,* **7,** 60, 196, 201, 212; and *Childe Harold,* **2,** 181n; reviews *Don Juan,* **6,** 213 and n; B.'s 'Letter to . . .' signed 'Wortley Clutterbuck', 214n, 215, 216, 224 and n, 236

Robertson, William, historian, **4,** 161

Robespierre, Maximilien François de, **1,** 16; **7,** 45, 80; **8,** 78n

Robin Hood, **3,** 224 and n

Robins, George Henry, auctioneer, **4,** 297 and n; **9,** *16 and n,* 32

Robinson, Lady Melbourne's servant, **3,** 155; **4,** 136 and n

Robinson Crusoe, **5,** 116

Robinson, Henry Crabb, **2,** 147n; **5,** 13n

Rocca, Mr., **3,** 231–2; **5,** 86 and n, 94, 260

Rochdale, **1,** 223, 232, 233, 234, 243; **2,** 8, 39, 40, 41, 45, 46, 47, 48, 51, 54, 55, 56, 57, 59, 61, 64, 71, 80, 85, 88, 93, 94, 95, 99, 101, 103, 105, 110, 127, 195, 201, 203, 215, 231n, 232, 234; **3,** 3, 81; **4,** 38, 39, 44; **7,** 69, 70, 71, 72, 73, 85, 94, 95, 110, 115, 116, 119, 120, 124, 202; **9,** 127, 155; **10,** 17, 37, 86, 151, 153, 159; lawsuit, **1,** 76 and n, 100, 102, 107, 146 and n, 181 and n, 235; **3,** 39; **7,** 122, 136; **8,** 34, 41, 62, 99, 117; **9,** 177; **11,** 49; Lancashire property, **1,** 163, 179; Hanson at, 174; **2,** 204; B. urged sale, **1,** 202, 207, 214; **11,** 25, 167; Hanson manager of estate, **1,** 275; B. to go to, **2,** 107; B. visited, 108, 109; value of, 114–15; **10,** 84; 8,256 acres, **2,** 115; B. wishes to sell, **3,** 22, 24, 25, 29, 33, 38, 53; **4,** 121, 140, 142, 143, 150, 163, 166, 179, 186, 189, 190, 200, 242, 253, 254, 255, 262, 275, 277, 300; **5,** 70, 139–40, 161, 230, 236, 245–6, 247, 257, 261, 272, 278; **6,** 6, 25, 34, 41, 42, 43, 49, 50, 52, 54, 57, 65, 79, 87, 114, 138, 222, 225, 228, 232; lawsuit lost, B. wants it sold at auction, **7,** 64, 144, 145; B. approves appeal, 146 and n, 149, 153, 158, 168, 190, 198, 239, 240; market tolls, 220; **9,** 106, 108, 111, 112, 114, 165, 177, 195, 199, 201, 219; **10,** 48, 51, 60, 74, 86, 91, 96, 110; suggested sale, **8,** 96; appeal of lawsuit, 181; **9,** 177, 188–9, 191, 206, 211, 214; **10,** 35 and n, 49, 53, 84, 98–9, 109, 136; and Dearden, **9,** 127, 128; **10,** 118, 124, 127, 150; Burdett and its management, **9,** 188; B. suggests survey, **10,** 86, 155; accommodation with Dearden, 35, 53, 73, 75, 77, 113, 124, 150; sale to Dearden, **11,** 35, 47 and n, 48n, 51, 55, 57, 74, 76, 77, 80, 82, 83, 85, 110, 116, 117, 135, 136, 144; B. going to, 159

Roche, Eugenius, ed., *Monthly Literary Recreations,* **1,** 129n, 130n

Rochester, John Wilmot, 2nd Earl of, 'To Lord Brocklehurst', **9,** 20 and n; **4,** 103

Rochfort, H. M. S., **9,** 212n, 218

Rodney, Admiral Lord, **1,** 244n

Rogers, 'Dummer', **1,** 39 and n

Rogers, Peter, **8,** 101

Rogers, Samuel, B.'s letters to, **2,** 152 (3), 160; **3,** 29, 33, 44; **4,** 61 (2), 73, 74, 121, 128, 133; **5,** 16, 17, 25, 55, 65, 85, 205; **6,** 16; **8,** 245; **11,** 180 (2); biog. sketch, **2,** 286–7; mentioned, 175; **3,** 29 and n, 49, 80, 101, 122, 127, 162, 207, 209, 213, 217, 231, 237, 238, 243, 247, 248, 250, 272; **4,** 64, 87, 115, 127, 139, 295; **5,** 124, 129, 177, 187, 188, 210, 248; **6,** 6; **7,** 250; **8,** 29n, 78, 201, 219; **9,** 12, 16; 'a likeness to the death', **1,** 6; **5,** 277; 'restore him to the Catacombs', **1,** 10; **6,** 13; conciliator between B. and Moore, **2,** 119; B.'s admiration for, 122, 129; invites B. to meet Moore at dinner, 123, 285; dinner with Hodgson and B., 127, 128, 129; friendship with B., 131, 152, 179; at Coleridge's lectures, 140 and n, 141 and n, 142, 147 and n, 149; man of taste, 143,

Rogers, Samuel—*continued*
146; **3**, 107 and n, 130, 214; poet and
man of society, **2**, 179; on tour in
the north, 192 and n; and B. and Lord
Holland, 281; *Giaour* dedicated to,
3, 44 and n; abused by women, 47;
Thurlow's poem to, 54 and n, 55; **5**,
250; abused everybody, **3**, 70; with
Madame de Staël, 73; B. jealous of
Moore's letters to, 81, 82; to judge
translators of *Charlemagne*, 97 and n,
130 and n; rated high as poet by B.,
220; **5**, 201, 265; **6**, 10; saw Sligo
letter on *Giaour*, **3**, 230; tried to
reconcile B. and Carlisle, 255; in
Hunt's *Feast of the Poets*, **4**, 50 and n;
advised suppression of *English Bards*,
59, 320–1; **5**, 241; attacked by the
Courier, 65; asks for help for Godwin,
16 and n, 17, 18; 'the black drop of
his liver,' **6**, 13; to come to Italy, 23;
and Sotheby, 243; B.'s lines on, **7**,
181 and n, 223; **9**, 213 and n; **10**,
18; B. called him venerable, **8**,
100 and n, 101, 102, 109, 132; in
Venice, 247, 250; kind to Sheridan,
9, 20; B. on his character, **8**, 132–3;
218; **9**, 27, 53, 66, 152; at Bologna,
50, 66; his gossip on Murray, 55, 56,
84; at Florence, 56, 66, 80, at
Certosa cemetery with B., 66;
visited B. at Pisa, 152; attacked by
Coleridge, **11**, 179; head by Denon,
197; his habits, 198; his character
assassination, 198; his 'liver-com-
plaint', 197; 'Pleasures of Mum-
mery', 198; *Columbus*, **3**, 34, 62 and
n, 169 and n, 224n; *Human Life*, **6**,
109; **8**, 132; *Italy*, **7**, 225–6n; **8**,
152n; *Jacqueline*, **4**, 126n, 133 and n,
138 and n, 145, 150, 152, 156, 157,
173; **5**, 239, 266; **8**, 73 and n; **11**,
196; 'Ode to Superstition', **4**, 181n;
Pleasures of Memory, **2**, 123, 286; **3**,
62 and n, 107 and n, 201; **8**, 132, 152
and n; *Poems*, reviewed by *Quarterly
Review*, **3**, 107 and n, 108; by
Edinburgh Review, 224 and n
Rohan, Cardinal de, **3**, 16 and n
Rolliad, **2**, 221 and n; **3**, 208n
Romagna, **6**, 122, 127, 128, 134, 145,
168, 181, 189, 240; **7**, 42, 47, 49,
137, 155n; **8**, 36n, 43, 45, 106, 109n,
138, 151n, 154, 157, 197; **9**, 98, 148,
149, 150, 167; **10**, 14, 121, 122, 130,
169, 177, 191n
Romagnuoles, **8**, 14, 34
Romaic, (*See also* Greek language), **1**,
238; **2**, 5n, 29, 32, and n, 33, 37, 46,
59, 60, 75, 102 and n, 104, 107, 115,
125, 128, 130, 134, 135, 136, 151,

178, 197; **5**, 166; **10**, 168, 180, 211;
11, 42, 59; Dr. Clarke knows little
of, **2**, 117
Romaika (Greek dance), **3**, 58 and n;
11, 223
Roman Emperors, **8**, 106–7
Roman History, **4**, 112
Roman women, **7**, 153 and n
Romanelli, Dr., **2**, 14–15, 19
Romans, **2**, 71, 123; **4**, 27; **7**, 113
Romans, Epistle to the, **11**, 56 and n, 58
Rome, **3**, 218; **4**, 93, 313; **5**, 53, 76,
136n, 146, 147, 152, 183, 191, 197,
210; **6**, 17, 18, 35, 43, 66, 146,
173n, 180, 182, 232; **7**, 132, 160,
202, 206, 211, 219, 257; **8**, 12,
13, 14n, 15, 53n, 107, 154, 159, 164,
170; **9**, 20, 42, 49, 51, 66, 116, 167n,
210, 217, 235; **10**, 151, 153, 169; **11**,
165, 216; Zantachi in, **1**, 235n;
Hobhouse gone to, **5**, 137–8, 140,
141, 144, 173, 174, 181; B. going to,
168, 181–2, 194, 197, 204, 208, 210,
211, 212, 214–15; B. delighted with,
219, 221, 233; B. in, 219–27;
Hobhouse's knowledge of, 263;
Hobhouse at, **10**, 14; **11**, 163, 165;
B.'s trip to, 166, 190; antiquities,
229
Romilly, Sir Samuel, B.'s letter to: **5**,
50; mentioned, **3**, *225 and n*; **5**,
138n; **7**, 208; B.'s enmity, **1**, 11; **5**,
26n; **6**, 78n, 90, 150, 167, 209; and
B.'s separation, **3**, 225n; **5**, 26 and n,
34–5, 50–1; counsel for Lady Byron,
26 and n, 34–5; **6**, 90; elected M.P.,
59n, 90; his suicide, 78n, 80, 81, 82,
84, 88n, 90; **11**, 170; employed by
Murray, 227
Romulus, **7**, 236
Rood, Ann (later Mrs. Fletcher), maid
to Lady B., **4**, 309 and n; **5**, 23 and n,
63 and n
Roper, Major, duellist, **7**, 178 and n
Roque, Dudu and Phokion, **2**, 13 and n
Rosa Matilda, **4**, 50, 95, 100n
Roscius, **2**, 203
Roscoe, William, **9**, 16; Lives of
Lorenzo the Magnificent and Pope
Leo X, **4**, 162 and n; *Lorenzo de
Medici*, **8**, 16n, 201n; ed. of Pope,
201 and n
Rose, George, **2**, 196 and n
Rose Glacier, **5**, 102, 106
Rose, William Stewart, B.'s letter to,
6, 38; mentioned, **2**, 196n; **5**, *262n*;
6, 26, 30, 78, 109; **7**, 46, 47, 54, 57,
97, 194, 225, 226; **11**, 191; marriage
to Italian, **6**, 18 and n; B.'s liking for,
20, 38 and n; *The Court and Parlia-
ment of Beasts*, 24 and n; *Letters from*

the North of Italy, **5**, 262n; **6**, 240 and
n; **7**, 202 and n
Rosebery, Lady, w. of 4th Earl, elope-
ment, **4**, 225 and n, 227
Rosel, Elizabeth and Gervase, **1**, 82n
Rosetta, **3**, 213n
Ross, Mr. (B.'s tutor), **8**, 108
Rossetti, Christina, **5**, 295
Rossetti, Dante Gabriel, **5**, 295
Rossetti, William Michael, **5**, 295
Rossi, Lieut., sells B. a dud horse, **6**,
219–20
Rossini, printer, **9**, 150
Rossini, Gioachino Antonio, feted in
Venice, **6**, 132; *Barber of Seville*, **7**,
87 and n; **11**, 231; *La Cenerentola*, **7**,
197 and n; *La Gazza Ladra*, **11**, 226;
Otello, **6**, 13, 18
Rotherham, **3**, 132, 138
Rothery (Rossoe), **2**, 215 and n
Rotten Boroughs, **8**, 121n
Rousseau, Jean-Jacques, **1**, 13, 94n, 171
and n; **3**, 195, 225n; **5**, 80n, 98, 215;
8, 54, 148; his novels seductive, **1**,
13; **10**, 68; and Mme Epinay, **7**, 167;
contrasted with B., **9**, 11–12; stoned
and banished, **10**, 109; and Baron
d'Holbach, **11**, 228; *Confessions*, **5**,
209; 'Letters of an Italian Nun', **1**,
94n; *La Nouvelle Héloise*, **3**, 151 and
n; **5**, 81, 82, 98, 209
Rowe, Nicholas, *Fair Penitent*, **2**, 143
and n, 144, 149; *Tamerlane*, **9**, 155
and n
Rowley and Capron, **10**, 153
Roxburghshire, **9**, 102n
Royal Academy, **4**, 96n; **6**, 173n
Royal Astronomical Society, **2**, 33n
Royal Geographical Society, **8**, 151n
Royal Naval Hospital, **4**, 189n
Rubens, Peter Paul, B. on, **5**, 73, 74–5,
213
Rubicon, **6**, 130, 160
Ruddiman's Grammar, **8**, 108
'Rule Britannia', **2**, 180n
Rulhières, Claude de, Epigram, **6**,
209–10
Rumelia, **2**, 132; **11**, 40, 135
Rundell, Maria Eliza, *Domestic Cookery*,
3, 238 and n; **6**, 29
Ruota, Count, on B., **9**, 42
Rupprecht, **7**, 106
Rural Sports, **1**, 142 and n
Rusconi, Cardinal Antonio, **7**, 50, 134;
8, 185 and n; **10**, 130; B.'s relations
with **7**, 47 and n, 51, 78, 118, 131,
237, 246, 247, 248, 249; his character,
73; at his wit's end, 137; and the
Carbonari uprising, 177; and the
Guiccioli, separation, 155, 164, 243;
orders arrest of liberals, **8**, 16; B.

queried by, 124, 131; and arrest of
B.'s servant, 140 and n, 142 and n,
143; poor people petitioned on behalf
of B., 156
Rush, Dr., **8**, 229
Rushton, Robert, B.'s letters to, **2**, 157,
158, 232; **3**, 20; mentioned, **2**, 232;
4, 41n; instructed by Mayfield, **1**,
194; B.'s attachment to, *187 and n*;
in B.'s will, 202n; **2**, 71, 232; taken
to prostitutes, **1**, 203–4; to go abroad
with B., 204 and n, 206 and n; sent
home from Gibraltar, 221–5; Turkey
unsafe for him, 235, 244; Mrs. B. to
care for him, 252; rudeness to Susan,
2, 157, 158; to be found a place at
Rochdale, 232, 234; to be employed
by Webster, **3**, 81, 88 and n, 89, 106,
110
Rushton, Mr., f. of Robert, B.'s letter
to, **1**, 222; mentioned, **4**, 41 and n
Rushton, Miss, **1**, 251 and n, 252
Russell, Bertrand, **3**, 226n
Russell, Lord John (later 1st Earl
Russell), **3**, *226 and n*; **11**, 196n
Russi, **7**, 176 and n; **8**, 45
Russia, **3**, 93, 99; **4**, 132n, 298n, 302n;
5, 294; **10**, 92; **11**, 185
Russia, Czar of, **8**, 12n
Russia, Emperor of, **4**, 125n, 128n
Russian courage, **7**, 169
Russians, **1**, 249, 254; **2**, 22, 84; **7**,
236; **8**, 40n; **10**, 171n; **11**, 84n, 85n,
147
Rusticucci, Jacopo, **6**, 131; **7**, 68n
Rutland, Henry, 5th Duke of, **1**, 67n;
4, 127n; **6**, 134n; marriage, **1**, 52n
Rutland, Duchess of (Lady Elizabeth
Howard), **1**, 52 and n
Ruyter, Michel Adriaanzoon van de, **3**,
212 and n
Ryder, Lady Susan (later Lady
Obrington), **4**, 267 and n
Rymer, Thomas, **8**, 115

Sadi, Persian poet, **4**, 30n
Sadler's Wells Theatre, **4**, 153
Sagrati, Marchesa, **9**, 217; **10**, 56 and n,
81
Sainte-Croix, Guillaume J., Baron de,
Mystères de paganisme, **8**, 237 and n
Saint-Germain, Mlle de, **3**, 147n
St. Albans, Duchess of, **2**, 108n, 159
St. Alban's Mercury, **2**, 260
St. Angelo's, prison of, **6**, 130; **7**, 97
St. Anthony, **5**, 253; **7**, 128 and n
St. Antonio of Padua, **7**, 57
St. Apollonari, **7**, 177
St. Athanasius, **4**, 109, 172
St. Aubyn, J. H., **5**, 110 and n, 112,
155, 163, 205, 258; *Mazza, 110n*

St. Aubyn, Sir John, **5**, 110n, 163, 258
St. Bartholomew, **6**, 145
St. Catherine, **10**, 105
St. Clair, William, on Parry, **11**, 217–18; *That Greece Might Still Be Free*, 27n, 108n, 128n, 146n
St. Crispin, **1**, 194 and n
St. Dionysius, **11**, 91
St. Dunstan's church, **2**, 105
St. Euphemia, **11**, 18, 30
St. Francis of Assisi, **4**, 28 and n; **7**, 229
St. George transport, **8**, 23
St. George's Channel, **2**, 125
St. George's Church, **4**, 237
St. Gingo, **5**, 220, 264; **6**, 126
St. Gothard, **9**, 210
St. Helena, **5**, 215n; **7**, 50; **9**, 26; **11**, 228
St. Hubert, **4**, 121
St. James, Parish of, **8**, 207n
St. James's Coffee House, **7**, 50, 63
St. James's Ledger, **5**, 172
St. James's, London, **4**, 108, 163, 257
St. James's Park, **4**, 154n
St. James's Square, **3**, 225; **10**, 229
St. James's St., **2**, 57, 155, 201, 234, **7**, 192, 257
St. James's, [Church], **3**, 63n
St. John, **6**, 207
St. John, Henry, Viscount Bolingbroke, **2**, 114
St. John's, **7**, 201
St. John's College, Cambridge, **1**, 172n; **2**, 22n, 179n; **3**, 190n; **11**, 226
St. Just, **3**, 218
St. Lambert, Francois, Marquis de, *Saisons*, **8**, 42 and n
St. Luke, **10**, 52 and n
St. Luke's Church, **6**, 75
St. Luke's Hospital, **2**, 265 and n; **3**, 168 and n
St. Luke's Theatre, **6**, 40
St. Mark, **8**, 198 and n
St. Mark's, (Venice), **5**, 133, 145, 179, 182, 203; **7**, 143, 201; **9**, 26
St. Mark's horses, **6**, 92
St. Mark's lion, **6**, 75 and n
St. Matthew, **5**, 186
St. Matthew, **7**, 172n
St. Mawes (fort), **1**, 209, 210
St. Nicholas, **3**, 94n
St. Paul, **1**, 148, 240; **2**, 127; **5**, 201, 238; **7**, 60, 201; **11**, 56, 58
St. Paul, *Epistle to the Corinthians*, **8**, 237; **11**, 164
St. Paul's Cathedral, **1**, 250–1 and n; **5**, 179; **7**, 243 and n; **8**, 193n
St. Paul's, Dean of, **3**, 22n; **8**, 193n; **11**, 222
St. Peter, **1**, 15; **5**, 216, 227; **8**, 229
St. Peter's, (Rome), **5**, 191; **6**, 146

St. Petersburg, **3**, 93, 95, 232n; **5**, 208, 277n; Don Juan in, **10**, 12
St. Sophia, **1**, 250 and n, 251
St. Stephen, **5**, 151; **7**, 128 and n
St. Ursula, **2**, 232; **3**, 124 and n
St. Vincent, **7**, 178n
Salamanca, Battle of, **2**, 216 and n
Salamis, **2**, 27; **9**, 48; **11**, 41, 45 and n
Salfi, **8**, 14n
Salisbury, James Cecil, Earl of, **3**, 171 and n, 215
Salle, Eusèbe de, **8**, 114n
Sallust, **4**, 169; Cataline Conspiracy, **8**, 14
Salmasius, Claudius, **4**, 278 and n
Salona (Amphissa), **11**, 134n, 137, 139, 141, 142, 144, 146, 151
Salora, **1**, 230
Salsette, frigate, **1**, 235–41, 242n, 247 and n; **2**, 3, 7, 30, 42; **3**, 15
Salthill, **3**, 56, 59; **4**, 160, 271 and n
Saluzzo, Madame, **10**, 83
Saluzzo, Villa, **9**, 204, 209; **10**, 86
Salvo, Marquis de, *Travels in the year 1806 . . .*, **1**, 224 and n
Samarkand, **2**, 91
Samos, **11**, 31
Samuel, **5**, 253; **11**, 197
San Antonio Abate, **7**, 128 and n
San Benedetto Theatre, **6**, 19, 77, 132
Sanders, George, painter, **1**, 197n, 206n; **2**, 224 and n, 234; **3**, 10, 33, and n, 41; B.'s portrait not delivered, **1**, 243, 251; **2**, 4, 18
Sandi, **7**, 131
San Domenico, **7**, 243
Sandri, on Teresa's decree, **7**, 130–1
Sandt, Charles, **6**, 104 and n; **7**, 113 and n; **10**, 180 and n
Sanfedisti, **8**, 17
Sandwich, John Montagu, 4th Earl of, **2**, 32n
San Lazzaro, (St. Lazarus), **5**, 130n, 146, 152, 157n, 165; **6**, 9n
San Leo, **8**, 180 and n
San Marco, Albergo di, **8**, 246
San Marco, Piazza, **5**, 129n
San Marino, **8**, 106
San Sebastian, **3**, 90n, 180n
Santa, **6**, 92
Santa Chiara, **7**, 129, 143, 152, 221; **8**, 81, 242; **11**, 78
Santa Croce, **5**, 218
Santa Maria Antica, **5**, 126n
Santa Maura (Lefkas), **1**, 246; **11**, 90
Sanuto, Marino, **8**, 161 and n; *Cronica*, **6**, 207n; **7**, 238n; *Vite dei Dogi*, **7**, 131 and n, 132, 141–2; **8**, 59n
Sappho, **1**, 246n
Saracen's Head, **4**, 49; **5**, 262
Saracens, **6**, 149

Saraci, Spiro (Andreas), **2**, 48 and n, 153n, 157 and n, 167 and n; **11**, 221

Saranzo (Soranzo? Seranzo?), **6**, 40, 238; **7**, 79, 135; **8**, 131

Sardinia, **1**, 221, 223, 224, 225, 237, 247, 255; **3**, 29; **11**, 157

Sardinia, King of, **7**, 184n; **8**, 21

Sardinia, Kingdom of, **9**, 175 and n

Sartorini, **6**, 210

Sass, Lt., **11**, 119n, 124, 125

Satan (Zatanai), **4**, 93 and n; **8**, 230; **9**, 53; B. compared to, 11

Satanic School of Poetry, **9**, 98 and n

Satirist, The, **1**, 136 and n, 167n; **3**, 84 and n; review of *Childe Harold*, **2**, 65n, 225 and n, 229; reviewed *Giaour*, **3**, 69 and n, 197 and n

Saturn, **6**, 22

Saunders, Mr., **7**, 39 and n

Savage, B.'s dog, **1**, 120, 123n

Savage, Richard, **6**, 85; **9**, 11

Savile Row, **9**, 73; **10**, 153; **11**, 148

Savioli Palazzo, **6**, 201

Savoy, **5**, 81

Sawbridge, Col., **1**, 205 and n, 214n, 222, 223; **4**, 259, 265 and n, 270 and n, 276; **5**, 245, 247, 278; **6**, 222n

Saxons, **7**, 61

Scalabrino, Luke, **6**, 81

Scaliger, **5**, 126

Scamander, **1**, 238; **4**, 326

Scarlett, James, legal counsel, **10**, 66, 72

Schadau, Chateau de, **5**, 100

Scheideck, **5**, 102, 205, 268

Scheldt, **5**, 217

Schiller, Johann Christoph von, **5**, 100; **8**, 25; incest theme, **3**, 196 and n, 199; *Fiesco, Robbers*, 245 and n; *Geisterseher*, **5**, 203 and n

Schinas, Dr. Demetrius G., **5**, 182; **11**, 228

Schlegel, August Wilhelm von, **5**, 88; **8**, 40, 225; at Coppet, **5**, 86 and n, 260 and n; accused B. of plagiarism, **8**, 164 and n, 172–3; on Alfieri and Molière, 164–5 and n; B. met at Coppet, 164–5, 167, 172–3; *Lectures on Dramatic Art*, 165 and n; B. refused to flatter, 167, 172–3; his bust by Tiecke, **9**, 26

Schlegel, Karl Wilhelm Friedrich, *History of Literature*, **8**, 38 and n, 39

Schreckhorn, **5**, 268

Schultess-Young, Henry Schultes, *The Unpublished Letters of Lord Byron*, **1**, 26

Schwarzenburg, **3**, 246

Schwerin, **11**, 85n

Scio, **2**, 102n

Scipio, **3**, 147; **4**, 302

Scotch deeds, **7**, 69, 240; **10**, 97, 114, 127, 135, 144, 153, 155

Scotland, **1**, 75; **2**, 38, 133, 136, 156, 244; **3**, 119, 182; **4**, 20n, 146, 154, 297; **8**, 73; **9**, 87; **10**, 97, 125n; **11**, 134; B. planned trip to, **1**, 131–2 and n; **4**, 138 ,162, 165; Mr. Gordon of, **1**, 220

Scott, Alexander, B.'s letters to, **6**, 150, 162, 166, 167, 177, 178, 182, 190, 204, 212, 218, 224; biog. sketch, 278–9; mentioned, **6**, 144 and n, 183n; **7**, 17, 27 and n, 105; swims with B., **6**, 51, 54, 55; **8**, 81, 82

Scott, Fallowfield, attorney, **4**, 307

Scott, John, editor of *London Magazine*, **8**, *99 and n*

Scott, Captain John, **11**, 15, 21, 29, 30, 39; and brig *Hercules*, **10**, 194, 201, 205, 214

Scott, Thomas, b. of Sir Walter, **5**, 182 and n

Scott, ed., *Arabian Nights*, **4**, 62n

Scott, Sir Walter, B.'s letters to, **2**, 182; **9**, 85, 131, 153; biog. sketch, **4**, 358; mentioned, **1**, 2, 14; **3**, 97, 217, 230n; **4**, 84n, 85, 86, 87, 107, 164, 198, 253n, 297; **6**, 47, 95; **7**, 45, 175, 178; **8**, 144, 145n; **9**, 30, 94, 142n, 151, 156; B. read his novels 50 times, **1**, 20; **8**, 13; B.'s fondness for his novels, **7**, 48, 98; **8**, 13; B.'s Athenian skulls given to, **2**, 59n; 'Gilpin Horner', 113 and n; editor of Anna Seward's letters, 132 and n; admired by Prince Regent, 180n, 182 and n, 183; praised *Childe Harold*, 182n; meeting with B., 286; **4**, 287n; B. accused of imitating, **3**, 141 and n; burlesque of *Lay of the Last Minstrel*, 202n; admired by B., 208–9, 271; **8**, 13, 23, 61, 88, 207, 219, 238; **9**, 85–7; compared with B., **3**, 209n, 250; pecuniary misfortunes, 219–20; octosyllabic verse, **4**, 153; cruise to the Orkneys, 151 and n, 152; taxation, 298; and *Christabel*, 318–19, 321 and n; recommends Maturin to B., 336n; **5**, 37 and n, 201; **9**, 35; alias Peter Pattieson, **5**, 171n, 191; reviewed 3rd Canto of *Childe Harold*, 178n, 183n, 185, 192, 198, 204; **9**, 85 and n, 86; called 'Ariosto of the North' by B., **5**, 255, 266; admired W. S. Rose, 262n; B.'s view of, as poet, 265; reviewed 4th Canto of *Child Harold*, **6**, 84; made baronet, **7**, 83 and n; his head on Murray's seal, **8**, 23, 61; *Cain* dedicated to, 198 and n, 205; **9**, 54 and n, 86; ignores reviews of himself, 55; attacked by B. in *English*

147

Scott, Sir Walter—*continued*
    Bards, 86n; sends B. *Halidon Hill*,
    10, 40 and n; character defended by
    B., 189–90; *The Abbot*, **7**, 204, 207,
    212, 214; **9**, 58; *The Antiquary*,
    quoted by B., **1**, 2; **5**, 109, 112 and n;
    8, 88; **9**, 21 and n, 31 and n; **10**,
    125n, 143 and n; *The Black Dwarf*, **5**,
    171n; **8**, 33 and n; *Bold Dragoon*, **10**,
    137 and n; *Border Minstrelsy*, **4**,
    151n; *The Bride of Lammermoor*, **7**,
    48 and n, 61 and n; **8**, 106 and n;
    'Cadyow Castle', **11**, 220; *Glenfinlas*,
    224; *Guy Mannering*, **4**, 264; **5**, 112n;
    8, 88; **10**, 149 and n; *The Heart of
    Midlothian*, **9**, 87 and n; **10**, 146 and
    n; **11**, 46n; *Helvellyn*, **2**, 192 and n;
    Ivanhoe, **7**, 48 and n, 83, 113; *Kenil-
    worth*, **8**, 16, 103; **9**, 97 and n; *Lady
    of the Lake*, **2**, 20, 182; **8**, 228 and n;
    Lay of the Last Minstrel, **1**, 227; **2**,
    182; **4**, 321n; **8**, 112 and n; **9**, 18 and
    n; **11**, 186 and n; *A Legend of
    Montrose*, **7**, 48 and n, 76 and n, 77,
    85 and n, 194 and n; **10**, 181 and n;
    Lord of the Isles, **4**, 201 and n, 252,
    280n; *Marmion*, **1**, 179n; **2**, 46, 182
    and n; **3**, 145–6; **4**, 107; **5**, 22 and n;
    7, 226 and n; **11**, 174 and n; *The
    Monastery*, **7**, 48n, 83, 158, 172, 200,
    201, 204, 212, 214, 217, 225 and n;
    9, 58; *Old Mortality*, **5**, 171n; **7**, 69
    and n, 71, 74; **8**, 46 and n, 148 and n;
    11, 41 and n; *Peveril of the Peak*, **10**,
    123; *The Pirate*, **9**, 87; *Quentin
    Durward*, **11**, 46 and n, 125n; *Rob
    Roy*, **6**, 123 and n, 132n, 137 and n;
    7, 70 and n, 75 and n, 83 and n; **8**,
    18, 43 and n; **9**, 87 and n, 154 and n;
    Rokeby, **2**, 191 and n, 197; **3**, 209
    and n; *Tales of My Landlord*, **1**, 20;
    5, 171n, 182, 184, 206, 220, 233,
    240, 275; **6**, 77; **7**, 201; **8**, 13, 16, 33,
    46; *Waverley*, **4**, 146; **5**, 112n, 150n,
    182n, 206 and n; **6**, 194 and n; **8**, 74
    and n, 88, 236 and n; **9**, 45 and n, 101
    and n, 154 and n, 164 and n; **11**, 82
    and n, 234
Scott, Lady, **9**, 87
Scott, Mrs., **4**, 306
Scott, Sir William, **3**, *90 and n*
The Scourge, **2**, 65 and n, 67
Scrofes, **11**, 88, 91, 92
Scrofe rocks, **11**, 86, 124
Scroggs, Sir William, **11**, 49 and n
Scrope, Sir Carr, Bart, **8**, 122 and n
Scudéry, Madeleine de, **4**, 130;
    Artamène, **2**, 194 and n
Scutari, **2**, 114; **11**, 35; Pasha of, **2**, 21,
    114, 125
Scylla, **11**, 172

Scythia, **8**, 208n
Scythians, **10**, 116n
Seaham, **2**, 175, 284; **3**, 153, 179; **4**,
    78, 174, 178, 179, 180, 181, 185, 186,
    187, 190, 191, 199, 202, 207, 208,
    211 and n, 214, 216, 217, 218, 220,
    222n, 223, 224, 225, 227, 228, 235,
    238, 245, 246, 247, 249, 255, 256,
    257, 261, 262, 288n; **5**, 15, 66; B. at,
    4, 228–31, 249, 258–80; B. offered
    as residence, 303
Sebastiani, Count, (?), **5**, *14 and n*; **10**,
    41
Sebright, John, **1**, 162n
Séchéron, **5**, 78, 80
Segati, Marianna, 'happiest—unlawful
    couples', **1**, 8; **5**, 141; appearance,
    129n, 130, 133–35, 141, 145; less
    obdurate than the language, 138; B.
    satisfied with his liaison, 143, 148,
    152 153, 155, 160, 162, 186, 188–9,
    193; fight with her sister-in-law,
    166–7, 172–3, 175; portrait (lost),
    175 and n, 179, 203; cared for B. in
    illness, 190; at La Mira with B.,
    234–5, 238; B.'s relationship with
    ended, **6**, 25, 40, 42, 49; illness, 37;
    her encounter with the Fornarina,
    194
Segati, Pietro, **5**, 129n, 166–7
Seid Ali, **3**, 58
Selim III, Sultan, **3**, 58n
Sellasia, Battle of, **11**, 70n
Selwyn, George, **9**, 97 and n
Semiramis, Queen, **4**, 290; **6**, 90; **7**,
    258; **8**, 147, 192
Semple, Mr., **3**, 195
Sénantes, Mme de, **3**, 147n, 148n
Seneca, **8**, 27; *Troades*, **2**, 89 and n
Seraglio, **1**, 242, 251
Seraglio Point, **1**, 247
Serassi, Pier Antonio, *Torquato Tasso*,
    8, 53 and n
Serchio, **9**, 185, 186, 192n, 193
Sergent-Marceau, Antoine François,
    10, 165 and n
Sergent-Marceau, Madame, B.'s letter
    to, **10**, 164; mentioned, *165 and n*
Sestos, **1**, 237 and n, 240, 242, 243,
    246, 247–8, 250, 253, 255; **2**, 18, 34,
    53, 59; **8**, 80; **11**, 157
Sestri, **9**, 203n; **10**, 13, 57, 102
Settle, Elkanah, *Absalom, Senior*, **8**,
    164n; 'Empress of Morocco', 164
Sevenoaks, **1**, 176n
Seven Towers, **1**, 241, 251
Seven Years War, **9**, 30
Seville, **1**, 2, 217, 219; **5**, 118
Seward, Anna, **2**, *132 and n*; **9**, 34;
    'Elegy on the South Pole', **8**, 215;
    Memoirs of Dr. Darwin, 47 and n

Seymour Road, **4**, 124n
Sgricci, Tommaso, *improvvisatore*, **5**, 119 and n, 125 and n; **7**, 47, 51
Shadwell, Mr., **9**, 112, 188, 193, 194, 198, 209, 212
Shakespeare, William, **5**, 60, 131; **6**, 42, 95, 123; **8**, 93, 109, 200; **9**, 11; **10**, 189; **11**, 193; B. quotes frequently, **1**, 2; B.'s speech Day declamation, 69n, 166n; life of, 154n; Coleridge's lectures on, **2**, 138n, 140n, 141 and n, 147, 149; in Drury Lane Address, 210, 219, 221; Malone's edition, **3**, 80n; B.'s opinions on, **4**, 50, 84–5, 301; B. considers him worst of models, **8**, 152; loves a quibble, 188; *Antony and Cleopatra*, **3**, 207 and n, 256 and n; **7**, 57 and n; **8**, 225 and n; **11**, 228; *As You Like It*, **2**, 201; **6**, 46 and n; **8**, 29 and n, 105 and n; **11**, 235; *Coriolanus*, **2**, 149; **4**, 61 and n, 173 and n; **5**, 24 and n, 25; **6**, 56, 106 and n; **7**, 194 and n; **8**, 133 and n; **9**, 81 and n, 213 and n; **10**, 17 and n; **11**, 171 and n, 225; *Cymbeline*, **3**, 25n; *Hamlet*, **2**, 28, 205n; **3**, 75, 219 and n, 230n, 243 and n, 244, 246, 255 and n, 257; **4**, 51 and n, 53, 93 and n, 94–5, 104–5, 212; **5**, 25 and n, 85 and n, 209, 215; **6**, 20, 63, 124 and n, 148, 207; **7**, 71 and n, 112 and n, 194 and n, 254 and n; **8**, 66 and n, 121 and n, 156 and n, 214, 218 and n; **9**, 71 and n, 80 and n; **10**, 118 and n; **11**, 147 and n, 159 and n, 228; *Henry IV, Part I*, **1**, 4; **3**, 146, 206 and n, 252; **4**, 76 and n, 284 and n, 323–4 and n; **5**, 116 and n, 177 and n, 250 and n; **6**, 145n, 207 and n, 217n; **7**, 50, 170 and n, 190, 218 and n; **8**, 20 and n, 55; **9**, 33 and n, 66, 87 and n, 95, 104 and n; **10**, 67 and n, 180 and n; **11**, 25 and n, 32 and n; *Henry IV, Part II*, **1**, 216 and n; **3**, 210 and n, 212, 245; **4**, 253 and n; **5**, 250 and n; **6**, 98 and n; **7**, 179 and n; *Henry V*, **2**, 44, 46, 256 and n; **3**, 153, 209; **4**, 73 and n; **6**, 210 and n; **7**, 82 and n, 118 and n; **5**, 172; **11**, 228; *Henry VI, Part III*, **3**, 107 and n, 246; **10**, 157 and n; *Henry VIII*, **6**, 89; **7**, 73 and n; *Julius Caesar*, **3**, 243 and n; **7**, 115 and n; **9**, 23 and n; *King John*, **7**, 102 and n; **8**, 250 and n; *King Lear*, **1**, 69n, 146n, 166 and n; **3**, 246 and n, 257; **4**, 85; **8**, 120 and n, 189 and n; **9**, 196 and n; **10**, 157 and n; *Love's Labour's Lost*, **9**, 11 and n; *Macbeth*, **1**, 96, 182 and n, 241 and n; **2**, 76, 110, 214 and n, 219 and n;

3, 25n, 38, 219 and n, 243 and n, 246, 250, 257; **4**, 17, 27 and n, 52 and n, 53 and n, 85, 93 and n, 133 and n, 146 and n, 153 and n, 155, 177–8 and n, 235, 242, 280n; **5**, 44 and n, 84, 116 and n, 146 and n, 152 and n, 253; **6**, 23, 34, 80 and n, 101, 114, 143 and n, 256 and n; **7**, 24 and n, 68 and n, 84 and n; **8**, 32 and n, 107 and n, 115, 181 and n; **9**, 153 and n; **10**, 167 and n, 176 and n; **11**, 73 and n, 184 and n, 225, 227, 229, 230; *Merchant of Venice*, **2**, 210n; **4**, 316; **5**, 39, 129, 146 and n, 159 and n, 203, 232, 243, 246 and n, 248 and n; **6**, 41, 106 and n, 143; **7**, 79 and n; **8**, 28 and n, 229 and n, 237 and n; **10**, 160 and n, 169 and n; **11**, 172, 228, 229, 234; *Merry Wives of Windsor*, **1**, 216 and n; **5**, 123 and n; **6**, 188; **10**, 65 and n; *Midsummer Night's Dream*, **5**, 52 and n; **6**, 175n; **11**, 229; *Much Ado About Nothing*, **1**, 162 and n; **2**, 141 and n; **3**, 11, 12, 160; **9**, 213 and n; **10**, 52 and n; **11**, 20, 220, 234; *Othello*, **2**, 257 and n; **3**, 82 and n, 145; **4**, 104 and n, 114, 115 and n, 116 and n, 118, 167 and n, 178 and n, 181 and n, 226 and n, 313, 314 and n, 316, 322 and n; **5**, 56, 83, 142 and n, 152 and n, 165 and n, 203, 248 and n, 257 and n; **6**, 18, 70; **8**, 104, 115, 250 and n; **9**, 119 and n, 165 and n, 199 and n; **10**, 32 and n, 67 and n, 81 and n; **11**, 86 and n; *Richard II*, **4**, 181 and n; **6**, 149 and n; *Richard III*, **2**, 212n, 245; **3**, 184 and n, 216, 229, 244, 250; **4**, 27, 49, 50 and n, 57, 63 and n, 77 and n, 85, 99 and n, 104 and n, 110, 175 and n; **5**, 165 and n; **8**, 43 and n, 115, 145 and n, 155; **10**, 49 and n; **11**, 86 and n; *Romeo and Juliet*, **3**, 219 and n, 257; **5**, 123, 126, 127, 132 and n, 173 and n, 206; **7**, 118 and n; **8**, 45; **9**, 41 and n; *The Taming of the Shrew*, **5**, 22 and n; *The Tempest*, **1**, 109; **6**, 67n; **9**, 209 and n; *Troilus and Cressida*, **6**, 47n; **9**, 14 and n; *Twelfth Night*, **2**, 207 and n; **6**, 168; **9**, 12 and n, 118 and n; **11**, 231; *Two Gentlemen of Verona*, **4**, 114 and n
Shannon, Lady Sarah, **3**, 51 and n
Sharp, Richard ('Conversation'), **3**, 162 and n, *216 and n*, 226; **5**, 205 and n; **8**, 19 and n; interview with Windham, **3**, 219 and n
Sharp, William, engraver, **4**, 164 and n, 167; **11**, 187
Shee, Martin Archer, B.'s letter to, **4**, 96; *Commemoration of Reynolds*, 96n

Sheerness, **2**, 60
Sheil, Richard Lalor, *The Apostate*, **5**, 238 and n
Shelbourne, William Petty, 2nd Earl of, **6**, 86
Sheldrake, T., and B.'s club foot, **1**, 41, and n, 43
Shelley, Clara, **5**, 296
Shelley, Harriet, **6**, 252n
Shelley, Mary (née Godwin), B.'s letters to, **9**, 205; **10**, 11, 33, 34, 108, 112; biog. sketch, **5**, 296; mentioned, **1**, 1; **2**, 282; **5**, 228n, 294, 297–8; **6**, 126; **7**, 162; **8**, 104, 190; **10**, 83–4; **11**, 155; approves B.'s arrangement for Allegra, **8**, 103, 112–13; quarrel with B., **9**, 202n; **10**, 205–6; postponed voyage, **9**, 205 and n; and Mrs. Mason, 205 and n; ridiculed Taaffe, 236; and Trelawny, 237; B. to be her banker, **10**, 11; possible provision for, 16; made copies of B.'s poems, 33n, 81, 90; not living in B.'s house, 52, 76–7; residing with the Hunts, 69, 77; B.'s appeal to Sir Timothy for, 78–9; B. to finance her journey through Hunt, 205; and Mavrocordatos, **11**, 215; *Frankenstein*, **5**, 296
Shelley, Percy Bysshe, B.'s letters to, **7**, 162; **8**, 103, 163, 171, 189, 202; **9**, 78, 147, 160; biog. sketch, **5**, 297; mentioned, **1**, 10; **2**, 16n, 282; **5**, 136n, 143; **6**, 46; **9**, 102n, 161n; praised by B., **1**, 11; **8**, 132; **10**, 79; forgeries of his letters, **1**, 26; defends Eaton, **3**, 185n; support of Godwin, **5**, 16n; to Chillon with B., 80n; **6**, 126; willing to correct proof for B., **5**, 90; and Murray, 90, 106; B.'s opinion of, 107, 162; **9**, 119, 189–90; **10**, 69; and MS of *Childe Harold*, **5**, 113, 115; death of wife, 162; at Geneva, 162, 294; at Este, 264n, 295; alleged child by Claire, 295; **7**, 191n; **8**, 97n; influence on and friendship with B., **5**, 296; visit to B. at Ravenna, **8**, 163 and n, 171 and n, 176n, 183 and n; writes to B. about Allegra, **6**, 7, 14; to send Allegra, 20, 25, 37; at Milan, 37; 'League of Incest', 76, 82, 126; agitated by ghost stories, 125 and n, 126; his courage, 126; Eldon's judgment against, 252 and n; deprived of custody of children, **7**, 121; 'crazy against religion and morality,' 174; B. called him 'Shiloh', 174 and n, 191; told B. of death of Keats, **8**, 102; B. on his poetry, 103, 104n, 162; urged B. to write a great poem, 104;

approved of placing Allegra in convent, 112–13; and Teresa, 176n, 184, 204; refused entrance to Duomo, 180 and n; Stockdale his publisher, 181n; rented Casa Lanfranchi for B., 189–90; cared for B.'s business in Pisa, 189–90, 202–3; proposed tutor for Teresa, 204–5; a visionary, **9**, 30; and auto-da-fé, 78n, 79n, 81; B.'s 'fellow serpent' jest, 81; and deed of B.'s sale of *Memoirs*, 84–5; and Leigh Hunt, 95 and n, 110n, 218; **10**, 66; signed himself atheist, **9**, 97 and n; his skeptical influence on B., 119n, 122n; belief in immortality, 121; and Masi affray, 128n, 160 and n; his boat, 137n; **10**, 11, 44 and n, 84; and Tita, **9**, 147n, 178 and n; death of Allegra, 148n; death at sea, 184 and n, 185 and n, 186, 187, 189, 190, 218; **10**, 13, 25, 33n, 105 114; cremation on beach, **9**, 192n, 197 and n, 198; preservation of his heart, 197; his financial affairs, 202, 218; his will, 202 and n, 205; **10**, 16, 77, 79, 158; attacked by Hazlitt, **9**, 216n; and *The Liberal*, 234; and Medwin, 235; and Taaffe, 236; his furniture, **10**, 11; discovered B.'s weaknesses, 25n; B.'s feeling for, 34; B. will not accept his legacy, 205–6; letter to B. from England, **11**, 227; custody of children, 233; *Adonais*, **1**, 11; **8**, 162; *Cenci*, **7**, 174 and n; **8**, 103, 104n; *Hellas*, **11**, 215; 'Hymn to Intellectual Beauty', 155; 'Mont Blanc', 155; *Prometheus Unbound*, **8**, 104 and n; *Queen Mab*, **6**, 252 and n; *Revolt of Islam*, **6**, 83; **7**, 174
Shelley, Sir Timothy, B.'s letter to, **10**, 78; mentioned, **5**, 296; **10**, 16, 77, 108, 112; and his son's debts, **9**, 202–3, 205n; B.'s appeal to for Mary, **10**, 78–9
Shenstone, William, **4**, 164
Shepherd, **2**, 84
Sheppard, John, B.'s letter to, **9**, 75; mentioned, 75n
Sherburn, George, ed., *Correspondence of Alexander Pope*, **8**, 148n
Sheridan, Richard Brinsley, biog. sketch, **3**, 272; mentioned, **1**, 113; **3**, 82, 129, 249, 250; **4**, 26, 74, 105n, 296n, 297n, 313, 330; **9**, 190n; **10**, 142n; B. quotes frequently, **1**, 2; amusing gossip about, 19; anecdotes of in 'Detached Thoughts', 21, 22; **8**, 245 and n; **9**, 13, 14, 15–16, 17–18, 20, 32, 33, 48; his Drury Lane Theatre burned, **2**, 20 and n; alluded to in Drury Lane Address,

223, 225n; ceased to write, 210; on Whitbread, **3**, 54 and n; conversation, 207–8, 238, 247, 248, 273; sentimentality, 239; his drunkenness, **4**, 121–2, 326–7; **5**, 188; **6**, 12; **9**, 15; death, **5**, 82n, 83; **6**, 243; **8**, 246; Moore's life of, **5**, 201 and n, 207; **6**, 47–8, 68 and n; his name at Harrow, 68; as orator, **9**, 13, 14; his wit, 14–17, 48; his liking for B., 14, 16; on death-bed, 20; softened Hanson, 32; and his creditors, 32, 33; *The Critic*, **2**, 195, 207 and n; **3**, 239; **4**, 50 and n, 51, 78 and n; **10**, 141 and n; **11**, 197; 'Monody on Garrick', **2**, 219–20 and n; **3**, 239; **9**, 15; *Pizarro*, **7**, 184 and n; **11**, 230; *The Rivals*, **2**, 14, 201, 219 and n; **6**, 125 and n, 127 and n, 149 and n, 220 and n; **7**, 154 and n, 211, 212; **8**, 18 and n, 101, 211 and n, 215 and n; **9**, 125n; **10**, 140 and n, 176; **11**, 125 and n, 229; *School for Scandal*, **3**, 155, 239; **5**, 72n, 82n; **7**, 61; **9**, 15; **10**, 199; *A Trip to Scarborough*, **2**, 227 and n; **3**, 104n, 249 and n
Sheridan, Thomas, s. of Richard Brinsley Sheridan, **2**, 20 and n
Sheridan, Thomas, the actor, **7**, 229
Sherwood (forest), **2**, 166; **7**, 119
Sherwood, Neely and Jones (publishers), *Waltz*, **3**, 41 and n
Shetland Islands, **4**, 151n
Shiraz, **4**, 269
Shirleys, **9**, 105
Shore, Jane, **7**, 159, 171
Shreckhorn, **5**, 106
Shrewsbury, **2**, 136n; **3**, 130n, 150n
Siam, **10**, 230
Sicily, **1**, 192, 223, 224, 225, 237, 247, 255; **2**, 7, 33, 236, 258; **3**, 86n, 89, 93; **6**, 226; **11**, 29, 157; Lady Melbourne's son in, **3**, 23
Siddons, Mrs. Sarah, **2**, 147 and n, 225n; **3**, 250n; **4**, 112n, 215 and n, 216, 337; **5**, 261n; **6**, 23; **8**, 30; **9**, 31, 34; **11**, 197; retirement, **4**, 290n; as 'Belvidera', **5**, 203n, 261n
Sidmouth, Henry Addington, 1st Viscount, **1**, *186 and n*; **6**, 227 and n
Sidney, Sir Philip, **2**, 249; **3**, 62n
Sidon, **2**, 39
Sierra Morena, **1**, 216
Silenus, **6**, 12
Silius Italicus, **8**, 200
Silvestrini, Fanny, B.'s letter to, **6**, 119; go-between, 117, 118, 120n, 121, 135, 139, 142, 247, 250, 254, 255, 258, 259; **7**, 143, 161, 162, 209, 210

Simmenthal, **5**, 100, 205
Simois, **4**, *326*
Simon, a German, **6**, 245
Simplon, **5**, 93, 94, 113–14, 115, 117, 188, 206; **6**, 39, 73, 74; **9**, 210
Sinclair, George, **1**, 156 and n; **9**, 43–4
Sinclair, Sir John, **1**, 156n; **4**, 162; **9**, 43
Sind, **11**, 20n
Sinigaglia, **8**, 131
Siri and Willhalm, bankers, **5**, 136, 139, 158, 171, 195, 196, 204, 209, 225, 274; **6**, 6, 7, 41, 48, 58, 151, 162, 163, 166, 191, 198, 203, 210; 242, 251, 254, 255, 260, 262; **7**, 78, 79; **8**, 70, 71, 75; **10**, 76n, 112; **11**, 192, 195
Sir Jacob, *see* Milbanke, Sir Ralph, and Noel, Sir Ralph
Sirmio, **5**, 123 and n
S[irota?] Pasha, **11**, 34
Sismondi, Jean Charles Léonard Simonde de, **7**, 132; **9**, 74; **11**, 198; *De la Littérature du Midi de l'Europe*, **3**, 195 and n, 252 and n; **4**, 161 and n, 167; *Histoire des Républiques Italiennes du Moyen Age*, **4**, 161 and n, 167; **8**, 152
Sisseni (Sessini), Giorgio, **11**, 128 and n, 138 and n
Sittingbourne, **2**, 59; **5**, 71
Sitwell, Lady Sarah Caroline (née Stovin), **3**, 140 and n, 141; **4**, 124 and n; marriage, 97 and n; Greek song, 97n
Sitwell, Sir Sitwell, **3**, 140n
Six Mile Bottom, **3**, 83 and n; **4**, 237 and n, 276, 281
Skepticism, **5**, 216
Skilitzy, Constantine, **10**, 210n
Skinas, Dr., see Schinas, Demetrius G.
Skinner, John, *Theological Works*, **2**, 174n
Skull cup, **1**, 277 (second printing); **3**, 56
Skulls, (Athenian), **2**, 59
Slave trade, **3**, 189n
Sligo, 2nd Marquis of (formerly Lord Altamont), **1**, *92 and n*, 152n, 159; **2**, 3 and n, 160; **9**, 67; succeeded father, **1**, 152n; with B. in Greece, **2**, 3–4, 7–8, 9, 16, 22, 24; **11**, 157, 158; his brig and entourage, **2**, 5–6, 11, 13–14; on way home, 49; in Ireland, 132; alleged abduction of a seaman, 117 and n, 118; travel plans, **3**, 27, 28, 82, 83, 87n, 90, 93, 95, 115n, 230; on source of *The Giaour*, 102 and n, 105, 155n, 200, 230; **9**, 80 and n; **11**, 186 and n; in trouble with the Navy, **3**, 155n

Sloane, Lady G., *see* Stanley, Lady Gertrude Sloane

Sloperton cottage, **5**, 200n; **6**, 24n

Smart, Christopher, *Universal Visitor*, **3**, 67 and n

Smedley, Rev. Edward, *Churchman's Epistles*, **7**, 201 and n

Smiles, Samuel, *A Publisher and His Friends*, **4**, 294n, 333n; **5**, 105n, 134n, 258n; **8**, 193n; **9**, 212n; **11**, 166n

Smith, Miss, actress, **4**, 330 and n; **9**, 36

Smith, Mr., B.'s indebtedness, **2**, 99

Smith, Messrs (creditors?), **4**, 265 and n

Smith, Newstead tenant, **4**, 293 and n, 299

Smith, Abel (?), **1**, 122 and n

Smith, Catherine Lucy (later Lady Stanhope), **3**, 116n

Smith, Mrs Constance Spencer, **2**, 132n; **3**, 154; **8**, 26 and n; love affair with B., **1**, *224 and n*, 239, 240; **2**, 198 and n, 199

Smith, Edmund, Johnson's Life of, **9**, 69 and n

Smith, H. B., **1**, 163n

Smith, Sir H. (Henry?), **1**, 162 and n; **7**, 234 and n

Smith, Horace, **9**, 119n; *First Impressions*, **3**, 20 and n

Smith, James and Horace, *Cui Bono* (parody of *Childe Harold*), **3**, 7n, 11n; *Horace in London*, 20 and n; *Rejected Addresses*, **2**, 221n, 228 and n, 235; **8**, 182 and n

Smith, Sir Sidney, defence of Acre, **2**, 181 and n; alleged liaison with Princess of Wales, **3**, 25n, 26

Smith, Sydney, **4**, 252; his 'Tory Virgin' story, **3**, 214 and n

Smith, William, denounces Southey, **9**, 97

Smollett, Tobias, **1**, 173; **6**, 91, 94; works compared to *Don Juan*, **1**, 13; 'Smelfungus', **4**, 171 and n; *Humphrey, Clinker*, **3**, 94 and n; **4**, 156 and n; **5** 253; **7**, 101; **8**, 237 and n; **9**, 209; *Peregrine Pickle*, **5**, 73; **6**, 253; **9**, 188 and n; *Roderick Random*, **4**, 256 and n; **6**, 96, 234, 253; **10**, 68, 98 and n; 'The Tears of Scotland', **2**, 211 and n; *Travels in France and Italy*, **4**, 171n

Smut, bulldog, **1**, 132

Smyrna, **1**, 225, 234–6, 237, 240, 242, 249, 250; **2**, 3, 7n, 17, 18, 32, 42, 102n, 198, 261; **3**, 75; **10**, 180; **11**, 17, 157, 216; Lord Aberdeen's explorations, **1**, 254n

Smyth, Professor William, **2**, 92 and n; **3**, 63 and n

Snuff boxes, sent to B. at Bologna, **6**, 221, 223; **10**, 185; B. trying to sell, 194–5, 200

Society of Antiquaries, **2**, 29n, 33n, 133n, 156n

Society of Arts, **5**, 58n

Society of Friends, **11**, 214

Society for the Diffusion of Useful Knowledge, **1**, 255n

Society for the Suppression of Vice, **1**, 195 and n

Socinian, **1**, 161

Socrates, **1**, 21, 148; **2**, 29; **8**, 35; **9**, 47

Sodom, **6**, 65, 143; **7**, 25n

Sodomites, **7**, 51–2

Sodomy, **1**, 208, 238; **6**, 207

Soliman Pasha of Baghdad, **3**, 58 and n

Solomon, **3**, 52, 164; **4**, 63, 105; **5**, 133; **8**, 12; **9**, 96; **10**, 103

Solomon, Samuel, *Guide to Health*, **7**, 229 and n

Somalian, Fr. Sukias, Armenian Friar, **5**, 235

Somerset, Edward Adolphus, 11th Duke of, **5**, 87n; **11**, 185n

Somerset, Charlotte Hamilton, Duchess of (w. of 11th Duke), B.'s letter to, **11**, 185; mentioned, **4**, 128 and n; **5**, 87 and n; **11**, 185n

Somersetshire, **5**, 138

Somerville, Major William Clarke, B.'s letter to, **6**, 123; mentioned, *123n*

Somerville, Miss, **5**, 82, 83, 84; in *Bertram*, 82n

Sommerville, Lord, **5**, 182

Sommery, Mlle de, **3**, 195 and n

Sophocles, **3**, 221; B. compared to, **9**, 11

Sorelli, Guido, Italian version of *Sappho*, **8**, 25 and n

Sotheby, William, B.'s letters to, **4**, 311, 313; mentioned, **2**, *128 and n*, 129, 131; **3**, 49, 214; **4**, 122n, 311n; **5**, 209, 212; **6**, 28, 192, 243; **7**, 82, 98, 172, 183; in *English Bards*, **1**, 194; row with Drury Lane Committee, **5**, 29 and n, 30, 205 and n, 208, 210; his ignorance of Italian, 229, 253; B.'s opinion of, 229, 238, 252–3, 263; anonymous note to B. on *Chillon*, 252–3; **6**, 18, 24, 33, 35; B. ridicules, **5**, 259; ignorance of languages, **6**, 3–4; 'bustling Bother-by' in *Beppo*, 35 and n, 36; **7**, 73; member of Alfred Club, **9**, 22; a bore, 29; on Coleridge's distress, 206, 208; *Darnley*, **5**, 259 and n; *Farewell to Italy*, **6**, 3n; *Five Tragedies*, **4**, 91 and n, 315 and n; *Georgics*, (translation

from Virgil), **2**, 128n; *Ivan*, **4**, 91n, 118n, 311 and n, 313–14, 315, 316, 319, 323, 334; **5**, 29n; recommended by B., 205n, 253; rejected by Drury Lane, 205n, 206, 259 and n; **6**, 24, 35; **9**, 35; **11**, 165 and n; *Oberon* (trans. from Wieland), **2**, 128n; **5**, 252 and n; *Orestes*, 259; *Saul*, 205 and n, 240, 253; **6**, 27 and n; 'Song of Triumph on the Peace', **4**, 118 and n

Sotheby catalogue, **11**, 192n

South America, **6**, 172; **8**, 36, 126n; **9**, 41, 49, 173 and n, 174, 178, 198, 215; **10**, 30n; B.'s plan to emigrate, **6**, 212, 225–7, 228, 232, 236, 240, 241, 242, 246, 249; possible origin of B.'s interest in, 123 and n; B. thinks of going to, **7**, 15

South Atlantic Quarterly, **9**, 162n

Southcott, Joanna, **4**, *164 and n*, 167 and n, 171, 172, 324; **5**, 267; **7**, 174n

Southerne, Thomas, **3**, 109; *The Fatal Marriage*, **10**, 176 and n

Southey, Robert, B.'s letter to, **9**, 102; mentioned, **1**, 158; **2**, 101n; **3**, 16n, 60 and n, 168, 206; **4**, 84n, 97n, 122n, 164, 253; **6**, 98; **7**, 82, 253; **8**, 145, 193; a Parish-clerk, **1**, 10; **4**, 85; 'League of Incest' gossip, **1**, 10; **6**, 76, 82–3, 126; **7**, 102; B.'s hatred of, **1**, 11; **6**, 76, 82–3, 104, 126, 192; possible contributor to *Edinburgh Review*, **1**, 177 and n; as S. says, 182; and Kirke White, **2**, 76n; unsaleable works, **3**, 101; appearance, 122, 127, 214; compared with Scott, 209n; B. on, 220; **5**, 220–1, 265; **8**, 207; *Don Juan* dedication, **6**, 68, 76, 91n, 94, 105, 123, 127; and Mary Wollstonecraft, 76; **9**, 97; writes for *Quarterly Review*, **6**, 83 and n; attacks reviewers, **8**, 163 and n; B.'s note on, 203–4; B. on his *Vision*, **9**, 62, 98 and n; abused in *The Two Foscari*, 86, 95 and n, 104; and Longman, 89; prolific author, 94; letter to *The Courier*, 95 and n; B.'s reply, 95 and n, 96–100, 100n; article in *Quarterly*, 96; on B. as leader of 'Satanic School', 98 and n; B.'s challenge to duel, 102 and n, 109–10, 114 and n, 115, 117, 160 and n; and B.'s reply to *Blackwood's*, 190 and n; not aware of B.'s charity, 206–7, 208; marriage to Miss Fricker, 207 and n; B. suspects of influencing Murray, **10**, 17; B.'s intended duel with, 89n; ribald reference to in *Don Juan*, **11**, 171 and n; *The Curse of Kehama*, **2**, 137; **5**, 259

and n, 277 and n; 'The Devil's Thoughts' (with Coleridge), **3**, 240n; *Life of Nelson*, 214; 'Queen Orraca and the Five Martyrs of Morocco', **2**, 138 and n; *Roderick*, **4**, 235 and n, 255n; *Thalaba*, **1**, 127n; Victory Odes, **5**, 220; *A Vision of Judgment*, **8**, 229 and n, 230, 236, 240; **10**, 13n, 80, 81; *Wat Tyler*, **5**, 220 and n, 221; **6**, 253 and n, 256; **9**, 97 and n; **10**, 81

Southwell, **3**, 125 and n; **9**, 37; Mrs. Byron rented house at, **1**, 44n; B. at, 44–8, 63–8; B.'s girls in, 48, 51n, 94 and n, 103–4 and n, 126 and n, 131 and n, 157; theatricals at, 51; B. hates, 57, 125, 127, 131, 135; Pigot family in, 172n, 277

Spa, **8**, 161, 170

Spain, **1**, 223, 237, 239, 241, 247, 255; **2**, 18, 53, 54, 74, 84, 91n, 106, 114, 146, 162; **3**, 90n, 119, 213n, 232n; **4**, 146, 161; **5**, 71, 200, 213; **8**, 36; **9**, 41, 49; **10**, 92; **11**, 157; compared to Turkey, **1**, 232; Spanish women, 216, 217–21; Spanish men, 216, 218; B. wishes to return, 217, 218; revolution in, **7**, 36, 76, 77, 78, 81–2, 155n, 190, 210, 218, 237; **8**, 79; **9**, 30; **10**, 90, 91, 133n, 138, 196; **11**, 57; in 1809, **7**, 236; travel books, **8**, 219; B. thought of going there, **10**, 114, 118; Pietro eager to go to, 143

Spalding, **7**, 212

Spaniards, **8**, 34, 48; **9**, 48; superior to Portuguese, **1**, 250

Spanish Cortes Constitution, **11**, 78

Spanish courage, **7**, 169

Spanish language, **5**, 115, 116, 123, 174; **6**, 225

Sparrow, Lady Olivia, **10**, 65

Sparta, **2**, 23; **6**, 12; **8**, 100

Spartan, ship, **6**, 105

Spartans, **2**, 16n; **8**, 188; **11**, 74

Spectator, **2**, 56

Spence, Joseph, reviewed in *London Magazine*, **8**, 111n; reviewed in *Quarterly* by Gilchrist, 199n; *Anecdotes of Books and Men*, **7**, 217n, 223; **8**, 14, 16, 21, 53n, 61, 111n; *Observations . . . and Characters of Books and Men*, **6**, 4 and n

Spencer, Lord Charles, **4**, 116n

Spencer, Georgiana Dorothy, **1**, 125n

Spencer, Lady Henrietta Frances (later Lady Bessborough—*see under*)

Spencer, John, 1st Earl of, **2**, 174n

Spencer, George John, 2nd Earl of, **3**, 31

Spencer, Lady, w. of 1st Earl Spencer, **2**, 174 and n

Spencer, Lady, w. of 2nd Earl, **3**, 31 and n, 46–7
Spencer, Dowager Lady, Sheridan on, **9**, 15
Spencer, William Robert, **4**, 116 and n; **9**, 22 and n, 29; B. reviews his poems in *The Monthly Review*, **2**, 156n; **9**, 42 and n
Spenser, Edmund, **2**, 210; **3**, 168; **4**, 13, 50
Spenserian stanza, **5**, 262; **6**, 134; **11**, 183
Spezia, **9**, 149, 178, 184n, 185, 187, 189, 190; **10**, 102
Spetsas, **11**, 30
Spider (British vessel), **1**, 226, 229n; **2**, 7 and n
Spineda, Countess, **6**, 62, 92
Spinelli, Spina, **7**, 47, 51
Spinninghouse prison, **5**, 168; **7**, 154 and n, **11**, 228
Spinoza, Baruch, **2**, 89, 136; **4**, 82
Spoletto, **5**, 233
Spooney, *see* Hanson, John
Spreti, Villa, **7**, 149, 152, 155
Springhetti, Angelo, **5**, 105, 129
Spurzheim, Johann Christoph, **4**, 182 and n
Stackleberg, Otto Magnus Freiherr von, **2**, 27n
Stackpole and Cecil, duellists, **7**, 178 and n
Stadium, **1**, 3; **2**, 37
Staël, Albert de, killed in a duel, **3**, 86 and n, 94
Staël-Holstein (later de Broglie), Albertine, **9**, 22
Staël-Holstein, Madame Germaine de (née Necker), B.'s letters to, **3**, 184; **5**, 87, 88; biog. sketch, **3**, 272–3; mentioned, **1**, 9, 13; **3**, 68, 136, 187–8, 228, 238; **4**, 28, 74, 83; **6**, 127n; **8**, 26; **9**, 19, 26; **10**, 68, 130, 140; 'frightful as a precipice', **1**, 9; **4**, 122; the immaculate, **1**, 13; **10**, 68; her shifting politics, **3**, 66; called the 'Epicene', 66 and n; essay against suicide, 73, 160; **4**, 26; and her son's death, **3**, 86 and n, 94; yawned over humour of Falstaff, 131; B.'s buffooneries about, 131, 207, 242, 247; pleased by B.'s note in *Bride*, 184 and n, 226–7, 235; character of her society, 231, 241, 244, 247; called B. a demon, 236–7; as an author, **4**, 19, 25; comments on B., 33; and John Murray, 71, 72; expelled from Paris, 158; kind and hospitable to B. at Coppet, **5**, 85, 86 and n, 92, 94, 109, 111, 124, 206–7; told B. about *Glenarvon*, 85; brilliant as ever, 86;

marriage to M. de Rocca, 86 and n; marriage of her daughter, 86 and n; tried to reconcile B. and wife, 88; gone to Paris, 114; compared to Countess Albrizzi, 148; B. urged Murray to publish, 204–5n; death, 205n, 256, 260; and Lewis, 206; **9**, 18; her letters, **5**, 258, 293; and B.'s separation, **7**, 96, 188; and Constant, 161 and n, 163 and n; **8**, 54; **10**, 167; lion of London in 1813, **8**, 29; and Schlegel, 166–7, 172; likens B. to Rousseau, **9**, 11; quizzed by Sheridan, 14; and the Dandies, 22; at Sir Humphry Davy's, **11**, 180n; *Considerations sur la Révolution Française*, **5**, 205 and n; *Corinne*, **1**, 8; **6**, 215 and n, 248; **7**, 18 and n, 38; **8**, 170, 213, 242; *De l'Allemagne*, **3**, 96 and n, 184 and n, 185, 224 and n; admired by B., 181 and n, 211, 231–2; *De la Littérature*, **9**, 152 and n
Stafford, Granville Leveson-Gower, 1st Marquis of, **3**, 232n; **4**, 267n
Stafford, George Granville Leveson-Gower, 2nd Marquis of, **3**, 236 and n, 237n
Stafford, Marchioness of, **3**, 236 and n, 254; **4**, 131 and n, 218 and n; 'Scotch Politician', 212 and n
Staines, **4**, 271
Stair, John W. Dalrymple, 7th Earl of, **3**, 85; **4**, 105 and n, 262 and n; marriages, **3**, *85n*
Stamboul, **1**, 242; **2**, 33; **5**, 210
Stanhope, Charles, 3rd Earl of Harrington, **11**, 218
Stanhope, Charles (later 4th Earl of Harrington), styled Lord Petersham, **3**, 106, *117 and n*, 126, 128, 133; **10**, 48 and n
Stanhope, Charles, 3rd Earl, 'Jacobin', **3**, 55n, 229
Stanhope, Lady Hester Lucy, **2**, *21 and n*, 49–50; **4**, 215
Stanhope, Col. Leicester, B.'s letters to **11**, 64, 86, 137; biog. sketch, 218; mentioned, **10**, 48; **11**, 73, 88, 113, 117, 119–20, 121; doctrinaire Benthamite, **10**, 230; arrival in Cephalonia, **11**, 64n, 65, 68; B. recommends him to Mavrocordatos, 71; at Missolonghi, 80; B. acting in harmony with, 83; and Greek Committee, 101, 103; and Parry, 109; joint letter with B. to Mavrocordatos, 105–6; and *Greek Telegraph*, 111n; his reports to Greek Committee, 125, 136, 139, 146; and newspapers in Greece, 132 and n, 138; at Athens, 137n, 138n; on Greek Loan Com-

mission, 146n; 'Typographical Colonel', 217, 218; *Greece in 1823 and 1824*, 104n, 218

Stanhope, Phillip Henry, 4th Earl, **3**, 106 and n, 116 and n, 133

Stanley, consul, **6**, 164

Stanley, Lady Gertrude Sloane (née Howard), **4**, 124; **11**, 225

Stanley, Zorina, *see* Harvey, Isabel

Staremberg, Count (Prince), **3**, 97 and n

Stark Library, **11**, 235

Statius, **8**, 200; *Thebais*, **9**, 126 and n

Staubach, **7**, 113

Steele, Richard, **4**, 11

Steevens's Coffee House, **6**, 211; **9**, 19, 28

Stendhal, *see* Beyle, Henri

Stepney, Tom, **11**, 159

Sterling, Charles, **10**, 213 and n

Sterling, James, British Consul, B.'s letter to, **10**, 11; mentioned, 213n; **11**, 56

Sterne, Laurence, letter to Ignatius Sancho, **9**, 49 and n; *A Sentimental Journey*, **3**, 165n, 229 and n; **4**, 171 and n; **7**, 62; *Tristram Shandy*, **3**, 87 and n, 134 and n; **8**, 33 and n, 246 and n; **10**, 150; **11**, 155

Sternhold, T. and Hopkins, J., *Psalms*, **4**, 173 and n, 220, 330; **8**, 226 and n; **9**, 11, 59

Stevens, servant, **5**, 105; **6**, 20

Stevens, A., *Madame de Staël, A Study*, **3**, 211n

Stevens, Gen. Edmund, **11**, 18n

Stevens, George, B.'s letter to, **11**, 96; mentioned, 95, 96, 109

Stevenson, Sir John, **3**, 79n; **4**, 277n; composer of music for *Irish Melodies*, 298 and n, 323 and n, 330

Stewart, Princess Annabella, **1**, 273; **2**, 68 and n

Stewart, Dugald, **1**, 214n

Stickles, John, **5**, 144n; **11**, 160 and n, 172

Stietz, Col., **10**, 211, 212

Stith, Mrs. Catherine Potter, B.'s letter to, **9**, 161; asks B. for a 'souvenir', 161–3, 162n, 164, 171

Stith, Major, **9**, 162

Stockdale, John J., **8**, 177 and n, 181 and n

Stockholm, **5**, 147

Stockton-on-Tees, **4**, 238, 255, 256

Stoddart, (Sir) John, **4**, 321n

Stoke Newington, **4**, 294n

Stornaris, **11**, 143

Stothard, Thomas, **4**, 292n

Stott, Robert (Hafiz), **4**, 269n

Stoven, Sir Frederick, B.'s letter to, **11**,
129; mentioned, 89 and n, 90, 100 and n, 115 129n,

Stovin, James, **4**, 97n

Strabo, *Geography*, **2**, 102n, 134

Strabonic controversy, **2**, 38

Strahan, William, **6**, 29

Strané, consul at Patras, **1**, 229 and n, 230, 232, 233; **2**, 6, 7, 8 and n, 9, 10, 11, 16, 19, 21

Strangford, Percy Clinton Smythe, Viscount, **1**, 137, 158

Strasbourg, **5**, 77

Strauss, Guiseppe, B.'s courier, **9**, 169 and n, 180

Street, Thomas George, ed. *The Courier*, **3**, 90n; **7**, 214 and n

Strephon, Mrs., **7**, 65

Stroelling, painter, **10**, 137

Stromboli, **11**, 29

Strout, Alan Lang, *John Bull's Letter to Lord Byron*, **6**, 257n; **8**, 145n

Stuart, Capt., R.N., **5**, 181

Stuart, Sir Charles (later Baron Stuart de Rothesay), **5**, 229 and n; **10**, 174; Irish Committee, **9**, 183 and n

Stuart, Charles Edward, **8**, 14n

Stuart, Daniel, owner of *Morning Post* and *Courier*, **3**, 90n; **7**, 214n

Stuarts, **7**, 198, 204

Stuttgart, **11**, 223

Stuyvesant, Peter, **8**, 53

Styles, Rev. John, **9**, 100n

Suetonius, **4**, 169; *Caligula*, **8**, 119 and n

Sugden, Mr., **4**, 328 and n

Suleyman of Thebes, **2**, 262

Suli, **1**, 229, 233; **11**, 158

Suliotes, B.'s letter to, **11**, 115; mentioned, **2**, 114, 123; **11**, 17, 23, 41, 54, 87, 92, 109, 119n, 124, 125; bravest of Greek soldiers, **1**, 23; **11**, 35; B. to pay, 31, 35, 92, 94 and n, 95, 102; liking for B., 35; B.'s aid to, 57; want B. to join them, 73; B.'s influence with, 80, 84, 85; refused to march against stone walls, 91n, 143, 145; B. angry at and disillusioned with, 112 and n, 123; under Gamba's command, 115; B.'s quarrel with, 145

Sulla, **11**, 225

Sullee (B.'s Servant), **2**, 13

Sultans, Millingen physician to, **11**, 216

Sun, The, **4**, 51, 314n; **5**, 58n

Sunderland, **4**, 279

Sunium (Sunion, Sounion), **1**, 237; **2**, 29n, 37

Surrey, **9**, 18n

Surrey, Earl of, **4**, 198n, 212

Surrey Gaol, **1**, 10; **4**, 52; **6**, 46

Surrey Institution, **6**, 100n

Surrey Theatre, **8**, 68n
Sussex, **10**, 97
Sutherland, Elizabeth, Countess of, **3**, 236n
Sweden, **3**, 107; **4**, 161n, 284
Swedenborg, Emanuel, **2**, 98; **4**, 324
Swedes, **8**, 95
Swedish language, **9**, 31
Swift, Jonathan, **1**, 217; **2**, 45n, 114, 221n; **4**, 263; **5**, 66, 119–20; **6**, 85, 125; **8**, 16 and n, 33 and n, 43; **9**, 32, 96; 'die at top first', **6**, 214; 'Clever Tom Clinch Going to be Hanged', **5**, 200 and n; *The Grand Question Debated*, **9**, 191 and n; *Gulliver's Travels*, **11**, 168 and n; Partridge-Bickerstaff papers, **6**, 214n; *Polite Conversation*, **9**, 85 and n
Swimmer (?), Dr., **1**, 51 and n
Swinburne, Henry, *Travels in the Two Sicilies*, **2**, 155 and n
Swiss, The, **5**, 78; **8**, 20n, 48; **11**, 139, 227
Switzerland, **4**, 93; **5**, 53, 76, 82, 123, 170, 182, 187–8, 191, 201, 205, 268, 294, 295; **6**, 82, 229n, 230; **7**, 100, 123; **8**, 11, 20 and n, 47, 54, 112, 125, 139, 157, 158, 159, 167, 168, 175, 178, 179, 180, 214, 221; **9**, 17, 22n, 41, 96, 97, 98; **10**, 77, 109, 130, 167, 180; 'League of incest' in, **1**, 10; English in, **5**, 132, 163; *Manfred* written in, **11**, 164
Sydenham, **2**, 128, 147 and n
Sydney, **11**, 221
Sydney, Algernon, **8**, 119 and n
Sykes, **5**, 224
Sylla (Sulla), **1**, 20; **3**, 218, 256; **4**, 93; **5**, 168; **9**, 41; B.'s 'greatest man', **8**, 106
Symonds, Capt., **11**, 62
Syria, **2**, 38
Syriac language, **5**, 130

Taaffe, John, B.'s letters to: **9**, 78, 129, 131 (3), 133; biog. sketch, 236; translation of *Divine Comedy*, 63, 64, 90 and n; his *Commentary* on Dante, 63–4, 90 and n, 122, 123, 126, 157; and auto-da-fé, 78, 81; fall from horse, 80; eager to be published, 81, 90, 122, 123; Masi affray, 129 and n, 130–1, 133 and n, 140, 143, 157, 180; **10**, 102–3; called Falstaaffe, **9**, 131; going to Egypt, 150; and Madame de Regny, **10**, 56n
Tabriz, **6**, 244n
Tacitus, **3**, 81, 173; **4**, 161, 214; **7**, 63; *Agricola*, **4**, 169 and n
Tagus River, **1**, 215 and n, 218; **8**, 81
Talavera, battle of, **1**, 221n

Tahiri, Dervise (Dervish), **2**, 13, 29, 262 and n; **6**, 96
Talleyrand, **2**, 196
Talleyrand, Mme, **6**, 18
Tamerlane, **9**, 155
Tamworth, Lord and Lady, **4**, 289 and n
Tartars, **1**, 227
Taruscelli, Arpalice (Tarruscelli), **6**, 40 and n, 62, 92, 124 and n; recommended to B.'s friends, **8**, 77, 83–4, 86, 101, 129 and n, 130
Tarutino, battle of, **11**, 85n
Tasso, Torquato, **3**, 97, 221; **5**, 211, 217; **6**, 4, 81, 148, 158; **8**, 53 and n, 210; his washing list, **6**, 145–6; *Gerusalemme Liberata*, **2**, 108 and n, 238n; **5**, 245; **6**, 170n; **7**, 229; **8**, 39 and n
Tassoni, Alessandro, **7**, 255; *La Secchia Rapita, Tenda Rossa*, 255n
Tattailin, Count, **9**, 215n
Tatler, The, **4**, 11
Tattersall, John Cecil, **1**, 65 and n, 109 and n; 'Davus' of 'Childish Recollections', 145 and n, 146; B.'s letters to offered to Murray, **8**, 227
Tavernier, Jean Baptiste, **5**, 104
Tavistock, Marquis of, **1**, 125 and n, 139; **7**, 168; **9**, 16
Tayler, Ann Caroline, **1**, 144n, 173n, 276; **4**, 213n
Tayler, Archdale Wilson, **4**, 213n
Tayler, Matilda, **1**, 276; **3**, 187n, 202n
Tayler, Mrs., **4**, 213 and n
Tayler, Tu, **4**, 215 and n
Taylor, (ed. Pausanius), **5**, 74 and n, 80
Taylor, Billy, **2**, 31
Taylor, John, ed. *Morning Post*, B.'s letters to: **4**, 305, 314, 322; mentioned, 305 and n; owner of *The Sun*, 314 and n; *Records of My Life*, **11**, 232
Tegg, Thomas, **5**, *143 and n*
Tehran (Tahiran), **3**, 27; **6**, 244n
Telegrafo Greco, **11**, 218; its motto, 132 and n, 134
Telephus, **11**, 85n
Tell, William, **8**, 48
Temple Bar, **4**, 273; **9**, 26
Templeman, Giles, **4**, 259, 266
Ten Commandments, parody, **7**, 196 and n
Tenedos, **8**, 82
Tentora, **6**, 92
Teotochi, Antonio, **5**, 293
Tepelene, (Tepeleen), **1**, 226 and n, 237n; **2**, 21 and n, 113, 114; **4**, 113; **5**, 76; B.'s description of, **1**, 3, 227
Teresa, maid to Count Guiccioli, **7**, 20 and n, 23, 29–30, 31, 32–3, 33n, 34, 36

Terni, Fall of, **5**, 211, 216, 233
Terra Incognita, **2**, 89
Terza rima, **6**, 46
Tetbury, **2**, 219, 221, 223
Tetuan, **1**, 221
Thackeray, William Makepeace, *Vanity Fair*, **3**, 71n, 94n; **5**, 109n
Thames, **2**, 207; **3**, 211; **7**, 16n; B. swam in, **1**, 132, 247n
Thaskalio, **2**, 5
Thebans (Greek servants), **2**, 103
Thebes, **1**, 237; **2**, 262; Mufti of, 27; (Egypt), 39
Themistocles, **8**, 48; **9**, 48; **10**, 181; at Magnesia, **7**, 50
Theodoric, **7**, 39
Theodorosian, Fr. Sarkis, Armenian Friar, **5**, 235
Theresina of Mazzurati, **6**, 92
Thermopylae, **9**, 48
Thersander, **11**, 85 and n
Theseus, Temple of, **2**, 13 and n; **8**, 109
Thibet, **2**, 199
Thisbe, **2**, 112
Thistlewood, Arthur, Cato St. conspirator, **6**, 187n; **7**, 62 and n, 113 and n
Thomas, money-lender, **1**, 205 and n; **2**, 62; **4**, 259, 291 and n, 337; **10**, 147; **11**, 161
Thomas and Riley, money-lenders, **2**, 154 and n, 155
Thomas, & Co., **5**, 278
Thomas, Dr., **11**, 100 and n, 115, 141
Thompson, Mr., **2**, 190
Thompson, Alexander, *The Family Physician*, **10**, 13
Thomson, George, B.'s letter to: **3**, 113; and Moore's *Irish Melodies*, 113 and n
Thomson, J., B.'s letter to: **3**, 121; mentioned, 121 and n, 234
Thomson, James, **4**, 13; Alfred, **2**, 180n, 221n; 'Verses occasioned by the death of Mr. Aikman', **8**, 42 and n
Thornton, Thomas, **2**, 106, 115
Thorogood, debt-collector, **4**, 333
Thorwaldsen, Bertel, bust of B., **5**, 235 and n, 243 and n; **7**, 44, 60, 202; **8**, 85–6, 111; **9**, 20–1, 55, 63, 69, 122 and n; B. on, 213
Thoun, **5**, 100, 103, 205
Thrale, Henry, **3**, 247n
Thrale, Mrs., **11**, 235
Thrasimene, **9**, 48
Throll, Mr., **2**, 153
Thurlow, Edward, 1st Baron Thurlow, **7**, 84; **9**, 28
Thurlow, Edward Thurlow, 2nd Baron, **3**, 220; poem to Rogers, 54 and n, 55; **5**, 250 and n; Moore reviews his

poems, **4**, 156 and n, 172 and n, 201; reference to B., 209 and n
Thyrza (Edleston), **2**, 116n, 139–40, 164n; **4**, 308n; B.'s poetic name for Edleston, **11**, 178
Tiberius, Emperor, **2**, 97; **3**, 234; **8**, 12n, 37, 107, 211; B. compared to, **9**, 11
Tibullus, **5**, 36
Ticknor, George, visits B. in London, **4**, 299 and n; **11**, 229
Tierney, Hon. George, **3**, *237 and n*; **6**, 86; **10**, 140 and n
Timbuctoo, **2**, 89; **6**, 244n
Times, The, (London), **3**, 21n, 55; **5**, 165; **11**, 155
Timon of Athens, **9**, 11
Tindall, Dr., **11**, 72 and n, 82, 94, 146 and n
Tindall, James, **4**, 105n
Tip, Augusta's dog, **5**, 65 and n, 98, 127
Tipperary, Dr., **11**, 46 and n
Tiraboschi, Geronimo, **8**, 41 and n
Tiretta, **6**, 45n, 255
Tisiphone, **1**, 74
Tita, *see* Falcieri, Giovanni Battista
Tithonus, **5**, 210
Titian, **8**, 19; **9**, 50; portrait of Ariosto, **5**, 213, 217; Venus, 218
Titus, **8**, 107
Titus (New Testament), **11**, 33n
Tivoli, **5**, 233
Tixal, **2**, 240
Tobacco, **2**, 221 and n; **3**, 213; **7**, 167, *see also* Byron, tobacco
Todd, Dr., **9**, 132
Todd, H. J., 'Oxoniensis', **9**, 151n
Toderini, Giovanni Battista, *Della Letteratura Turchesca*, **3**, 104n, 106–7, 111
Toledo, **11**, 84n
Toledo swords, **3**, 78, 82n
Tollemache, Capt. John, RN, duellist, **7**, 178 and n
Tomline, Sir George Pretyman, Bishop of Winchester, **3**, *22 and n*; **11**, 222; *A Refutation of Calvinism*, **3**, 22n
Tomline, William, **11**, 222
Tonson, Jacob, **2**, 30; **3**, 41; **6**, 29; **7**, 42, 113
Toobonai Islanders, **10**, 90
Tooke, John Horne, **1**, 186n; **2**, 235; **3**, 219, 249; **7**, 45; **8**, 102; **9**, 16
Tooke's Court, **5**, 142
Tories, **1**, 16, 113n; **3**, 66, 242n, 247n; **4**, 18, 37n, 38, 46; **6**, 59n, 86, 208, 227n; **7**, 213, 222; **8**, 74, 83; **9**, 183; **10**, 166n
Torlonia, B.'s Roman banker, **5**, 195, 196, 225 and n

Tory government, **1**, 177n; **2**, 196n, 216n
Toryism, **5**, 159, 160, 205, 220n; **6**, 77
Toulouse, **4**, 102n
Tower of London, **6**, 146; **7**, 149
Town Talk, **2**, 254 and n
Townsend, Rev. George, *Armageddon*, **2**, *82 and n*; *Poems*, 82n
Townsend, Mr. (Col. Wildman's representative), **6**, 74n, 87
Tozer, Rev. Mr., **4**, 164 and n
Trafalgar, Battle of, **8**, 12n; **9**, 48
Trajan, **8**, 107
Tranchemont, Captain, **4**, 209
Travel books, *see* Byron, views on, travel books
Traveller, The, **8**, 83n, 108n
Travis, Archdeacon George, **4**, 168 and n
Travis, Signor, merchant Jew, **5**, 276
Treaty of Paris, **7**, 184n
Trebia, **9**, 48
Tree, Miss, actress, **6**, 97
Trelawny, Edward John, B.'s letters to: **9**, 192 (2), 203, 204; **10**, 11, 25, 36, 39, 44, 45, 199, 203; biog. sketch, **9**, 236–7; mentioned, **5**, 110n, 296–7, 298; **9**, 184, 186; **10**, 206, 211; and B.'s boat, **9**, 137 and n, 203 and n, 204; and Taaffe, 143–4; and Roberts, 187n; cremation of Shelley and Williams, 192n; and Medwin, 235; **11**, 23n, 137 and n, 218; and the *Bolivar*, **10**, 12 and n, 25 and n, 43–4, 46 and n, 75, 165–6; B. kept him from assaulting Taaffe, 103; B.'s failure to write him, 199; invited by B. to go to Greece, 199, 203; to come from Leghorn on *Hercules*, 201, 203, 204–5; on the *Hercules*, 210n, 211; trip to Ithaca, **11**, 18n; his black servant, 31 and n; in the Morea, 23 and n, 33, 38, 57; treated well by Greek Government, 52, 53; at Athens, 134n, 137 and n, 138 and n; *Letters* . . ., ed. Forman, **9**, 137n; *Recollections of Byron and Shelley*, 237
Trent (river), **4**, 47; **10**, 52
Trevanion, Mr., B.'s letter to: **5**, 117; mentioned, 117 and n, 127
Trevanion, Sophia (w. of Admiral Byron), **1**, 53n, 135n, 165n, 195n; **5**, 117n
Trevanions, the, **1**, 165n, 191
Treviso, **6**, 62, 117, 121; **7**, 132
Trevoux, **8**, 140 and n
Tricoupi, Spiridion, **11**, 38, 150; delivered B.'s funeral oration, 138 and n
Trieste, **1**, 224; **2**, 216; **6**, 184, 240, 243, 245; **10**, 76, 179, 180; **11**, 17
Trinity Chapel, **1**, 88n

Trinity College, Cambridge, **2**, 29n; 82n, 96n, 124n, 173, 215n, 282; **3**, 147; **4**, 100n, 144n; **7**, 45, 154n, 225n, 230, 232, 234; **8**, 24; **11**, 220; B. entered name, **1**, 69, 71, 78n; B.'s life at, 78ff.; B.'s rooms, 79 and n; Mansel Master of, 81n; B.'s classmates, 110n, 121n; B. to stay another year, 134; B. first met Matthews at, 277 (2nd printing)
Trinity College, Dublin, **2**, 284
Trinity Review, **1**, 79n
Tripolitza (Tripolis), **2**, 16 and n, 262n; **10**, 181; **11**, 22n, 23, 25, 26, 33, 45 and n, 157; Sligo going to, **2**, 6, 8; B. going to, 8; massacre of Turks at, **11**, 39n
Troad, **2**, 34, 53, 92, 262; **11**, 22, 30, 157; B. visited, **1**, 236, 237, 238 and n, 247, 250, 255; **4**, 325
Trojan War, **7**, 31
Troppau, Congress of, **7**, 235 and n, 256
Troy, **1**, 238, 242, 243; **2**, 3; **3**, 26, 215, 234 and n; **4**, 97n, 103; **5**, 76; **6**, 23n; **8**, 21–2; **11**, 85n; existence disputed, **8**, 22 and n; **11**, 30
Trumpington, **3**, 197
Truro, **11**, 222
Tucker, Norman, **11**, 111n
Tucker, Surgeon, **2**, 54 and n, 58
Tulk, Mr., **9**, 25
Tully, **3**, 207
Tully, Richard, *Court of Tripoli*, **8**, 186 and n
Tunbridge Wells, **2**, 183n, 187 and n; **8**, 11
Turcolimano, **2**, 37n
Turin, **3**, 147n, 148n; **4**, 93; **5**, 214; **6**, 141; **8**, 14n; **10**, 55, 61, 81, 106; **11**, 223
Turkey, **1**, 227n, 228; **2**, 53, 163; **3**, 110–11, 119; **4**, 213, 325; **5**, 116, 157n, 173, 200; **7**, 192, 222; **8**, 122; **10**, 76; **11**, 157, 220; Hobhouse's prospects in, **1**, 208; B. travelling in, 226, 233, 234–57, 237; B. likes, 232, 237; women inaccessible in, 241; B. saw much of, 244, 247, 251; **2**, 17; Fletcher not adapted to, 34; Turkish rosary, **3**, 35; Hobhouse as traveller in, 97; bigotry in, 119; Turkish drawings, 224; B. thinks of going to, **7**, 15; armies, 236; Turkish brig of war, **11**, 114, 124, 126; burying grounds, **1**, 251; corvettes, **11**, 76, 80; Turkish courage, **7**, 169; Turkish fleet, **1**, 242 and n, 243; **11**, 16, 23, 33, 40, 100, 148, 150; beaten by Greeks, 65, 66; blockades Missolonghi, 102; frigates, 86–7, 90, 91

158

and n; Turkish girl and *Giaour*, 186 and n; Turkish language, **2**, 115 (*see also* Byron, languages); Turkish, prisoners, returned to Patras by B. **11**, 98–9; prisoners returned to Prevesa by B., 116, 117, 118, 120, 124; prisoners freed by B., 126, 129; Turkish vessel, B. nearly wrecked in, **1**, 229, 232, 233, 240; taken by Greeks, **11**, 34; Turkish war, **8**, 180; Turkish women, **2**, 46, 79; **5**, 130

Turks, **2**, 7n, 9, 24, 35, 36, 37, 40, 43, 47, 75, 83, 113, 182; **4**, 321; **6**, 12, 149; **9**, 17; **10**, 92, 139n, 169, 171n, 180, 229; **11**, 22n, 71, 72, 80, 104n, 128n; B.'s attitude toward, **1**, 17; Greeks to unite against, 23; boys not safe among, 222; description of, 227; pay attention to birth, 228; and Albanians, 230; difference between English and, 238; regular features, 249; at war with Russians, 249, 254; **2**, 22; Greeks inferior to, **1**, 250; no precedence of rank, 256n; B.'s servants, **2**, 4; bathing habits, 14; army in Acarnania, **11**, 23, 30; retired from siege of Missolonghi, 34; attack on Missolonghi, 40; massacre of at Tripolitza, 39n; victories, 54; not much war activity, 58; massacre of Greeks on Chios, 59n; compared to Greeks, 70; released Bombard, 90, 91; planning attack on Missolonghi, 107, 110, 131, 132; B.'s narrow escape from, 125

Turner, J. W. M., **3**, 4n

Turner, William, fails to swim Hellespont, **8**, 80–2, 83 and n; *Tour in the Levant*, 80 and n

Tuscany, **3**, 239n; **8**, 14, 175, 179, 180, 211, 214, 235, 245; **9**, 95, 98, 149, 179 and n, 181, 193, 197, 202; **10**, 55, 130, 152, 154, 174, 184, 186, 203; **11**, 78

Tuscany, Duke of, **8**, 21

Tusculum, **7**, 228; **8**, 108; **11**, 233

Tweeddale, George Hay, 8th Marquis of, **3**, *153 and n*

Twiddie, Mr., **1**, 150 and n

Twiss, Horace, **2**, 191 and n, 193; **4**, 116; **5**, 131 and n; **6**, 192; **9**, 22

Twiss, Richard, *Travels through Portugal and Spain*, **5**, 131n

Tyers, Thomas, tracts on Pope and Addison, **8**, 110 and n

Tyler, Capt., **9**, 156

Tyler, Wat, **7**, 44, 63, 81 and n; **9**, 97

Tylney Long, Catherine, **4**, 79n

Tyndale, *see* Tindall, Dr.

Tyrconnel, 2nd Earl of, **4**, 29n

Tyre, **2**, 39

Tyrol, **6**, 245, 246, 249, 253

Tyrtaeus, **1**, 176 and n

Tyrwhitt, Thomas, **11**, 227

Ugolini, Paulo, **10**, 107 and n

Ugolino, Count, Pisan partisan, **8**, 18–19, 39; **9**, 74

Ulysses, **3**, 8; **11**, 18

Unidentified Correspondents, B.'s letters to, **1**, 247; **2**, 63, 178; **3**, 19; **4**, 11, 30, 58, 98, 135, 296, 303, 304, 334; **5**, 23, 67, 87, 129, 153; **6**, 74

Union Club, **9**, 23; **11**, 156 and n

United Irishmen, **3**, 249n

United States of America, **10**, 87; **11**, 35

Universal Visitor, **3**, 67 and n

University College, Oxford, **4**, 271n

Upper Berkeley St., **3**, 6

Upper Grosvenor St., **8**, 25

Upton, William, **8**, 224 and n; **9**, 36 and n; *Words of the most Favourite Songs*, **6**, 27n

Urbini, surgeon, **7**, 248

Ursula, **6**, 189, 190

Usurers, *see under* Byron, debts

Utica, **7**, 62 and n

Uxbridge, Lord, **5**, 70, 277n

Vacca Berlinghieri, Andrea, B.'s letter to, **10**, 193; mentioned, **5**, 164 and n, 179 and n; **9**, 169, 181; B. asked him to recommend surgeon, **10**, 193–4, 203

Valentia, Arthur, 8th Viscount and 1st Earl of Mountnorris, **2**, 125, 128, 148; **3**, 216n; **4**, 67 and n; **10**, 113n; marriage of his daughter to Webster, **2**, 126 and n; 287

Valentia, George Annesley, Viscount (later 2nd Earl of Mountnorris), **2**, 50, 124 and n, 128, 131; **9**, 22; to stand for Wexford, 108 and n

Valeriani (Valeriano?), servant, **6**, 251; **7**, 128–9, 130

Valerius Maximus, *Facta et Dicta Memorabilia*, **6**, 91; **7**, 153n; **10**, 90n

Validé, **1**, 250–1n

Valletta, **2**, 126

Valley of Sweet Waters, **3**, 180 and n

Valpy, Abraham John, **5**, 142 and n; **8**, 118 and n, 177 and n

Valpy, Rev. Dr. Richard, B.'s letters to, **2**, 133; **4**, 98; mentioned, **2**, *133 and n*; **11**, 187 and n, *225*

Valsamachi, Capt., **11**, 91 and n

Vanbrugh, Sir John and Cibber, Colley, *The Provoked Husband*, **4**, 62 and n, 66 and n; *The Relapse*, **2**, 227 and n; **3**, 104n, 249n; **6**, 12n

Van Dieman's Land, **9**, 215; **10**, 171

Vandyke, Sir Anthony, **5**, 74

Varennes, **11**, 227
Vasilidi, **11**, 150n
Vassall, Elizabeth (later Lady Webster and Lady Holland), **2**, 281
Vasari, Giorgio, *Lives of the Painters*, **5**, 213n
Vathy, Ithaca, **11**, 18n
Vatican, **5**, 227
Vauxhall, **2**, 92; **3**, 75 and n; **11**, 221
Vaud, **5**, 100
Vaughan, Susan, B.'s letter to, **2**, 159; pretty Welsh girl, 131 and n; B. enamoured of, 151 and n, 155 and n, 157; B. deceived by, 158, 159, 160, 163
Vavassour, Mrs., **6**, 175 and n
Vega Carpio, Lope Felix de, **5**, 206 and n; **8**, 14; **9**, 93
Veglioni, **8**, 44
Velati, the Capon, **7**, 153
Velasquez, Diego de Silva y, **5**, 213
Veli Pasha, **1**, *226 and n*, 231n; **2**, 24, 262n; **3**, 206; **5**, 214; **7**, 236; B. to visit, **2**, 8; **11**, 157; gave B. a horse, **2**, 9, 11, 17, 19, 27, 33, 37; his homosexual advances to B., 9–10, 11, 114; on way to the Danube, 16, 21
Vendiamini, **6**, 39–40
Venetian dialect, **5**, 130, 133, 138, 193, 248; **6**, 23; **7**, 143n; **9**, 19
Venetian profanity, **6**, 97 and n
Venetians, **4**, 321; **5**, 147, 179, 182, 213; **6**, 11, 23
Venezuela, **6**, 123n, 225, 228, 236; **9**, 173n
Venice, **2**, 216, 285; **3**, 218; **4**, 93, 172, 269; **5**, 76, 80; **7**, 14, 39; **8**, 15 and n; **9**, 24, 88, 148, 235; **10**, 77, 112, 130, 192; **11**, 17; B. describes life in, **1**, 3; **6**, 43–4, 65–6; 'the greenest island', **1**, 3; **5**, 129; B. to go to, 117, 118, 121, 122, 123, 126, 127; B. in, 128–216, 229–79; **6**, 3–143, 224–59; B.'s life in, **5**, 129–30, 131, 132–3; Carnival in, 133, 143, 151; **11**, 163; theatres in, **5**, 133, 140, 142 and n, 143 and n, 151, 152; **6**, 65; B.'s contentment in, **5**, 135–6, 140–1, 144, 155, 162; **6**, 17, 43–4, 66; state of morals in, **5**, 145, 147–8, 152, 155–6, 189; not so many English in, 187, 191; city is decaying, **6**, 17; Gritti Palace, 25n, 37; Palazzo Mocenigo, 25 and n, 43, 65, 254; not liked by the English, 65; B. to retain his establishments, 65–6; Grande Bretagne Hotel, 74 and n; B. to leave, 124, 125, 134, 141, 247; B. leaving for Ravenna, 142, 143n; returning to the ocean, 205; B.'s opinion of, 229, 231, 237; **8**, 125,

131; a Sea-Sodom, **6**, 262; Guiccioli in, **7**, 17, 20; B. knew it well, 194; an 'ocean-Rome', **8**, 186 and n; comedies of Goldoni, **11**, 189 and n; B. to return to, 190, 192
Venice papers, **8**, 118
Venus, **6**, 206n
Venus de Medici, **5**, 211, 216, 218
Vernon, **7**, 154
Verona, **5**, 122, 123, 126, 127, 128, 129, 132, 137, 146, 147, 183, 206, 211, 233
Verona, Congress of, **10**, 81n, 94 and n
Vertot, René Aubert de, histories of revolutions, **4**, 161 and n
Vestri, Luigi, **8**, 15 and n
Vestris, Gaetano, **1**, 159n
Vesuvius, **2**, 170; **4**, 269; **5**, 210, 229; **7**, 98, 193
Vevey, **5**, 81, 82, 95, 97
Viareggio, **5**, 296; **9**, 184n, 192n, 192–3, 194, 197, 202, 236; **10**, 62
Vicari, Geltrude, **6**, 176 and n, 186, 189; **7**, 20 and n, 22, 186; **8**, 16 and n, 168, 249
Vicenza, **5**, 132, 206, 211; **11**, 163
Victor, Claude, Duc de Belluno, at Talavera, **1**, 217n, 221n
Victoria, Queen, **2**, 185n, 283; **6**, 18n; **9**, 72n
Victory (Nelson's ship), **10**, 30n
Vienna, **2**, 199; **3**, 91n, 197; **4**, 182n; **5**, 14n, 179, 182, 294; **7**, 20, 239; **8**, 25n, 38n; **9**, 26; **11**, 35
Vienna, Congress of, **4**, 132n, 283n
Vigo Lane, **1**, 243, 251; **2**, 18
Villiers, Mrs. George, **4**, 19, 22
Vincent, E. R., *Ugo Foscolo, An Italian in Regency England*, **6**, 172n
Vincenzo, *see* Papi, Vincenzo
Vincy, Baron de, **5**, 104
Viner, Samuel, **1**, 185
Viney, Mr. (?), **4**, 222, 223
Virgil, **8**, 200; **5**, 126; birthplace, 211 and n; *Aeneid*, **1**, 115, 118, 125 and n; **2**, 90–1, 137 and n; **3**, 205 and n; **4**, 239 and n, 302 and n; **7**, 83, 110 and n, 183 and n; **9**, 103 and n; **10**, 81n; **11**, 234; *Eclogues*, **2**, 33 and n; **3**, 217 and n; **4**, 17 and n, 173 and n; **7**, 81 and n; **10**, 67 and n, 68 and n; *Georgics*, **4**, 118n, 311n; **5**, 123n
Viscillie (Basili), **1**, 228 and n; **2**, 10 and n, 13, 29, 262 and n
Visconti, Ettore, **5**, 125 and n
Vitelloni, Countess, **7**, 65
Vittoria, battle, **3**, 73n, 75n, 90n
Volage, frigate, **2**, 44, 51, 48–59
Volpiotti, Constantine, **11**, 151 and n
Voltaire, François Marie Arouet de, **1**, 14, 15; **2**, 89n, 98 and n; **3**, 45n; **4**,

93; **5**, 45; **6**, 77, 91; **7**, 101 and n, 103, 113; **8**, 54; **9**, 20n, 100, 116; epitaph on, **3**, 117–18; Ferney, **5**, 277n; B.'s note on, **8**, 162, 192; 'très gai', but wrote tragedies, 31; unpopular, **10**, 109; *Candide*, **3**, 111; **4**, 139 and n, 144 and n; **5**, 168, 248; **6**, 144; **9**, 24 and n; *Oeuvres Complètes*, **5**, 199 and n, 215–16; *Voyages de Scarmentado*, **4**, 139 and n; **7**, 51; *Zaire*, **8**, 162

Vondel, Joost Van, *Gysbrecht van Amstel*, **2**, *112 and n*

Von Stackelberg, Otto Magnus Freiherr, **2**, 27n

Vostitza (Aigion), **2**, 6 and n; **3**, 253; **11**, 104n

Wadd, William, *Modern Poets*, **3**, 60n

Waddington, Samuel F., Radical, **8**, 240 and n

Wagram, **9**, 48

Waite, dentist, **3**, 245; **5**, 80, 135 and n; **6**, 17, 223 and n; **7**, 113, 150; **11**, 28; death, **7**, 227, 228

Wakefield, Gilbert, **3**, 126n, 242n; *Correspondence*, **6**, 12 and n

Waldegrave, Lady Charlotte Maria, **3**, 4n

Waldegrave, James, 2nd Earl, *Memoirs*, **8**, 71 and n, 112, 144, 187, 189, 211

Waldie, Jane (later Mrs. Watts), **9**, 67; *Sketches Descriptive of Italy . . .* **7**, 173 and n, 183 and n; **8**, 136, 162, 178

Wales, **2**, 38, 93, 244, 251, 255; **11**, 160

Wales, Prince of, (*see also* Prince Regent and George IV), **1**, 47n, 165; **2**, 80n, 85n, 86, 123n, 215n, 285; **3**, 71n, 79 and n, 109n, 117, 272; **4**, 189n, 253n, 274n

Walker, Mr., **4**, 160; possible buyer of Newstead, 186, 188; **11**, 189 and n

Walker, John, *Rhyming Dictionary*, **4**, 109

Walker, Keith, **1**, 79n

Wallace, Capt., **1**, 165 and n, 184 and n, 187; **2**, 8 and n, 28 and n; **9**, 19

Wallachia, **11**, 71, 215

Walleden, G. (?), B.'s letter to, **2**, 153 and n

Walpole, Horace, 4th Earl of Orford, **2**, 170n; **3**, 4n; **6**, 11; *Historic Doubts . . .*, **4**, 50 and n; *Horace Walpole's Letters*, ed. Peter Cunningham, **11**, 232

Walpole, Rev. Robert, B.'s letter to: **2**, 190 and n; mentioned, 190n, 197

Walpole, Sir Robert, **8**, 111

Walsh, William, **2**, 49, 55; friend of Pope, Ode to King William, **7**, 232

Walworth, Sir William, **7**, 44, *81 and n*

Wansford, **4**, 49, 227

Wantley, Dragon of, **3**, 79 and n; **11**, 159 and n

Wapping, **3**, 90

Warburton, William, **8**, 201; and Pope, **9**, 145n; *A Vindication of Mr. Pope's Essay on Man*, 146 and n

Ward, John William (later 1st Earl of Dudley and Ward), B.'s letter to, **4**, 306; mentioned, **1**, *214 and n*; **3**, 170, 173, 216; **4**, 45, 54, 306 and n; **5**, 260, 272; **6**, 5, 89; **7**, 154 and n; **9**, 14, 19, 20, 22, 36; **11**, 179; member of Alfred Club, **2**, 125 and n; dines with B., Moore and Rogers, 128 and n; B. invited to dine with, 129, 130; B. much with, 131; lent Drummond's *Œdipus Judaicus* to B., 140; has left town, 148; review of Horne Tooke's life, 235 and n; reviews Rogers' works, **3**, 62 and n, 107n; and Wakefield-Fox correspondence, 126 and n, 242 and n; projected trip to Holland with B., 176 and n, 180, 184, 187, 218, 223, 231, 234; B.'s liking for, 182, 215, 242; gone to Scotland, 182; epigram on, 182 and n; B.'s pun on, 227; tried to reconcile B. and Carlisle, 255

Wardle, Col. Gwyllym, charges against Duke of York, **1**, *179 and n*; **2**, 194n

Ware, **7**, 16

Warrington, Lancashire, **2**, 188n; **4**, 272

Warton, Joseph, **6**, 31; **8**, 201; **10**, 83; **11**, 231

Warton, Thomas, **2**, 54; Ode in honour of George III's birthday, 221n

Warwick, Richard Neville, Earl of, **3**, 209 and n

Warwickshire, **2**, 105; **3**, 226n

Washington, D.C., **3**, 229

Washington, George, **1**, 20; **3**, 218; **4**, 104n; **8**, 40n; **9**, 49, 174; **11**, 44, 84

Waterford, **2**, 132n, 218

Waterford, Lady (née Hussey), **4**, 29 and n

Waterhouse, Anne, **1**, 82n

Waterhouse, Mr. and Mrs. John, **8**, 140 and n

Waterloo, Battle of, **4**, 302 and n, 312; **5**, 70–1, 76, 82, 169, 202; **6**, 132; **7**, 84 and n; **9**, 26, 48; **11**, 190n

Waterpark, Richard Cavendish, 2nd Baron, **3**, 123 and n

Watier's Club, the 'Dandies', **4**, 117 and n; **9**, 22, 36–7; **10**, 41, 141

Watkins, John, and B.'s attack on Moore in *English Bards*, **9**, 190 and n; *Memoirs of . . . Lord Byron*, 190 and n, 191

Watson, George, **2**, 13 and n
Watson, George (later Taylor), *The Profligate*, **7**, 200 and n
Watson, Major, **1**, 172 and n
Watson, Richard, **2**, 136, 140; *An Apology for Christianity*, 136n; **11**, 179
Watson, Robert, *Philip the Second*, **4**, 161 and n
Watts, A. A., B.'s alleged plagiarisms, **8**, 166n
Way, Mr., **2**, 168
Webb, J., B.'s letter to, **10**, 152; to sell B.'s snuff boxes, 152
Webb, Joseph, **3**, 185n
Webb, W., B.'s letter to, **9**, 202; banker, 116, 202 and n
Webb & Co., B.'s letter to, **10**, 103; B.'s bankers, **9**, 203, 206, 217; **10**, 19, 26, 42, 71, 74, 92, 112, 113, 118, 151, 154, 177, 178, 186, 187, 200, 210; **11**, 16, 26, 49, 53, 55, 56, 62, 65, 93, 94, 109, 152, 153; to sell B.'s snuff boxes, **10**, 103, 152, 159
Webb and Barry, **11**, 57, 80, 81
Webster, Lady Frances (née Frances Caroline Annesley), B.'s letter to, **10**, 106; mentioned, **1**, 10, 171n; **3**, 81, 89, 216n; **5**, 101n; **6**, 66, 69, 174, 176 and n; **10**, 113n; Platonism 'in some peril', **1**, 5; **3**, 136; 'seal is not yet fixed', **1**, 8; **3**, 145; B. 'spared' her, **1**, 9; **3**, 146–7, 148, 152, 154; **5**, 28n; conflict of B.'s relation with, **1**, 19; conjugal contempt for husband, **2**, 126 and n, 131; relations with husband, 128; **3**, 116, 129, 142–3, 144, 145, 146, 147, 149; about to produce an heir, **2**, 131, 138, 148; B.'s lines to, 200n; **11**, 225; B.'s flirtation with, **2**, 284, 287; her sisters, **3**, 116, 141, 142, 147, 151, 153, 208, 237n, 241; **4**, 29, 31–2, 34, 36; 'very like Christ!', **3**, 116; her character, 116, 124, 129, 133, 142–3, 147; and Petersham, 117, 126, 128, 133; invites Augusta to Aston Hall, 126n, 127; progress of B.'s affair with, 133–57, 171, 173–4, 205, 209, 221; love and billiards, 134, 136; exchanged notes with B., 135; **4**, 29; not without passion, **3**, 136, 137, 138, 143, 146; nearly a scene at dinner, 140–1; B. willing to elope with, 143, 144, 146, 149, 152; at Newstead, 145–7; her caressing system, 147; correspondence with B., 151, 154, 157, 171, 173–4, 209, 221; uses words 'effusions' and 'soul' too often, 154; as Zuleika, 195n; and B.'s portrait, 224 and n; 'To Genevra',

240n; B.'s involvement with, **4**, 16 and n, 22 and n, 23, 77n; B.'s sonnets to, 17n; 'embarrassed with constancy', 20; distraction from Augusta, 21 and n; letters to B., 22 and n, 31, 34, 129; stopped at first tense of verb 'aimer', 28–9; with B. at Newstead, 31–2; in Paris, 310, 312 and n, 313; at Brussels and Paris, **5**, 28n; Moore on her character, 28n; alleged adultery with Wellington, 28 and n; **10**, 48n; called on Augusta, **8**, 217; B.'s letters to offered to Murray, 227; and Petersham, **10**, 48n; B.'s comments on, 95, 102; miniature portrait, 95 and n; B.'s attempt to reconcile her and Webster, 95 and n, 101–2, 106–7, 129, 174; B.'s suppressed stanza on, 198
Webster, Sir Godfrey, **1**, 165 and n; **2**, 28n, 241 and n; divorces his wife, 281
Webster, James Wedderburn, B.'s letters to: **1**, 199; **2**, 62, 63, 78, 86, 107, 138; **3**, 81, 88, 105, 110, 115, 118, 126, 172; **4**, 35, 67, 75, 83, 88, 124, 310, 312; **5**, 68; **6**, 43, 65, 173, 227; **10**, 18, 82, 95, 97, 100, 106, 109, 119; biog. sketch, **2**, 287; mentioned, **3**, 126, 251; **6**, 176; **9**, 73; **10**, 108, 198; his children scream in low voice, **1**, 6; **3**, 116; his absurd character, **1**, 10; **2**, 78–9, 124, 125, 126, 128, 131; 'Bold Webster', **1**, *171 and n*; **2**, 50, 114, 125, 148; **11**, 160; marriage, **2**, 50, 126n, 148; quarrel with B. over carriage, 62, 63–4 and n, 78–9; **11**, 160 and n; controversy with the press, **2**, 125–6, 128; 'noble subject for cuckoldom', 126, 131; leases Aston Hall, **3**, 81 and n, 114 and n, 122 and n; takes Rushton into service, 81, 88 and n, 89, 110; death of his son, 106n; his jealousy, 116, 128, 129, 133, 135, 141, 143; treatment of his wife, 116, 117, 129, 133, 134, 135, 138, 141, 142, 144, 149, 155, 193, 221; affair with the Countess, 123–4, 127, 128, 129, 132; his boasting, 136; at Newstead, 137, 145–6; B.'s loan to, 138–9, 144 and n, 152, 172 and n, 212; **4**, 83–4, 124, 259; **5**, 68 and n; in scrape with ex-tutor, **3**, 139–40; tried to match B. with his sister-in-law, 147, 151, 153; possible duel with B., **4**, 16n; deceived by wife, 29; wanted to defend B., 75; and Lady Caroline Lamb, 310, 312–13; philanderer, 312n; obtains damages from Baldwin, **5**, 28n; replies to *Quarterly*, 169 and n, 172, 176, 182; writes B.'s epitaph, 176, 185; mania

for publishing, 208; B. described life in Venice to, **6**, 65–6; attempt to reconcile the Byrons, 227–8; **7**, 111; his bond, 71; **10**, 48–9, 60–1, 98, 99, 153, 174; B. lampooned by Hobhouse about, **7**, 99, 224; visit to B. in Genoa, **10**, 18–19, 48–9; knighted, 48, 57, 100 and n; B. on, 48–50; and Lady Hardy, 49–50, 101, 102, 129, 130, 131; effort at reconciliation with wife, 95 and n, 101–2, 106–7, 109, 129, 174; B. declines endorsing his bills, 97–8, 99; brought news of Portsmouth trial, 119n; ran away with wife's children, 174; writing on Habeas Corpus, **11**, 166 and n; *Waterloo and other Poems*, **5**, 111 and n, 112 and n, 169n, 187, 193, 199; **11**, 163 and n

Webster, John, *The White Devil*, **7**, 122–3, 123n, 124

Wedderburn, Sir A., grandfather of James, **2**, 287

Weimar, **10**, 213, 214; **11**, 216

Welbeck Street, **10**, 30 and n

Wellesley, Sir Arthur (later Duke of Wellington), *see also* Wellington, Duke of, **2**, 142n, 216n; at Talavera, **1**, 217n, 221n; **2**, 91n

Wellesley, Richard Colley Wellesley, Marquis, **3**, *232 and n*

Wellesley, William Pole, marriage, **2**, 142 and n; **4**, 79 and n

Wellington, Arthur Wellesley, Duke of, **3**, 180, 232n; **4**, 79n, 90; **8**, 225 and n; **10**, 39n; victory at Vittoria, **3**, 73n, 75n, 90n; and Harriette Wilson, **4**, 88n; masked ball in honour of, 135 and n, 136; **9**, 36–7; **10**, 141; B.'s opinion of, **4**, 302 and n; **7**, 228; **9**, 49; **5**, 72 and n, 202; accused of adultery with Lady Frances Webster, 28 and n; alleged assassination attempt, **6**, 165n; attacked in *Don Juan*, **9**, 182–3, 183n; **11**, 197; and Webster's libel suit, **10**, 48 and n; Hunt's stanzas on, 133 and n; tavern signs, **11**, 170

Welwyn (Herts), **2**, 252

Wengen Alp, **5**, 101, 102, 106, 188, 205, 268

Wentworth, Mr., possible buyer of *Bolivar*, **9**, 186 and n

Wentworth, Thomas Noel, 2nd Viscount, **4**, 223, 225, 303; **5**, 46; pleased with B., **4**, 185, 197, 199, 240; Annabella to be his heir, 186, 208, 230, 285, 289, 309n; urges lawyers to hasten marriage, 227, 228; called on B., 236, 238, 239; his longevity, 260, 264–5; his illness and

death, 285, 288 and n, 289, 291, 294; his will, 289, 291, 297, 309n; his estate, **9**, 105n, 108, 109, 110, 111, 112, 145n, 152, 155; his illegitimate son, T. Noel, **10**, 14–15, 54n, 203n

Werry, Francis, B.'s letter to: **11**, 177; mentioned, 177n

West, William Edward, B.'s letters to: **9**, 211, 214; to paint B.'s portrait, 162 and n, 164n, 174, 198; proposed engraving, 211 and n, 214; portrait of Teresa, 211; portraits of B. and Teresa, **10**, 18 and n, 198

West Charlotte St., **11**, 187

West Indies, **1**, 135; **11**, 31

Westall, Richard, **3**, 33 and n; portrait of B., 41, 198; **4**, 296; **11**, 187 and n; drawings for *Don Juan*, **7**, 165 and n, 168

Westbrook, John, **6**, 252n

Westcombe, Mr., **3**, 133

Westminster, **3**, 249 and n; **5**, 138n; **6**, 27n, 59n, 60, 88 and n, 96n, 106n, 107; **8**, 144n, 209; **10**, 202; Hobhouse won parliamentary seat, **1**, 275; Parliamentary election, **7**, 16n, 49, 62, 70, 78, 213; Hobhouse standing for, **11**, 168 and n, 169, 170

Westminster Abbey, **4**, 254n; **5**, 218; **6**, 67, 97; **10**, 157

Westminster Bridge, **2**, 207

Westminster Hall, **9**, 13

Westminster School, **4**, 235

Westmorland, 10th Earl of, **1**, 221n; **2**, 173n; **3**, 271; **4**, 120n

Westmorland, Countess of (née Jane Saunders), B.'s letter to: **3**, 67; mentioned, **1**, *221 and n*; **3**, 65, 71; **4**, 34 and n, 37; **5**, 215, 241, 272; **11**, 164

Weston, Capt., B.'s letter to: **6**, 75

Wetterhorn, **5**, 101, 102

Weybridge, **9**, 18n

Wexford, **2**, 108

Wharton, Gerard Blisson, **4**, 300 and n; **5**, 30, 52 and n, 57, 65, 66, 69; **10**, 114n

Wharton and Ford, **4**, 300n

Wheatley, Mr., **8**, 227

Whigs, **1**, 16; **2**, 180n, 183n, 211n, 281, 285; **3**, 79n, 80n, 214n, 242, 247n; **4**, 296n; **6**, 26, 47, 86, 165, 208, 233; **8**, 74, 229, 230; **9**, 15n, 19, 32; **11**, 59n; view of war in Peninsula, **1**, 218n; Hobhouse a liberal, 275

Whig Club, *see* Cambridge Whig Club

Whig society, **1**, 18–19; **3**, 128n; **4**, 120n, 126n

Whiston, John, **5**, 156 and n

Whiston, William, f. of above, **5**, 156 and n

163

Whitaker, Mrs., **1**, 122 and n
Whitbread, Samuel, **2**, *211n*, 212 and n, 213–14; **3**, 67; **4**, 122; **5**, 93, 135n; **6**, 82; **9**, 14; manager of Drury Lane Theatre, **3**, 15, 73; **4**, 296 and n, 297; **11**, 181; Drury Lane address contestant, **3**, 54n; death, **4**, 302, 305n
Whitby, Capt., **8**, 54 and n, 55
White, Henry Kirke, **2**, *76 and n*, 82; **4**, 332 and n; **8**, 163 and n; **9**, 76
White, Lydia, **3**, 214 and n; **6**, 46
White & Cochrane, **3**, 61
Whitefield, George, **6**, 97
Whitefriars, **6**, 29n
Whitehall, **3**, 23; **4**, 238 and n, 239, 242
Whitehead, Paul, **11**, 219
Whitehead, William, **1**, 161n
Whittington [?], **2**, 157
Whittington, Richard, **3**, 15; **4**, 241 and n; **6**, 163, 168
Whittingham and Arliss, publishers, **4**, 316 and n
Whitton, G. B., **10**, 16, 78
Whitton Park, **4**, 276; **5**, 51; **6**, 75, 101; **7**, 114, 216, 224; **10**, 61, 202
Wieland, Christoph Martin, **8**, 25; *Oberon*, **4**, 118n, 311n; **5**, 252 and n
Wilberforce, William, **4**, 327 and n; **6**, 47, *96* and n, 96–7; **9**, 14, 15, 41; **10**, 23; **11**, 132 and n
Wilbraham, Mr., **1**, 206
Wildman, Major Thomas, B.'s letter to: **6**, 81; purchaser of Newstead, **5**, 70 and n, 71, 277–8, *277n*; **6**, 49, 57, 59, 72, 74, 79, 81, 87
Wilkes, John, **1**, 161n; **7**, 45
Wilks, Robert, **7**, 61
William, servant to Mrs. Byron, **1**, 48 and n
William II, **5**, 218
William III, **9**, 197n
William IV, **9**, 72n
Williams, Edward Elleker, biog. sketch, **9**, 237; mentioned, **5**, 110n, 298; **9**, 121n, 204; and Shelley, 102n, 137n, 235; drowned at sea, 184 and n, 185, 186, 187, 189, 190; cremation, 192n, 197, 236; and Trelawny, 236; on B., 237
Williams, Jane, **9**, 237
Williams, William, *Journal of Llewellin Penrose*, **3**, 176 and n, 186 and n, 189; **4**, 160
Williams & Co., **9**, 75
Wilmot, Anne (née Horton), w. of Robert John W., **3**, 140n; **4**, 97n, 124n, 290n; **5**, 47n
Wilmot, Sir John Eardley, **3**, 69n
Wilmot, Robert John, B.'s letters to: **5**, 47, 49 (2), 50; **6**, 5; mediator in B.'s separation, **5**, 47n, 48–50, 55, 61,

232; **11**, 169 and n; elected M.P., **6**, 61 and n
Wilmot, Mrs. (née Barberina Ogle, later Lady Dacre), **3**, 214 and n; **4**, 311; *Ian*, *290 and n*; **5**, 259 and n; **6**, 28
Wilson, Dr., **10**, 185n
Wilson, Mr., offer to buy Newstead, **5**, 230, 236, 237, 245–6, 261; **11**, 167
Wilson, Harriette, B.'s letters to, **4**, 88; **7**, 64, 100; claims to have met B., **4**, *88 and n*, 135n; B. sends her fifty pounds, **7**, 64, 100–1; *Harriette Wilson's Memoirs*, **9**, 21n
Wilson, John, 'Christopher North', **4**, 84n; **6**, 84, 126; **7**, 60n; **10**, 81n; 'Noctes Ambrosianae', *Blackwood's Magazine*, **3**, 217n; reviews *Manfred*, **5**, 269 and n; possible reviewer of *Don Juan*, **6**, 257 and n; abused by Murray, **7**, 49; B.'s *Prose Observations*, 83, 96–7; alleged author of reply to article in *Blackwood's*, **9**, 58 and n; *Isle of Palms*, **8**, 219
Wilson, Sir Robert Thomas, **10**, *114 and n*, 196
Wimbledon, **6**, 200
Winchester, Bishop of, **3**, 22n; **5**, 147
Winchelsea, **3**, 249n
Windham, William, **1**, *186 and n*; **3**, 219 and n; **9**, 14
Windsor, **1**, 247n; **4**, 80n
Windsor Castle, **1**, 63n; **6**, 146
Wingfield, John, **1**, *101 and n*, 109n, 119, 154, 176; **3**, 34n, 106n; death, **2**, 69 and n, 70, 77, 81, 84, 92–3, 118n, 119n, 120n; B.'s letters to offered to Murray, **8**, 227
Wingfield, Richard, **3**, 106n
Winthrop, Benjamin, barrister, **4**, 271 and n, 272–3, 275, 276–7, 282
Wintz, General de, **11**, 27 and n
Wirtemberg, **10**, 180
Wirtemberg, King of, **3**, 158
Witt brothers, Corneille and Jean de, **3**, 212 and n
Wolcot, John, *Peter Pindar*, **1**, 174n; **2**, 49
Wollstonecraft, Mary, **6**, 76, 82, 126; **9**, 97; *Vindication of the Rights of Women*, **5**, 293–4
Wolseley, Sir Charles, Bt., **6**, *211 and n*
Wolsey, Cardinal, **3**, 158
Woodfall, Henry Sampson, *Junius's Letters*, **2**, 250 and n
Woodhouselee, Alexander Fraser Tytler, Lord, **1**, *112 and n*, 113
Woolriche, Dr. Stephen, **4**, 243 and n
Woolwich, **3**, 73n
Worcester Cathedral, **8**, 215
Worcestershire, **9**, 15n

Wordsworth, William, **2**, 138, 215n; **3**, 206, 214n, 217n, 220; **4**, 51, 84 and n, 164, 274; **8**, 56, 207; **11**, 158; 'a man-midwife', **1**, 10; **4**, 85; 'powers to do about anything', **1**, 14; **4**, 167; parodies of, 68n, 84n; B. on, 317 and n, 324–6; **5**, 13; **11**, 198; more admired than read, **5**, 252; his disciples, 267; Shelley influenced B. to read, 297; Hunt's view of, **6**, 47; stanzas on in *Don Juan*, **7**, 82; disparagement of Pope, 114n; called 'Turdsworth' by B., 158, 167, 168, 253; **8**, 66, 68; parody by Reynolds, **7**, 171 and n, 207 and n; **10**, 130n; *The Excursion*, **4**, 157, 324, 325n; 'Goody Blake and Harry Gill', **2**, 44; *Lyrical Ballads*, **4**, 324; *Peter Bell*, **7**, 167; *Poems* (1807), **1**, 129 and n, 130; **9**, 42 and n; *Poems* (1815), **4**, 325 and n; *The White Doe of Rylstone*, **5**, 187, 199

Worgman (jeweller), **1**, 161

Worthing, **1**, 97, 98; **2**, 154

Wousky (dog), **1**, 94 and n

Wrangham, Rev. Francis, **4**, 128 and n, 129; ed. Plutarch's *Lives*, **8**, 127 and n

Wraxall, Mr., robs Sir William Drummond, **6**, 132

Wraxall, Sir Nathaniel, *Historical Memoirs . . . 1772–1784*, **6**, 140 and n

Wright, Capt., **9**, 116

Wright, Col., **11**, 93, 95

Wright, J. M. F., *Alma Mater; or Seven Years at the University of Cambridge, by a Trinity-Man*, **1**, 79n

Wright, Mr., **10**, 108, 150, 159

Wright, Walter Rodwell, **1**, 248 and n; **2**, 20n; Consul-General in Ionian Islands, 111 and n; *Horae Ionicae*, 92; Ode to the Duke of Gloucester, 92n, 93

Wyatt, Benjamin Dean, **4**, *254n*; and Newstead, 254

Wych, grocer, **8**, 11

Wycherley, William, *The Country Wife*, [*Girl*], **3**, 42n; **11**, 223

Wye river, **2**, 215–16

Wylde and Co., **1**, 149n, 196n

Wymondham, **1**, 203n, 205 and n, 223; **2**, 8, 38n, 39, 72

Wynn's Hotel, Falmouth, **1**, 205

Xenophon, *Retreat of the Ten Thousand*, **1**, 21; **8**, 13, 14

Xeres, **1**, 219–20

Xerxes, **1**, 115; **8**, 36, 106

Yani, **2**, 12

Yanina, *see* Janina

Yankees, **3**, 256

Yale Library, **4**, 97n

Yarmouth, Francis Charles, 6th Marquess of Hertford and 18th Earl of, **3**, *71n*, 72; **5**, *109 and n*; patron of pugilists, **3**, *94 and n*

Yeni-Cami (New Mosque), **1**, 250n, 251n

Yorick, **5**, 77

York and Albany, Frederick Augustus, Duke of, **1**, 132, 197n; **2**, 180n, 194 and n, 199, 255 and n; **3**, 255n; **4**, 33n, 54n, 87n; **9**, 18n

York Minster, **11**, 155

Yorke, Capt., B.'s letter to, **11**, 101; mentioned, 100 and n, 101 and n

Yorkshire, **2**, 27n; **3**, 81n, 138, 151, 167; **4**, 90, 228, 230n; **11**, 185

Yorktown, **8**, 40n

Yosy, Madame A. de, **10**, 64, 70; *Switzerland . . .*, 22 and n, 23

Young, Edward, **1**, 113; **9**, 11; *Conjectures on Original Composition*, **8**, 16 and n; *The Revenge*, **1**, 63 and n, 170 and n; **5**, 188n; **8**, 115 and n

Ypsilanti (Hypsilantes), Alexander, **11**, 39n

Yugoslavia, **8**, 12n

Yungfrau (Jungfrau), **5**, 94, 101

Yusuff Pasha, B.'s letter to, **11**, 97; mentioned, 111 and n

Yverdun, **5**, 104

Zaimes, Andreas, **11**, 143 and n, 145, 148, 149, 150

Zambelli, Lega, B.'s letter to, **7**, 46; mentioned, **6**, 254; **9**, 208; **10**, 83, 88, 161; **11**, 153; B.'s secretary, **7**, 11 and n, 22, 23, 28, 30–1, 33, 46–7, 125, 131, 134, 135, 137, 143, 146, 147, 151, 161, 164, 186, 210; **8**, 19, 28, 160, 168, 169, 170, 184, 188, 213; **11**, 115 and n, 116, 137 and n; B.'s steward, 63; and Villa Spreti, **7**, 149, 155, 156; trusted by B., **8**, 46; responsible for delays, 190, 199, 202, 212, 242; preparing to leave Ravenna, 222, 235, 243; leaving for Pisa, 244, 247

Zambelli, Mrs. (Fanny Sylvestrini), **7**, 28

Zambieri, **6**, 92

Zantachi, Andreas, **1**, 235 and n; **2**, 10 and n, 13 and n, 16, 29, 32n

Zante, **2**, 33, 43; **3**, 115; **10**, 195, 200; **11**, 15n, 16n, 17, 26, 31, 40, 41, 45, 63n, 65 and n, 69, 78, 86n, 89 and n, 90, 94, 100 and n, 118, 129n, 146n

Zara, Siege of, **7**, 132

Zea, **2**, 5, 8, 16

Zeno, **1**, 148

Zenobia, **6**, 90

Zhukovsky, Vasili Andreevitch, *The Minstrel*, **11**, 85n
Zinanni, Count, **6**, 152, 178
Zinanni, Countess, **7**, 37, 193; **11**, 233
Zinanni, Contessa Placidia, 1st wife of Guiccioli, **6**, 276
Zinanni, Signora, **6**, 136
Zitza (Zitsa), **1**, 226 and n
Zograffo, Demetrius, **2**, 48 and n, 60, 102, 118, 124, 130; **5**, 75; in B.'s will, **2**, 71; Arnaut dialect, 84, 102, 103, 113 and n; Hobhouse's travel book, 113 and n, 129 and n, 150, 155 and n, 162; to return to Greece, 153n, 167, 262 and n; and Greek insurrection, **8**, 211; **9**, 23
Zoroaster, **2**, 26
Zoroastrian, **2**, 89
Zuleika, **3**, 164, 195 and n, 196n, 199, 205, 206
Zuyder Zee, **3**, 212